THE ARMY IN INDIA AND THE DEVELOPMENT OF FRONTIER WARFARE, 1849–1947

STUDIES IN MILITARY AND STRATEGIC HISTORY
General Editor: Michael Dockrill, Reader in War Studies, King's
College, London

Published titles include:

Nigel John Ashton
EISENHOWER, MACMILLAN AND THE PROBLEM OF NASSER:
Anglo-American Relations and Arab Nationalism, 1955–59

G. H. Bennett
BRITISH FOREIGN POLICY DURING THE CURZON PERIOD,
1919–24

David A. Charters
THE BRITISH ARMY AND JEWISH INSURGENCY IN PALESTINE,
1945–47

Paul Cornish
BRITISH MILITARY PLANNING FOR THE DEFENCE OF
GERMANY, 1945–50

Robert Frazier
ANGLO-AMERICAN RELATIONS WITH GREECE: The Coming of
the Cold War, 1942–47

Brian Holden Reid
J. F. C. FULLER: Military Thinker

Stewart Lone
JAPAN'S FIRST MODERN WAR: Army and Society in the Conflict
with China, 1894–95

Thomas R. Mockaitis
BRITISH COUNTERINSURGENCY, 1919–60

Roger Woodhouse
BRITISH FOREIGN POLICY TOWARDS FRANCE, 1945–51

Studies in Military and Strategic History
Series Standing Order ISBN 0–333–71046–0
(*outside North America only*)

You can receive future titles in this series as they are published by placing a standing order.
Please contact your bookseller or, in case of difficulty, write to us at the address below with
your name and address, the title of the series and the ISBN quoted above.

Customer Services Department, Macmillan Distribution Ltd
Houndmills, Basingstoke, Hampshire RG21 6XS, England

The Army in India and the Development of Frontier Warfare, 1849–1947

T. R. Moreman
Lecturer in War Studies
King's College
London

in association with
KING'S COLLEGE, LONDON

First published in Great Britain 1998 by
MACMILLAN PRESS LTD
Houndmills, Basingstoke, Hampshire RG21 6XS and London
Companies and representatives throughout the world

A catalogue record for this book is available from the British Library.

ISBN 0–333–69541–0

First published in the United States of America 1998 by
ST. MARTIN'S PRESS, INC.,
Scholarly and Reference Division,
175 Fifth Avenue, New York, N.Y. 10010

ISBN 0–312–21703–X

Library of Congress Cataloging-in-Publication Data
Moreman, T. R.
The army in India and the development of frontier warfare,
1849–1947 / T.R. Moreman.
p. cm. — (Studies in military and strategic history)
Includes bibliographical references and index.
ISBN 0–312–21703–X (alk. paper)
1. North–west Frontier Province (Pakistan)—History, Military.
2. India. Army—History. I. Title. II. Series.
DS392.N67M67 1998
355'.0095491'2—dc21   98–18858
                                                              CIP

This book is printed on paper suitable for recycling and made from fully managed and sustained forest sources.

10   9   8   7   6   5   4   3   2   1
07   06   05   04   03   02   01   00   99   98

Printed and bound in Great Britain by
Antony Rowe Ltd, Chippenham, Wiltshire

To Susie and my parents for all their love, support
and encouragement over the years

Contents

Table of Figures

Acknowledgements

I would like to thank the staff of the following archives and libraries for their friendly assistance with my research: the Oriental and India Office Collections, London; the British Library, London; the Public Record Office, Kew; the Royal United Service Institution, Whitehall; the Liddell Hart Centre for Military Archives, King's College London; the National Army Museum, Chelsea; the Staff College library, Camberley; the Imperial War Museum, Lambeth; the Gurkha Museum, Winchester; the Dorset Military Museum; the United Service Institution of India, New Delhi; the Royal Engineers Institution, Chatham; the Royal Air Force Museum, Hendon; the Royal Air Force Historical Branch, Whitehall; the Ministry of Defence Library, Whitehall; the Institute of Historical Research; the School of Oriental and African Studies, Senate House Library and finally King's College Library. Crown copyright is acknowledged for citations from records from the Public Record Office and Oriental and India Office Collections. I also wish to thank the Trustees of the Liddell Hart Centre for Military Archives for permission to quote from papers held in their collections. The late Sir Torqhuil Matheson kindly allowed me access to his father's papers, while the Indian Army Association and Frontier Corps Association provided useful assistance. My work would not have been possible with generous financial support awarded by the Department of War Studies and the University of London Grant Committee. Thanks also to David and Alison Kilby, Peter and Cei Conlan, Paul and Ruth Bailey, John Gearson, Tim Peacock and Raffi Gregorian whose encouragement and friendship has been greatly appreciated. Moira Parry also deserves a special thank you for proof reading early versions of this book. My particular gratitude goes out to my friends and colleagues in the Department of War Studies for their help, comments and friendly criticism – Dr Michael Dockrill, Dr Brian Holden Reid and Dr Andrew Lambert, as well as Professor Peter Marshall, Dr Keith Jeffery and Dr Doug Peers. I owe a particular debt to my supervisor, Professor Brian Bond, for his advice and support.

All errors of fact and interpretation are, of course, the responsibility of the author alone.

T.R. Moreman

List of Abbreviations

Adj.-Gen.	Adjutant General
AHQ	Army Headquarters
AQ	*Army Quarterly*
Brig.	Brigadier
Brig.-Gen.	Brigadier General
CAF	Civil Armed Forces
Capt.	Captain
CGS	Chief of the General Staff
CJ	*Cavalry Journal*
CO	Commanding Officer
CRF	Chitral Relief Force
Col.	Colonel
DAQMG	Deputy Assistant Quarter-Master General
DMM	Dorset Military Museum
GOC	General Officer Commanding
GOI	Government of India
GSI	General Staff, India
GSO1	General Staff Officer Grade 1
IWM	Imperial War Museum
JRA	*Journal of the Royal Artillery*
JRUSI	*Journal of the Royal United Service Institute*
JRCAS	*Journal of the Royal Central Asian Society*
JSAHR	*Journal of the Society for Army Historical Research*
JSS	*Journal of Strategic Studies*
JICH	*Journal of Imperial and Commonwealth History*
JUSII	*Journal of the United Service Institution of India*
L. of C.	Line of Communication
L/MIL	Military Department Papers, India Office Library and Records
L/P&S	Political and Secret Department Records, India Office Library and Records
L/WS	War Staff 'WS' Series files, India Office Library and Records
Lt.	Lieutenant
Lt.-Col.	Lieutenant-Colonel
Lt.-Gen.	Lieutenant-General

LHCMA	Liddell Hart Centre for Military Archives, King's College London
Maj.	Major
Maj.-Gen.	Major-General
MT	Motor Transport
NCO	Non-Commissioned Officer
NAM	National Army Museum
NWFP	North-West Frontier Province
Offg.	Officiating
PIF	Punjab Irregular Force
PFF	Punjab Frontier Force
PPRE	*Professional Papers of the Corps of Royal Engineers*
PRO	Public Record Office, Kew
Proc. RAI	*Proceedings of the Royal Artillery Institution*
Proc. USII	*Proceedings of the United Service Institution of India*
QMG	Quarter Master General
RA	Royal Artillery
RAF	Royal Air Force
REJ	*Royal Engineers Journal*
RP	Road Protection
RSQJ	*Royal Signals Quarterly Journal*
RUSI	Royal United Service Institution
SCL	Staff College Library
SSI	Secretary of State for India
TA	Territorial Army
TEF	Tirah Expeditionary Force
TEWT	Tactical Exercise Without Troops
USM	*United Service Magazine*
WO	War Office Papers, Public Record Office

Glossary of Indian/Pushtu Words

Algad	water course
Anna	$\frac{1}{3}$ of a rupee
China	spring
Chaplis	grass sandals
Chigha	village pursuit party
Crore	ten million
Dara	defile or pass
Faqir	religious mendicant
Gasht	patrol
Ghazi	Muslim who devotes his life to killing non-infidels or fighting unbelievers
Ghar	mountain peak
Jihad	religious war – equivalent to a crusade
Jirga	tribal assembly
Kach	an alluvial flat on the bank of a stream
Kafila	caravan
Kamar	cliff or precipice
Kandao	mountain pass
Khassadar	tribal levy
Kot	walled hamlet
Kotal	pass
lakh	ten thousand
Lashkar	tribal war party (not usually applied to less than 200 men)
Maidan	plain or large open space
Malik	tribal representative or elder
Mullah	Muslim priest or holy man
Narai	pass
Nullah	small ravine
Raghza	plateau on the edge of a valley
Sangar	stone breastwork
Shin	green
Spin	white
Tangi	defile or gorge
Tauda	warm

Toi	stream
Tor	black
Warsak	spur of a hill
Zam	river
Wuch	dry
Ziarat	shrine

Introduction

Throughout the nineteenth and early twentieth centuries, the British and Indian armies, along with a wide range of locally recruited irregulars, were almost constantly engaged in a series of testing military campaigns to expand and protect the far-flung British Empire. As Brian Bond has noted 'for only two years between 1856 and 1899 were the guns silent.'[1] These military operations varied widely in scale and extent, although they can be broadly classified as campaigns of conquest or annexation, campaigns to suppress insurrections and punitive campaigns in response to aggression. To generations of British officers and men such operations represented the staple fare of the imperial armies. Indeed, in many respects involvement in conventional European conflicts, for which the British armed forces primarily organised, trained and equipped, was an aberration from the normal course of military events. The insistent demands of Empire meant imperial troops had to deal with the often conflicting requirements of fighting in deserts, jungles, open plains and mountains against varying opponents whose military organisations, arms and equipment changed with often bewildering rapidity. Most operations were first and foremost, however, campaigns against nature during which commanders and troops had to surmount immense difficulties imposed by the terrain, climate and vast distances that that had often to be traversed. To complicate matters intelligence regarding imperial opponents and local geography were often meagre or non-existent. Transport and supply problems, moreover, meant British officers had to be particularly skilled at moving and maintaining troops in areas often ravaged by disease. Such fighting represented a distinctive genre of military operations that always differed from European military requirements. To the Victorian master of colonial or 'savage' warfare, Major-General Sir Garnet Wolseley, the conduct of such operations represented 'an art in itself' requiring specific tactics far from different from those suited to 'civilised' opponents.[2]

Following the First World War the characteristics of imperial conflict changed as emphasis shifted to controlling vast subject populations and guarding troubled imperial frontiers, requiring the development of new military skills and training to maintain order. These post-war operations were collectively described by new generations of officers and men as 'imperial policing', during which British armed forces contained internal threats to imperial authority employing methods very different from conventional military operations. Yet in some areas more traditional forms of colonial warfare still persisted. As Lieutenant-Colonel CE Vickery pointed out in the *Army Quarterly* in 1923:

> The soldier of to-day may look round and bemoan the absence of any fresh countries that might afford a potential outlook for his energies and for his training. Certainly the halcyon days of 1880 to 1910 are gone and their equal will not be seen, but there will remain for many years wars and rumours of war on the frontier of India and elsewhere on the marches of the empire.[3]

This experience of traditional 'real soldiering' within and along the periphery of Britain's varied imperial possessions in Africa and Asia shaped the organisation and ethos of the British armed forces and formed the dominant experience of most serving officers.

Yet the manner in which the British armed forces conducted colonial military campaigns has attracted comparatively little serious attention from either military or imperial historians, in contrast to that directed towards conventional European campaigns.[4] Most military historians remain decidedly Eurocentric looking towards the conventional battlefields of the First and Second World Wars, and have paid only lip-service to the insistent demands of Empire. Apart from the work of several British and American academics interested in the origins of the methods so successfully employed in post Second World War counterinsurgency campaigns, studies of how British imperial troops adapted to, fought and trained for small wars or imperial policing operations during the inter-war period are marked by their absence.[5] As Ian Beckett has argued, low-intensity conflict has always enjoyed a relatively low status in the study of war, both amongst professional soldiers and new generations of academic military historians.[6] This reflects an enduring dismissive attitude amongst serving officers and the military establishment in England towards the British Army's imperial role, who instead focused on contemporary European *grande guerre*, which was professionally more rewarding and always regarded as the primary justification for the army's existence. As a result the British armed force's organisation, training and equipment was determined primarily by the 'threat' of war with a European power rather than warfare in the British Empire. The sheer diversity of conditions encountered in the Empire and the short duration of most campaigns made it difficult to formulate lessons of universal and lasting importance. By default, most officers believed, the lesser was contained in the greater and as such they looked towards the perceived lessons of contemporary modern European warfare dismissing as insignificant campaigns in which imperial troops enjoyed a decisive superiority in weapons and during which out-dated tactics were often resurrected. What could a serious professional soldier learn after all from fighting against poorly armed and ill-disciplined 'savages' who knew nothing of modern military skills or training? In some quarters it was believed that experience gained in the Empire could be positively harmful. As Colonel Lonsdale Hale, former Professor of Military History at the Staff College at Camberley, noted in 1889, 'An officer who has seen service must sweep from his mind all recollections from that service, for between Afghan, Egyptian and Zulu warfare and that of Europe, there is no similarity whatever. To the latter the former is merely the play of children.'[7] Such an approach meant that when most British Army officers fought in the Empire they did so without specific instruction, relying instead on 'on-the-spot' improvisation and pragmatic adaptation to local conditions. This robustly pragmatic approach, an emphasis on 'down-to-earth', practical soldiering and the inherent flexibility of the regimental system also contributed to that fact that lessons learnt by British service officers from colonial conflicts were seldom recorded for the benefit of future generations.[8]

Most imperial historians have also largely ignored how European armies trained for and conducted colonial warfare, despite the central role military power often played in the establishment and maintenance of imperial rule. Attention has focused on the relative ease with which numerically inferior bodies of British troops inflicted massively disproportionate casualties and rapidly defeated indigenous opponents. D.R. Headrick's identification of rifles and machine guns as decisive 'tools of penetration' rather than other important factors such as the organisation, tactics and training adapted by imperial troops for colonial warfare has led to widespread acceptance that superior technology was the predominant reason for European military success.[9] To an extent David Omissi has followed a similar line in his seminal study of the RAF and air policing during the inter-war period, although he is rather more justified regarding aircraft as local populations could only hope to lessen the impact of aircraft on the battlefield rather than acquire them themselves.[10] Peter Burroughs has also attributed this lack of interest amongst imperial historians to the unappealing character of traditional didactic and antiquarian military history which attracted little interest from scholars working in other fields.[11] Rather than examining European armies, most recent studies of colonial campaigns have focused on indigenous responses to European armies.[12] A notable exception is a thought provoking study written by Howard Bailes who has examined how continental models of military organisation and colonial warfare affected the reform of the Victorian army.[13] Most historians discussing colonial conflict still rely heavily upon an authoritative and comprehensive work originally published in 1896 written by a serving British officer discussing how imperial troops conducted small wars.[14] Charles Callwell's *Small Wars: Their Principles and Practice* has justifiably been described as the only 'truly distinctive' work produced by an officer of the Victorian Army and also 'a minor classic of compression and sophistication', but it should not be regarded as the sole source of information regarding the conduct of Britain's small wars.[15] Despite some recent signs of growing interest as Michael Howard has pointed out much work remains to be done on the how the British armed forces approached their duties as an imperial gendarmerie.[16]

The Army in India – composed of British and Indian army units – merits particular attention from historians interested in colonial conflict, as it conducted a long a series of colonial military operations during the nineteenth and twentieth centuries in support of imperial interests. It has been all too readily assumed that the training of the garrison of the subcontinent followed exactly the same pattern of the British Army at home, despite it being an almost entirely separate military organisation. Yet as R. Haycock has pointed out British arms in India developed in a manner distinct from that of the army in England, under direct War Office control, requiring an investigation in its own right.[17] As several important newly published studies of the military in British India have demonstrated the composition, organisation and training of the Indian Army was dictated primarily by its role in maintaining imperial rule in the subcontinent from internal and external threats.[18] Service in India also had a significant impact on British units. While stationed in the subcontinent, British regiments – serving on tours of duty lasting up to sixteen years – shared the training schemes and priorities as their Indian counterparts, under the direction of the local military authorities. These were often very different from that given to regiments on the home establishment or serving elsewhere in the British Empire. During the nineteenth and twentieth centuries imperial units in India primarily carried out the military tasks of maintaining internal security and policing the extensive borders of Britain's most important imperial possession and, rather more unofficially, conducted military operations elsewhere in the Empire in support of imperial interests. For example, Indian troops served overseas in Abyssinia, Malta, Perak, East and West Africa, the Sudan and Egypt as well as providing garrisons for other imperial colonial possessions.[19] The vast majority of campaigns fought by imperial troops in India, however, took place along the land frontiers against a variety of opponents whose arms, military organisation and equipment differed widely. Indeed, in microcosm, warfare on India's extensive frontiers mirrored conditions elsewhere in the British Empire with imperial troops involved in desert, jungle and mountain operations requiring tactics, organisation and training different from conventional European warfare. Such fighting taught imperial troops many lessons that also had a considerable influence on campaigning elsewhere in the British Empire. Despite the frequency of such operations and flourishing interest in South Asian military history in recent years, most historians have shied away from discussing events on the battlefield and the mundane details of training and doctrine for the Army in India's special roles. As Doug Peers has recently pointed out it is striking how few contributions to the military history of South Asia venture near the battlefield and often completely ignore the fact that armies are raised, trained and designed to fight and frequently did so.[20]

The mountainous no-man's-land between the administered areas of India and Afghanistan on the North-West Frontier of India in particular was the scene of repeated 'small wars' and punitive expeditions, providing British and Indian troops with a source of sustained experience in conducting military operations against one particular type of tribal opponent. Warfare against the intractable trans-border Pathan tribes necessitated the permanent commitment of large numbers of regulars and a range of irregulars recruited from the local population to tribal control along the administrative border with tribal territory. In common with other imperial frontiers, the North-West Frontier marked the limited of conquest and direct administration of British India, as well as forming the most strategically sensitive border of the Empire. It combined a local and immediate problem of raiding and tribal control with a serious perceived external threat from Imperial Russia (later the USSR) and Afghanistan. In many respects the former represented a far more difficult problem than that of foreign invasion. As a result the trans-Indus areas of the Punjab and later the North-West Frontier Province (NWFP) remained an area apart from the rest of India, requiring distinctive administration in which policing and tribal control took on a strong military aspect and rule was based on the frequent display and use of military power.[21] The maintenance of imperial rule along this unsettled border required the conduct of repeated military operations against the trans-border Pathan tribes dating from the annexation of the Punjab in 1849 until the end of the British Raj in August 1947.[22] The inability of the local political administration to pacify the tribal areas, forced recourse to controlling or managing them by means of fines, blockades of tribal territory and punitive military operations ranging in scale from minor skirmishes to major campaigns involving tens of thousands of men. Between 1849–1914 there were over 52 punitive operations in tribal no-man's-land as well as almost incessant small scale operations associated with what became known as the 'watch and ward' of the administrative border against the depredations of tribal raiding gangs. As Philip Mason has observed, these operations represented the staple fare of the Indian Army during the Victorian period, as well as providing imperial troops with perhaps more sustained practical experience of colonial warfare than in any other part of the British Empire.[23] During the nineteenth century the maintenance of imperial rule by British and Indian troops along this unsettled border led to the development of a distinctive frontier style of policing and military operations against elusive tribal guerrillas. This was distinctive style of low-intensity war fighting that exerted an important influence on the organisation, equipment and training of imperial units. The conduct of what was known to British officers in India alternatively as tribal warfare, hill warfare, mountain warfare, trans-border warfare or more commonly during the twentieth century as frontier warfare posed a range of unique military problems far different from that encountered during conventional European warfare, other 'small wars' or from prior experience of large scale campaigns fought on the Indian plains. Indeed, in some respects they were in advance of contemporary European practice. Operations conducted against the independent tribes were especially hampered by limited intelligence, endemic diseases, climatic extremes and scarcity of water and food, severely complicating the transport, supply and administration of imperial troops. In comparison, the local population was particularly well adapted to fighting under such difficult conditions. As Charles Callwell summed up in 1899: 'Hill warfare may fairly be said to constitute a special branch of the military art' and indeed 'almost the most trying which disciplined soldiers can be called on to undertake.'[24]

This book charts the changing characteristics of the military operations conducted by the British armed forces against the trans-border Pathan tribes on the North-West Frontier. It is not, however, simply a battle narrative or a campaign history like most earlier studies, although extensive use has been made of examples from various operations fought in tribal territory. Rather it examines how the localised armed forces raised in the Punjab and later units of the Army in India adapted to the distinct problems encountered by imperial troops operating in tribal territory and explains how specialised principles and minor tactics were evolved at the 'sharp end' during repeated encounters with the trans-border Pathans. The main part of the book then traces the history of the evolution and refinement of this distinctive approach to colonial conflict from 1849 until the end of the British Raj in 1947, spurred on by improvements in tribal military effectiveness and the adoption of modern weapons, equipment and training by the imperial armies. Unlike other colonial conflict this study demonstrates that military technology did not confer a decisive advantage on imperial troops who instead had to be given specialised training in the distinctive form of tactics required in tribal territory. In particular, this book concentrates on how such military methods were 'passed on' to successive generations of British and Indian officers and men in the form of official doctrine by means of specialised manuals and training that was very different from that carried out elsewhere in the British Empire.

1 The Punjab Irregular Force and the Origins of Hill Warfare, 1849–78

The annexation of the Punjab in 1849, following the Second Sikh War, brought the British administration in India into direct contact with the disparate Pathan tribes inhabiting the lengthy chain of mountains marking the physical boundary between India and Afghanistan for the first time. The rugged, barren and arid mountains of the North-West Frontier stretched 704 miles along the border of the Punjab, rising generally in height from the Sulaiman range and the Gumal pass in the south to Chitral and the Pamirs in the far north.[1] This belt of mountainous terrain varied in width between twenty and two hundred miles and was pierced by four main passes that followed the course of the Kabul, Kurram, Tochi and Gomal rivers. These formed the main arteries of trade and migration, as well as the historic invasion routes into India (See Figure 1). The character of the terrain varied widely along the length of the border. At Chitral, in the far north, the terrain consisted of deeply incised wooded valleys and mountains that reached a height of over 20,000 feet.[2] Further south, in Dir, Swat and Bajaur inhabited by the Yusufzai, Tarkani and Utman Khel tribes, the mountains were intersected by fertile valleys that varied in breadth from the wide alluvial expanses in the Lower Swat, Panjkora and Rud valleys to narrow glens of the upper branches of these rivers' tributaries. The height of the mountains, offshoots of the Hindu Kush, rapidly increased from 2,000 feet at the junction of the Swat and Panjkora Rivers to 15,000 in the north-west and to 22,000 feet in the north-east of the region.[3] The area to the north of the Khyber Pass, inhabited by the Mohmand tribes, consisted of desolate, broken rugged foothills varying between 3,000–5,000 feet in elevation, intersected by flat open valleys scored by deep dry nalas.[4] In the vicinity of the Khyber Pass the comparatively low-lying hills were divided by steep and precipitous gorges that rose steadily in height towards the Safed Koh range and the Tirah massif, inhabited by the Afridi and Orakzais tribes, that separated the Khyber Pass and Kurram Valley. Tirah itself consisted of a mass of hills linked to the Safed Koh range interspersed by long narrow steep valleys containing significant areas of cultivation. Lateral communications between the valleys was difficult as there were only a few passes through the hills.[5] The low-lying Kurram Valley represented a dramatic contrast from the mountains, stretching 73 miles long from Thal to the Peiwar Kotal pass that linked it with Afghanistan. It was inhabited by the Turis (Shia Muslims) who were frequently in conflict with the more orthodox (Sunni) surrounding tribes.[6] Further south, Waziristan consisted of a tangle of rugged hills and ravines rising towards the Suleiman range of mountains

Fig. 1.   The Principal Tribal Areas of the North-West Frontier of India *c.* 1900

in the east. These hills were generally low-lying, with the exception of Pir Ghal at 11,517 feet and Shuidar at 10,942 feet, but were so rugged that they were generally inaccessible except on foot. In central Waziristan the comparatively well-watered mountains were wooded and covered in dense scrub and supported the majority of the local population. This area was primarily inhabited by the Mahsuds and Wazirs, together with the smaller Bhittani and Daur tribes (see Figure 2).[7] Although many perennial rivers and streams existed, water was scarce throughout the mountains limiting cultivation. In the foothills vegetation was limited to a scattering of stunted bushes and trees. In upland areas the hills were partially covered

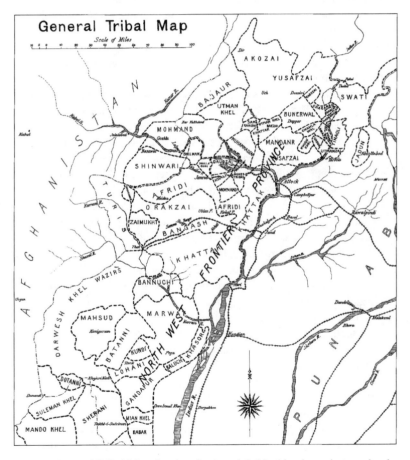

Fig. 2.   General Tribal Map showing the areas inhabited by the main trans-border Pathan tribes

with scrub jungle, dwarf palm, ilex, and fir trees along with some grassy uplands that provided grazing for flocks of sheep and goats. The climate was extremely vigorous. During the summer intense heat was experienced in the foothills and lower valleys, although the temperature fell considerably at night at higher altitudes. During the winter, heavy snow and rainfall made the valleys often impassable, and the intense cold forced many of the inhabitants to migrate to warmer lowland areas until the weather improved.

The Pushtu-speaking Pathan tribes inhabiting tribal territory shared ethnic, linguistic and religious ties with the inhabitants of Afghanistan, to which country they owed nominal allegiance. Tribal society was intensely democratic and vigorously opposed any encroachment into the hills perceived to threaten its way of life. The Yusufzai, Mohmands, Afridis, Orakzais, Mahsuds and Wazirs and other small tribes were united by a shared language, but otherwise were internally divided and normally incapable of combining due to religious, ethnic and political differences. Each tribe was subdivided into small sections or clans and in turn into smaller family groups.[8] The code of Pukhtunwali governed Pathan society, representing tribal law within each community and directing relations between tribes and sections. Tribal society stressed egalitarianism and the right of individuals to resort to violence to settle disputes and support the personal pursuit of power, status and honour. The tribes spurned leadership beyond the loose control exercised by tribal elders in council (*jirgahs*). To a large degree every man was a law unto himself and actively pursued his own aims unrestricted by societal controls. As a result the trans-border Pathan tribes existed in a state of perpetual internal conflict, or what anthropologists have termed 'ordered anarchy.'[9] The insistent demands of the Pathan code of honour and the institution of the feud militarised tribal society resulting in constant tribal and sectional warfare and endemic personal feuding. Individual tribesmen were always heavily armed for self-defence and constantly sought to acquire arms and ammunition to prosecute feuds against their neighbours. Tribal settlements, clustered in the valley floors near the few cultivable patches of ground, were carefully sited for defence and heavily fortified against attack. Small hamlets, dotted along the valleys, formed the home of a single family in which fortified towers, normally over 30 feet in height, formed a refuge of last resort in the event of tribal attack. Feuding exacerbated the poverty and lack of alternative employment in the hills. Agriculture was limited to a few herds of livestock and small patches of cultivation yielding maize, barley and rice, forcing the transhumant tribe to live in an almost symbiotic relationship with the settled areas on the plains. The heavily armed Pathan tribes posed a constant menace to the security of the trade routes through the passes into Afghanistan and an immediate and insistent threat to the border areas of the Punjab. From time immemorial the tribes had charged for safe conduct through the passes into Afghanistan and raided the adjacent plains to seize money, livestock and goods as the growing Pathan population was unable to subsist in the barren border hills.[10]

The maintenance of imperial rule in the border areas of the Punjab presented the British Board of Administration, appointed to govern the area, with a complex problem. When it assumed control the trans-Indus areas were in a state of virtual anarchy and trans-border Pathan raiders operated with virtual impunity from the safety of the surrounding hills. Villages along the border were strongly fortified and their inhabitants heavily armed for self-protection. Indeed, the former Sikh government had only been able to collect revenue in the area at swordpoint using large numbers of troops. The immediate concerns of the Punjab authorities were to consolidate British rule within the border, protect their subjects from raids, keep open the trade routes and to ensure the internal security in the newly annexed areas. A system based on conciliation backed by force of arms, intended to control the border and maintain internal order, replaced the arbitrary punitive measures hitherto employed by the Sikhs. Tribal independence was recognised and they were actively encouraged to trade with British India, given access to medical and other assistance and allowed to enlist in the ranks of the police and military forces to promote friendly relations. British officials were also expressly forbidden to go into tribal territory to minimise incidents in what became commonly known as the 'close border' policy. Tribal *maliks* (headmen) and *jirgahs* were encouraged to seek the advice of the deputy commissioners appointed to administer the six border districts, Hazara, Peshawar, Kohat, Bannu, Dera Ismail Khan, and Dera Ghazi Khan, in the resolution of disputes, and to colonise land within the settled areas. It was also soon realised that the payment of allowances to the hill tribes gave the political authorities a lever by which to exert control and a means to replace raiding as a main source of tribal livelihood.[11]

THE PUNJAB IRREGULAR FORCE

The military threat posed by an estimated 100,000 heavily armed Pathan fighting men to the security of the Punjab meant that other measures were also immediately undertaken to protect and control the inhabitants of the border areas. On 18th May 1849 Sir Henry Lawrence was empowered by the Governor-General, Lord Dalhousie, to raise a force for the protection of the western frontier and to ensure internal security while the strength and deployment of a permanent military garrison of the Punjab was determined.[12] Ten regiments – five infantry and five cavalry – were raised at stations throughout the Punjab during the summer and autumn of 1849, collectively designated the Punjab Irregular Force (PIF), intended for general service in the Punjab and Trans-Indus provinces and organised and equipped on similar lines to other irregular regiments in the Bengal Army. A British Commandant and three officers were appointed to each regiment, selected from the regular Bengal, Bombay and Madras armies, several of whom had served during the First Afghan War and had some experience of the frontier tribes. Indian officers and NCOs were recruited from the families of local chiefs on both sides of the border, while the rank and file consisted of a mixture of Sikhs, Punjabi Muslims, Dogras and both cis- and trans-border Pathans organised in mixed companies. This new force was bolstered by the permanent addition of three Light Field Batteries, raised from the former Sikh Durbar Horse Artillery, each equipped with six conventional 9lb smooth-bore guns and a 24lb howitzer.[13] Following initial uncertainty as to whether it should come under the command of the regular Bengal Army, the PIF was finally placed permanently under the direct control of the Board of Administration of the Punjab, regarding its organisation, training and employment. Writing in October 1850, Lord Dalhousie, the Governor General, explained that his object in excluding the PIF from military control was to 'secure for the local Government the full and complete control of military means sufficient to effect any object which political considerations may, in their judgement, render it expedient to secure on that distant frontier.'[14] This decision to localise the PIF solely for duty in the Punjab gave the Board of Administration almost complete control of the troops stationed along the border, enabling it to quickly respond to raids or other developments without constant recourse to the central government for military support. To carry out its specialised duties each infantry and cavalry regiment was given a permanent establishment of mules, camels and followers, as no organised commissariat system existed west of the River Indus, materially increasing their effectiveness by enabling them to respond at an hour's notice to internal unrest or tribal raids.[15]

The PIF, under the command of Brigadier John Hodgson, was given full responsibility for the 'watch and ward' or security of the administrative border stretching between Kohat and Mithunkote. Two infantry regiments, one cavalry regiment and an artillery battery were garrisoned in each district and were held at instant readiness to stop tribal incursions, maintain internal security in the border areas and prevent outlaws from taking refuge in the nearby hills. A chain of forts and outposts were steadily built along the length of the border between Dera Ghazi Khan, Dera Ismail Khan, Bannu, Kurram, Kohat, Asnee and Bahadur Khel. They were linked by a military road running parallel to the border that allowed troops to be shifted rapidly from area to area in response to tribal incursions. Cavalry regiments, along with small detachments of infantry, were dispersed in a chain of small mud forts, blockhouses and outposts that blocked valleys, ravines and other lines of approach leading down from the hills used by raiding gangs. The intervening ground between these posts was systematically patrolled by cavalry detachments to deter raids, gather intelligence and attempt to intercept parties of marauders following attacks on local villages. Although reasonably effective, these detachments were too few and too heavily encumbered to police the line of the ill-defined border effectively. Outpost duty provided valuable practical training denied to the rest of the regular army requiring initiative, resourcefulness and physical fitness. Many of the duties involved in the 'watch and ward' of the border were more civil than military in character involving PIF troops in a range of tasks supporting the local civil administration that considerably strengthened the latter's authority. Infantry regiments garrisoned frontier cantonments and forts, guarded treasuries and jails, furnished escorts, safeguarded cattle and livestock, and protected the lives and property of British subjects living near the border. Local magistrates were empowered to call out troops in the event of tribal raids or local discontent. United under the orders of the local government, close co-operation was ensured between civil and military officers in the pacification of the trans-Indus areas. Indeed, military and police duties were synonymous during the 1850s and the denial of safe refuge in the surrounding hills to outlaws escaping British justice always formed an important part of the PIF's duties. Several Commandants were assigned civil duties in addition to their military work. Captain John Coke, for example, was both Deputy Commissioner of Kohat and CO of the 1st Punjab Infantry. As a result of this constant service along the border both officers and men of the PIF steadily acquired a detailed knowledge of the tribes, their language, and customs which proved of inestimable value in the performance of their joint political and military duties.[16]

Peshawar District, opposite the mouth of the Khyber Pass, was the only part of the border entrusted to regular British and Indian troops of the Bengal Army stationed in the Punjab, who were primarily responsible for defending against a conventional Afghan attack. As these duties were of a more regular nature large numbers of conventionally organised, equipped and trained troops were permanently garrisoned in the area and were retained under the direction of the Commander-in-Chief in Bengal. During the early 1850s, forts were constructed and garrisoned by troops of the large Peshawar Brigade at Abazai, Michni, Shabkadr and Fort Mackeson. Unlike further south, the immediate defence of the border of Peshawar and Kohat districts was entrusted to the civil police, distributed in a line of small towers and outposts, while the Corps of Guides was made responsible for the protection of the Eusufzye border from raiding.[17]

The political authorities, the PIF and the Bengal Army at Peshawar, however, were unable to provide complete security against tribal incursions along the lengthy and poorly defined border, despite a defensive system consisting of 15 forts, over 50 outposts and over 12,800 irregular and 10,821 regular troops in 1855.[18] The length of the uninhabited border, the broken scrub-covered terrain in the foothills, the close proximity of tribal territory and the location of many villages and areas of cultivated land well in advance of the outposts meant that a system of passive defence had limited effectiveness. It proved difficult to safeguard the local inhabitants as the administrative border between tribal territory and the plains was ill-defined and because many of the Pathan tribes owned land and lived on both sides of the border. Skirmishes regularly occurred between hostile tribesmen and British troops and villagers, who raided the settled areas as they had under the prior Sikh regime, burning villages, stealing property, seizing hostages as well as murdering several British officers.[19] In many cases the political authorities successfully curbed these activities by suspending allowances, punitive fines, the seizure of hostages and economic blockades of tribal territory. However, the ultimate sanction available to the Board of Administration in dealing with particularly recalcitrant tribal sections rested on force of arms to restore order and British prestige.

During the 1850s the PIF, and those regular troops stationed in Peshawar District, mounted a succession of counter-raids and punitive 'butcher and bolt', 'harry and hurry' and 'tip and run' military expeditions across the administrative border into the hills in response to serious tribal incursions resulting in a state of almost constant warfare. A total of 15 punitive expeditions were carried out between 1849 and 1855 against the Kohat Pass Afridis, Mohmands, Miranzai tribes, Utmanzai Waziris, Hassanzais, Ranizais, Utman Khel, Bori Afridis, 'Hindustani Fanatics', Shiranis, Kasranis, Michni Mohmands, Aka Khels and Orakzais, to exact punishment for offences committed in British territory and to demonstrate imperial troops ability to penetrate their hills at will. It was soon clear during these operations that the conduct of expeditions in tribal territory, however, posed a range of difficult operational and political problems.

Indian columns had to operate in virtually unknown country without the benefit of maps or reliable guides and initially with minimal intelligence regarding the fighting strength of the tribes. It proved particularly difficult to identify an objective that would enable Indian troops to achieve a decisive victory and thereby secure a lasting settlement as no organised government, capital city or towns existed in tribal territory. This meant the fighting men of a tribe or their villages and crops therefore represented the only tangible objective for an Indian column. However, when Indian troops approached, the local inhabitants normally abandoned their homes and dispersed into the surrounding hills, leaving their fighting men to conduct guerrilla warfare making it impossible for Indian troops to inflict serious casualties and thereby compel them to surrender. The proximity of Afghanistan or other neutral tribes, moreover, provided sanctuaries for women, children and livestock and areas where fighting men could rest and regroup. Additionally, the independent tribes were often given active support by Afghan and neighbouring tribes with food and fighting men. As a result, Indian troops were forced to exact punishment by seizing livestock and destroying villages, fortified towers, water tanks, buried reserves of food and standing crops or else to remain in temporary occupation of an area until hunger, exposure or the necessity to sow crops compelled the tribe to pay fines of money or weapons. Such measures gave hill warfare a distinctive character very different from prior operations carried out by British and Indian troops departing from the accepted principles of 'civilised warfare'. As Sir Richard Temple explained in 1855:

> When an expedition is undertaken, then *if* the enemy were to assemble in force and take up a position and offer battle, they could be attacked and defeated, and their discomfiture might suffice as punishment, without any further measure. In *that* event the affair would be conducted after the manner of regular warfare. In civilized warfare, force is directed against the armed enemy and his defensible positions, but not against his country and subjects, who may be morally unconcerned in the hostilities and innocent of offence. *But this is not civilized warfare*; the enemy does not possess troops that stand to be attacked, *nor* defensible posts to be taken, *nor* innocent subjects to be spared. He has only rough hills to be penetrated, robber fastnesses to be scaled, and dwellings containing people, all of them to a man concerned in hostilities ... To spare these villages would be about as reasonable as to spare the commissariat supplies or arsenals of a civilized enemy.[20]

Although frequently criticised by British officials and soldiers on humanitarian grounds, there was little alternative available to punitive operations apart from the politically unacceptable alternative of occupying and administering tribal territory. Indeed, the destruction of lives and property often exacerbated conflict by increasing the desire for revenge in accordance with the tenets of Pukhtunwali and thereby ensured continued clashes between the trans-border tribes and imperial troops.

The rugged mountainous terrain in tribal territory was the main factor that dictated the conduct of hill warfare by causing a range of tactical, logistical and administrative problems. The steep and precipitous hillsides, interspersed by a succession of knife-edge ridges, rugged spurs, cliffs, and precipices, were impassable to organised bodies of men equipped with wheeled transport and cavalry. Indian columns were compelled to advance along narrow, winding, boulder-strewn river beds and valleys overlooked from vantage points in the surrounding hills. Valley floors were usually broken and intersected by deep ravines and troops frequently had to cross rivers and streams. During most of the year watercourses did not present an obstacle, but during winter after sudden, heavy rainfall they could be transformed into spates, capable of sweeping men and animals away. An absence of roads, broken terrain and scarcity of water made the movement of large bodies of troops difficult and time-consuming and meant the maximum distance a column could march in a single day was severely restricted. The few existing tracks through the hills were usually only narrow pathways, winding through defiles and over difficult mountain passes often requiring considerable improvement by sappers and miners or pioneers before they could be used.

Indian columns operating in tribal territory had to carry large quantities of stores, food and fodder as only small quantities of meat, corn, rice, straw, grass, or firewood could be foraged from the barren hills. Hardy pack mules and camels were the only form of transport capable of moving across the broken terrain, but they placed severe administrative and logistical constraints on expeditions that were in many respects a more serious check on operations than tribal resistance and dominated the conduct of operations in the hills. Slow-moving columns of pack animals were normally forced to advance in single file lengthening the line of march, causing continual stoppages and delays while being difficult to protect. Casualties amongst the transport animals by enemy action or disease could be sufficient to impede or bring to an end military operations. A large proportion of the carrying capacity of pack transport, moreover, was devoted to carrying forage for the animals themselves, whose protection, care and management was of particular importance as troops were completely dependent upon them during a hill campaign. As there was a limit to the number of men and pack animals that could be moved over one road in daylight, large forces normally had to be broken into several columns and moved by separate routes. The movement, protection and supply of columns dependent on pack transport also limited their maximum strength to no larger than four or five battalions, a mountain battery and a company of sappers. Such a force moving in single file normally stretched over nine miles in length and required approximately 5,000 mules to supply it in the field for only a short period of time. Indeed, transport and supply difficulties made it imperative that no larger a force than was absolutely necessary was employed in the mountains.

Endemic diseases and the harsh climate could also hamstring the conduct of military operations in tribal territory. Sickness and mortality rates amongst imperial troops and followers from malaria, sandfly fever, dysentery, diarrhoea, enteric fever, typhoid fever, pneumonia, bronchitis and cholera, were often greatly in excess of the casualties inflicted during the course of fighting. Heat-stroke during the summer and intense cold with heavy snowfalls during the winter dictated when and where operations could take place and led to heavy casualties that could incapacitate entire units. Animal transport was also highly susceptible to disease: surra, anthrax, rinder-pest, foot and mouth, and sore feet and backs through bad husbandry could bring an operation to a halt. The scarcity of water also acted as a powerful constraint that limited the areas in which British columns could operate and the length of time they could remain in the hills.[21]

The military characteristics, tactics and arms used by the Pathans also determined the tactics employed by Indian troops. Tribal society lacked any formal military organisation in a European sense. However, when an external threat overrode the internal divisions that normally prevented the tribes from acting together, the fighting strength of a Pathan tribe or section would unite to form a *lashkar* ('war party') whose characteristics reflected the loose social and political organisation of tribal society. *Mullahs* (priests) settled internal differences and arranged truces between individuals or families at feud, allowing a tribe to decide a plan of campaign, the number of men to be provided by each section, a rendezvous and date of assembly and to choose a leader. The size of *lashkars* varied widely from small parties to several thousand men, although the capacity of the surrounding area to support a force dictated its maximum size. A *lashkar* normally lacked regular leadership, discipline, organisation or any form of organised transport or supply arrangements. Command normally devolved on a charismatic individual or religious leader with sufficient influence or personal leadership to weld the fighting men together. The acephalous and egalitarian nature of Pathan society, however, precluded

effective leadership over any extended period of time. Individual tribesmen would report equipped with their own arms, ammunition, blanket
and food at a chosen place to form the *lashkar*, which would also be
accompanied by unarmed men and boys who carried food, ammunition
and wounded and acted as reinforcements employing discarded weapons
when fighting men were killed or wounded. A *lashkar* was incapable of
maintaining itself in the field for a period longer than ten days and, once
the supplies carried by individual tribesmen were exhausted, they had
either to return home or forcibly requisition food, water and ammunition
from local villages. It would also lose what limited cohesion it possessed
if defeated, as its discredited leaders lost all authority and were unable to
rally the tribesmen or organise further opposition. *Lashkarwals* would disperse to their homes carrying their dead and wounded, mourn their losses
and wait while tribal *jirgas* deliberated the need for further action. These
factors meant the strength of a *lashkar* therefore was liable to fluctuate
wildly in accordance with its mercurial morale, the state of its provisions
and the success of the fighting in progress. Despite these inherent defects
lightly equipped *lashkars* enjoyed a considerable tactical and strategic
advantage over Indian troops as they were less circumscribed by supply
and transport difficulties.[22]

Those martial skills developed and refined by individual tribesmen
during years of feuding and inter-tribal warfare were tribal *lashkars'* main
source of strength. Accustomed to fighting from youth, individual Pathan
tribesmen were physically fit, skilled at skirmishing, fieldcraft and the use
of arms and were inured to local diseases. Unlike imperial troops, tribesmen were intimately acquainted with the local terrain, paths, and resources.
Tribal clothing – grass *chaplis* (sandals), baggy trousers, flowing grey shirts
normally bound with leather ammunition belts and untidy pagris – and their
skill in utilising the hillsides for cover and concealment made it difficult to
spot tribesmen skirmishing over the hills. Tribal tactics were particularly
well adapted to the terrain and their own military characteristics. *Lashkars*
normally attempted to hold defensive positions at ridges or passes which
were heavily fortified with *sangars* (rock breastworks), sited to allow
frontal and flanking fire on the probable line of advance of an attacking
force, where they would mount a determined resistance. Each man fought
according to personal judgement once fighting began, exploiting the terrain
for cover and concealment, advancing or retiring as an engagement developed. Pathan tribesmen would seldom remain to fight at close-quarters with
the assaulting troops and, if their flanks, rear or line of retreat were threatened, would disperse into the surrounding hills before an organised pursuit
could be mounted. *Lashkars* excelled at desultory hit-and-run guerrilla

warfare, attacking isolated parties of troops, raiding convoys on the lines of communication, sniping foraging parties, and attacking rearguards at the end of each day's operations. When the situation offered a prospect of success the tribesmen would seize the opportunity to attack with considerable élan and engage in hand-to-hand combat. Their speed and mobility across the rough, precipitous terrain effectively enabled *lashkars* to ebb and flow around Indian columns and easily evade attacks by organised bodies of troops, giving them the freedom to choose the time and place for an attack and to keep the initiative.

Indian tactics were also dictated by the locally manufactured long knives, swords and firearms employed by trans-border Pathan *lashkars*. The vast majority of the tribesmen initially encountered by British forces were armed with a variety of swords, knives and shields, making them reliant on combat at close quarters. Following the First Afghan War the Pathan tribes had steadily acquired a large number of matchlock or flintlock *jezails* – a crudely manufactured muzzle-loading rifled musket – whose range and accuracy outclassed the Brown Bess percussion muskets initially employed by Indian troops.[23] They initially gave tribesmen a distinct qualitative advantage in small arms, allowing *lashkars* to harass British columns from out of range without effective reply. The procurement of such firearms steadily altered tribal methods from reliance on shock tactics and hand-to-hand combat to guerrilla warfare against Indian columns. However, *jezails* were not as highly effective as many officers and men against which they had been used believed. Tests on two *jezails* purchased in the Khyber Pass in 1875, by the Adjutant-General for Musketry, indicated that both weapons were crudely manufactured, inaccurate and had an effective range of only 300 yards.[24]

The officers and men serving in the PIF quickly learnt by trial and error 'on the job' that hill warfare had special characteristics of its own and that conventional tactics, training and equipment devised for operations on the Indian plains against similarly armed, organised and trained troops, were of little use in tribal territory. Indeed, it was soon apparent that military operations against the trans-border Pathan tribes represented a distinctive form of warfare requiring the development of operational principles and specific minor tactics for each arm of service. Fortunately the ranks of PIF regiments at the beginning included several officers with prior experience of the tribes, dating from the First Afghan War, who could provide initial guidance in the tactics of mountain warfare against a tribal opponent. This was complemented by advice and local knowledge provided by locally recruited officers, NCOs and men already accustomed to fighting in mountainous terrain.[25]

The frontier regiments soon learned that tribal *lashkars* were unwilling
to engage in a stand-up fight with Indian troops. As Major John Nicholson,
Deputy Commissioner at Bannu, noted in September 1853: 'It is not the
policy and never has been the practice of any of the tribes on this frontier
to meet our troops openly in the field. Any operations in which this force
has been engaged have been skirmishing of greater or less magnitude, on
broken or hilly ground.'[26] As a result the infantry bore the brunt of fighting
in tribal territory and quickly learnt to employ light infantry skills in place
of ponderous formal battalion drill, with its reliance on iron collective discipline, close-order line and column formations that dominated training in
the regular Bengal Army. It was simply impossible to maintain close-order
infantry formations or exploit disciplined massed firepower across the
broken hillsides, making it essential to employ loose, flexible, skirmishing
tactics utilising the ground for cover and concealment, modelled on those
used by their Pathan opponents. This also meant they had to develop the
individual skills of marksmanship and fieldcraft and be sufficiently physically fit to move quickly over the hillsides carrying their arms, ammunition and equipment. A direct corollary of such dispersion on the battlefield
was that officers and men had to be self-reliant, well-motivated and
capable of exercising considerable individual initiative in comparison to
those serving in the regular army. To carry out their role as light infantrymen changes were made in arms and equipment issued to frontier regiments. Personal equipment was reduced to a minimum light marching
order and men frequently wore *chaplis* in place of boots to increase their
mobility. A less conspicuous khaki uniform was adopted by infantry regiments in January 1853, instead of the heavy and easily noticeable scarlet
clothing used in the Bengal Army, that provided effective camouflage
against the brown backdrop of the arid border hills.[27] The smoothbore percussion musket, with which the majority of the infantry regiments were
initially equipped, also proved unsuitable for fighting in the hills. Its short
range, inaccuracy and heavy weight placed Indian troops at a marked disadvantage when opposed by lightly equipped tribesmen armed with
jezails. During skirmishing in the hills bordering the Derajat the marked
superiority of the 1st Punjab Infantry's rifles – a regiment with arms, green
uniforms and equipment modelled on the 60th King's Royal Rifle Corps
(which had served at Peshawar in 1849–50) – was quickly demonstrated.
In May 1853 Brigadier General Hodgson requested that the light companies in each infantry regiment should be armed with similar weapons, so
that they could be brigaded together to form a corps of riflemen in event of
an emergency and placed on equal terms with *jezail* armed tribesmen.[28]
Although it was felt that a small proportion of muskets should be kept in

case of a major incursion into the plains or hostilities with Afghan troops, this request was widely supported by political and military officers accustomed to tribal tactics.[29] As Major J.D. Macpherson, Military Secretary to the Punjab Government, pointed out: 'The drill also of Rifle Corps give the men a great superiority over soldiers trained to the Battalion exercise. In the one case the men are taught to act singly, to take advantage of all cover, to rely on the excellence of their weapon.'[30] Two regiments were completely re-armed with two-grooved Brunswick Rifles so that rifle regiments could be stationed permanently at Kohat, and in the Upper and Lower Derajat, in addition to the flank companies of the remaining units. Although slow and difficult to load in comparison to the musket, the greater accuracy and range of 200–300 yards enabled Indian troops to oppose tribal *lashkars* on equal terms for the first time.[31] The number of Brunswick rifles issued to the infantry steadily increased until, by 1856, four complete infantry regiments and the light companies of the remaining four had received the weapon.[32]

It also proved impossible to employ conventional horse-drawn wheeled road-bound field artillery in mountainous areas. Two specialised mountain artillery trains, modelled on units improvised during the Nepalese and First Afghan War, were raised by the Bengal Army during the early 1850s and equipped with ordnance – 3lb guns, 24lb howitzers and $4\frac{1}{2}$-inch mortars – capable of being broken down and carried in small loads by pack mules. Those guns that equipped the Peshawar and Hazara Mountain Trains were capable of coming quickly in and out of action in the hills at very restricted positions.[33] They rapidly demonstrated their utility during the Hassanzais expedition on the Black Mountain prompting a request by Brigadier Hodgson in October 1852 that a mountain train should be added to the PIF, but instead two 3lb mountain guns were attached to the light field batteries stationed at Kohat and Bannu.[34] The relative immobility of mountain batteries when compared to infantry units and the strain they placed on transport and supply arrangements, meant that they normally formed a small component of any force operating in the border hills. This paucity of guns, lack of shell power and the difficulty of ammunition supply meant the main fighting had to be carried out by the infantry, with mountain guns tasked to provide invaluable close fire support in both the attack and defence. An absence of opposing artillery and the short range of tribal *jezails*, however, allowed the mountain gunners to break batteries into two gun divisions that operated in close proximity to the forward troops. Artillery enjoyed an unprecedented moral superiority over tribesmen unaccustomed to its employment, magnifying the normally limited physical impact caused by its small-calibre shells that were often unable to dislodge defenders entrenched behind *sangars* or engage tribesmen hidden behind hill crests. Indeed great care had to be taken not to employ artillery batteries too early in a battle for fear that they would drive off the tribesmen and prevent a general engagement with a *lashkar*.[35]

Unlike other units the PIF's cavalry regiments were seldom employed in punitive expeditions due to the vulnerability of horsemen in the mountains, except for an occasional detached squadron to safeguard the line of communications, escort convoys, and for orderly work. An opportunity to use the arme blanche in hill warfare was rare and the cavalry were relegated primarily to the duties of watch and ward of the administrative border during which they developed considerable mobility and skill at moving over difficult ground. Cavalry had a valuable moral effect on the tribesmen out of proportion to its physical impact, since the majority of the hill tribes were unaccustomed to horses. On several occasions small bodies of horsemen successfully dealt with large raiding parties operating out of the safety of the hills.[36]

The frontier regiments and batteries of the PIF quickly adapted to local conditions and devised specialised tactics to conduct an attack in the hills, protect columns on the march, protect columns when halted at night and to govern the conduct of withdrawal in contact with hostile tribesmen that were dominated by the twin principles of offensive action and the maintenance of security. The maintenance of the offensive throughout operations against the tribes was accepted as a basic principle of hill warfare, to exploit *lashkars'* lack of cohesion, demoralise its members and take advantage of the superior discipline and training of Indian troops. Attacks on a large scale were an exception, however, rather than the rule except at the beginning of a campaign when tribesmen normally occupied strong defensible positions blocking a line of advance into the hills. A combination of a frontal attack with an enveloping movement on one or both flanks was frequently employed to force tribesmen out of strong defensive positions when they stood to fight and to inflict heavy casualties on a retreating *lashkar* which normally bolted when its line of retreat was threatened. Initially the short range of Pathan matchlocks and *jezails* meant flanking attacks had only to cover relatively short distances with little loss of life and delay. Attacks or retirements were made in bounds up spurs or along ridges by dispersed infantry who carefully avoided low ground or re-entrants where they could be fired upon from above or surrounded. Reserves and supports moved closely behind the firing line, providing covering fire as an attack progressed and using flanking fire to clear *sangars* and breastworks. A close-order line was still required shortly before an enemy position was reached in case Pathan swordsmen counter-attacked. Hill warfare normally necessitated the dispersion and the decentralisation of command and control to give Indian columns the degree of flexibility required when operating across difficult terrain. Most fighting frequently devolved into a series of separate unrelated skirmishes, rather than a formal set-piece encounter under the direct control of senior officers.

Indian columns operating in tribal territory otherwise seldom encountered serious resistance from *lashkars*. Instead, opposing tribesmen normally concentrated on attacking and harassing Indian columns as they marched through tribal territory. The comparative immobility of Indian columns to tribal *lashkars* exposed them to attack from the flank, rear and directly against the vulnerable pack transport which made ensuring all-round security of special importance. The essence of the tactical problem lay in ensuring the security of the main body of a column and protecting its long, vulnerable train of pack transport from attack from the surrounding hills. It was quickly discovered that the key lay in controlling the flanking ground and dominating the surrounding area by 'crowning the heights' on either side of the route of march with small parties of troops who occupied all high ground or tactically important features within effective *jezail* range of a column (300 yards). Tribesmen were seldom prepared to attack uphill and were wary of moving in the vicinity of piquets, although these positions were normally fortified with *sangars* that protected against sniping or direct assault. A ring of piquets provided all-round defence to the main body of the column as it moved along the valley floor denying positions from where tribesmen armed with *jezails* could fire on the troops and blocking nullahs and covering lines of approach to the valley below that could be used by swordsmen. Piquets protecting the flanks of an advancing column would rejoin the main body once the rear guard had passed out of effective range of their position, which could then be safely abandoned to the enemy. The evacuation of a piquet was often the point of greatest danger as tribesmen sought to seize the vacant position and attack the retreating detachment. During a withdrawal the main body of the piquet would retire with speed downhill leaving a small party consisting of an officer or NCO and a handful of men who would make as much noise as possible and then quickly retreat from the position once the rest of the piquet had rejoined the column. If casualties were suffered it became axiomatic to immediately counterattack to recover dead and wounded and to reoccupy the position. Piqueting required a high degree of physical fitness, drill, co-ordination, intelligence, and personal skill if the 'crowning' of the heights along the line of march was to proceed without impeding a column's progress and ensure complete security. The selection of the tactical features that needed to be piqueted and the routes by which detachments should advance across the intervening ground, required an officer with a practised and skilful eye in the advance guard. The posting and withdrawal of piquets led to the development of elaborate codes and drills by the PIF to prevent tribal attacks on imperial troops or undue delay for columns on the march. The premature evacuation of a piquet, for example, could endanger the security of an entire column or the other piquets and necessitate rapid counter-attacks to recover the position from the enemy that might delay an entire operation.

The protection and security of British encampments at night was based on similar principles as those used to protect a column on the march. The mountainous terrain forced troops, followers and pack animals to encamp on the valley floors, where sufficient level ground and water was available, but such locations were vulnerable to sniping as they were always commanded by the surrounding hills and the ground was often poorly suited to defence. The surrounding heights dominating a camp were held by small detachments of troops, occupying *sangars*, ordered to hold the position overnight to deny the tribesmen sniping positions and dominate lines of approach to the encampment below. During the hours of darkness piquets could not provide complete protection, however, from sniping at close range, attacks by tribesmen who infiltrated the outer ring of defences or thieves intent on stealing rifles or equipment from Indian troops. The defence of the main body from a surprise attack was ensured by the construction of elaborate field defences encompassing the limits of the encampment. A perimeter wall or breastwork, built from rocks, stores, or bales of fodder, backed by a trench was constructed to stop tribesmen rushing a camp, to provide cover from sniping, to prevent rifle thieves from infiltrating an encampment and provide shelter for sleeping troops. Infantry units were deployed along the length of the perimeter while the central area was reserved for the transport, cavalry or other non-combatant units. Within its walls, messes and sleeping places were often dug down into the ground or surrounded by *sangars* to protect against sniping into the densely packed perimeter camp. The construction of such elaborate defences, however, was time-consuming and meant that columns had to encamp long before nightfall in order to allow sufficient time for their completion while it was still light. Despite these serious drawbacks the importance of such perimeter defences was demonstrated on numerous occasions when large parties of swordsmen penetrated the surrounding ring of piquets and launched desperate attacks on the troops in the valley below.

The conduct of a withdrawal in contact with hostile tribesmen, an operation that occurred frequently, was the most difficult phase of an expedition in tribal territory during which the heaviest fighting normally occurred. A *lashkar* normally interpreted a withdrawal as a sign of success causing the scale and intensity of attacks to dramatically increase. The superior mobility of tribal skirmishers and local knowledge gave them an advantage in pressing a retirement which normally left commanding positions in tribal hands from where heavy fire could be delivered on the withdrawing imperial troops. As a rearguard gradually retired it had to be covered by infantry and artillery in successive layback positions until out of effective range of the tribesmen. Such operations required considerable skill, discipline, intelligence, careful control and eye for the ground by officers in order to be achieved without loss. Mountain artillery normally acted as the mainstay of a withdrawal, leap-frogging back from successive firing points in the same manner as the infantry. The brutality tribesmen often meted out to British or Hindu prisoners exerted a powerful influence on hill warfare. Mutilation of the dead bodies of imperial troops was commonplace, while captured soldiers were liable to be castrated or otherwise disfigured before being put to death. Any dead and wounded left behind during operations necessitated rapid counter-attacks as a result to recover casualties before they fell into tribal hands. As the numbers of wounded increased, so the pace of the retreat would slow as men were encumbered with dead, wounded and rifles which could not be allowed to fall into tribal hands.

These principles and minor tactics devised by the PIF to conduct what became known as hill warfare were a practical, pragmatic and highly effective response to local conditions. During the 1850s its regiments carried out the majority of hill campaigns alone giving it an unrivalled expertise in mountain warfare. By 1857 some of its units had participated in no less than 20 different expeditions or skirmishes with the trans-border tribes. As it was free from the overall direction and straitjacket of the regular military authorities, its units were able to quickly adapt their arms, equipment and training to meet the specialised local military requirements of mountain warfare. A permanent establishment of regimental pack transport was critical in ensuring the success of military operations in which so much depended on transport and supply, allowing PIF units to move quickly and with comparative ease through the border hills. As a result of the PIF's permanent commitment to the watch and ward of the border, both officers and men out of necessity also gained an intimate knowledge of tribal territory and its inhabitants. During such operations and while on outpost duty both British and Indian officers learnt to exercise a degree of

initiative and self-reliance unknown in the regular army. A high state of
efficiency was maintained during Brigadier-General Hodgson's tenure
of command, who ensured that both regiments and batteries frequently
exercised their men and transport in full marching order near their cantonments as if engaged against hostile tribesmen.[37] The resulting close co-
operation and mutual understanding that developed between its regiments
and batteries, high standard of training and esprit-de-corps within the force
that developed added considerably to its effectiveness. Isolated from the
mainstream of military life in India by distance and the Indus river, and
relieved only between the border cantonments, its officers and men developed a high standard of professionalism devoted solely to local political
and military requirements. Indeed, despite the harsh conditions in the
border cantonments, the unrivalled opportunities for active service and its
growing reputation meant competition was fierce amongst officers to serve
in its regiments and batteries.

In comparison, the regular Bengal Army regiments and British units
that garrisoned Peshawar District, trained solely in conventional operations, lacked knowledge of tribal tactics or suitable transport, equipment
and training adapted to the exigencies of mountain warfare. Armed with
muzzle-loading muskets, clothed in scarlet uniforms and accompanied by
large quantities of baggage, regular troops proved highly vulnerable in the
hills. Knowledge of mountain warfare could only be acquired through
close contact with the PIF in the field or had to be bought by experience
by the successive commanders and regiments posted to Peshawar District
at a high cost in lives, reputations and prestige. Columns composed of
regular troops employed in the hills lacked a similar degree of mobility as
PIF units, as prior to 1861 no standing transport was maintained by regular
units during peacetime and it had to be extemporised before each campaign. The collection of sufficient animals, carriage and followers in the
Punjab often delayed operations for several weeks. As SS Thorburn later
observed:

> In hill fighting the garrison was only strong through numbers and disci-
> pline. In fact, no troops in the Bengal army were adapted for guerrilla
> warfare in the mountains: Britishers and Hindustanis alike were plains-
> men, not cragsmen, and neither moved unless accompanied by immense
> baggage trains. Owing to these disabilities expeditions launched from
> Peshawar were infrequent, and when undertaken were very costly,
> formal, and ineffective campaigns carried on close to a base within our
> border rather than the rough-and-ready sort of marching customary in
> the Derajat.[38]

The periodic relief of units carried out every two or three years within the Bengal Presidency militated against the assimilation or dissemination of local knowledge regarding tribal territory and its inhabitants as well as practical experience of mountain warfare. Any information gained through practical experience was soon lost before it could be passed on to the rest of the regular army, as units returned to the mainstream of professional soldiering in India with its emphasis on conventional European warfare.

The success with which the frontier regiments and batteries policed the administrative border and conducted punitive operations in tribal territory was reflected in 1855, when the PIF assumed responsibility for the watch and ward of the border between Mardan and Abbottabad, with Peshawar District intervening between its existing garrisons at Kohat and in the Derajat. To carry out these duties the strength of the force was steadily augmented during the 1850s to five regiments of cavalry, six regiments of Punjab infantry, the Corps of Guides, four regiments of Sikh infantry, three Light Field Batteries, two mountain trains and a garrison battery.[39] The isolation of the PIF from the rest of the Indian Army along the remote border of the Punjab had wider significance during the summer of 1857, following the outbreak of mutiny within the ranks of the Bengal Army, when its regiments and batteries formed the backbone of the force despatched from the Punjab to central India, the North-West Provinces and Oude to suppress the rebellion. Its training, experience and rough and ready organisation proved ideally suited to operations on the Indian plains, refuting claims that troops trained solely to mountain warfare were incapable of holding their own in conventional military operations. Indeed, it was so successful that it later formed the model on which the whole native army was reorganised during the 1860s.[40]

When the fighting in central India ended the PIF quickly resumed the watch and ward of the administrative border, replacing tribal levies raised during the war. Despite its vital role in suppressing the Mutiny, the independence of such a large number of men outside the jurisdiction of the Commander-in-Chief was questioned during the ensuing reorganisation of the Indian Army.[41] The resulting discussions reflected the perceived military and political importance of a localised force being maintained in the Punjab. Brigadier-General Sir Neville Chamberlain, the PIF's current commander, emphasised the joint political and military role of the force and stressed the importance of localisation to maintain its intimate knowledge of the frontier and its inhabitants. He argued that its men had become accustomed to mountain warfare by repeated operations against the trans-border tribes and that by experience, organisation, recruitment and training the PIF was now ideally fitted for conducting military operations against the hill tribes. The Commissioner of Peshawar, Captain W. James, was more effusive in his support, emphasising the unique character of the fighting in which it was employed:

> Everyone who has been engaged on expeditions on this frontier must admit that it is a peculiar kind of warfare, requiring special training of officers and men. Independent of the harassing duties attendant on campaigning everywhere, there are peculiar difficulties to be encountered in the hills on the border, and which are overcome by practice only. I have no hesitation in saying that troops freshly and indiscriminately brought to the work must fail; even physically they would break down. I can assure the Government that I have seen sepoys of the Regular Army *shot down and cut down* on the hill side perfectly helpless, whilst their comrades of the Irregular Force have been driving the enemy up a neighbouring hill; and if we look to smaller matters (which in truth make up the efficiency of the whole) we shall see how the Irregular of the Punjab Force excels his comrade of the Regular Army ... It is necessary to occupy many points, and to keep up communications with them all; this involves the detachment of many parties, and Native Officers and Non-Commissioned Officers are frequently Commanding small but important posts, requiring intelligence, care, and prudence of mind, and knowledge of the enemy's tactics to extricate themselves from. Such incidents are unobserved generally, but the enemy is acquainted with them, and they frequently tend, as much as more open signs of power and skill, to the successful result of the day; and to establish a wholesome fear of our men.

Such wholehearted support for the PIF contrasted sharply with the biting criticism he reserved for regular Bengal Army regiments:

> Conceive a General had never before seen an expedition of the kind, with a force which found itself on the frontier in ordinary course of relief!! Supposing the General and his Officers to be even superior to the ordinary men; – we require no prophetic skill to calculate the rest – not aware of the style of the enemy's warfare, of the nature of the country he is about to penetrate, of the arrangements found by experience to be required for the efficiency and comfort of his men, of the weak points of our organisation under such circumstances, of the manner in which the enemy can most readily inflict loss on us, of the arrangements for the wounded, and above all of what men can and what they cannot do, it would be a miracle if he avoid a disaster ... Nothing which I have said can, I trust, be considered in any way disparaging to

the officers of the other divisions of the army. I simply assert that, while the main principles of war must be the same anywhere, yet its details are necessarily dependent on the character of the enemy and that these can be mastered only by experience and practice: any attempt to theorize will prove abortive, and just as peculiar training is necessary for the various departments of the same profession in civil life, so it is essential in the Army.[42]

Despite the Commander-in-Chief's continued objections, the PIF remained under the orders of the Punjab Government.[43] Although major changes were implemented in the regular Indian army during the 1860s, the organisation of the PIF remained essentially unaltered during the early 1860s apart from a reduction in the strength of its regiments and their attendant transport.[44] Following the disbandment of various Military Police battalions and levies serving in the Punjab, Sir Neville Chamberlain became responsible for the entire system of border defence in May 1862 outside the confines of the Peshawar District. A new Frontier Militia was recruited from Pathan tribesmen living on both sides of the administrative border to provide alternative employment to raiding and to enlist local support. Henceforth the line of outposts in the Bannu, Dera Ismail Khan, Dera Ghazi Khan and Rajanpore districts was placed under the control of the commandants of the PIF cavalry regiments while the militia – 403 horsemen and 217 infantrymen – garrisoned intermediate posts either alone or in conjunction with troops. Members of the militia provided local knowledge, acted as guides and collected valuable intelligence regarding raids and offences committed by the trans-border tribes which considerably increasing the efficiency of the troops in their duties in peace and war.[45]

The military effectiveness of the PIF was maintained primarily during the early 1860s by frequent practical experience combined with the large cadre of seasoned officers and men remaining in its ranks, despite heavy casualties during the Mutiny, who 'passed on' their knowledge of hill warfare to new subalterns, while Indian officers, NCOs and men disseminated their own experience to successive generations of new recruits. A Standing Order issued by Brigadier-General Chamberlain on 1st October 1862 directed that the commanding officer of each infantry regiment should move his troops into camp each year for the purpose of light infantry training on the hill sides nearby each station. This proved a highly successful form of practical training for the PIF's specialised duties, accustoming the troops to light infantry skills and the special training required during operations over mountainous terrain. In addition, they provided British and Indian officers with the opportunity to organise and

control each unit's baggage, equipment, pack transport, and hospital establishments under operational conditions. Such training was deemed of
special importance due to the complex administrative requirements of
hill warfare and to reduce the amount of transport accompanying the
regiments in the field.[46] Training was given added realism when mock
fights were held between opposing parts of the regiments, simulating
attack, defence and retirements from positions in the hills. Annual inspections of the border outposts, cantonments and each regiment and battery
by the commander of the PIF frequently coincided with the light infantry
training camps, providing him with an opportunity to assess the performance of his units under simulated active service conditions and to ensue
tactical uniformity.[47]

THE BENGAL ARMY AND MOUNTAIN WARFARE

The conduct of mountain warfare on the North-West Frontier did not completely escape professional attention within the regular army during the
1860s. When the hastily formed Eusufzye Field Force – consisting of
5,000 men and 18 guns – assembled during the autumn of 1863 for punitive operations against the colony of 'Hindustani Fanatics' at Sitana it represented the largest force assembled on the North-West Frontier since the
First Afghan War. Six PIF infantry regiments, the Queen's Own Corps of
Guides and two mountain trains from the Derajat and Kohat garrisons
formed the backbone of the force which was bolstered by two regular
British and three Indian regiments and a single artillery battery. When
these units arrived it soon became apparent that their equipment and transport were inappropriate for the planned operations. Mules and equipment
had to be borrowed from PIF light field batteries to make the Royal
Artillery battery effective. As the punitive expedition ventured into the
mountains it immediately encountered difficulties as the hastily collected
transport, baggage and heavy equipment accompanying the regulars
slowed movement to a crawl.[48] The advance finally ground to a halt at the
Umbeyla Pass when the force was attacked by over 15,000 Swati,
Bunerwal and Hindustani tribesmen emboldened by its slow progress
through the mountains. On 22nd October it assumed the defensive under
sustained tribal attack, altering the entire plan of campaign and transforming a minor expedition into a major war. Heavy fighting continued for two
months for the possession of Crag Piquet, Eagle's Nest, and Conical Hill,
which dominated the position in the Umbeyla Pass. Tribal *jezails* out-
ranged the muskets and Brunswick rifles used by Indian troops and

provided effective covering fire to swordsmen utilising the network of ravines, rocks and broken wooded terrain to close and engage in hand-to-hand combat with troops defending the breastworks and *sangars* blocking the pass.[49] The key to the position, Crag Piquet, changed hands on three occasions, with heavy losses on both sides, before it was finally recaptured by Indian troops.[50] Deadlock continued during October and November 1863, focusing the attention of Sir Hugh Rose, the Commander-in-Chief, and the Governor-General on the operations and provoking calls for an ignominious withdrawal back to the plain. After two officers were sent by the Commander-in-Chief to report on the situation, reinforcements were despatched from the regular army including two British and three Indian regiments.[51] The strengthened Eusufzye Field Force finally took the offensive in November and the destruction of the village of Malka on 22nd December ended the campaign. However, this was after it had suffered 238 killed and 670 wounded, which represented the highest losses ever inflicted on Indian troops during a campaign on the North-West Frontier.[52]

The hard fighting at Umbeyla campaign briefly focused interest of officers serving in the Bengal Army on the requirements of hill warfare, as well as some providing further British and Indian troops with practical experience of the inherent difficulties of military operations against a 'savage' tribal opponent in mountainous terrain devoid of roads. Several books and lectures appeared in its aftermath discussing the military requirements of hill warfare. An essay on mountain warfare was published in England in 1866, using examples from the 1816 Gurkha War, the First Afghan War, Umbeyla and European mountain warfare, intended to redress the meagre amount of information on the subject currently available to officers serving in India. In this book Lieutenant Charles MacGregor recommended that 'everything should be done to raise the efficiency of our own soldiers, by subjecting them beforehand to practice of the style of warfare in which they will soon be engaged, by nerving them gradually to the hardships they will have to undergo, and by equipping them in the manner most suited to the climate and features of the enemy's country.'[53] Those problems inherent in an Indian mountain campaign were discussed at length in a detailed study of the Umbeyla campaign written by Colonel John Adye, who was highly critical of the effectiveness of conventionally organised, trained and equipped Indian troops in mountain warfare. This experienced officer pointed out:

> Offensive Mountain warfare, in a hostile unknown region, is the prosecution of a difficult art under most trying circumstances. All the ordinary obstructions to successful campaigning present themselves in an

aggravated form. Whether in climbing steep ridges, or in forcing rocky defiles, the advantages of ground and the knowledge of locality are in entirely the favour of the enemy. They not only hold the commanding points, but the very habits of their daily life render them particularly adapted to irregular fighting. The well-fed soldier of the plains, on the other hand, toiling wearily over the unwanted difficulties of the ground, find that the advantages of the regular formations and severe drill are of little avail under conditions antagonistic to normal routine.[54]

In particular, the dearth of appropriate transport to carry food, ammunition and medical stores was heavily criticised, since it had represented the Achilles heel of the regular army throughout the campaign. Adye concluded by suggesting that British troops should be given experience of hill warfare and that organised transport should be provided for all troops at frontier stations.[55] In April 1867, the attention of the influential Royal United Services Institute (RUSI) in London was directed to the lack of knowledge and appropriate training for mountain warfare in India amongst British officers. Major George Fosbery of the Bengal Staff Corps complained that while the French army had learnt from its service in Algeria, the British Army had ignored 'lessons' gained in India. He pointed out that:

Comparatively few English officers know what Indian mountain fighting means; the remainder, when brought face to face with a brave, numerous, and formidable enemy, on ground very different from the valleys of Aldershot, or the plains where so many of our triumphs have been won, are apt to find the ordinary regulations, manuals, and drill books less than what is necessary for ordinary success. English courage and English resources eventually win the day, but both courage and resources are often wasted in the winning. True, we have men such as Neville Chamberlain, Reynel Taylor, Wilde, Vaughan, Green, Probyn, Keyes, Brownlow, and others, whose very names are a terror to the tribes with whom we are in contact; but they are so, not merely because they are brilliant soldiers or diplomatists, but because they possess special knowledge, not possessed by the rest of our Services; an experience, too, which unhappily dies with them.[56]

Despite this concern displayed in India and England following the Umbeyla campaign, knowledge of mountain warfare bought at heavy cost by British and Indian regiments was soon lost as they returned to the mainstream of professional soldiering in India with its emphasis on instruction for operations against conventionally organised, trained and equipped European troops.

During the 1860s the PIF was kept on a permanent war footing and maintained a high degree of efficiency given the likelihood of further operations against the Pathan tribes. This was facilitated by further specialised training and the publication of the PIF's Standing Orders and a collated volume of Brigade Circulars in 1865, which provided 'Piffer' officers with a source of guidance and a means of standardising training in the duties required in the trans-Indus areas.[57] Although its organisation otherwise remained unaltered, later that year the PIF was redesignated the Punjab Frontier Force (PFF) after the irregular system was adopted throughout the Indian army.[58] The amount of transport and baggage accompanying its regiments, however, was a growing source of concern to its commander. In July 1867 a new Standing Order laid down a maximum scale of one camel and three mules for each company to maintain mobility in the hills, with an additional 32 camels allowed to carry regimental stores.[59] To assess the performance of frontier units in exercises involving all three arms of service and to monitor the amount of regimental baggage in the field a new experiment was tried, when the commander of the PFF proposed in September 1867 that manoeuvres should be held for the border garrisons during the coming cold season. As Brigadier General Alfred Wilde observed:

> It has been my desire for some years past to inspect occasionally the troops of this Brigade in 'Camps of Exercise,' instead of visiting them year by year in cantonments; the object being to enable me to supervise more fully the working condition and saddles of the mounted branches, and the public cattle and camp equipage of the Infantry. It will also give me the opportunity to exercise the Cavalry and Artillery in rough and unknown ground, and to practise the Infantry on the hill side as light troops.[60]

During the winter of 1867–68 Camps of Exercise were held for the garrison of Kohat at Goombut, for the garrisons of Bannu and Dera Ismail Khan at Amakhail and for the garrisons of Dera Ghazi Khan and Rajanpore at the outpost at Harrand. A series of exercises and inspections were conducted at each location directly supervised by Brigadier-General Wilde, who declared the camps an unqualified success and proposed that similar manoeuvres be held in the future. He concluded his final report: 'I believe the exercising of the troops on the hill side, in parts of the country not often visited by the Officers of the Force, has done good and afforded the younger Officers of Regiments some idea of the difficulties attending all Military operations in mountainous countries.'[61]

When a punitive expedition was assembled for operations against the Akazais and Hassanzais clans inhabiting the Black Mountain in October-

November 1868, it consisted primarily of regular British and Indian troops from stations in the Punjab and North-Western Provinces in a deliberate endeavour to extend practical experience of hill warfare to the regular Bengal Army and to prevent weakening the border garrisons. The scale of equipment taken by the Indian regiments was deliberately kept at a minimum, mindful of the earlier experience at the Umbeyla Pass. A Field Force Order, issued at the start of the campaign, laid down: 'The success of all military operations on mountainous countries depends, in a marked degree, on the organization of the Columns employed. The advance of British troops unencumbered with tents or baggage cannot be long checked by the Hill tribes.'[62] However, the dearth of appropriate training and experience in hill warfare amongst the selected regular regiments concerned the commander of the expedition. In September 1868 Major-General Wilde circulated a memorandum to regimental COs in the Hazara Field Force containing guidance regarding skirmishing, the role of artillery and piqueting when opposed by a tribal opponent.[63] Both brigade commanders were also specifically instructed to ascertain that all COs understood the 'spirit of the orders' and to ensure they acted in accordance with them in the field.[64] It was perhaps fortunate that the Hazara Field Force encountered little resistance during the three-week-long campaign on the Black Mountain, although a considerable improvement was evident over prior operations involving regular troops. The reduced scale of baggage and the number of camp followers normally accompanying regular units materially increased their mobility, indicating that regular units were capable of undertaking a mountain campaign as long as sufficient preparations were made beforehand.[65] Sir William Mansfield, the Commander-in-Chief, enthusiastically observed:

> A great lesson has been learnt in mountain warfare which should never be lost sight of in future hill campaigns in India; it being certain that in all such operations, the presence of heavy trains and comparatively useless baggage is more fatal to the initiative of the General in immediate command than any positive resistance it may be in the power of the enemy to offer.[66]

Despite this sanguine view the commander of the Hazara Field Force was less optimistic regarding the lessons of the campaign. In May 1869 Wilde submitted a detailed letter to the Commander-in-Chief that outlined the type and quantity of carriage, provisions and equipment required to fight in the mountains, pointing out that the recent operations had been hampered by the absence of rifled ordnance, four different types of small arms, insufficient equipment adapted to mountain warfare and the lack of organised and armed camp followers. Although several of these defects were being rectified, he warned that the amount of transport and equipment required by imperial troops was tending to increase. Clearly Wilde was aware that it was impossible to keep regular troops in a permanent state of readiness for hill warfare due to the great expense, but he noted that it would be possible to equip and raise columns within a reasonably short space of time if suitable equipment was kept close at hand. Wilde pointed out:

> I would remark, that the Government cannot expect a permanent peace on the North-West Frontier; encounters with the tribes ... will periodically occur, and be successfully met; in the event, however, of the slightest check to our troops, as at Umbeylah in 1863–64, the disturbing influence amongst the fanatical and disaffected inhabitants of our frontier districts makes it a paramount duty in the military advisers of the Government, to be prepared to overcome very formidable combinations. I advocate preparedness in equipment and carriage, to enable the Local Government to strike a blow, readily and effectively at the shortest notice, and, at the same time, to have means at hand to move up to the base of operations the necessary supports, without which, no force should ever be permitted to enter the passes, even for a day; ... these simple and warlike tribes owe their power of resistance to the nature of their country, and the general absence of centralization, making it often difficult to subdue them at a blow, and rendering it necessary to conquer them man by man. In mountainous countries, regular troops cannot fight in close order, and their superiority is often imperilled by novel positions they find themselves suddenly placed in. My object in writing this letter is to induce Government to adapt our soldiers, by exercise in the hills, and by organization in equipment and carriage, to these new conditions of Indian warfare.

In conclusion, the PFF's commander noted: 'The North-West Frontier of India, like Algeria and the Caucasus is, as regards the science of war, a field yielding special wants and experience.'[67]

The Hazara campaign did not lead to any serious endeavour, however, to adapt the organisation, equipment and training of the Bengal Army to these 'new conditions' of Indian warfare, apart from prompting a further abortive attempt by Sir William Mansfield in August 1869 to absorb the PFF into its ranks. To support his case the Commander-in-Chief argued that there was now no difference between the duties of the frontier regiments and that of the regulars and blamed its independence for the fact that information regarding the tribes, independent territory and the repeated military operations along the border had been lost to the rest of the Bengal Army.[68] Although supported by Brigadier General Alfred Wilde, with the proviso that the force would remain localised in the Punjab to maintain its intimate knowledge of the tribes and the border, this suggestion was once again strongly resisted by the Government of the Punjab who feared the force would lose its distinctive character if it was absorbed into the line.[69] Despite the opposition of the Commander-in-Chief the PFF therefore remained a separate unit solely for frontier service under local command although steps were undertaken to raise regular mule trains and two RA mountain batteries for service in tribal territory.[70]

THE 1870–71 FRANCO-PRUSSIAN WAR AND THE ARMY IN INDIA

The Franco-Prussian War diverted attention in India from local military requirements of mountain warfare and directed it towards the study of strategy and tactics used against similarly equipped, organised and trained European troops. After 1870 the 'Prussianisation' of the drill books dominated training in both India and England and focused professional attention back to conventional military operations to the exclusion of all other forms of warfare.[71] This tendency was reinforced by the fact that many observers attributed the defeat of the French Army in 1870 to the effects of Algerian military experience. An anonymous contributor, writing for the influential Wellington Prize Essay competition in 1872, mirrored similar views within the British Army to its own colonial experience, observing: 'The service which our soldiers have seen in India, or China, or New Zealand, will not stand them in much stead; the lessons gathered in such warfare, unless read with great intelligence, might prove rather the reverse of useful, just as the Algerian experience, there is reason to believe, was positively injurious to the French army.'[72] During the 1870s new systems of drill and training were introduced for the Indian army, modelled on the Prussian system emphasising musketry, attacks by infantry swarms and the use of skirmishers.[73] In many ways these new skirmishing tactics were similar to those developed by the PFF for military operations against the border tribes. As General Luther Vaughan noted in his memoirs: 'When many years later the Franco-Prussian war came and the world – surprised by the great superiority of the German troops – inquired how it was brought about, we on the frontier smiled to find how, by the use of a bit of common sense and freedom from red tape, we had anticipated a great deal of what was best in the German system of training.'[74] Both the standard training manuals used by British and Indian troops, the *Field Services and Exercises of Infantry*, and the various unofficial books used for instruction focused on the lessons drawn from continental military practice under conditions far different from the requirements of warfare in India.[75] The new in-house periodical of the Indian Army, the *Proceedings of the United Services Institution of India* (*Proc. USII*), reflected the emphasis now placed on the lessons of conventional European warfare. Few of its articles even mentioned colonial military requirements in terms of tactics and training. Although several pieces of literature appeared addressing the general conduct of mountain warfare for regular troops engaged in operations on the North-West Frontier, they had limited impact on the mainstream of military thought in India.[76]

The fact that the Bengal Army still only provided the comparatively small and ever-changing garrison of Peshawar District, despite growing fears that the security of British India was threatened from Afghanistan and beyond, meant that the PFF's regiments and batteries still shouldered the burden of watch and ward during the 1870s. Its units remained responsible for garrisoning the majority of the forts and outposts scattered along the Punjab border, periodically moving from cantonment to cantonment in the trans-Indus areas in the course of reliefs. By 1870 its strength had grown to that of a large division of all-arms (despite being classified as a brigade command) consisting of 12 infantry regiments, five of cavalry, four light field batteries, two mountain batteries, and one garrison battery and the attached Frontier Militia.[77] The likelihood of further skirmishes in the hills ensured its infantry regiments were among the first in India to be issued with muzzle-loading Enfield rifles between 1869–71, with greatly superior range to their current small arms, giving them a real technological edge in armament over the tribes for the first time.[78] Both the Peshawar and Hazara mountain batteries had also already been re-equipped with bronze 7lb rifled mountain guns in 1869 with greatly improved range and accuracy, while four guns and their equipment were placed in store at Kohat for the Light Field Batteries which retained smoothbore guns.[79] Yet PFF units had little opportunity to test the effectiveness of its new arms as during the early 1870s the independent tribes were generally quiet.

This period of relative peace meant theoretical instruction in hill warfare assumed growing importance for the PFF as opportunities for active service were now generally few and far between. Most of the training and garrison duties carried out henceforth by the PFF during this period of relative calm differed in few respects from those performed by the line army and the force slowly began to lose the distinctive 'rough and ready' character that had hitherto differentiated it from the Bengal Army.[80] Following the annual

The Army in India

inspection in 1872 the commander, Brigadier General Charles Keyes, complained that its regimental commandants now paid too much attention to the drills laid down in the battalion exercise and smartness, rather than to the 'essential qualities requisite for the special service of the Frontier'.[81] This problem was exacerbated when, after being reorganised in 1873–74, the militia and civil police took over many of the PFF's outpost duties along the administrative border, denying its units a source of active training and experience. Most frontier troops were withdrawn as a result from outposts and concentrated at cantonments at which they were held in immediate readiness to respond to any major tribal incursions.[82] This decision meant that to maintain a high standard of efficiency the system of annual training camps carried out near their cantonments assumed a new significance for the frontier regiments.[83] Several larger manoeuvres were also carried out in the trans-Indus areas by Brigadier-General Keyes similar to those introduced during the 1860s. A Camp of Exercise was held at Paniala, for example, during January–February 1874 for the garrisons of Dera Ismail Khan and Edwardesbad. During this period of practical training across rough terrain in the Sheikh Budin range of hills units practised attacks on and the defence of mountain passes.[84] Instruction of officers was also facilitated later that year by the publication of a detailed official history of prior frontier expeditions, written by Colonel William Paget, Commandant of the 5th Punjab Cavalry, with information 'as might render the work a valuable guide to those who might have future dealings with those turbulent neighbours'. This survey was, unfortunately, little more than a dry narrative of earlier campaigns. It did little to collate practical lessons for British officers serving either in the PFF or the regular army, except for the publication of extracts from orders issued by Brigadier-General Chamberlain.[85] The primary importance of practical instruction for units deployed in the border areas was still clearly recognised by the local political authorities. After another Camp of Exercise was successfully held at Zam, near Dera, in March 1876 Ismail Khan, the Military Secretary to the Punjab Government, declared:

> So much time is now taken up in musketry and other duties, which confine the troops to their cantonments, that the Lieutenant Governor is afraid the important and essential duty of teaching regiments how to face an enemy on the hill side, has in a great measure to be set aside … much of the efficiency of the force depends on this kind of training; and he thinks, that whenever the musketry course has finished, no economy ought to be allowed to stand in the way of giving to each regiment and battery some exercise in the hills, under the guidance of the Brigadier-

General Commanding. Indeed ... the special character of the force cannot be maintained without it.[86]

In October 1876 the two remaining Light Field Batteries in the frontier force were re-equipped with 200lb-weight steel 7lb muzzle-loading rifled mountain guns and permanently reorganised as mountain batteries two months later, finally making all the PFF's units capable of operating with comparative ease in tribal territory.[87] Despite this measure and various other efforts undertaken to maintain effectiveness, a growing number of outside observers were increasingly critical of the PFF, believing that it had lost the high standard of training and efficiency that had characterised its regiments since the occupation of the Punjab.[88]

The hostility of the Jowaki Afridis finally provided both the PFF and the regular garrison of Peshawar District with a practical opportunity during the winter of 1877–78 to assess the effectiveness of their training, breech-loading small arms and modern rifled mountain, field and heavy artillery in hill warfare. It was almost immediately clear during fighting in the Bori Valley that Snider and Martini-Henry breech-loading rifles and modern rifled artillery conferred a decisive technological advantage. Throughout these operations Indian columns brushed away large Afridi *lashkars* with comparative ease and moved at will through the hills.[89] After suffering heavy casualties the Jowakis reverted to hit-and-run tactics and sporadic long-range rifle fire using a handful of captured Enfields.[90] Following the fighting on 8th December, Brigadier-General Campbell Ross reported: 'The Afridis appear to have found that their traditional tactics were absolutely useless against the arms and disciplined soldiers opposed to them, and with the exception of a few individuals, none of them on this occasion attempted to hold their ground or fire upon our men during their retreat.'[91] Nine-pounder rifled field artillery firing from positions on the Shergadra ridge forced the tribesmen to abandon strong defensive positions, covered parties of infantry destroying villages and towers and totally prevented the Afridis from following up withdrawing troops.[92] Only 11 dead and 50 wounded were suffered by imperial units throughout the campaign which achieved complete success. The Military Secretary to the Punjab Government declared:

The results obtained prove most conclusively that the coercion of any hill tribe is now a matter of comparative ease and certainty. Our own troops have gained confidence in their weapons, whilst not only the Jowakis, but the whole Afridi tribe, now know that they cannot safely venture within range of our rifles, which carry so much further than their own weapons.[93]

Such views were supported by other officers who agreed that rifled 'arms of precision' and mountain, field and heavy artillery had important implications for infantry tactics, the composition and size of columns required for operations in the border hills. As Captain John Trotter concluded in an article in the *Proceedings of the United Service Institution of India*: 'It seems probable that two compact brigades of thoroughly disciplined infantry, armed with breech loading rifles and with a strong proportion of artillery will always be found at least as efficient for service against the Afridis as a whole Corps d'armée.'[94] Indeed, to a large extent modern rifles compensated for the lack of knowledge of the specialised tactics of hill warfare amongst the regular troops employed in the Bori Valley, counterbalancing the strategic inferiority they suffered in terms of intelligence, immunity to disease, and transport and supply difficulties when operating in tribal territory.[95]

2 The Army in India and Mountain Warfare, November 1878–April 1898

A large proportion of the regular Army in India was introduced during the Second Afghan War to the operational and tactical exigencies of mountain warfare against a tribal opponent. Most of the extended fighting in the bleak, treeless and precipitous hills of Afghanistan and along the extended lines of communication through tribal territory, in 1878 and 1879–80, was very different from those conditions envisaged in the standard military text-books on which training in India had hitherto been based.[1] At the beginning of the campaign it is simply incorrect to say regular British and Indian troops had an authoritative doctrine or system of training for mountain warfare, although, as already noted, a code of tactics and body of experience had been devised and refined by the PFF since 1849.[2] Despite the fact that information relating to the conduct of hill warfare was circulated inside the PFF and passed on informally within its units by means of an 'oral tradition', Standing Orders and specialised training, it had not been published outside its regiments or batteries or made readily available to those British and Indian regulars stationed in the northern Punjab. Although some officers and men in the Bengal Army had some personal experience of hill warfare gained while serving alongside PFF regiments, relevant information had only been disseminated in an ad-hoc manner by word of mouth to the rest of the army. Several factors explain this apparent anomaly. As the PFF was still retained under the independent administrative control of the Punjab Government, rather than the military authorities, it was not responsible for the circulation of tactical information beyond the few regulars that had fought alongside it on active service. The small scale of the early military expeditions against the trans-border tribes and the remoteness of tribal territory are also responsible. As long as PFF units could cope with fighting the frontier tribesmen with limited outside assistance, there was simply no need to develop a tactical doctrine for training the rest of the British and Indian armies. The system of regimental reliefs in Peshawar District, moreover, prevented regular units gaining sustained experience or building up a cadre of trained officers, NCOs or men with personal knowledge of mountain warfare, the trans-border Pathans and the border hills. As a result of these factors the experience and lessons learnt from fighting on the North-West Frontier remained locked in the minds of individual officers who had served in the border areas, or was scattered in the pages of published memoirs and was therefore lost to the regular army as a whole.

When hostilities broke out the PFF's regiments and batteries formed a large part of the troops deployed in Afghanistan. Four mountain batteries, three cavalry regiments, four infantry regiments and the Corps of Guides were immediately placed under the command of the military authorities by the Government of the Punjab. Throughout the two campaigns, heavy reliance was placed on these highly trained and experienced units, whose equipment was ideally suited to operations in mountainous terrain.[3] For example, they formed the mainstay of Major General Frederick Roberts' Kurram Field Force when it advanced towards the Peiwar Kotal at the beginning of the campaign. Apart from the British mountain batteries and the current garrison of Peshawar District, who had participated in the recent Jowaki and Utman Khel operations, the majority of British and Indian regiments from stations on the plains were composed of inexperienced and untrained men who knew little of mountain warfare and lacked sufficient equipment or transport adapted to service on the North-West Frontier. Only two mule trains and eight mountain batteries – two British and six Indian – existed in the regular army at the beginning of the campaign specifically organised, trained and equipped for operations in mountainous terrain. It was soon apparent these were insufficient as the scale of the extended operations undertaken in Afghanistan increased.[4] Other units had to learn the rudiments of mountain warfare while on active service or else rely on the training given at the discretion of individual commanders. For example, before the attack on Ali Masjid, Major-General Sir Sam Browne, a senior PFF officer, circulated a memorandum to the 1st Division at Peshawar outlining methods for an attack on a position, an advance in the hills, piqueting, skirmishing tactics and musketry against dispersed tribal *lashkars* on the mountain sides.[5]

The Second Afghan War demonstrated to regular Anglo-Indian troops that the tactics and training devised for European conditions were unsuitable when employed against a 'semi-civilised' opponent.[6] As Lieutenant Martin Martin critically observed: 'The study of tactics in India is generally conducted (longo intervallo) after the European or Prussian model, i.e. it assumes an enemy possessing breech-loading arms ... It is hardly necessary to say this was not the practical experience of the Afghan campaign.'[7] Indeed, in many ways the Afghan war was simply another punitive hill campaign on a large scale during which orthodox European tactics gave way progressively to those more suited to 'savage warfare', although to some extent the initial operations against Afghan regulars did conform more to conventional warfare.[8] Following the fighting at Ali Musjid and the Peiwar Kotal, however, the rapid dissolution of the regular Afghan army meant that the invading Indian columns were primarily opposed by poorly-armed tribal levies against which advanced tactical formations, derived from the experience of facing breech-loading rifles in Europe, were clearly inappropriate.[9] The decisive technological superiority enjoyed by imperial troops equipped with 'arms of precision' largely compensated for the strategic superiority in terms of supply and communications enjoyed by the Afghan irregulars. Martini-Henry and Snider breech-loading rifles and rifled mountain, field and heavy artillery enabled numerically inferior columns of imperial troops to brush away vastly superior numbers of tribesmen and to inflict massive casualties. As Lieutenant Charles Robertson observed:

> The tables have been turned since the days when the deadly *jezails* used to harass our men, who were powerless to reply. The change is dead against all accepted rules of tactics in Afghanistan. If a Pathan can crouch behind a rock and shoot you in safety, he enjoys himself amazingly; but he hates risk, and of there is any chance of your shooting him instead, the sport is entirely spoiled in his eyes.[10]

Skirmishing was placed at a premium on the Afghan mountain sides, making those light infantry tactics devised for use against European troops, armed with breech-loading rifles and artillery, of some relevance during the fragmented fighting which occurred. A combination of frontal offensives, flank attacks and turning movements successfully cleared Afghan regulars and irregulars from out of their defensive positions in the mountains. It proved difficult, however, to exercise effective command or control of the scattered Indian troops on the hill sides and few Indian officers possessed sufficient initiative or skill to fight effectively in small detachments out of the direct control of British officers. As Major James Colquhoun later observed after participating in the attack on the Peiwar Kotal: 'A line of skirmishers extended in a pine wood over a rocky hillside is soon lost to the view, nor can the officers do much as regards its superintendence, when, excepting those close to hand, their men cannot be seen. Fighting under these circumstances becomes a series of hand-to-hand combats.'[11] Attacks by imperial troops were therefore prone to fall into disarray as they became strung out on the mountain sides, out of control of their officers, and the thin skirmishing lines were in turn vulnerable to counter-attacks by Afghan swordsmen. All too often such advancing troops also masked the fire of their own comrades moving up in support.[12]

Afghan tribesmen, without modern firearms and artillery, were still formidable opponents who relied heavily on shock tactics supported with often ineffective rifle and *jezail* fire against British and Indian troops. It was, however, found to be impracticable to maintain Indian troops in extended skirmishing order, which lacked sufficient solidity or cohesion to meet charges made by swordsmen.[13] To most officers it became apparent that the best formation when opposed by masses of swordsmen, intent on hand-to-hand fighting, was the close-order shoulder-to-shoulder line, which allowed the maximum development of fire and gave sufficient solidity to the ranks to receive a massed attack. For one officer this seemed to herald a return to the line, 'the old formation so dear to British arms', as perhaps best suited for mountain warfare against a 'savage' opponent rather than the dispersed skirmishing formations laid down in the training manuals in the aftermath of the Franco-Prussian War.[14] For example, at Ahmed Khel, British and Indian troops deploying into an extended attack formation for an attack on a strong defensive position, were charged by cavalry and thousands of Ghazi swordsmen and Sir Donald Stewart's force only narrowly escaped defeat when a line formation was improvised, rallying squares were formed by the reserves and both heavy and field artillery were hurriedly committed to the battle. An estimated 2,000 dead and wounded Afghan tribesmen were left on the battlefield following the engagement, whilst British casualties only amounted to 17 killed and 124 wounded.[15] Not all operations were so one-sided. At Maiwand on 27th July 1880, for example, the tables were turned when Afghan troops and irregulars led by Ayub Khan inflicted a decisive defeat on a poorly handled brigade of British and Indian troops.[16]

THE LESSONS OF THE SECOND AFGHAN WAR

The Second Afghan War confirmed many of the lessons that had been learnt by the PFF and the mountain artillery since 1849, with particular regard to offensive tactics and the importance of piquets, perimeter camps and skirmishing. Moreover, it acquainted many British officers with the special conditions and requirements of warfare in mountainous terrain for the first time. Throughout the fighting, PFF regiments and batteries demonstrated their proficiency in mountain warfare, refuting accusations that the efficiency of the force had declined during the 1870s. As the Government of the Punjab concluded in 1879: 'The records of the two

Kabul campaigns show conclusively, and the fact is acknowledged by every military authority of position, that the best troops for work in mountainous country like Afghanistan, are those which have been accustomed throughout their service to military duties on the border.'[17] It also brought the mountain artillery into prominence. During the war the British and Indian mountain artillery batteries had been heavily employed as they possessed the only type of ordnance capable of operating in Afghanistan, other than on the Kandahar line where field and heavy artillery was also employed. General Roberts' decision to accompany the force sent from Kabul to relieve Kandahar in August 1880 with only mountain batteries in particular had attracted considerable public and professional interest both in England and India.[18] Two mountain batteries equipped with new 2.5″ screw guns – tested in the Kurram Valley – were added to the regular Indian establishment after the war increasing the number of permanent British mountain batteries stationed in India to six.[19] To help train the growing number of mountain gunners, a manual of mountain artillery drill was published in India for the first time in 1882, although it contained a meagre amount of tactical information for officers new to operations against the trans-border Pathan tribes and concentrated more on the interior economy of the mountain artillery batteries and technical questions.[20]

The tactical lessons of the fighting in Afghanistan for the rest of the regular Army in India were, however, mixed and often contradictory. While the skirmishing tactics devised for European warfare were vindicated, they had been frequently discarded by British officers for close order formations to meet massed attacks by Afghan swordsmen. To a limited extent, however, the war had lessened the impact of European military thought in India, by exposing the limitations of conventional tactics in mountainous terrain against opponents reliant on hand-to-hand combat. It also stimulated a growing realisation that the tactics and arms of an opponent had to be taken into account in addition to the terrain when determining suitable tactics. It did not provide a catalyst, however, for the development and dissemination of tactics and appropriate training for hill warfare throughout the British or Indian armies. Nevertheless, officers and men in a large number of regiments, especially those in the Bengal Army, had now gained practical experience of military operations against the trans-border tribes.

Those 'lessons' derived the recent fighting were viewed solely by the military authorities in terms of their relevance to conventional military operations. Several officers quickly reminded their peers that the adoption of close order formations was an aberration and potentially disastrous in the face of breech-loading rifles.[21] The example of the French Army and the events of 1870–71 were still fresh in the minds of many British officers. Lieutenant Martin Martin summed up the consensus of opinion in India:

> It seems unlikely that many hints can be gained from our late experience which would be useful to us in any European struggle, and further, that our late practice should be conscientiously studied least we may haplessly engraft the faults of self confidence into a system which is very far from perfection. It is then hardly in the political, strategical or tactical aspects that much practical information can be added to our knowledge, but rather in the perfection of the organisation, equipment and use of the several combatant arms and subsidiary departments.[22]

Many of the tactical lessons learned as a result were discounted in India. As General Sir Orfeur Cavenagh noted in 1882: 'If the Indian Army is to prove a source of strength instead of weakness to the Empire, it must be prepared to meet the best troops of civilized Europe, for the struggle to check the invasion of Hindustan may take place in Egypt or in Asia Minor.'[23] No sooner had troops arrived back in barracks than their attention became focused, once again, on preparing to meet a 'civilized' opponent as the perception of a Russian threat to the security of British India steadily increased, leaving the PFF to shoulder once again the burden of the watch and ward of tribal territory. Further factors also explained the failure to disseminate a doctrine for mountain warfare in the aftermath of the Second Afghan War. The marked superiority of the 'arms of precision' used by the British and Indian troops masked the need to develop specific training adapted to warfare against tribal opponents. In addition, the number and scale of frontier campaigns decreased during the early 1880s, doing little to encourage the dissemination of appropriate tactics to the rest of the Indian Army.

The fighting in Afghanistan and various other 'small wars' fought by British troops in Africa since 1879 did stimulate a growing awareness of the distinct general requirements of colonial warfare. Several experienced officers questioned the emphasis placed on conventional European warfare in training as the tactics and attack formations laid down in the training manuals were either completely inapplicable or required considerable modification to meet the altered conditions of colonial warfare. An examination of the military requirements of colonial warfare was spurred on by British defeats at Isandhlwana and Maiwand. In an essay published in the *Professional Papers of the Corps of Royal Engineers* in 1881, Lieutenant Reginald de Costa Porter pointed out the difficulty of systematising such disparate experience although he believed that certain broad principles existed of value to British officers.[24] A succession of other articles appeared in the English service press during the early 1880s discussing the conduct of what was increasingly referred to as 'savage warfare', reflecting a growing realisation that appropriate training should be devised and implemented during peacetime to meet Britain's imperial commitments.[25] During the mid-1880s the square was widely accepted as an authoritative battle formation against opponents reliant on shock tactics and hand-to-hand combat, after its repeated successful employment by British troops in South Africa and the Soudan. However, a reversion to such an outdated tactic, long abandoned in European warfare, provoked an extended debate in the service press in England revealing a wide diversity of opinion regarding the conduct of colonial warfare and a growing realisation that Britain's military obligations differed from those of other continental powers.[26] The comments of Colonel H.H. Knollys, editor of the *United Service Magazine*, in 1884 perhaps were indicative of changing attitudes in England towards imperial military operations:

> Of more immediate and practical use to a British officer than the tactics to be adopted against a well-armed, well-trained enemy, are those suitable for employment against a savage foe, such as the Ashantees, the Zulus, the Afghans, or the Soudanese, for the reason that regular warfare is with us exceptional, while a campaign against a uncivilized foe in some parts of the world may be considered chronic.[27]

Those lessons derived from recent colonial campaigns formed the subject of the prestigious RUSI prize-essay competition in 1887. In the winning essay, Captain Charles Callwell discerned both tactical and strategical lessons from Britain's disparate colonial military operations since the Crimean War. While he argued that colonial wars bore no comparison with that in Europe, Callwell explicitly recognised that strategical, tactical and logistical lessons of significance could be derived from colonial campaigns that would be of value for British troops serving throughout the Empire, including India.[28] A significant omission for officers serving in India was any mention of the trans-border Pathan tribes, although it was recognised that the training of the British and Indian troops should be partly based on 'savage' warfare against opponents very different from those envisaged in the official training manuals. It was clearly impossible to employ a square formation in the border hills of the Punjab due to both the terrain and the large target it would present to tribal *jezails*. The discussion regarding the appropriate tactics for colonial warfare did not, however, have an appreciable impact on official training either in England or India during the mid-1880s, which still remained based primarily on the lessons of the 1870–71 Franco-Prussian War.

THE FORWARD POLICY AND THE ARMY IN INDIA

The Pendjeh incident in 1885 and the threat of war with Russian troops in northern Afghanistan, however, already had had important implications for the organisation and deployment of troops on the North-West Frontier. It also immediately ensured the emphasis being paid to conventional military training against similarly organised European troops was reinforced. At a series of large camps of exercise, held by the regular army during the 1880s and 1890s, British and Indian troops trained intensively for operations against Russian or Afghan troops.[29] For the first large numbers of regular troops were deployed during the 1880s in the Punjab in preparation for a possible campaign in Afghanistan. The presence of 14,036 men in the ranks of the PFF along the border outside the jurisdiction of the Commander-in-Chief in India, however, was a glaring anomaly that prompted repeated requests for their assimilation into the Bengal Army during the early 1880s as the likelihood of war in Afghanistan increased.[30] To many officers it now appeared that the PFF had lost its formerly distinctive role, moreover, following a decline in the number of punitive expeditions since the Afghan war, the extension of British administration in Baluchistan, and with the pacification and disarmament of the trans-Indus districts of the Punjab. In August 1886 it was finally incorporated into the Bengal Army, after the Government of the Punjab was assured it would maintain its close connections with political officers and the militia. This decision finally gave the Commander-in-Chief complete control of all the troops along the border and made the Army in India solely responsible for military operations against the tribes for the first time. However, despite the change in overall command, the frontier regiments retained their distinctive character and remained localised solely for duty in the Punjab.[31] The threat of external attack also had important implications for policy towards independent territory and relations with the trans-border tribes following the adoption of the 'scientific frontier' in Afghanistan as the basis of Indian strategy in 1888 in the event of a Russian invasion. Henceforth the safe passage of the Field Army and its maintenance in Afghanistan focused military attention on fostering and securing the support of the trans-border Pathan tribes living astride the main lines of communication through the mountains and exploring the border hills, transforming a hitherto local problem into one of strategic importance.[32]

The PFF, supported by various locally enlisted militias and levies, still trained primarily during the 1880s for its specialised duties in the watch and ward of tribal territory, despite now being part of the regular army. In accordance with Standing Orders each year its regiments still went into the hills nearby their cantonments specifically to practice light infantry skills and the minor tactics of hill warfare.[33] Now that large numbers of regular troops were deployed closer to tribal territory the conduct of mountain warfare was a subject of growing interest to regular officers serving in India. Those lessons derived from the experience of mountain artillery batteries were examined for the first time outside official channels in the service press. For example, their organisation, equipment and training was discussed at length in the *Proceedings of the Royal Artillery Institution* in several essays submitted for its 1887 annual prize essay competition. [34] The military authorities, however, made no endeavour to issue formal guidance to the large number of batteries deployed in India. Writing in the *United Service Magazine* the following year Captain Henry Simpson could still complain with some justification about the continuing lack of official instruction apart from the meagre information laid down in the *Manual of Mountain Artillery Drill*. In an endeavour to help rectify this glaring omission he provided a brief summary of mountain artillery tactics based on European manuals and his own personal experience.[35] Other officers were firmly convinced that important lessons could be derived from Indian experience. As Major E.J. de Latour, a former commander of the Hazara Mountain Battery, pointed out in 1889: 'The proceedngs of foreign mountain batteries are certainly interesting but hardly as instructive as those of our own service, if only for the reason, that of late years few nations have had the same practical experience in mountainous countries.'[36]

The Black Mountain Expedition in September–October 1888 once again exposed the limitations of training for mountain warfare in India.[37] Before the operation began the military authorities clearly realised that most of the sixteen regular British and Indian regiments selected for the forthcoming operations in Hazara lacked knowledge of frontier fighting. For example, as a large number of inexperienced officers were serving in 2nd Brigade, the Commander-in-Chief in India specifically instructed Major-General William Galbraith to personally warn them about the minor tactics needed in tribal territory.[38] Most units still had to rely on the officers and men of three frontier regiments that fought alongside them for guidance in hill warfare or that gleaned from Standing Orders and a memorandum, containing information about fighting in the hills originally written by Brigadier-General Alfred Wilde in 1868, that was circulated shortly before operations began.[39] However, the decisive technological superiority of British firearms – Sniders, Martini-Henrys, Gatling guns and mountain artillery – still masked the need for appropriate training during the 1880s for regular troops. Throughout the campaign, the poorly-armed tribes avoided direct confrontation and attempted to come to close quarters with the troops on only a few occasions. At Kotkai on 24th October 1888 No. 4 Column was attacked by a mass of swordsmen who were mown down by rifles and Gatling guns before they could engage in hand-to-hand combat. Following this engagement, the Hazarawals abandoned open resistance to imperial troops. As Major-General Sir John McQueen remarked: 'The severe lesson learnt by the tribesmen in this action broke down all organised opposition, and in facing the other columns, the enemy confined themselves to guerrilla warfare in thick forest, a trying style of fighting which was productive of numerous casualties to our troops, but in which the enemy suffered severely and soon lost heart.'[40]

During the late 1880s and early 1890s the 'forward policy' adopted by the Government of India provoked a series of campaigns against the transborder Pathan tribes, which led to the commitment of a growing number of regular British and Indian troops, without training or prior experience of hill warfare, alongside PFF regiments on the North-West Frontier. The concurrent campaigns which took place along the Takht-i-Sulaiman, the Samana Ridge, the Black Mountain, Hunza and Nagar stimulated professional interest in the exigencies of hill warfare in England and India, coinciding with a growing acceptance during the 1890s in the service press of the importance of experience derived from colonial military operations.[41] A detailed account of the 1891 Miranzai campaign appeared in the JRUSI in 1892 as it 'affords a very typical example of the kind of warfare which officers serving in India may find themselves called upon to take part in.' During the campaign it was still all too apparent that the Orakzais *lashkars* were at a marked disadvantage fighting against imperial troops. As Captain Alexander Mason, the official historian of frontier expeditions, confidently observed:

Since the Jowaki campaign in 1877–78 a revolution has taken place in the matter of frontier expeditions, and the ill-armed tribesmen are now beginning to see that it is certain destruction to try and stand up against breech-loaders. In the days of the Brown Bess things were different, and they were then able to meet us with a weapon which, if not so good in some respects, yet the matter of range was equal to, if not better than, our own, and at Ambela they were able to inflict heavy loss on our troops. The advent of the Snider and then of the Martini has, however, altered all this, and now they are beginning to understand that to be shot down at 1,000 yards or more by breech-loaders when your own weapon is a muzzle-loader which may possibly carry an erratic bullet 300 yards, is a one-sided business and a game that does not pay … It is now, therefore, becoming a safe maxim that if a Pathan tribe has once fairly stood up to fight breech-loaders, it will never do so again.[42]

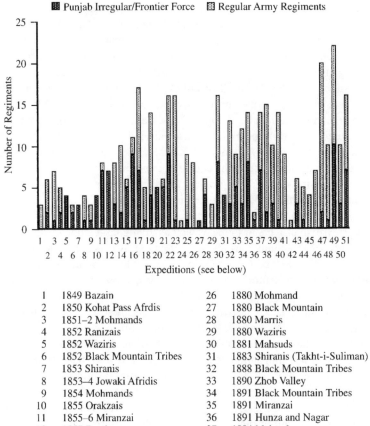

■ Punjab Irregular/Frontier Force   ▨ Regular Army Regiments

Fig. 3. Proportion of Punjab Irregular Force/Frontier Force and Regular Army Regiments employed during expeditions against trans-border Pathan tribes, 1849–1908

Later the same year an attack on a detachment of troops constructing a road, however, provoked further operations against the Orakzais. Writing after the second Miranzai campaign one commentator noted: 'A second time General Lockhart showed how easily and effectively a thoroughly well organised, scientifically armed, smartly led British force can brush away superior numbers of ill-disciplined, disorganised, poorly armed tribesmen.'[43] Further to the north, however, during the Hunza-Nagar campaign, Indian troops had been opposed when attacking Nilt Fort by tribesmen armed with Russian Berdan, Martini-Henry, Snider, Spencer and Winchester rifles in addition to local matchlock *jezails* for the first time in sufficient quantities to affect the course of the fighting.[44]

The increasing number and growing size of military expeditions on both the North-Western and North-Eastern frontiers of India involving a higher proportion of regular troops stimulated a growth of professional interest amongst British officers in India, as well as giving large numbers practical experience of mountain warfare (see Figure 3). It was apparent to many officers that the 1889 edition of *Infantry Drill*, which emphasised conventional European warfare and contained little more than one sentence suggesting the use of close-order drill when facing poorly armed opponents reliant upon shock tactics, was of limited interest to units currently engaged in mountain warfare.[45] For the first time a paper dealing with mountain warfare was published by the JUSII in 1892, though symptomatically it was a translation of a paper written by a French officer from the *Journal des Science Militaires*, based on European military experience. Major Henry Simpson, who contributed the article to the United Service Institution of India, pointed out that there was no text book on the conduct of mountain or other forms of 'rough' warfare available in India and appended a list of French and German books on the subject which he recommended to interested officers.[46] For the first time the specific requirements of warfare on both the North-Western and North-Eastern frontiers of India were discussed in a series of articles and books written by officers serving in India. Writing in 1892, Captain Herbert Cox, for example, justifiably complained that there was insufficient guidance in the Drill Book on jungle warfare in the hills of Burma, where Indian troops endeavoured to bring to battle elusive bands of dacoits.[47]

The 1892 provisional edition of *Infantry Drill* on which training was now based did include a section that discussed the conduct of colonial warfare, but it referred solely to tactics in terms of close-order formations that were clearly inappropriate in mountainous terrain. Indeed, these were a liability against increasingly better armed Pathan tribes, whose tactics did not rely on massed assaults. For the first time the term 'savage warfare', employed to describe colonial campaigns in the military press during the 1880s, was officially recognised and was used to denote the entire class of operations conducted against poorly-armed tribesmen throughout the British Empire.[48] It also accepted that certain modifications, necessitated by the differing conditions encountered by imperial troops, were of sufficient importance that they should be studied separately. This section was a first step towards discerning authoritative principles, but to officers eager for more precise instructions it was too limited to be a really useful guide to training. Other guidance provided by non-official literature available in India, however (primarily intended to aid officers preparing for promotion examinations), still either lacked any guidance for colonial warfare or was based on Sudanese experience that had little relevance for officers on the Punjab border.[49]

The conduct of mountain warfare along India's extensive frontiers was discussed at length in the United Service Institution's influential annual prize essay competition for 1892–93. Two essays were published which outlined the intrinsic problems posed by the climate, terrain, transport and supply for regular troops operating across India's North-Western and North-Eastern borders and went on to attempt to discern general principles to govern the conduct of future operations and peacetime training. In a telling critique the Gold Medal prize winner, Major George Bulloch of the Devonshire Regiment, lambasted the military authorities' failure to provide a suitable training doctrine, and criticised the unsatisfactory nature of instruction for the young officer in hill warfare. In a lengthy paper he noted that insufficient attention was paid to mountain warfare and suggested that British troops should make use of the period spent in the hills to escape the intense summer heat on the plains to ensure they were physically fit and practise piqueting, *sangar* building and field firing to guarantee uniformity of drill and training. Bullock concluded:

Nearly every year some portion of the army is engaged in more or less important operations in the hills. Yet of these operations there is seldom to be found a satisfactory history. The lessons learnt, the mistakes made, the steps taken to rectify these mistakes, may be recorded for the benefit of Head-Quarters Staff, but they are not published in any form which is generally available for the army. The young soldier who wishes to study mountain warfare in India, has to be content with a very few books as a rule, and those are not always obtainable, being old and often out of print. It is not a subject of instruction at garrison classes, and what is known of it is chiefly derived from experience, and from the training so many officers have had in many a mountain war.

But is this satisfactory? Should not the lessons of the past be collected, and available for all to learn?

Should not the warfare we are likely to engage be a subject of study, in
preference to a warfare in which our army seems never likely to engage?

The lines of our military education has been laid down too much by
those whose eyes are dazzled by the great wars of the Continent, and
forget that the work we have to perform is equally arduous, requires as
careful a study, and that the material for that study are to be found in
our own 'little wars'.[50]

In the second published essay Captain Francis Carter of the Royal
Berkshire Regiment attempted to chart the historical development of
expertise in mountain warfare, in the clear belief that valuable lessons
could be derived from past experience. This officer stressed the importance of greater preparation for hill warfare, especially in terms of the provision of training manuals, and suggested the addition of special notes on
the requirements of jungle, desert, and mountain warfare to the Drill Book.
However, he also recognised the intrinsic practical difficulty of laying
down any precise tactical instructions for imperial troops for such varied
operational conditions.[51]

A succession of articles appeared in the service press over the next few
years describing recent operations and discussing the development of a
doctrine and appropriate training for hill fighting, reflecting growing professional interest and awareness of the specific requirements of colonial
warfare in India. Although the 1893 Drill Book was regarded as a considerable improvement on the earlier edition it still lacked any guidance on
jungle, desert and mountain warfare that many officers clearly desired.[52]
Writing in the *Proceedings of the Royal Artillery Institution*, for example,
in 1893 Major Henry Simpson once again urged that the theory and practice of mountain artillery tactics and irregular warfare in general should be
taught to the officers and men in mountain batteries stationed in India and
England. To do so he recommended a French pamphlet to complement the
artillery drill books after noting that nothing had been published in English
on mountain and irregular warfare since 1875.[53] This display of interest in
the conduct of colonial warfare did not have any appreciable impact on the
mainstream of military training in India, however, which was still predicated on a conflict between similarly organised, trained and equipped
troops. The only troops to receive specialised training remained the frontier force or mountain artillery batteries.[54] Most regular British officers
still had to learn 'on the job' or from experienced frontier soldiers when
deployed in the border areas. The following year the JUSII prize essay

competition focused on the difficulties of devising suitable training pro-
grammes for an army operating in widely differing theatres of war and
against opponents that changed with bewildering rapidity. Captain Francis
Carter, the prize-winning author, reiterated his belief that the military
authorities had failed by not providing the bulk of British and Indian
troops with appropriate training for local requirements, with emphasis
instead being placed on training along continental lines. He noted that
additional information was required to complement that already contained
in the Drill Book and suggested the inclusion of an authoritative 'Indian
Appendix' containing hints and precepts dealing with operations against
tribesmen on the frontiers of India that could become the recognised
authority on the subject. Carter went on:

> Until the present drill season, however, I believe no attempt has been
> made ... to exercise troops with a view to warfare other than that
> against civilized foes in fairly open, level, or partially heavy country.
> Mountain and jungle warfare against savage tribes has, in all our big
> camps, been an unknown factor ... That some of our troops are
> extremely proficient in Guerrilla and Mountain Warfare, there is no
> doubt; but this is due more to experience gained during the ever fre-
> quent little frontier wars, rather than to the intuition given in times of
> peace; and in many cases, 'ere officers and men have become thoroughly
> 'aguerri' to this description of fighting, they have had to undo a great
> deal learnt on the parade ground, and start afresh with experience and
> common sense as their guides in lieu of the drill book. I remember full
> well, during one campaign, after many little brushes with the enemy
> and not a few night attacks, a Sikh Officer asked me if we were ever
> going to advance against the enemy in 'pucca (real) attack formation.'
> This remark is instructive as showing within what narrow grooves the
> instruction imparted to our soldiers has been laid.[55]

He concluded by pointing out that the present system of training and drill
books were palpably incomplete and needed revision to reflect imperial
requirements.[56]

The JUSII published a second essay submitted for the 1894 prize essay
competition the following year that argued in a similar vein. In a lengthy
essay Captain William Hamilton of the East Lancashire Regiment recognised that instructing British and Indian troops in mountain warfare posed
certain practical difficulties for the Army in India given the limited
number of hill stations with nearby terrain suitable for training purposes
and officers accustomed to hill warfare. Moreover, the wide differences in
the armament and tactics of various 'savage' opponents also militated

against the development of a system of widely applicable training for warfare along the frontiers of India. Hamilton observed:

> Our troops, it may be urged, have had so much practice in fighting savage tribes, that tactical instruction in such a matter is superfluous. This is true to a certain extent, but the experience gained by part of the army in India requires to be imparted to the whole. There are no text-books on the subject and the literature of savage warfare though fairly full is not generally accessible. It would, I think, be of undoubted assist-ance if the accumulated experience gained in many wars with many kinds of savages were crystallized in the form of a short official text-book; meanwhile the personal knowledge and experience of individuals must be our guide ... While it would be a work of supererogation to teach the troops of the Punjab Frontier Force, for instance, how to fight Pathans or to instruct the Burma battalions in the subtleties of jungle warfare, the experience of recent hill campaigns shows that some pre-liminary instruction is certainly required in many cases, and especially in the case of British or Native regiments new to the work required.[57]

Clearly the development and adaptation of training to the varied exigen-cies of colonial warfare around the British Empire, and more immediately on the frontiers of India, posed a complex problem. For the time being Hamilton believed that experienced officers represented 'the natural teach-ers in the theory of savage warfare,' and proposed a detailed programme of progressive training commencing with a few companies and working up to a full brigade of all arms. Small camps of instruction should be held, at such places as Ranikhet or the Murree Hills, he suggested with a skeleton enemy provided by men accustomed to tribal tactics as well as the estab-lishment of permanent schools to provide combined tactical training in hill warfare at which troops could be instructed for a month each autumn. Those articles published by the JUSII during 1894–95 were a significant recognition of the importance of appropriate training and indicated some of the fundamental problems involved in devising suitable training for regular troops in such a specialist form of warfare.[58] Despite such detailed suggestions, the Adjutant-General in India made no attempt to formally alter the existing system of training to reflect the growing awareness of the peculiar requirements of warfare on the North-West Frontier or to absorb the lessons of the early 1890s. Apart from a small pamphlet published in 1894 written by Major Oswald Radford, Commandant of the 4th Punjab Infantry, for probationary officers serving in the Punjab and the Standing Orders of PFF regiments, no sources of guidance in mountain warfare were readily available for British officers.[59]

The steady extension of British influence in tribal territory during the mid-1890s brought the Army in India into further conflict with the trans-border tribes. A mixed Mahsud and Wazir *lashkar*, for example, attacked troops escorting a party delimiting the Durand Line at Wano on 4th November 1894, successfully overrunning the camp.[60] The ensuing punitive expedition, carried out primarily by highly trained and experienced PFF regiments, traversed Waziristan during the winter of 1894–95 destroying villages and seizing food and livestock. It suffered a only 23 casualties during skirmishes with the poorly-armed local tribesmen who were unable to offer effective resistance.[61] This operation was soon followed by the mobilisation of the 1st Division in March 1895 to relieve the beleaguered British Agent and garrison at Fort Chitral. The Chitral Relief Force, under the command of Major-General Sir Robert Low, totalled 15,000 men equipped with modern weapons that included Maxim machine guns and Lee-Metford rifles, further increasing the disparity in armament between imperial troops and local tribesmen.[62] On 3rd April, for example, the majority of the estimated 12,000 tribesmen defending the Malakand Pass were armed with swords or resorted to rolling boulders down the mountain sides at the advancing British troops, while the remainder possessed a handful of muzzle-loading and breech-loading firearms.[63] Tribal *sangars* and breastworks were clearly marked with standards allowing rifle volleys, mountain artillery and Maxim machine guns to exact a heavy toll of the defenders. As one observer observed: 'The Maxims playing from right and left of the gorge created an ideal picture of a civilised attack on a savage enemy.'[64] At the cost of only 60 casualties the 2nd Brigade captured the position after killing over 500 of the comparatively poorly-armed defenders.[65] Apart from some minor fighting at the Panjkora River, sniping of camps at night and attacks on small parties and individuals during the advance up the Swat Valley the decisive defeats inflicted at the Malakand and at Khar on 4th April ended all major resistance. Fort Chitral was finally relieved by a column of Imperial Service Troops advancing from Kashmir, restoring peace to the border after a six-week campaign. This operation indicated, however, that the technological superiority enjoyed by British arms was on the decline, when both the Imperial Service Troops from Kashmir and the defenders of Fort Chitral were opposed by tribesmen armed with Sniders and Martini-Henry rifles qualitatively superior to their own weapons.[66] When Dir Fort was also captured evidence was also found indicating the tribes were actively seeking to secure their own 'arms of precision' and revealing the existence of a lucrative arms trade on the North-West Frontier.[67]

Both the 1894–5 Waziristan Campaign and the 1895 Chitral Campaign demonstrated once again the importance of the Army in India studying hill warfare, especially after new garrisons were established in tribal terri- tory. Further lectures, articles and books appeared in print during 1895 describing these campaigns, that attempted to deduce lessons from the recent fighting on the North-West Frontier.[68] Two articles that appeared in England and India were particularly significant. At a lecture at the RUSI in London, Major Francis Carter noted that recent operations in India could be characterised exclusively as mountain warfare and stressed the need for training and preparation for future campaigns. His lecture provoked a lengthy discussion during which General John Gordon called for the publi- cation of a condensed record of experience gained in mountain warfare by British forces and emphasised the value of small wars for instructing officers in initiative, eye for ground and common-sense.[69] A detailed article also appeared in the JUSII in 1896 discussing hill warfare con- ducted on both the North-Western and North-Eastern Frontiers of India, which noted that Indian troops lacked suitable equipment and training. Its anonymous author pointed out that each enemy's tactics needed to be studied and copied by imperial troops as they were suited to the terrain, and that losses had been suffered unnecessarily because of a lack of appro- priate training.[70] Both official manuals and non-official text books contin- ued to emphasise pragmatic adaptation to local conditions or advocated the use of the square in open terrain. As Lt.-Colonel Edward Gunter observed in his *Outlines of Modern Tactics*: 'The methods employed must vary with and be adapted to those of the enemy, to his fighting character, weapons, to the description of country, and to the object to be attained. No rules could, therefore, be of universal application.'[71]

This growing professional concern about the conduct of 'small wars' displayed in the military press in England and India clearly indicated that the brief section on 'savage warfare' in *Infantry Drill* was no longer regarded by many British officers as a sufficient basis of instruction. The degree to which attitudes had changed was indicated when in 1896 a leading military theorist and 'crammer' openly called for instruction in Britain's imperial military requirements. As Thomas Miller Maguire observed: 'While looking at the stars we tumble in a ditch, and while lost in wonder at how to move effectively from Strasbourg, Mayence, and Metz towards Paris with many divisions of cavalry and armies consisting each of from three to eight corps, we may forget how to handle a few bat- talions in the passes of the Suleiman Range or in the deserts of Upper Egypt.'[72] During the 1890s the War Office had received a growing number of requests for guidance in the conduct of 'small wars', from officers serving throughout the Empire.[73] A small manual published under the auspices of the Intelligence Department, written by Britain's acknowledged leading authority on the conduct of colonial warfare, was a direct response. Captain Charles Callwell's *Small Wars: Their Principles and Practice* represented the first detailed study solely devoted to the military requirements of Britain's colonial campaigns. It dealt at length with the peculiar tactical and strategical exigencies of colonial warfare and stressed that unmodified European methods were unsuitable for military operations in the Empire. As Callwell observed: 'The conduct of small wars is in fact in certain respects an art by itself, diverging widely from what is adapted to the conditions of regular warfare, but not so widely that there are not in all its branches points which permit comparisons to be made.'[74] Although the book was clearly useful to the Indian Army, with its discussion of the general requirements of colonial warfare, it still did not specifically address the peculiar tactical requirements of the North-West frontier against the hill tribes. Despite this important omission it was favourably reviewed by the JUSII during 1896 and recommended as a 'valuable text-book' in light of the marked increase in military operations throughout the Empire, but it was not widely available to officers serving in India until after the close of the century.[75]

THE GREAT FRONTIER RISING, 1897–98

During the summer, autumn and winter of 1897–98 large-scale tribal risings broke out along the length of the North-West Frontier that stimulated intense professional interest about the specific military requirements of colonial warfare in India. On 10th July 1897 fighting started when a British Political Officer and his military escort were unexpectedly attacked by Madda Khel Wazir tribesmen during a *jirga* at Maizar in Northern Waziristan. Heavy losses were inflicted on the surprised troops before they escaped to Datta Khel. Major-General George Corrie Bird immediately advanced into Waziristan with two brigades (composed primarily of frontier regiments) to punish those section implicated in the attack, overawe the surrounding tribes and to prevent unrest spreading along the frontier. Although these disturbances was quickly suppressed by the Tochi Field Force during the summer without serious resistance, unrest quickly spread along the rest of the North-West Frontier, transforming what initially appeared a minor incident into an all-out war with the trans-border tribes.[76] On 26th July the isolated fort at Chakdara was surrounded by thousands of Swati tribesmen, who then attacked the British garrison at the

Malakand Pass. The initial assault overran part of the position, but heavy fighting continued for possession of the remainder between 26th and 30th July 1897 while reinforcements were rushed to support the hard-pressed Indian troops. Hand-to-hand fighting occurred reminiscent of earlier frontier campaigns against men predominantly armed with knives and swords, but a handful of other tribesmen armed with Martini-Henry rifles inflicted significant casualties on the defenders.[77]

On 2nd August the hastily mobilised Malakand Field Force relieved the embattled garrison at Chakdara and then conducted punitive operations in the Swat Valley throughout August, but without encountering serious resistance.[78] An attack on the fort of Shabkadr in Peshawar District on 7th August by Mohmand, Utman Khel, Mullagoris and Afghan tribesmen, however, suddenly widened the scope of hostilities. During September the Malakand Field Force and the newly mobilised Mohmand Field Force commenced operations to punish those tribesmen responsible for the attack. While two brigades of the Malakand Field Force moved southwards through Bajaur and Mohmand country, further British and Indian troops advanced northwards from British territory via the Gandab Valley to join forces. The advance brigade of the Malakand Field Force reached Nawagai without encountering any resistance, but the 2nd Brigade was unexpectedly attacked at Markhani on the night of 14th/15th September by Mamund tribesmen, effectively dislocating the entire plan of campaign. While the 3rd Brigade halted awaiting reinforcements, Brigadier-General Patrick Jeffreys' 2nd Brigade was diverted into the Mamund Valley to punish those local tribesmen responsible for the attack. The fighting that ensued between 15th and 30th September against *lashkars* armed with a significant number of Martini-Henry and Remington rifles was dramatically different from that in Waziristan and at the Malakand. Instead of attacking at close quarters Mamund tribesmen relied on long-range rifle fire to harass Indian columns, only launching attacks in strength when they began to withdraw at the end of the day's fighting. These tactics proved highly successful and during heavy fighting near Inayat Khel on 16th September the 2nd Brigade lost 150 killed and wounded, which represented the highest loss suffered by the Indian Army on the North-West Frontier for twenty years.[79] A portion of the force went missing during the withdrawal and was benighted in a small village several miles from the perimeter camp during this operation, causing considerable alarm until it arrived back the following morning.[80] Operations in the Mamund Valley continued with the destruction of villages and fortified towers, but few casualties were inflicted on the opposing tribesmen. On 21st September Brigadier Jeffreys summed up the problem encountered by his troops: 'We can do a lot of damage and kill a few men but we cannot make a bag. They retire on our advance right up the hills, fire at long range 1,800 to 2,000 yards, and as soon as we commence to withdraw down they come from rock to rock.'[81]

The 3rd Brigade of the Malakand Field Force did not escape tribal attention. It was also attacked on the night of 19th and again on 20th September at Nawagai by over 3,000 swordsmen, who attempted to rush its entrenched perimeter camp under the cover of rifle fire from the surrounding hills. Although the assault was conducted with considerable tactical skill, it was repulsed by shrapnel and rifle volleys with heavy casualties under illumination provided by star shells. Thirty-two casualties, including Brigadier-General Josceline Wodehouse, however, were suffered within the encampment and 133 transport animals were also killed or wounded.[82] When the Mohmand Field Force advanced up the Gandab Valley from Shabkadr in Peshawar District it encountered little resistance, and at Lakarai on 21st September it established contact with the Malakand Field Force. The Badmanai Pass, occupied by the Adda Mulla's *lashkar*, was captured by the combined force which then destroyed the tribal stronghold at Jarobi, against only desultory opposition from the tribesmen. At a *jirga* on 28th September Mohmand representatives finally agreed terms, bringing an end to the fighting, but the Mohmand Field Force remained in the area until all the outstanding fines had been collected. Although the operations in the Mamund Valley dragged on during September, tribal resistance declined after heavy casualties were inflicted on a *lashkar* during further heavy fighting around Agrah and Gat villages on 30th September against well-armed tribesmen exploiting the difficult terrain.[83] Following the destruction of the village at Badalai on 3rd October active operations against the Mamunds ended and after the proscribed fines were collected imperial troops withdrew into British territory towards the end of the month.[84] On several occasions during the operations against the Mamunds, however, the limitations of training given to regular British and Indian troops had been exposed. Writing on 7th October 1897, Sir Bindon Blood pointedly observed: 'There is no doubt that our officers and men have much to learn in regard to keeping together, and seeing to mutual support, and to the ground, when they get away from direct authority. All the mishaps that have occurred here are traceable to carelessness on these points – which is brought out by the superior smartness of the enemy.'[85]

The Waziristan, Swat, Bajaur and the Mohmand operations were a prelude to the largest and most difficult campaign fought by the Army in India in 1897–98. While operations were in progress in Mohmand country unrest spread southwards during August to affect the Afridis and Orakzais who inhabited the strategically important area between the Khyber Pass

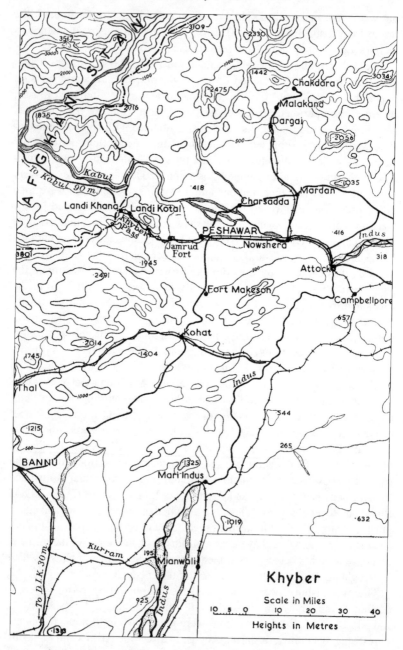

Fig. 4.   The Khyber Pass and Surrounding Area

and Kurram Valley. On 23rd August Afridi *lashkars* attacked outposts and forts in the Khyber Pass held by the locally recruited levies (see Figure 4). The Khyber Rifles successfully resisted until 25th August, but following the death of two influential senior Afridi officers they then surrendered with the loss of the garrison's Snider rifles and 50,000 rounds of reserve ammunition, closing the Khyber Pass. Skirmishes continued throughout August and September along the Samana ridge and in the Kurram Valley. In mid-September the forts on the Samana ridge were attacked in strength by a mixed Afridi and Orakzai *lashkar*. On 12th September Fort Saragarhi fell to the tribesmen with the loss of the entire garrison of 21 sepoys from the 36th Sikhs who refused to surrender. Other isolated forts were successfully relieved by a force from Kohat under General Sir Arthur Yeatman-Biggs, who then concentrated on ensuring the security of the local border from further attacks. The Kurram Valley was also the scene of serious fighting. At Sadde on 16th-17th September, a camp occupied by the 1st Brigade was attacked by 2,000 Massuzai tribesmen, who were repelled with heavy casualties after they attempted to rush the perimeter.[86]

The punitive expedition which assembled at Shinawari during September and October 1897, to conduct operations against the Afridis and Orakzais, represented the largest concentration of imperial troops ever deployed on the North-West Frontier. It was expected that the two tribes – with an estimated combined fighting strength of 40–50,000 men – would offer strong resistance as they were comparatively well armed with breech-loading rifles bought with income from subsidies and military salaries and as their *lashkars* included many reservists, pensioners and deserters from the Indian Army aware of the tactics employed by imperial troops.[87] To complicate matters this part of tribal territory remained virtually terra incognita, despite being only 60 miles from Peshawar, and the approach of winter placed severe time constraints on any operations. The Tirah Expeditionary Force (TEF), under the command of General Sir William Lockhart, accordingly consisted of two divisions consisting of infantry, cavalry and mountain artillery totalling 34,506 troops, 19,858 non-combatant followers and 34,000 assorted pack animals to transport and supply it in the field.[88] Further line-of-communication troops were also deployed to maintain the flow of supplies and reinforcements 73 miles back across the Indus to a railhead at Khushalgarh. Two other columns were also formed to operate respectively in Peshawar District and the Kurram Valley, while another brigade was held in reserve at Rawalpindi. An acute shortage of trained transport officers, attendants and pack animals, however, delayed the initial advance as other expeditions had absorbed all the available organised transport units. The poor quality of the transport units that were finally cobbled together was widely recognised, seriously reducing the mobility of the force and severely complicating the tactical and administrative conduct of the following operations.[89] The 3rd Sikh and 3rd Punjab Infantry were the only PFF regiments, along with the No. 1 (Kohat) and No. 2 (Derajat) mountain batteries, to serve with the force during the campaign, due to ongoing operations elsewhere and the large number of Afridi sepoys enlisted in the ranks of its other regiments whose loyalty was questionable.[90] Several regular British and Indian units had served in tribal territory before in 1895 – the 2nd Battalion King's Own Scots Borderers, 1st Gordon Highlanders, 15th Sikhs and the 1/3rd and 2/4th Gurkhas – or earlier had formed part of the Mohmand Field Force. The vast majority, however, were from cantonments 'down country' on the Indian plains lacking any experience or knowledge of the requirements of hill warfare and whose training was based solely on the Drill Book. For example, the 2nd Battalion Derbyshire Regiment had served in India for fifteen years, but only one or two officers had ever been west of the River Indus during that period.[91] A small section outlining appropriate tactics was included in the Standing Orders issued by the headquarters of the TEF at the beginning of the campaign, which covered skirmishing and other elementary hill training.[92] When the force concentrated at Shinwari the vast majority of the British regiments were given their first rudimentary introduction to the tactics of hill warfare. Captain Arthur Slessor noted: 'One morning by way of variety the Battalion was taken out to practice the attack, in the direction of the Kotal, and realized very forcibly that the pretty little manoeuvres and formations of the parade ground or ordinary field day on the plains have to be chucked overboard when it comes to scrambling about hills like the side of a house, as was the case with most things laid down in the Infantry Drill.' 'In fact, the first thing the British soldier has to do,' the same author went on, 'when he goes on active service, is as a rule, to renounce the drill-book, like the devil and all his works, and start to learn his trade afresh.'[93]

When the Second Division reconnoitred the route into Tirah in strength on 18th October it launched a successful attack on tribesmen occupying the precipitous ridge at Dargai that dominated the line of advance. Following the demolition of the enemy defences, however, it abandoned the position and returned to Shinawari later that afternoon.[94] When the main column commenced its advance on 20th October it found Dargai once again occupied in strength by Afridi and Orakzais tribesmen armed with Enfield, Snider and Martini-Henry rifles. The attack carried out at Dargai on 20th October 1897 by Brigadier-General Francis Kempster's 3rd Brigade – against Lockhart's orders – graphically illustrated the impact rapid-firing modern 'arms of precision' had on the conduct of hill warfare. When the assaulting troops attempted a frontal attack on the position, they were unable to cross a narrow neck of ground below the ridge that was swept by intense rifle fire from the heights above.[95] A series of costly assaults carried out without success by five battalions of infantry illustrated the difficulties of attacking a fortified position defended by resolute tribesmen armed with modern rifles. The fire of massed batteries of mountain artillery was unable to dislodge or suppress the riflemen hidden in crevices in the cliff or in carefully constructed *sangars*. Later that day Dargai was finally captured when the Gordon Highlanders and 3rd Sikhs made a concerted rush across the neck, forcing the tribesmen to hurriedly abandon the ridge. The scale of the casualties inflicted on the TEF at Dargai, 172 killed or wounded, was unprecedented and indicated that the decisive technological superiority in firearms enjoyed by imperial troops since the Jowaki campaign had ended.[96]

Dargai represented the last major set-piece engagement of the Tirah Campaign. Neither the Afridis nor Orakzais made any attempt to hold the easily defensible passes which led towards Maidan in strength, and instead conducted a delaying action against the TEF as it moved across the Chagru Kotal.[97] Imperial troops advancing towards the Sampagha Pass through the Khanki Valley were heavily sniped by riflemen hidden on the hill sides along the line of march and skirmishes occurred each day between small groups of tribesmen and foraging parties. It soon became apparent that the possession of modern rifles by the tribes would greatly complicate the conduct of military operations in Tirah. Afridi marksmen hidden in the pine-covered hills commanding the valley inflicted over 50 casualties during the night of 25th October against the occupants of Karappa Camp, who at General William Symons' direction had neglected the elementary defensive precaution of 'crowning the heights' or building adequate perimeter defences surrounding the camp.[98] The vulnerability of the densely packed perimeter camp to long-range rifle fire led to the hurried construction of large fortified piquets, each containing a company of infantry on the surrounding heights at a distance of one mile from camp. Their size reflected the continued expectation that massed attacks would be made by tribal swordsmen. Within the camp the construction of shelter trenches and protective walls provided a partial solution to sniping and diminished the number of casualties amongst the combatant troops. However, the transport animals could not so easily be protected and suffered heavy losses, while the civilian followers took no precautions at all and had to be restrained from building fires that provided aiming marks for the snipers.[99] A small detachment of lightly equipped and specially trained

Gurkha Scouts, formed from men selected from the 3rd and 5th Gurkha
Rifles, attached to the TEF, however, proved a highly effective solution to
the problem by actively stalking the Afridi snipers harassing the camp.[100]
Skirmishes with Afridi and Orakzais *lashkars* made it readily apparent that
the majority of the TEF were considerably less efficient than the frontier
regiments who had hitherto monopolised the conduct of frontier warfare.
As one of Lockhart's Aides-de-Camp later observed in his memoirs: 'The
great part of the Tirah Expeditionary Force ... did not realise what it
meant to be confronted by an active and agile enemy who knew every inch
of his country and would be ready to seize every opportunity for turning
the tables on his civilised foe.'[101]

A combination of the administrative and logistical problems involved in
moving and supplying the TEF's two divisions in the barren hills dictated
the pace of the advance into Tirah. A week-long delay was imposed in the
Khanki Valley while the Second Division's pack transport crossed the
Chagru Kotal, new tracks were constructed or improved, and foraging
parties collected supplies of corn, straw, and wood from the surrounding
area. Due to the poor state of the steep paths and complete reliance on
pack animals the supply columns on which the TEF depended moved in
single file across the passes into Tirah at a snails' pace and had to be
heavily guarded from tribal attack. On 29th October the formidable
Sampagha Pass was captured with relative ease when a wide flanking
movement, combined with a bombardment by the largest concentration of
mountain artillery ever used in frontier warfare and a single rocket battery,
opened the route to Mastura Valley.[102] Two days later the Arhanga Pass
fell with similar ease, clearing the way to the heart of Tirah. This lack of
resistance at the passes clearly indicated that the tribesmen had learnt that
it was impossible to resist the combined strength of the punitive column in
open battle without heavy casualties. Instead, the *lashkars* waged guerrilla
warfare against the vulnerable columns of British and Indian troops
melting away before determined assaults, pressing their attacks during
withdrawals while all the time relentlessly harassing perimeter camps and
convoys.[103]

The 2nd Division entered the Maidan Valley on 31st October 1897,
confidently expecting that the Orakzais and Afridis would submit now that
British troops had penetrated to the heart of Tirah and lifted its much-
vaunted 'purdah'. Most of the inhabitants, however, had fled with their
livestock and valuables, leaving behind their fighting men.[104] Afridi and
Orakzais *lashkars* skilfully resisted the Indian troops in temporary occupation of Maidan, exploiting the nullahs, ravines and rugged terrain in the
area to make attacks on isolated bodies of troops. On the night of 1st

November they were particularly successful capturing from a badly protected convoy a regimental treasure chest and 12 boxes of Dum-Dum
ammunition which they then employed with deadly effect.[105] The perimeter camp at Maidan, containing the 2nd Division and a brigade of the 1st
Division, was regularly fired upon by Afridi riflemen. A steady toll of
dead and wounded was inflicted within the encampment each night by
snipers, requiring the hurried construction of elaborate field defences to
provide some protection, whilst the Gurkha Scouts stalked the marauders
who had penetrated the outer ring of defences.[106] The cumbersome so-
called 'flying columns' which moved out of the large encampment to
destroy villages, conduct surveys and forage for food and fodder were
continually harassed by snipers and were normally attacked in strength by
Afridi *lashkars* as they withdrew at the end of each day. As Colonel
Thomas Holdich observed:

> Afridi tactics by night were effective enough. They were almost more
> effective by day. Neither by night or by day would they trust themselves
> to open resistance or solid attack, but by day they could watch from
> their nests above the valley the scattered threads of transport moving in
> lines for foraging purposes, the little bands of scouts covering the
> survey party that was making its way slowly up the hillside, working its
> way comfortably within their range; or they could hang about the cliffs
> and woods whilst an advance in force was in progress, ready to mass
> themselves with most surprising rapidity on any luckless party that
> might get involved in the spider-web of nullahs ... This small brigade of
> bandits owed quite as much of their extraordinary mobility to the
> fewness of their numbers, as to their loose organisation and moun-
> taineering instincts. They simply played around the British force, and
> with the facilities with which they possess of attaining safe cover when
> too hard pressed, the hunting of them with an army of two divisions
> was not unlike hunting rabbits with a pack of foxhounds.[107]

To many British officers, aware that their own men were incapable of
doing the same, the skill with which the Afridis skirmished around the
imperial force was an object of open admiration.[108]

The close-order formations used by imperial troops to move and fight –
companies in extended order had only had a gap of half a pace between
each man – proved vulnerable to long-range rifle fire as they were too large
and conspicuous a target. Easily identifiable British officers were often
singled out by Afridi marksmen and suffered a high proportion of casualties during the campaign, materially reducing the effectiveness of some

Indian units. Indeed, it became a maxim amongst the British other ranks not to stand near officers or white boulders to avoid Afridi rifle fire as casualties mounted.[109] With regard to his opponents on 5th November General Lockhart declared: 'Moreover, it must be noted that even at present the Afridis and Orakzais appear to be as well armed as our own native troops, they have ample supplies of ammunition, they shoot with remarkable accuracy and they are adepts in skirmishing and guerrilla warfare. There are many pensioned or discharged officers and soldiers among them who doubtless impart the military training they have themselves acquired in the ranks of the Native Army.'[110] This was confirmed on several occasions when words of command taken straight out of the *Drill Book* were heard being used by Afridi servicemen to direct attacks on British troops. Much to the alarm of many observers, these ex-officers and NCOs provided effective leadership and discipline that considerably increased the tactical effectiveness of *lashkars* throughout the campaign.[111]

Those punitive and foraging operations mounted from Camp Maidan during November 1897 dramatically exposed poor leadership, insufficient training and limited knowledge about the peculiarities of hill warfare in both British and Indian regiments. It was all too apparent that the tactical training regimes in force in India were almost entirely inapplicable for the conditions encountered on the frontier. As one officer explained:

> We at once found out the deficiencies of our peace training. In the first place the system of attack which we had taken so much trouble to learn was quite out of place in the hills. In the second place we had not been in action five minutes before we found that volley-firing was useless, for the targets never remained in position long enough for us to go through all the elaborate preliminaries. In the third place, companies, and even sections, had to a great extent fight their own battles, for it was impossible to supervise them, and sometimes even to see them; and lastly both officers and men were very much at sea in the skirmishing tactics which the ground made necessary ... As regards the last, I must acknowledge that all were not tarred with the same brush, and some regiments, notably several belonging to the native army, were at home from the first ... Tommy Atkins was nearly as clever a skirmisher, although hardly as agile as his Pathan Comrade. But of course while he was learning his business, the losses were both heavy and unnecessary, and this is certainly a reflection on our system of training.[112]

The broken terrain made the stereotyped system of attack and retirement laid down in the Drill Books useless to British and Indian troops. Furthermore, the system of collective fire control and discipline, based on carefully directed and controlled volley firing, in particular proved singularly unsuited to fighting against widely dispersed Afridi skirmishers. In fact, it played directly into their hands on numerous occasions. Captain Ernest Maconchy graphically described the problems encountered on 9th December when the 21st Madras Regiment engaged the Afridis for the first time: 'Their fire discipline and the volleys were perfect but on the word "Ready" the Afridis would step out from behind the rock and get in two or three very accurate shots before the smoke of the volley disappeared when they stepped back under cover of the rock … This finally convinced me that volley firing was not the way to conduct hill fighting, however useful it may be against an enemy in the plains of India or even Europe.'[113] While the fighting proceeded British and Indian troops were forced to acquire the skills of individual marksmanship and snap-shooting and to assimilate the lessons of frontier warfare opposed to watchful tribesmen ready and willing to exploit the slightest mistake.

British and Indian troops in Tirah suffered a series of minor defeats at Afridi hands due to a lack of disseminated knowledge of the principles and tactics of frontier warfare. During its withdrawal from the Saran Sar ridge on 9th November, the 4th Brigade encountered serious difficulty when the rearguard, heavily encumbered with wounded, came under heavy attack at the end of the day's operations.[114] Ignoring advice given by experienced officers Colonel Robert Chaytor, the CO of the Northamptonshire Regiment, withdrew two infantry companies from the crest without leaving a small party to cover their retirement. The retreating officers and men were caught as a result on a congested mountain path by tribesmen on the crest above who inflicted heavy casualties on the troops as they attempted to join the main rearguard.[115] A small detachment wandered into a deep nullah during the ensuing confusion where they were killed and their bodies mutilated by 12–30 Afridi tribesmen who seized their Lee-Metfords and ammunition. On 11th December a Court of Enquiry convened at Camp Maidan to investigate the incident concluded that the troops lacked training and experience in hill warfare and that both Brigadier Richard Westmacott's and Colonel Chaytor's tactical dispositions had been poor.[116] In particular, Brigadier Richard Westmacott's decision to move too far along the Saran Sar crest was criticised, as it had delayed the entire day's operations and the later retirement to camp.[117] Sir William Lockhart was more explicit and identified the root cause of the losses suffered during the engagement. The GOC observed: 'I fully recognise that hill-fighting, especially in such difficult country as Maidan, is an art that can only be learnt by experience, and that British soldiers, especially those regiments that have not served before on the North-West Frontier, are at a serious disadvantage when opposed to Afridis, who are experts in guerrilla warfare, and who are lightly equipped and fully acquainted with the ground they work over.'[118] The Northamptons' senior officers simply lacked the training, experience and practical knowledge of the tribesmen's tactics that would have enabled them to withdraw success-fully under attack through such difficult terrain.[119]

The military operations continued in Maidan during November, although the Afridis were unable to secure successes against better led, trained and increasingly more experienced Indian troops. A force under the command of Brigadier Alfred Gaselee – an experienced 'Piffer' – successfully reconnoitred the Saran Sar ridge on 11th November and con-ducted the operation with such skill it denied the tribesmen an opportunity to inflict casualties on the column.[120] British regiments, however, still proved particularly vulnerable to tribal attacks, since both officers and men seemed incapable of adapting to frontier warfare. Their lack of expe-rience and training resulted in frequent tactical errors, which watching tribesmen were ready and willing to exploit. For example, the 3rd Brigade was badly mauled during its withdrawal from Waran through the Tseri Kandao Pass to Camp Maidan on 16th November after the rear guard was heavily attacked by the Zakka Khel Afridis. The reinforcements sent out to aid the retirement were benighted in a small village and during the confu-sion half a company of the Dorsetshire Regiment wandered into a deep ravine and were overwhelmed by the tribesmen.[121] Such losses made it apparent that to prevent the repetition of similar incidents British junior officers and NCOs urgently required some official guidance. Writing immediately after the incident Sir William Lockhart complained bitterly: 'This is the second occasion on which a British regiment has shown its inexperience of hill warfare, the first during the retirement from the first reconnaissance of the Saran Sar heights, when a proportion of the 1st bat-talion, Northamptonshire Regiment, allowed itself to become isolated, entered a deep ravine, and lost heavily in consequence.'[122] Those British regiments that had been roughly handled by the Afridis on the 9th and 16th November were addressed personally by the GOC who attempted to pass on some of the lessons of frontier warfare to the troops. Sir William Lockhart pointed out the necessity of keeping in touch and choosing suit-able ground when withdrawing in the face of a Pathan opponent and gave other hints regarding mountain warfare on the North-West Frontier.[123] On 18th November 1897 the headquarters of the TEF issued a memorandum to every unit listing principles governing the conduct of rearguards that, in effect, constituted an ad-hoc guide to the conduct of hill warfare.

It must be remembered that the Force is opposed to perhaps the best skir-mishers and best natural rifle-shots in the world; and that the country they inhabit is probably the most difficult on the face of the globe. The enemy's strength lies in his knowledge of the country, which enables him to watch our movements unperceived by us, and to take advantage of every rise in the ground and every ravine. Our strength lies in our dis-cipline, controlled fire, and mutual support. Our weakness lies in our ignorance of the ground, and the consequent tendency of small bodies to straggle and get detached. The moral of this is that careful touch must be maintained; and, should small parties become isolated from any cause, instead of seeking shelter in ravines where they offer themselves as sheep to the slaughter, they must stick to the open as far as possible. It is to be hoped that we may have the opportunity of wiping out all old scores with the enemy before many days have elapsed, and meanwhile there is no occasion for us to be depressed because some of us have been outnumbered and overwhelmed by the enemy.[124]

Issuing such guidance to the troops during the course of fighting was an open admission that the regular British and Indian regiments lacked appro-priate training for the operations in which they were engaged in Tirah. However, it is doubtful whether the memorandum had an appreciable influence on the conduct of the campaign and the regiments composing the TEF were forced to acquire experience and learn the lessons of hill warfare during the fighting, with the Afridis as their willing tutors.

The main body of the TEF broke camp and moved three miles to a new base at Bagh on 18th November from where operations continued to inflict punishment on the remaining hostile sections in Maidan. On 20th November the government's terms were announced to the tribes, including a fine of 50,000 rupees, restoration of Government property, forfeiture of allowances and the surrender of 500 breech-loading rifles, but few attempts were made to comply. While awaiting a decision by the tribes, punitive operations in Maidan continued directed against the Orakzais and Chamkanni section inhabiting the western side of Tirah. A successful reconnaissance of Dwa Toi between 22nd and 24th November was attrib-uted directly to the skilful handling of the rearguard by Brigadier Richard Westmacott and the growing experience of the mysteries of piqueting, perimeters and patrols amongst British officers, NCOs and men acquired as the result of a hard month's practical experience in Maidan. Such proficiency had, however, been dearly bought during the opening stages of the campaign when the tribesmen had been able to run rings around regular British and Indian troops.[125]

When the weather deteriorated and forage for the pack transport animals became increasingly scarce at the end of November the TEF began preparations to withdraw despite continued Afridi resistance. Heavy baggage, surplus stores, and excess personnel were sent back to Shinawari while the main body prepared to withdraw north-west towards Peshawar District. The two divisions cut themselves free from their fixed line of communications and began to withdraw in two separate columns on the 7th-8th December 1897. The 1st Division moved unopposed down the Waran and Mastura Valleys, but the 2nd Division's withdrawal via Dwa Toi and the narrow Bara Valley, in constant contact with Zakka Khel *lashkars*, resulted in the heaviest fighting of the campaign. On 11th December the 3rd Brigade came under accurate sustained sniper fire almost immediately after it left camp from Afridi marksmen armed with captured Martini-Henry and Lee-Metford rifles, who fired with deadly effect upon the vulnerable densely packed columns of troops, camp followers and transport animals. Due to a misunderstanding the leading brigade withdrew its route piquets before the 3rd Brigade arrived making it necessary to replace these positions under heavy fire from the tribesmen, mostly using rifles firing smokeless ammunition, whom it was impossible to locate on the broken hill sides. Colonel Robert Warburton noted: 'We were at the time under the cover of a high bank, and had no conception from where the bullets came or from what quarter the Afridi marksman fired his rifle. This is one of the advantages of your rifle with the smokeless powder falling into the hands of Jack Afridi ... You are made to feel the bullet long before you hear the crack of the rifle.'[126] The time-consuming piqueting of the heights on either side of the route of march, together with driving snow, sleet and rain slowed the pace of the withdrawal, which became progressively disorganised as the straggling, unarmed and frozen camp followers tried in desperation to reach the safety of the perimeter camp established at Sher Khel. As darkness fell tribal attacks intensified, and the heavily encumbered rearguard was forced to take shelter overnight in a nearby village unsupported by the badly mauled main body of the brigade which reached camp apparently unconcerned about its comrades. The Zakka Khel were elated by their success, having killed or wounded 41 troops and 100 followers (together with 150 baggage animals) belonging to the now badly demoralised 3rd Brigade.[127] A series of desperate attacks on the 2nd Division's rearguard and continual sniping began when the march resumed on the 13th December as the Afridis seized their last opportunity to oppose the heavily encumbered imperial troops. One correspondent graphically described the intense fighting during the retreat:

Road there was none, but the river bed. For four days and nights it was an unbroken rearguard battle, and the masses of troops and transport were the constant mark and quarry of vicious snipers. At times the baggage train became an uncontrollable mass, more or less bogged in the rice fields that skirted the water-way ... Time and time again the situation became so critical that the Medical Officers marching with the wounded became combatants in hand-to-hand struggles. The rearguard and flank-guards were fighting without respite from sun up until nightfall.[128]

Zakka Khel Afridi riflemen, moving parallel to the withdrawing imperial columns along the hills, once again inflicted severe losses on the Indian troops, camp followers and transport animals from ranges of 1,800 yards using captured Lee-Metfords and ammunition. The badly disorganised, haggard and gaunt troops of the 2nd Division finally joined the Peshawar Column at Swaikot on 14th December but had lost during the withdrawal a further 33 killed and 133 wounded.[129]

The Tirah campaign dragged on into 1898 as the Peshawar Column and the 1st Division carried out further operations in the Khyber Pass and the Bazar Valley, while the 2nd Division reorganised within Peshawar District. Despite the destruction of houses, villages and large quantities of foodstuffs in Tirah and a blockade of tribal territory, several Afridi sections continued to resist attacking outposts, intercepting convoys and destroying telegraph lines. A steady toll of casualties were inflicted on imperial troops by Zakka Khel riflemen when various abandoned forts and outposts along the length of the Khyber Pass were re-occupied during January.[130] Throughout the spring, desultory fighting continued while a settlement was negotiated at a series of *jirgahs* attended by Lockhart and tribal *maliks*. Another 'regrettable incident' unfortunately occurred on 29th January 1898 at Shinkamar, when the premature retirement of a piquet due to misunderstood orders resulted in heavy casualties amongst the 36th Sikhs and the King's Own Yorkshire Light Infantry.[131] The threat of a renewed campaign in Tirah, however, at last led to a settlement with the remaining hostile sections in April 1898. On 6th April the TEF was finally disbanded, although three brigades remained near the Khyber Pass to ensure the final payment of outstanding fines.[132] Despite its victorious conclusion, the protracted and indecisive fighting had forcibly demonstrated that the Army in India had much to learn regarding the conduct of military operations against a tribal opponent and indicated that several trans-border Pathan tribes had acquired sufficient of their own 'arms of precision' to profoundly alter the conduct of mountain warfare.

3 The Lessons of Tirah, May 1898–August 1914

Many serious defects were exposed in the organisation, equipment and particularly the training of the Army in India throughout the 1897–98 frontier risings. During the most serious outbreak of resistance to British rule since the Mutiny, nearly the entire strength of the Field Army was mobilised, involving the deployment of over 59,000 regular troops, 4,000 Imperial Service Troops, and 118 guns in parts of the Pathan borderland that were still virtually terra incognita.[1] Imperial troops suffered 470 dead, 1,524 wounded and ten missing in action during the extended fighting, losses exceeding those suffered during the Second Afghan War.[2] Despite the benefits of Dum-Dum bullets, machine guns, search lights, a rocket battery, field and mountain artillery, the large Anglo-Indian force encountered serious, albeit uncoordinated, resistance from the trans-border Pathan tribes. The Tirah Campaign proved the most difficult and protracted military operation during the rising – costing the Army in India 287 dead and 853 wounded – despite initial expectations in many quarters that British and Indian troops would only be opposed by *lashkars* still reliant on hand-to-hand combat supported by limited *jezail* or occasional rifle fire.[3] In his final report dated 24th February 1898 Major-General Sir William Lockhart summed up the difficulties encountered by imperial troops:

> No campaign on the frontiers of India has been conducted under more trying and arduous circumstances than those encountered by the Tirah Expeditionary Force. Its operations have been carried out in a country destitute of roads, the physical configuration of which is such as to present the maximum of difficulty to the movement of regular troops. The enemy were for the most part skilled marksmen, exceptionally active and well armed and expert in guerrilla tactics. While avoiding serious resistance to the advance of the troops they have lost no opportunity of harassing both on the march and in bivouac, a system of fighting admirably suited to the nature of the country, and which has necessarily occasioned us considerable loss, not only in action, but also from toil and exposure.[4]

Perhaps the most striking feature of the fighting was the dramatic improvement in the military effectiveness of Afridi *lashkars*. The large quantity of rifles captured by imperial troops or surrendered as part of the final political settlements, confirmed that in certain parts of tribal territory the size and quality of the tribal arsenal had dramatically improved.[5] Fighting in Tirah had graphically demonstrated the impact such 'arms of precision' had on the nature of frontier warfare, compounding the operational problems faced by regular troops operating in the border hills. During the withdrawal down the Bara Valley, the Zakka Khels Afridis' skilful use of a handful of captured Lee-Metfords had provided a portent for the future if they obtained further supplies of magazine rifles firing smokeless ammunition. Writing to the Viceroy on 16th December 1897, Lockhart warned: 'When the number of long range breech-loaders in the hands of the Afridis shall have reached a higher figure than at present, I think that the next invasion of Tirah will be perhaps the hardest piece of work that troops could ever be called upon to undertake. It is the accuracy of the fire, not the number of rifles, that has caused my recent losses.'[6] Despite possessing only a handful of modern rifles the Zakka Khel had revolutionised frontier fighting. As Colonel John Haughton explained shortly before his death at Shinkamar:

> Not many years ago, for instance, in a case like the march down the Bara valley, the baggage would have been quite safe; that is to say, the enemy could not have attacked it without coming down the hill, and thereby exposing themselves. Now the enemy, with Lee-Metfords & smokeless powder, make it very uncomfortable in the valley from the tops of hills up to 1800 yards on either side and we could not see them & thanks to smokeless powder, could not even see where they were, neither our rifle nor artillery fire could do much against scattered small groups. Of course, heights ought to be & were crowned; but, with an enemy armed with modern rifles, this entailed going great distances & crowning distant heights which, under former conditions could have been ignored. The work of the advanced & rear guards was enormous, and the enemy, being as active as cats and knowing the ground, enabled a few men with magazine rifles to make it hot for any party coming to crown a height; and, of course, by the time the party got to the top, with possibly several casualties, not a sign of the enemy was to be seen, till a vicious 'phit-phit' or two of a Lee-Metford told you he was on another height a half mile away.[7]

An enquiry conducted by the civil and military authorities in 1898–99 provided much food for though when it determined that the trans-border tribes possessed 49,000 firearms, including 7,700 breech-loading rifles firing government-pattern ammunition. Moreover, it indicated that the breech-loading Snider, Martini-Henry and Lee-Metford rifles in tribal hands had been obtained by capture or theft directly from the Indian Army, as gifts from the political department, by local manufacture using stolen components obtained from condemned government rifles or by means of an illicit trade in arms conducted in military cantonments throughout India during the 1890s.[8] Fortunately it appeared only a small number of the weapons in tribal hands were Lee-Metfords. It was perhaps ironic that the majority of weapons used so effectively against the Indian Army during 1897–98 had been obtained from the military and political authorities. Regarding the recent operations, Colonel Thomas Holdich observed in October 1898:

> They have taught us something of the nature of that new phase of trans-border military existence, which is rapidly developing on our borders, i.e., the existence of a people brave and warlike (as, indeed, they have ever been), becoming daily better trained and educated in military science, armed with weapons as good as ours, and just beginning to feel their way towards military combination under experienced leadership. All this puts an entirely new complexion on our little frontier fights of the future (for we cannot disarm them) ... Nothing stands still in the evolution of time, certainly not the military development of the Afridi, the Swati, the Bonerwal, the Afghan or the Wazir ... If we have purchased our recent experiences in Tirah somewhat dearly, we have at least secured much matter for useful reflection. Like the man in the fable who created a tiger, we have now to consider what to do with our creation.[9]

To the alarm of many British officials it quickly became apparent that controlling the arms traffic was impossible as new sources of supply replaced those within India.[10] Writing in September 1900, Lord Curzon warned: 'The fact is that, now that the Zulus and Matabeles have been subdued, and that the Dervishes have been defeated in the Soudan, there are no first class fanatics left anywhere in the world except on the Indian frontier, and it is these individuals unfortunately who by theft, smuggling, and otherwise, are gradually acquiring an armament not greatly inferior to our own.'[11]

LEARNING THE LESSONS OF TIRAH

The Tirah Campaign was fiercely criticised by the press in India and England during 1898, surprised by the difficulties encountered by imperial troops and the heavy losses which were sustained.[12] One anonymous author summed up popular opinion: 'Tirah is but the history of a failure, redeemed by the gallant pluck and endurance of the fighting ranks and their officers.'[13] News of relatively minor tactical defeats was magnified out of all proportion into major disasters for British arms while invidious comparisons were made between the Khartoum and Tirah campaigns, indicating that few observers appreciated the difficulties inherent in mountain warfare.[14] In mitigation Captain Fitzjames Edwards, former DAQMG of the 4th Brigade TEF, observed:

> On the whole the losses which have been incurred are only the natural result of operations undertaken by an army, many units of which had had no previous experience of frontier warfare, and no corps of which had had experience of an exactly similar mode of warfare before. You can't make war without suffering losses. The fact is the British public, and the army also, have got so accustomed to the small and comparatively bloodless campaigns on the Indian frontiers that when a campaign of greater magnitude takes place, and we are pitted against foes who are above the average of frontier tribesmen, both in cuteness and arms, we find the game of war is not so easy as we have been accustomed to expect.[15]

Most of the numerous 'petty mishaps' that had occurred in Maidan and elsewhere were primarily attributable to inexperience or a lack of more generally diffused knowledge and practice of the requirements of frontier warfare. As had been apparent during the Second Afghan War, apart from those British and Indian troops serving in mountain batteries, few regular units had had any specific training in mountain warfare unless they had fought in earlier campaigns. As a direct result of leaving frontier warfare as almost the sole prerogative of the PFF, specialised training for military operations on the North-West Frontier had been neglected by the rest of the Army in India. Despite being officially part of the Bengal Army since 1886, the PFF was still not prepared to share its knowledge with the regiments that had not served the same hard apprenticeship in the border hills. As Charles Callwell later observed:

> Mountain warfare was their business, and not that of the army of the 'plains', to which they scarcely belonged. What wonder if the lessons learnt in the rough school of the Khyber Hills found no place in the training manuals, but were jealously guarded as trade secrets in the standing orders of the regiments and batteries?[16]

The sheer scale of the tribal risings, however, meant that the PFF had been incapable of carrying out all the punitive operations unaided, leading to the mobilisation of large numbers of regulars whose training had been predicated solely on the basis of conventional European warfare.[17] Despite the Standing Orders issued by the HQ of the TEF at the beginning of the campaign and the rudimentary instruction while at Shinwari, casualties had been unnecessarily heavy as inexperienced troops repeatedly violated the principles or ignored the elementary minor tactics required in tribal territory and got into difficulties. Writing in March 1898, the TEF's Chief of Staff, Brigadier-General William Nicholson, observed: 'In the present campaign the regimental officers have behaved as gallantly as was to be expected, but many of them were new to the game and did foolish things until they learnt wisdom by Experience.'[18] Whilst Gurkha, Pathan and Sikh troops enlisted from hill districts were familiar with mountain fighting, British troops and Indian regiments recruited from the plains appeared quite out of place in the hills.[19] An absence of appropriate training was compounded by the fact that few British service officers were willing to take advice from experienced soldiers before the campaign began and their units suffered avoidable casualties as a result. This was highlighted when many senior officers later acknowledged that if they had had prior knowledge of and training in mountain warfare at the beginning of the campaign many 'regrettable incidents' and casualties could have been avoided.[20] In his farewell speech to the Indian Army on 21st March 1898 Sir George White, the outgoing Commander-in-Chief in India, focused on British units' lack of appropriate training for local Indian requirements:

> Although brilliant exceptions exist, the bulk of our infantry is insufficiently trained in the theory and practice of hill-warfare, the class of service for which the most constant and the most severe calls are made on our Army. It is true that at very many stations no ground exists where this can be practically taught, but there are others, especially those in the hills, where full opportunity for such training is afforded. In those latter cantonments the troops should be worked more consistently and for longer hours over the most difficult ground available, and practised in all the requirements and incidents in hill warfare, so that the officers and men may not only be acquainted with the theory of hill-fighting, but may also be at all times kept physically fit for it by constant practice.[21]

Such views were shared by many British officers that had served in the recent operations. Indeed, the Tirah Campaign stimulated a debate on the tactics of hill warfare in India and a dramatic re-evaluation of British methods in the aftermath of the fighting.

The United Service Institution of India at Simla was at the forefront of the professional debate during 1898 regarding the perceived importance of appropriate training for frontier warfare. At a lecture on the lessons of the campaign attended by the Viceroy, the acting Commander-in-Chief in India and other senior members of the Government of India on 28th June 1898, Colonel Henry Hutchinson, the Director of Military Training in India, called upon the institution to aid in collating the valuable experience gained during the 1897–98 operations in its annual essay competition, which could be incorporated as an appendix to a future Drill Book or in a manual devoted to hill warfare.[22] His views were openly supported by the Military Member of Council, who urged the introduction of practical camps of exercise and training for both staff and men in the tactics developed by the PFF. Major-General Sir Edwin Collen also observed: 'If we are to really profit by the experience we have had, the great thing is to collect all the evidence we can, to sift it, and to apply the lessons we learn, so that those who run may read.'[23] The emphasis placed on training in the tactics of the Drill Book to the complete detriment of those required for mountain warfare was roundly condemned during the ensuing discussion. As Major-General Gerald de Courcy Morton, the Adjutant-General in India, commented:

> It has always been a surprise to me that the authors of our drill-book have not devoted more attention and space to the tactical formations suitable to warfare with an uncivilised enemy. It will be within recollection of my military hearers that it was not until the introduction of the 1896 drill-book that what is there termed 'Savage Warfare' is even alluded to, and even then only one page is devoted to it; now as we have in the last forty-two years, since the Crimean War, been engaged with no civilised enemy, but on the other hand have been engaged in constant conflict with uncivilised tribes in New Zealand, Abyssinia, in the Sudan, the Cape, India and elsewhere, it seems strange that what is our normal condition has received so little consideration at the hands of those responsible for our military training, for, though we are told on page 128 of the drill-book that formations are to be adopted with reference to the nature of the enemy and the manner in which he is armed, it follows that those formations cannot be carried out unless troops are trained in them in times of peace, and that is where I think the lecturer has made a point and called attention to a defect in our training.[24]

The JUSII provided the main forum for discussion regarding appropriate tactics and training for mountain warfare against the trans-border Pathan tribes. A series of articles were published during the spring, summer and autumn of 1898 written by British officers who sought to discern further lessons from the campaigns and to examine precisely what training was required by British and Indian troops. These ranged from specific tactical proposals to detailed accounts of the recent operations intended to aid fellow officers.[25] To meet the immediate demand for guidance from concerned British officers, one of these articles, based on Colonel John Pollock's twenty years of practical experience serving with the 1st Sikh Infantry in the PFF, was published later the same year by the Institution as a pamphlet and sold at a price of two annas.[26] The USII quickly responded to the Director of Military Education's request and set the title of its 1898–99 influential prize-essay competition as 'The Tactical Principles and Details Best Suited to Warfare on the Frontiers of India'. It attracted eleven entries from officers who had served during the 1897–98 campaigns and who were intimately acquainted with modern frontier warfare. Four essays were published between 1899 and 1900 providing a detailed survey of the conduct of warfare along the extensive frontiers of British India. They contained detailed information regarding tribal territory, its inhabitants and the conduct of operations for all three arms of service against tribesmen armed with modern rifles. Moreover, they also provided information regarding military operations in the jungles and bush of the North-Eastern Frontier against opponents very different from the trans-border Pathans.[27]

Articles in the service press were complemented by a series of books written by war correspondents (many of whom were serving officers) who had accompanied the various punitive expeditions and sought to extrapolate detailed lessons from the conduct of the campaign.[28] Captain Leonard Shadwell, former correspondent of the *Pioneer* and *London Daily News,* in particular made direct comparisons between European and frontier warfare in a detailed didactic account of the Tirah Campaign written aboard ship while returning to England.[29] The clamour for a source of practical guidance prompted the publication of several unofficial text books on the conduct of military operations on the frontier, which formed a valuable stop-gap for imperial troops until the military authorities in India could officially respond. Those books and pamphlets published in England and India during 1898–99 took widely differing approaches ranging from detailed descriptions of tactics required across the border to more ambitious attempts to discern wider principles governing the conduct of 'savage warfare' throughout the British Empire. Captain George Younghusband's *Indian Frontier Warfare*, written before the 1897–98 campaigns, was largely based on experience gained between the Second Afghan War and Chitral Campaign. Though containing valuable information of general interest regarding the conduct of military operations along India's extensive frontiers, it did not discuss in any depth what impact tribal 'arms of precision' would have on hill warfare in the future. The preface written by Captain Walter James, Editor of the Wolseley series and a leading 'crammer', reflected contemporary wisdom regarding colonial warfare prior to the 1897–98 campaigns: 'Strategy is the same, whether used against Arabs or Frenchmen. The tactics differ as the weapons of the enemy differ. But the soldiers trained to meet the highest class of opponents are *ipso facto* better qualified to deal with the inferior.'[30] However, the majority of the books and pamphlets published in India were more up-to-date, reflecting an important awareness of the new characteristics of hill warfare. In the preface to a small manual published at Allahabad in 1898, Brigadier-General Charles Egerton noted:

> It is not claimed that these notes contain anything new or original, they merely comprise in a collected form the tactics which experience of others has found it best to adopt in the various situations which arise in the course of frontier expeditions, and are contained in some form or other of the Standing Orders of the Regiments of the Frontier Force, the conditions of service in which embrace wide opportunities for the study of this special subject. It is hoped that by placing the results of this experience in a collected form, some of the mistakes which so commonly occur in regiments which have no previous experience in hill warfare may be obviated.[31]

Lt.-Colonel Alfred Martin's small pamphlet – *Mountain and Savage Warfare* – followed a similar vein, containing little more than a brief resume of skirmishing, piqueting and the other minor tactics that had been so successfully employed by the 5th Gurkha Rifles during the nineteenth century.[32] Several officers were more ambitious in their analysis of the recent operations. In a much larger volume, Captain Edmund Peach postulated the existence of distinct principles underlying the conduct of 'savage' warfare throughout the British Empire which he believed were best illustrated in hill warfare, regarded by him as the most difficult of all such operations. In his *Handbook of Tactics for Savage Warfare* Peach divided the subject into 'savages' armed without arms of precision and those armed with rifles. Regarding the latter he noted: 'In this group we have conditions approaching more closely to those of warfare against regular troops. And they are conditions that we may expect to meet more and more in the future. For even savages march with the times, and we have had experience lately of how soon they learn to appreciate the power of long range and accurate weapons.'[33] A comparative approach was taken by Major Ernest Rodwell, who discussed both 'civilised' and 'savage' warfare in a collection of essays that made wide use of historical examples drawn from military operations on the frontier.[34] The dearth of general information available to British units regarding the frontier and its inhabitants was particularly noticeable, however, during the autumn of 1897. In response Lt.-Colonel Francis Plowden, the CO of the 2nd Battalion Oxfordshire Light Infantry, wrote a short guide for British regiments new to the border to remedy this problem containing general information and guidance regarding the appropriate tactics required during operations in tribal territory. It included sections on camps, transport, marches, convoys, advanced guards, rear guards, attacks, piquets, retirements and other details regarding the conduct of mountain warfare.[35]

These books, pamphlets, lectures and essays written by serving British officers after the Tirah Campaign shared common themes and ideas ranging from criticism of the Drill Book to detailed prescriptions of tactics and training required for 'savage' warfare. The 1896 Drill Book was roundly condemned by the majority of authors with regard to its emphasis on frontal attacks, volley firing, quarter-columns and apparent disdain for cover as these were irrelevant to Indian troops fighting in tribal territory. The tactics of conventional European warfare and the formations recommended for 'savage' warfare against opponents armed with close-quarter weapons in open terrain were dismissed as clearly inappropriate for operations on the Indian frontier. Although the Drill Book allowed considerable latitude in terms of the deployment of troops and stressed general principles applicable to all forms of war, most commentators agreed it contained insufficient guidance in the special military conditions encountered by Indian troops in mountainous terrain. All agreed that some form of special guidance was required for imperial troops in the principles and minor tactics of hill warfare, although whether that guidance should appear as an integral part of a new edition of *Infantry Drill* or as an Indian supplement remained a subject of discussion. The vast majority of the tactical proposals appearing in the military press were classic re-statements of the principles known and practised on the frontier by the PFF since 1849, although there was some discussion on various minor tactics on the frontier. The intricacies of piqueting, perimeters and patrols now had to be disseminated amongst the regiments of the regular British and Indian armies during peacetime. Such training was deemed of special importance since operations in tribal territory threw such responsibility on junior officers and NCOs. Indeed, a badly placed piquet or the clumsy handling of a small body of troops during a retirement by a junior officer or NCO during the 1897–98 operations had often been the cause of unnecessary and heavy loss of life. The value of the tactical and operational lessons derived from prior campaigns, known to the officers and men of experienced frontier regiments, was widely acknowledged. Regular troops had, for example, to be taught to mount attacks along the crests of converging spurs rather than in ravines where they would themselves be vulnerable to attack. In particular, guidance was required respecting the tactics developed to ensure the all-round security of a column on the march or while halted in tribal territory. Following the repeated Afridi successes in Tirah Maidan, the conduct of a withdrawal in contact with hostile tribesmen obviously also merited special attention.

The acquisition of 'arms of precision' and large quantities of ammunition by the trans-border Pathans necessitated important modifications to the principles and minor tactics of hill warfare developed by the PFF during the nineteenth century. When *jezails* had formed the main firearm used by the Pathans, tribesmen had had to approach Indian columns to relatively close proximity and, each time they fired, their position had been marked by a puff of black powder smoke. Now, when tribesmen used rifles firing smokeless ammunition, their positions were masked, making it difficult to mount outflanking or direct attacks until they could be located. Piquets, responsible for the protection of columns on the move and in encampments at night, now had to be positioned over 1,600 yards from the main body in order to ensure their protection from long-range Martini-Henry and Lee-Metford rifle fire. A single determined marksman could now impede the passage of an entire column through tribal territory and inflict significant casualties on both the troops and the vulnerable transport animals on which they depended. During the Tirah Campaign, however, it had also been found possible to reduce the strength of piquets from a company to 10–12 men, as tribesmen armed with modern rifles appeared unwilling to mount determined hand-to-hand attacks *en masse*. The vulnerability of perimeter camps to long-range sniping had also been graphically demonstrated in Maidan, but continued attacks by tribal swordsmen indicated that they could not be abandoned, forcing troops to attempt to augment the defences surrounding and within the encampments to shield themselves from rifle fire.

Dargai had graphically illustrated what could be expected when too closely grouped tactical formations were opposed by resolute tribesmen armed with modern rifles. Open formations proved indispensable throughout the fighting in Tirah. The necessity of greater tactical dispersion on the battlefield and increasing initiative, self-reliance, skill and intelligence on the part of the troops in the field during attacks and retirements in the face of a tribal opponent was evident. When opposed by some of the finest light infantry in the world, British regiments had to rediscover largely forgotten light infantry skills. The importance of skirmishing on the mountain sides by well-trained marksmen, making careful use of the ground for cover and concealment when fighting Pathan *lashkars* was recognised. Unfortunately, the section on skirmishing had been removed from the training manuals since the 1892 edition of the *Drill Book*. Individual and small-unit training therefore became the key to tactics in hill warfare when soldiers moved out of the direct command of their officers. In a general engagement, fire and manoeuvre was vital as the widely extended troops worked their way up the hill sides covered by their fellow infantry and the firepower of the mountain artillery. The efficacy of a flanking movement combined with a frontal assault against 'savage' opponents was reiterated again and again to exploit the lack of discipline and cohesion amongst Pathan *lashkars*. However, the range of modern rifles meant flanking attacks had to be mounted over wider frontages than before, becoming increasingly difficult and time-consuming. Scouts, or skirmishers, would be deployed before the advancing main body, although close order formations and cold steel still remained essential in the final stages of an attack, when it was possible tribal swordsmen might counter-attack. In addition, modern rifles compounded the difficulties encountered during withdrawals in contact with hostile tribesmen, increasing the number of casualties and making it difficult to break contact with the enemy.[36]

Many of the limitations of the current system of musketry training used by British and Indian troops were exposed and heavily criticised during the fighting. As Captain Alexander Campbell later observed: 'Trained as our soldiers were to fire volleys exclusively, they proved the excellence of their fire discipline and the deficiency in the system of their education, by omitting to load and fire except by word of command in a country and against an enemy and on occasions, when the volley was precisely not the description of fire to employ.'[37] The collective system of volley firing and musketry was roundly condemned in light of its obvious limitations against dispersed tribal skirmishers who presented fleeting targets to the infantry, and it became evident that Indian troops had to develop new systems of musketry training. Volley firing had to be replaced by individual marksmanship for which British and troops armies were not trained. Tirah led to the introduction of highly realistic live-firing exercises over broken, hilly terrain which placed emphasis on long-range fire, snap-shooting and firing at moving targets. As one contributor to the 1897–98 prize-essay competition observed: 'The first and main point to be attended to in the training of troops for frontier warfare is musketry instruction. To meet the frontier tribes on their own ground and in accordance with their methods of fighting, we require an army of skilled marksmen.'[38]

The Gurkha Scouts led by Lieutenant Charles Bruce had proved so successful in Tirah that the formation of permanent specialist light infantry units organised, trained and equipped solely for hill warfare was widely discussed. Throughout the campaign the results achieved by these three officers and 120 specially selected and trained men had been far out of proportion to the size of the force. As General Sir William Lockhart declared on 26th January 1898: 'During the present expedition the scouts drawn from the 3rd and 5th Gurkhas have proved specially valuable. Being trained mountaineers and accustomed to guerrilla warfare, they were able to climb the most precipitous hills, lie in ambush at night, and surpass the tribesmen in their own tactics.'[39] Later than month an additional battalion of Scouts was formed at Abbottabad 1898 as reinforcements for the TEF, consisting of 500 picked men from the 5th Gurkha Rifles, who were specially armed with Lee-Metford rifles for fighting against the Afridis.[40] The term 'scout' was essentially inaccurate, however, since these troops had acted as skirmishers, pursuing and engaging the tribesmen on their own terms, and had ignored conventional scouting duties. Debate within the Indian Army focused on the organisation best suited for scouts in the future: complete battalions, light companies, or individual men within each unit. The inherent difficulties involved in raising and maintaining British scout battalions were rapidly appreciated because of short service, the interchange of units between stations throughout the Empire and the necessity of having to rotate units between the plains and the hills because of the climate.[41] Similar problems were not so apparent for Gurkha or Indian troops who were normally stationed in India throughout their service. The importance of trained scouts within each battalion in hill warfare became widely recognised, but their training remained a bone of contention, especially in light of the later experiences during the Second Boer War.[42]

The lessons regarding weapons and equipment carried by the infantry were also carefully considered after the Tirah campaign. In particular, the heavy personal equipment carried by individual regular soldiers – boots, ammunition, great coats and rations – was heavily criticised and prompted attempts to reduce the amount carried in the field, although it was apparent that regulars would never be able to match the mobility of lightly clothed tribesmen carrying nothing but a rifle, a few cartridges and food. During the campaign the effectiveness of Lee-Metford rifles, now firing Dum-Dum pattern expanding ammunition originally developed following the Chitral campaign specifically to stop charging Pathan swordsmen, had been graphically confirmed.[43] However, captured Dum-Dum ammunition was used with equally deadly effect against imperial troops in Tirah.[44] An attempt to prohibit its use, however, in India following the 1899 Hague Conference – which banned its use in European warfare – prompted the military authorities to mount a vigorous defence, arguing that such ammunition was essential against 'fanatical savages' who did not recognise the laws of war and mutilated Anglo-Indian casualties.[45] Despite its abandonment elsewhere in the British Empire as a result Mk II Indian Pattern ammunition was manufactured and retained specifically for use by the Army in India in 'savage warfare' in tribal territory until 1902.[46]

Despite high expectations Maxim machine guns, which equipped British regiments and various posts, had once again failed to have any significant impact on the fighting, due to their heavy weight, unsuitable carriages and the dispersed fighting formations employed by *lashkars*. On a few occasions they had, however, proved useful. At Chakdara on 2nd August 1897, for example, they had inflicted heavy casualties on the tribesmen attacking the fort. Additionally, when employed *en masse* during deliberate attacks, such as at Landakai and the Bedmanai Pass during the Mohmand expedition, they proved effective, but more generally they were restricted to the defence of fixed posts and perimeter camps.[47]

The mountain artillery provided invaluable close support to the infantry throughout the fighting and were used, in particular, to suppress the fire of tribal riflemen. However, the short range of the guns employed, less than 500 yards, made them vulnerable to tribal riflemen during withdrawals, when most of the fighting took place. In particular, the 2.75-inch mountain artillery gun had been heavily criticised following the Tirah campaign due to its inability to suppress Pathan riflemen during the attack at Dargai on 20th October 1897, despite having fired over 1,300 rounds during the engagement. The flat trajectory and light weight of its shells made them largely ineffective against *sangars* or dispersed tribesmen taking advantage of rocks, boulders and crevices for cover.[48] Although used *en masse* at the Sampagha and Arhanga passes, most mountain artillery batteries had been broken down into small sections, usually of two guns, which were parcelled out to the foraging and reconnaissance parties operating in Tirah. An increase in the establishment of batteries in India was requested in February 1898 and again in 1899 as a direct result of the perceived lessons of the 1897–98 frontier campaigns as mountain artillery represented the only real qualitative advantage available to imperial troops now that the tribes had acquired modern small arms.[49]

Other types of artillery had supplemented the mountain batteries during the frontier rising. A Hale's rocket battery was hurriedly formed at the request of Sir William Lockhart for the fighting in Tirah. This new weapon was used at Dargai and Kharappa, but its missiles had more of a moral than material impact and considerable difficulty was found firing them accurately at long ranges.[50] Indeed, its rockets proved so 'erratic and unreliable' that at Lockhart's insistence they were quickly returned to base.[51] Conventional wheeled artillery batteries were also used against the tribes wherever possible. At the beginning of the fighting four guns of the 51st Field Battery had helped to repel the attack at Shabkadr, and other batteries were employed inside the administrative border. The 10th Field Battery penetrated deep into the border hills during the Malakand campaign, where its heavy guns were used with great effect against the tribesmen unaccustomed either to their range or the power of their shells.[52] An improvised elephant battery equipped with 12lb BL guns was also formed at Peshawar in case the TEF required heavy fire support in areas inaccessible to wheeled artillery, although it was never deployed.[53]

Except in the wide Kurram, Panjkora and Swat valleys, the 1897–98 operations had demonstrated once again the fact that cavalry had a limited role in hill warfare due to the mountainous terrain. During the fighting at Chakdara and the Malakand large numbers of tribesmen were caught in the open by Indian cavalry on several occasions and the continued psychological value of mounted shock action against men unaccustomed to horses had been demonstrated. The value of the arme blanche during these engagements had been reaffirmed, although the cavalry proved increasingly vulnerable to long-range rifle fire. As a result dismounted fire action began to replace traditional cavalry tactics in the hills, although cavalry was used to maintain the security of the line of march in British and Indian columns, for liaison duties and, on occasion, mounted charges. The weakness of dismounted cavalry armed with carbines against tribesmen equipped with rifles, however, had been displayed during the operations in Bajaur in the Watelai Valley when tribal riflemen had engaged them from long range without reply. During the fighting in the Kurram Valley, the Central India Horse and 6th Bengal Cavalry fought on foot while defending Sadde camp, where it was once again apparent that a better weapon than the short Martini-Henry carbine was required against opponents armed with rifles. A single squadron accompanied the TEF when it advanced into Maidan, which was soon relegated to the lines of communication as the terrain and the skirmishing tactics used by the Afridis limited the opportunities when it could be used with effect.[54]

Those lessons learnt in the Mamund Valley and Tirah Maidan were also discussed in the military press in England, with regard to the provision of appropriate training and also in terms of the experience gained from fighting against opponents armed with small-bore, long-range magazine rifles firing smokeless ammunition. Indeed, the Tirah campaign provided a valuable first source of information regarding the impact of the 'second firepower revolution' on the conduct of warfare in general, and was eagerly studied by military theorists in England. Opinion was divided, however, as to the importance of a specialised training manual for colonial warfare. In October 1898 during a lecture at the RUSI Major Arthur Yate launched a scathing attack on the failure of the military authorities to provide any instruction in North-West Frontier warfare or 'savage warfare' in general. After discussing at length the changed nature of frontier warfare and the merits of the various books and pamphlets published during 1898 in India and England he pointed out that officers could only acquire knowledge of frontier warfare by personal experience or by independent study.[55] Yate summed up the opinion of many officers when he condemned the military authorities for failing to provide an official training manual for either 'savage' warfare in general or Indian frontier warfare in particular. Referring directly to the TEF he observed that:

> Our best frontier officers and soldiers found themselves foiled and at times worsted by these unorganised guerrillas. Surely the inference to be drawn from this is that in the future Her Majesty's officers and soldiers must be systematically educated to meet these foes. It is not a matter to be left in the hands of irresponsible and unofficial essayists ... A manual of instruction for uncivilised warfare is required. Her Majesty's troops, and more especially those stationed in India and in our colonial possessions should be instructed and practised, not only in the exercises and manoeuvres prescribed for modern European warfare, but also in the irregular methods of fighting which must be adopted against uncivilised races.[56]

Other influential officers in England vigorously defended the Drill Book, aware of the growing pressure for amendments dealing with colonial warfare. At a lecture held by the Military Society of Ireland in March 1899, Lt.-Colonel GFR Henderson, Professor of Military History at the Staff College, stressed the wider significance of the lessons gained from fighting the Afridis, in a campaign against Russian troops. Additionally he defended the value of the existing Drill Book by emphasising its general importance for training of the British Army throughout the Empire:

> When troops find themselves on service under conditions with which their ordinary training has done nothing to familiarise them, and to which their ordinary formations are absolutely inapplicable, a cry is once more raised against the Drill-book. We have all heard it. At one

time, when the losses in desert fighting have been severe, it has been, 'Why does not the Drill-book teach us something about savage warfare?' At another, when the foe has been a mountaineer, 'Why does not the Drill-book teach us how to fight in the hills?' The next time it may be, 'Why does not the Drill-book teach us how to fight in the jungles of Africa, or in the swamps of China?' I think, however, that by anyone who looks at it as a whole, and not as a single campaign, the constant variety of ground, of climate, and of tactics, such complaints against the official teaching will hardly be approved. The Drill-book does not pretend to be an exhaustive tactical treatise. It is nothing more than a compendium of tactical principles adopted to almost every kind of warfare. They lay down a few rules for the most difficult of all operations, the attack and assault of a defended position over open ground, but that is all. It does not attempt to show how these rules must be modified under other conditions, for these conditions, as I have already said, are so infinitely diversified that it would be impossible in one volume to deal with them in detail.[57]

A similar view was expressed by Major-General Sir William Gatacre at the RUSI in October 1899, who argued that troops in England should be instructed in Indian hill warfare and emphasised the wider value of the skirmishing tactics used on the North-West Frontier. Although a firm advocate of specialised training, he believed that the recent experience should be applied to the existing Drill Book rather than devising special forms of drill for hill warfare.[58] The ensuing discussion revealed much about current attitudes in England towards the provision of manuals and training specifically for colonial warfare. The indefatigable Lt.-Colonel Francis Carter urged the military authorities to make fuller use of the facilities in England to train regiments preparing to serve in India, suggesting that suitable terrain existed near Aldershot where 'semi-civilised and savage wood and mountain warfare could be carried on'. Moreover, he complained that the Staff College at Camberley completely ignored colonial warfare before concluding:

> One would think that the British Army was every year engaged in fighting nothing but European foes. It is, however, very nearly half a century since we fought in Europe; whilst every day along the marches of our vast Empire the British soldier and his dusky companion in arms is fighting across mountains and deserts and through jungles and swamps, and it is training for that kind of fighting which we want for Tommy Atkins and his officers, as well as for our native troops.

General Sir John Gordon, chairing the meeting, concurred with the lecturer's views regarding the value of the existing Drill Book and concluded
the meeting by observing: 'I believe thoroughly in our Drill-Book. Its
principles, when properly applied, suffice for the world-wide field which
the British Army is constantly called on to act in. We do not require forms
or rules; principles are the only guide in war, and we must fit them to the
locality or enemy. We must study our enemy and his country. Each tribe,
each clan, has its characteristics and special tactics, and a knowledge of
these is half the battle.'[59] Despite such strong opposition, the importance
of officially sanctioned guidance was supported by other influential
officers in England. A second revised edition of *Small Wars: Their
Principles and Practice,* published in 1899, included a detailed chapter on
hill warfare for the first time, based on information derived from the
numerous books and pamphlets produced in India. Major Charles Callwell
acknowledged that hill warfare was a distinct form of military operation
and joined in the growing clamour for both practical and theoretical
instruction, after praising the first hesitant steps already undertaken in
India.[60] It was now for the military authorities in India and England to
decide whether the growing pressure from within the army for guidance in
the tactics of 'savage' warfare on the North-West Frontier should lead to a
change in the existing system of Drill Books and training used by the
Army in India.

THE OFFICIAL RESPONSE

The professional debate conducted in the pages of the JUSII and various
military periodicals in England clearly reflected the perceived importance
attached to the provision of appropriate training for hill warfare. As a
direct result of recent experience some practical training in the principles
and minor tactics of frontier warfare had already been undertaken for the
first time during 1898 by large numbers of regular troops temporarily stationed in a state of readiness at Peshawar, Nowshera and Rawalpindi
pending a settlement with the Afridis.[61] Those British and Indian regiments stationed in the Khyber Pass, for example, awaiting a possible
spring campaign were instructed in frontier warfare during training
enlivened by occasional sniping.[62] To provide initial guidance a training
syllabus was issued by the Commander-in-Chief in India during the
summer, which laid down a progressive and continuous system of instruction, from company to battalion level, for those troops stationed in the hills
to be supervised by the General Officer Commanding each district. It

recommended that schemes should be carefully prepared by Company commanders for each day's training, with a few men detailed as a 'skeleton enemy', and that whenever available mountain guns should train in co-operation with the infantry. The syllabus also laid down that the main objectives of company training were to provide elementary knowledge of the nature of hill warfare; to ground imperial troops in the first principles of the different forms of military operations in tribal territory; to make them physically fit and accustom them gradually to working in hilly terrain, working up to carrying the heavy weight of full field service equipment. Finally, it suggested that scouts should be selected to provide a cadre of highly trained skirmishers and marksmen to cover each company's operations. An 'Indian Army Order on Instruction in Hill Warfare' was also circulated, recommending four of the newly published unofficial books, pamphlets and lectures about 'savage' warfare on the frontier to act as guides for training purposes to the principles and minor tactics of frontier warfare. Both the syllabus and tentative guidelines, combining both theory and practice of hill warfare, were warmly welcomed within the Indian Army by officers eager to train their men specifically for operations in tribal territory.[63]

Elsewhere in India the conduct of colonial warfare formed the topic of study at several large exercises involving all three arms of service, facilitated when stations such as Quetta and those in the northern Punjab, for example, with suitable mountainous terrain in the immediate vicinity, were given large manoeuvre grants during the cold season of 1898.[64] A large 'Camp of Exercise in Hill Manoeuvres', attended by the Lieutenant General Commanding the forces in Bengal, took place in the hills at Almora and Ranikhet between 24th and 30th October 1898 that represented the first serious opportunity to study hill warfare on a considerable scale since the need for tactical training had been forcibly impressed on the Army in India by the Tirah campaign.[65] In March 1899 a similar 'Camp of Exercise in Hill Manoeuvres' was held in the Cherat-Attock hills in the northern Punjab. On this occasion troops belonging to the Rawalpindi and Peshawar Brigades practised advance guard duties, rear guard actions, piqueting and the other lessons derived from the 1897–8 campaigns under conditions approximating to active service. To add greater realism, they were opposed by a 'savage enemy' composed of the Pathan companies of the Queen's Own Corps of Guides, 24th, 25th and 27th Punjab Infantry, dressed in mufti, who harassed the regular troops exactly as if they were at home in tribal territory. Such skilled opponents made officers forcibly aware of the precautions required in hill warfare and quickly exploited errors made by imperial troops. These manoeuvres were declared an unqualified success, but this was hardly surprising since both brigades were composed of regiments that had served during the 1897–8 operations and therefore had practical experience of frontier fighting. They did, however, provide valuable experience and some guidance about suitable methods of instruction, indicating that progressive training at company, battalion and brigade level was required and that each battalion should spend fifteen days training at camps in the hills during October, November and December each year before proceeding to exercises that involved brigades composed of all arms. After the camp ended Brigadier-General Edmund Elles, GOC Peshawar District, singled out the importance of special training for British, Sikh and Punjabi regiments, as they lacked an 'intuitive' knowledge of mountainous terrain which he believed that Gurkhas, Dogras and Pathan units possessed, as well as suggesting that a pamphlet on hill warfare should be translated into Urdu for use by Indian officers and men.[66] Similar manoeuvres were held the following year near Nowshera and Khairabad for the Rawalpindi and Peshawar brigades, with similar success.[67] A 'skeleton enemy' – men from Pathan companies – once again added considerable realism to the exercise. Several went so far as to shower the attacking troops with boulders until they were restrained, with some difficulty, by their British officers before coming to blows with their Gurkha opponents![68]

Those lessons learnt and errors committed during the 1897–8 operations clearly convinced the military authorities in India that it was no longer possible to leave the regular British and Indian troops without official specialised training in hill warfare. Training carried out between 1897 and 1898 indicated what needed to be taught to imperial battalions regarding the tactics of mountain warfare in India. However, an officially sanctioned manual laying down definite tactical procedures to ensure uniformity of training throughout the Army in India remained a desideratum. While lecturing at the RUSI in London in January 1900 on the lessons of sixty years of frontier warfare, Major Arthur Yate reiterated his earlier concerns regarding providing a source of official guidance:

> I should be glad to see a good official manual on mountain and other forms of savage warfare, compiled and issued to the Army. We do require some definite source from which we can learn what hard experience has taught our predecessors. The military educational staff both in Great Britain and in India must surely feel the need for such a manual; for as everyone knows, more especially those who have to pass garrison class and tactical examinations, the subject is one that has to be studied.[69]

This widespread acceptance of the importance of an authoritative 'doctrine' and training for 'savage warfare' on the North-West Frontier finally led to the publication of an officially sanctioned manual intended to provide authoritative guidance to British and Indian regulars stationed in India. In 1900 a small pamphlet on mountain warfare was published by the Adjutant-General in India, whose contents reflected the recent perceived lessons of the 1897–8 operations that was intended to complement the existing Drill Book. It laid down various squad and company drills, emphasising the importance of skirmishing and the duties of infantry hill scouts. It also included company drill covering general principles of hill skirmishing, firing uphill and piqueting. Particular attention was directed towards conducting retirements in contact with a tribal opponent, stressing the need for independent movement, self-reliance and initiative on the part of British and Indian troops operating in the hills.[70] This represented a unique response to the military requirements of colonial warfare, devoted to local Indian conditions. A more comprehensive and enlarged manual – *Frontier Warfare 1901* – was published the following year specifically intended to provide guidance for military operations on the North-West Frontier. Major-General Edmund Elles, now Adjutant-General in India, noted in the preface:

> It must be understood that these notes on frontier warfare are in no way intended to be in supersession of the Drill Book but are written for the assistance of commanders when operating in broken and mountainous ground and are based on the experience gained in late frontier campaigns.

This manual contained guidance regarding the tactics required against a Pathan opponent for all three arms of service, although it copied the earlier pamphlet with regard to squad drill, skirmishing, scouting, company drill and retirements. An additional chapter dealt with battalion-level training, covering reconnaissance, flanking duties, advance guards, baggage and rearguard duty. Volley-firing was condemned as a waste of ammunition in hilly country, with independent fire recommended as the norm. The movement of large bodies of troops and the lines of communication on the frontier formed the subject of further chapters, although the manual referred primarily to operations by a single brigade in mountainous terrain. A whole chapter was devoted to the organisation, working and protection of the lines of communication, reflecting the transport and supply problems encountered when operating in tribal territory. The final section dealt with the principles governing the employment of mountain artillery in frontier warfare, recognising the need for greater employment of that arm now that the tribesmen had acquired modern small arms.[71] The Drill Book and its successor *Infantry Training*, however, remained the basis of the system of training for civilised warfare in India and still included a small section on 'savage warfare', containing information relevant to operations in open terrain which also stressed the importance of adapting to local conditions.[72] Other sources of information about frontier fighting also appeared outside official channels at the turn of the century. A further series of articles and unofficial text books dealing with fighting against the trans-border Pathan tribes were produced by officers directly concerned with the training needs of the army, including one volume written by Major-General Sir R.C. Hart who had commanded the 1st Brigade TEF in Tirah.[73]

Several of the 'regrettable incidents' and heavy casualties suffered amongst the pack transport animals were directly attributable to senior officers' ignorance of the tactical, administrative and logistical conduct of frontier warfare. In particular, the judgement and ability of some of the brigadiers and staff of the TEF was heavily criticised and some were accused of incompetence.[74] While those officers with prior experience of hill warfare, for example Brigadier-General Alfred Gaselee and Brigadier-General Richard Westmacott, had generally performed well, others experienced considerable problems.[75] In particular, Brigadier-General Francis Kempster was singled out for negligence during the withdrawal down the Bara Valley, when the rearguard and transport of the 3rd Brigade had been left behind benighted in a village outside the main encampment.[76] To be 'Kempstered' became a widely used term of disgust and 'I'm Kempstered if I do,' an expression of dissent amongst British officers, after his military career in India was abruptly concluded.[77] Initial steps were implemented after the operations to provide guidance for staff officers but, apart from a small manual written by Colonel John Nixon containing copies of various Standing Orders issued during prior frontier campaigns, information was scarce.[78] Garrison Classes, which taught regimental officers in India preparing for promotion examinations, covered frontier warfare for the first time in 1898, compelling officers to study the subject. Annual promotion examinations included questions that either made direct comparisons between the specialised requirements of hill warfare and European warfare or discussed the implications of improving tribal armament on the conduct of military operations or the requisite dispositions of a force operating in the border hills.[79] To rectify this dearth of knowledge the Staff College at Camberley included the administrative and operational conduct of hill warfare in its curriculum for the first time in 1899, with study based primarily on the recently revised edition of Callwell's *Small Wars: Their Principles and Practice*.[80] Practical instruction was given during Staff Tours held each year near Llanberis, Snowdon and Beddgelert in North

Wales, to illustrate the principles of hill warfare in terrain supposedly similar in some respects to that near Tirah.[81] As one experienced Indian Army officer on the staff observed, the relevance of these trips was debatable given the wide differences in terrain between the North-West Frontier and Wales; but such training did reflect an important new awareness of the distinct military requirements of the Empire.[82] To emphasise the different conditions between Staff Rides in England and military operations in tribal territory, the War Office published a detailed pamphlet in 1906 which discussed at length the details of mountain warfare in India intended primarily for officers without experience of the country.[83]

The Staff College established by Lord Kitchener in India in 1903, modelled on that at Camberley which replaced the Garrison Classes that had hitherto provided instruction to officers, unsurprisingly covered frontier fighting in some depth. While temporarily based at Deolali, a series of mountain warfare exercises and Staff Rides were held by the Senior Division in the Western Ghauts.[84] After permanent buildings were constructed at Quetta in Baluchistan the course included questions on tactics and Staff Tours in the neighbouring hills, and concluded with an annual tour of the North-West Frontier to study the Pathan tribes and terrain at first hand.[85] Those lectures originally written for the Staff College at Quetta formed the basis of a book written by Major W.D. Bird, a former instructor, on the principles of mountain warfare, which was published on his return to England in 1909.[86]

THE 1908 ZAKKA KHEL AND MOHMAND EXPEDITIONS

The effectiveness of the Army in India's new system of training in hill warfare was not tested immediately, as the North-West Frontier was comparatively peaceful following the 1897–8 campaigns. A combination of tribal exhaustion and Lord Curzon's endeavours to avoid punitive operations by progressively withdrawing Indian troops from posts established in tribal territory and replacing them with locally enlisted militia during the early 1900s, meant comparatively few clashes occurred between hostile tribesmen and imperial troops.[87]

The 1901–2 Mahsud Blockade was the last military operation carried out predominantly by Piffer regiments. On 31st March 1903 the PFF finally ceased to exist as a separate administrative unit, following the reorganisation of the system of commands on the North-West Frontier.[88] Although 'Frontier Force' was retained as part of their official designations, its regiments and batteries were now made available for service throughout India and overseas, although by training and tradition they were still regarded as experts in frontier warfare.[89] Henceforth the provision of manuals and specific training for hill warfare was even more essential, as the garrisons in the newly constituted North-West Frontier Province (NWFP) were filled by British and Indian regiments periodically rotated through the area as part of the normal system of regimental reliefs. New units arriving at the border cantonments had to quickly acquaint themselves with the intricacies of frontier warfare based on the instruction laid down in the training manuals and the advice of experienced officers, NCOs, and soldiers already serving in their ranks or in other units. As a result the principles and minor tactics of frontier warfare were closely studied by the local garrisons and those detailed for their immediate reinforcement in the event of war. Indeed, there was a veritable 'boom' of interest in this class of warfare, as a result of which it was hoped that the skills, training and traditions of the PFF would be 'passed on' to the rest of the army. Troops stationed in the border cantonments, formed into moveable columns ready to support the militia, regularly carried out 'savage warfare' exercises utilising training areas along the border hitherto monopolised by frontier regiments. In November 1903 the Bannu moveable column, for example, simulated its response to an attack on Kurram Garhi post by a party of well-armed tribesmen.[90] Instruction in hill warfare was also carried out at regimental level throughout India during the 1900s.[91] During the summer of 1906, units of the 5th (Mhow) Division carried out training, for example, in both bush and hill warfare.[92] Much preliminary instruction was possible, for example, in nearby Bakloh and Duneira in Lahore District, near Rawalpindi, on the Quetta plateau and in parts of Umballa District, where hilly areas were also available that could be employed for realistic exercises. Training those regiments stationed on the Indian plains in frontier warfare, however, posed certain intrinsic problems that had already been foreseen during the 1890s as suitable terrain was unavailable nearby most cantonments. British regiments were in a more favourable position, as they moved into hill stations annually to avoid the worst effects of the summer heat. The wide differences in terrain and vegetation between many hill stations, however, such as those on the Himalayan frontier and those in tribal territory, complicated instruction, but did not prevent units learning useful skills. Despite these drawbacks the system of reliefs meant that units otherwise denied frontier service could now become familiarised with border conditions in the most likely theatre of operations for the Army in India. However, the system also meant that troops were seldom in one location long enough to acquire a detailed knowledge of either the local terrain or the people, and were seldom able to achieve as high a standard of training and efficiency in mountain warfare as PFF regiments had during the nineteenth century.

The military authority in India's decision to prepare and issue manuals and implement training in frontier warfare to complement that laid down for European warfare had implications for the development of training for other classes of 'savage warfare' also at variance with that laid down in the Drill Book. A manual on jungle warfare written by Captain Arthur Taylor, specifically for Indian Army officers attached to Burma Military Police battalions, was published in 1902 which contained various extracts and references from the mountain warfare pamphlet prepared by the Adjutant General in India.[93] A series of articles and books also appeared discussing bush warfare, written by experienced British officers from both the Indian and British armies, which emphasised the importance of suitable training for officers seconded to the Foreign or Colonial Offices, as well as for the Indian Army regiments deployed in Africa.[94] *Frontier Warfare 1901* was complemented by a small appendix published in 1903 entitled *Bush Fighting. (An Appendix to 'Frontier Warfare')* intended to provide guidance for Indian regiments deployed on the North-Eastern frontier of India and the increasing number of officers and men from Indian regiments serving in east and west Africa. It included a 'Syllabus of Instruction in Bush Tactics' containing information on skirmishing and other skills required by imperial troops.[95] These two manuals were amalgamated in 1906 to produce a final authoritative manual governing the conduct of frontier warfare around the peripheries of India and for operations elsewhere in the British Empire. Sir Beauchamp Duff, the Chief of Staff, emphasised in the preface of *Frontier Warfare and Bush Fighting*: 'It must be understood that these notes … are in no way in supersession of the Training Manuals but are written for the assistance of commanders when operating in broken and mountainous ground and in Bush Countries and are based on the experience gained in late various campaigns.' Although the text and contents were identical in most respects to those of the earlier edition, it referred throughout the text to the current training manuals – *Infantry Training 1905*, *Combined Training 1905* and *Field Service Regulations* – produced to direct training in conventional military operations.[96]

The punitive expedition mounted against the Zakka Khel Afridis in February 1908, after a succession of large and well-organised raids had been perpetrated in Peshawar District, provided an opportunity to assess the effectiveness of the Army in India in frontier warfare. This operation, conducted under the command of Major-General Sir James Willcocks, represented a dramatic change from prior military operations during the

1890s and gave the Indian Army an opportunity to apply the principles
and minor tactics of frontier warfare learnt and practised since 1898. The
Bazar Valley Field Force, operating with a minimal amount of equipment
and mule transport, was mobilised in thirty-six hours and achieved complete surprise over the Zakka Khel, who submitted after punitive operations were carried out in the Bazar Valley between 17th and 24th February
1908. After having suffered only three dead and 37 wounded, which
Willcocks directly attributed to the high state of efficiency and training
which Indian troops had acquired, the column withdrew back across the
administrative border on 29th February 1908. The Zakka Khel had suffered casualties far in excess of those lost in the Tirah Expedition with
every family in the Bazar Valley suffering losses from amongst its fighting
men.[97] During the peace negotiations, the Zakka Khel openly acknowledged the improved fighting ability of the Indian Army. Lt.-Colonel
George Roos-Keppel noted: 'The Afridis, who are no mean judges of hill
fighting, express themselves amazed at the handling and conduct of the
troops as unlike anything they have seen or heard of, and the fact that they
have obtained no loot in mules, rifles, stores, or ammunition, on which
they confidently counted to compensate for their own losses, has given
them a strong distaste for expeditions conducted on these novel lines.'[98]
The Viceroy, Lord Minto, concurred:

> From a military point of view the most satisfactory features of the expe-
> dition were the ease and rapidity with which it was sent off without any
> dislocation of the separate commands, the excellence of the transport
> and supply arrangements, the signalling communications, and above all
> the unexampled efficiency of the troops themselves in their knowledge
> of hill fighting. They proved as good or even better than the Zakkas
> themselves among their own hills. It speaks volumes for the pains
> bestowed on their training. In 1897 the superiority of the tribes over us
> in the hills was very marked and we suffered heavily, whilst I believe
> the Zakka loss on the present occasion exceeds the whole tribal loss in
> the Tirah campaign and our own loss has been extremely small.[99]

Similar operations were mounted two months later against the Mohmands
and after another short campaign they submitted after suffering heavy
casualties. It was abundantly clear that the success of 'Willcocks' Week
End Wars' was a direct tribute to the improved light infantry and training
in hill warfare born of the frontier rising and vastly improved musketry
instruction in the Indian Army.[100] Both campaigns also provided valuable
experience for British and Indian regiments and represented an important
test of changes in the organisation, administration and training of the

Indian Army during the 1900s. They also provided confirmation that the
tribesmen now possessed large quantities of Martini-Henry and .303 rifles,
which they used with effect during night attacks and in sniping, although
on several occasions swordsmen still engaged in hand-to-hand combat.[101]

THE ARMY IN INDIA AND FIELD SERVICE REGULATIONS

The Zakka Khel and Mohmand punitive expeditions represented the last
major operations mounted against the trans-border tribes before the outbreak of the First World War. Nevertheless the insistent duties of 'watch
and ward' of the border ensured the garrisons in the NWFP maintained a
high level of military preparedness and trained primarily for frontier
warfare. To facilitate instruction a report on training carried out by Bannu
Brigade between 10th and 15th February 1908, for example, simulating an
attack on a frontier village followed by a withdrawal in contact with
hostile tribesmen, the construction of a perimeter camp and its defence
from a night attack, convoy escort duty and the duties involved in intercepting parties of tribal raiders, was circulated by Northern Command
later that year.[102] The Russo-Japanese War, the declining incidence of
punitive expeditions and the reorientation of British policy towards
Europe, however, led to a progressive decline of professional interest in
frontier fighting elsewhere in India following the boom of the early 1900s.
Apart from the independent frontier brigades in the NWFP, which carried
out training predicated on operations against a 'savage' opponent, the
mainstream of professional attention re-focused on training against a
'civilised' opponent as the subject lost its prior appeal. The approach taken
by the military authorities towards instruction for other, more specialised
forms of warfare also underwent a significant change.[103] An unquestioning
acceptance of the guidelines contained in the specialised frontier warfare
manuals by some regiments as the basis of all training had caused conster-
nation and alarm amongst the General Staff in India. In accordance with a
decision made at the Imperial Defence Conference in 1909, the specialist
frontier warfare manuals were cancelled in an endeavour to standardise
training regulations and the organisation, administration and training of
imperial troops throughout the Empire. Training in India was brought into
line with the rest of the Empire in 1911 with the adoption of *Field Service
Regulations* (*FSR*), *Musketry Regulations*, *Training and Manoeuvre
Regulations*, the training manuals of the various arms and the *Field
Service Pocket Book* as the basis of its organisation, administration and
training.[104] This decision met initial opposition in India, as many officers

misunderstand the principles underlying this change in approach and the fact that the draft section on mountain warfare in *FSR* was insufficiently comprehensive. A committee headed by the Director of Military Training, responsible for investigating these complaints and drawing up what was to be included in *FSR*, finally concluded that, while dividing the subject of instruction in frontier warfare between *FSR* and specialist training manuals was sound in theory, in practice it had caused considerable confusion.[105] At the Staff College at Quetta on 14th October 1912, General Sir O'Moore Creagh, the Commander-in-Chief in India, explained:

> Up to the time of the Tirah campaign 'mountain warfare' was looked on as a special prerogative of the Frontier Force, and was practically entirely neglected by the Army at large. After that campaign there was a violent swing of the pendulum in the opposite direction, and tendency rose to stereotype warfare into two distinct types, the character of the ground and of the enemy were often ignored, and the 'perimeter' camp especially became almost a fetish, so that at manoeuvres it was common to see troops crowded into such camps even when opposed by an enemy provided with artillery. The result was no doubt greatly due to the fact that the rules for frontier warfare were contained in a separate manual, for this manual was unfortunately accepted by many officers as containing all that was required. It was overlooked that it did not deal with *principles* at all, but only with such *modifications* of the principles as were necessitated by the topographical conditions and the character of the enemy on the frontier; and that the rules given were merely complementary to those contained in the ordinary training manuals.[106]

A revised edition of *FSR* appeared in 1912 containing various amendments especially intended for the Army in India and this became the primary source of tactical guidance regarding mountain warfare. A new chapter – entitled *Warfare in Uncivilized Countries* – began by noting that: 'In campaigns against savages the armament, tactics, and characteristics of the enemy, and the nature of the theatre of operations demand that the principles of regular warfare be somewhat modified; the modifications in this chapter are such as experience has shown to be necessary.' It contained sections covering both bush and mountain warfare, but the latter was restricted to six paragraphs covering protection on the march, protection when at rest, camps and bivouacs, general information and a section on piquets.[107]

The emphasis on conventional warfare during peacetime training did not completely obscure the fact that it was still incumbent on British officers to prepare for more specialised operations on the North-West Frontier.[108]

As one officer reminded his fellows: 'Situated as we are in India it is to be hoped that the pendulum will not swing too much one way, leading us to neglect continual practise of the plans and tactics mainly suitable for an encounter with unorganized tribesmen.'[109] Despite these changing training priorities in India, several new books were published providing an important means of expanding upon the limited information contained in *FSR* on mountain warfare. A detailed didactic study of the Tirah Campaign written by Colonel Charles Callwell appeared in 1911 – in his 'Campaigns and their Lessons' series – to exemplify a campaign conducted by regular troops against irregulars, in which tactics and training required for mountain warfare in India were described at length.[110] The following year a one-volume 'student's history', written by Captain Hugh Nevill, also appeared, intended to familiarise officers with campaigns on the North-West Frontier, to illustrate the principles of FSR and to provide a detailed account of the gradual changes of arms and tactics used by both the tribesmen and the Indian Army.[111] This was complemented by a general survey of operations and campaigns written by Colonel Harold Wylly in 1912 to provide information about the tribes, the borderland and prior punitive campaigns that had been conspicuous by its absence in 1897.[112] By 1913 professional interest in frontier warfare had fallen to such an extent that it was the subject of a lecture by Colonel William Venour, a highly experienced Frontier Force officer, at the USII. Venour called for a revitalisation of interest in such fighting and stressed its wider importance for both Indian and British troops:

> Since 1908 there have been no expeditions on the Pathan border and it seems that interest in this particular form of training has somewhat waned throughout the army as a whole. In the future, as in the past, this is the most likely form of fighting in which Indian troops may have to take part, and as long as they serve in India the same thing applies to British troops; and though they may have to train in Europe or any part of our Empire, still a knowledge of frontier warfare is a useful fighting asset to any unit under any conditions, teaching as it does initiative and self reliance.[113]

Venour justifiably questioned the wisdom of including instruction regarding frontier warfare in a single manual forming the basis of all infantry training throughout the Empire. The six paragraphs included in the 1912 edition of the *FSR* were of necessity so condensed that a considerable diversity in applying the principles existed amongst units and between different brigades regarding piquets and perimeter camps. As absolute uniformity in minor tactics was required in frontier warfare, he observed that these variations made imperial troops vulnerable to tribal attack. As a solution to the problem Venour suggested the addition of an Indian appendix to *FSR* and the creation of a training school to provide systematic training in the 'peculiarly Indian subject' of frontier warfare, modelled on similar lines as the Mounted Infantry schools held at Umballa and Poona.[114] In the ensuing discussion the Chief of Staff, Lt.-General Sir Percy Lake, noted the dangers inherent in too much specialisation in FSR, but it was clear that the majority of the audience supported the idea of a specialised school of instruction for frontier warfare.[115]

The Army in India contained by 1914 a large proportion of officers and men, despite such reservations, who possessed a sound working knowledge of the principles and minor tactics required on the North-West Frontier. Former PFF regiments provided a nucleus of highly trained soldiers with experience, training and a tradition of expertise in fighting against the trans-border Pathan tribes. Due to the system of periodic reliefs in the border garrisons a large number of regular regiments had acquired practical experience, familiarised themselves with local conditions and built up a cadre of officers, NCOs and men accustomed to the requirements of frontier warfare for the first time. The steadily increasing fighting strength, armament and military effectiveness of the trans-border Pathan tribes, however, remained a serious source of concern. In 1911 the General Staff in India estimated that more than six divisions would be required to deal with a general rising similar to that in 1897–98 or to secure the lines of communication in the event of war with Afghanistan.[116] It was increasingly apparent that frontier warfare would become more costly and protracted in the future, moreover, as *lashkars* assimilated further military training through service in the Indian Army or militias and acquired increasing quantities of modern breech-loading rifles and ammunition.[117] Despite the realisation that the military effectiveness of Afridi *lashkars* had been significantly enhanced by ex-servicemen in their ranks, however, large numbers of trans-border Pathans were still enlisted into the military. On 1st January 1908, for example, 10,600 trans-border Pathans were serving in the Indian Army and the various irregular forces raised in the NWFP since 1899.[118] Perhaps of greater significance was the growing availability of modern 'arms of precision' in tribal territory. Arms imported from the Persian Gulf via Afghanistan flooded the Pathan borderland during the early 1900s, with European rifles far superior to locally manufactured weapons. By 1909 the scale of the arms trade threatened the political and military stability of the North-West Frontier and posed a serious threat to peace, after large consignments of high-quality rifles, far better than the weapons which equipped the irregular forces responsible

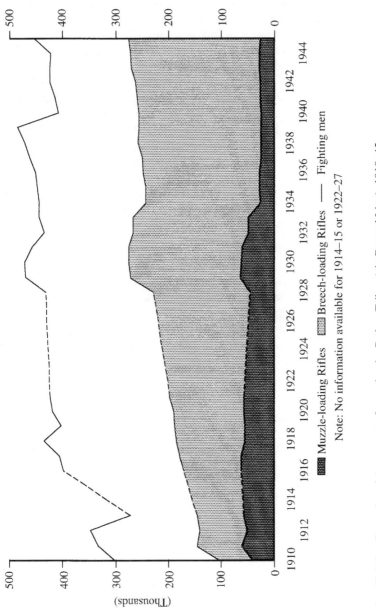

Fig. 5. Fighting Strength and Armament of trans-border Pathan Tribes (cis-Durand Line), 1910–45

for the 'watch and ward' of the administrative border, arrived in tribal territory. As a direct result the militias and Border Military Police had to be
hurriedly rearmed to keep pace with raiding gangs, and in 1910 the border
villages had to be issued with Martini-Henry rifles to defend themselves
against attack.[119] Later that year the first detailed investigation of the size
of the tribal arsenal estimated that the trans-border tribes now had a potential fighting strength of 301,596 men who were armed with 63,564 breech-
loading rifles and 40,270 muzzle-loading rifles.[120] Further investigations
confirmed that the tribal arsenal was still increasing (see Figure 5). A
blockade imposed by the Royal Navy and Royal Indian Marine and
amphibious operations mounted along the Mekran Coast successfully
interdicted the arms traffic across the Persian Gulf from Muscat by 1911,
but not before large consignments of modern rifles and ammunition had
transformed the military position on the North-West Frontier.[121] The
implications of the arms trade for frontier warfare in the future were
widely appreciated in India. Writing the same year, Fraser Lovat pointed
out:

> Our preventive measures came too late. The mischief is already done,
> and all we can now do is to prevent it spreading farther. The tribesmen
> on the North-West Frontier are now armed as they were never armed
> before, and we shall discover the results of our carelessness in the tale
> of the dead and wounded if we ever again have to send a big expedition
> into the hills between the Khyber and the Gomal.[122]

4 The Lessons of Waziristan, August 1914–October 1925

The insistent 'threat' posed by Afghanistan and the independent tribes led to the mobilisation and deployment of three infantry divisions and a cavalry brigade in the NWFP, in addition to the normal three frontier brigades and militia, throughout the First World War.[1] However, the quality of these troops steadily declined as the war progressed and highly experienced, long-service, pre-war regular regiments were sent overseas to France, the Middle East and East Africa. Those units that remained were steadily 'milked' of officers, NCOs and men, to act as instructors or replace casualties, and soon primarily consisted of reservists and raw recruits of doubtful fighting value. During 1915 the military effectiveness of the border garrisons started to seriously concern the General Staff in India, when unrest spread throughout tribal territory and the remaining regulars in the Field Army were replaced by newly-raised, under-officered and poorly-equipped Indian regiments, Imperial Service Troops and units of the Nepalese Contingent.[2] The inherent limitations of relying solely on the general principles and six condensed paragraphs on mountain warfare laid down in *FSR* to govern training were quickly exposed after partially trained TA battalions and new Indian regiments were deployed in the NWFP, whose officers lacked both experience and basic military knowledge. As a stop-gap measure a Mountain Warfare School opened on 21st May 1916 in response specifically to train TA officers and NCOs, who would in turn act as instructors at their own units in the principles and minor tactics of hill warfare. Four highly successful week-long courses were held at Abbottabad, Dharmsala, Lansdowne and Wellington, where a total of 27 officers and 108 NCOs were introduced to mountain warfare against a 'savage' opponent.[3] Training for more senior officers in the staff duties associated with mountain warfare also received attention at the Staff School established at Quetta for the duration of the war.[4]

When 1st (Peshawar) and 2nd (Rawalpindi) Divisions conducted operations along the Mohmand border in November 1916, employing BE2C aircraft and armoured cars for the first time, alarming differences in tactical procedures amongst their units were exposed.[5] At a conference held for senior officers in Delhi between 22nd and 24th February 1917, these were highlighted when the GOC 2nd (Rawalpindi) Division complained that a serious lack of uniformity existed in the application of the principles laid

down for the conduct of mountain warfare in *FSR* that represented a
source of confusion and danger in the field. Major-General William
Bunbury argued that it was necessary to lay down more definite rules as:
'Every teacher of mountain warfare and every writer on the subject
appears to have his own ideas, not so much to principles but as to how
they should be applied, and the result is that one finds different teaching
on certain points in every brigade and even in the battalions of a brigade.'
Opinion differed between units and formations, for example, about the
correct way of posting and withdrawing piquets and the relative merits of
piqueting slips or bayonet sentries. Although these only appeared 'trifling'
differences in procedure, he warned that they had resulted in serious casualties in the past. Despite his trenchant criticisms Bunbury remained a
strong supporter of *FSR*, although he now urged that definite rules should
be laid down to apply its abstract principles. The ensuing discussion
reflected the continued interest in the conduct of mountain warfare within
the Army in India. Major-General Sir Frederick Campbell, GOC 1st
(Peshawar) Division, took the opposite view when he warned of the
dangers of laying down precise details or specific tactics to be employed
on particular occasions. Other senior officers openly opposed any addition
to the manual, stressing the importance of relying solely on general principles universally applicable to all forms of warfare. The Director of Staff
Duties and Military Training responded by pointing out that the
Commander-in-Chief was, in principle, strongly opposed to the publication of a special manual or any additions to *FSR*. Brigadier-General
Hubert Isacke pointed out all units and formations just needed to ensure
that they based their instruction on sound principles and that more light
would be thrown on the points that had been raised now AHQ had decided
to re-open the mountain warfare school at Abbottabad.[6] Lt.-General Sir
Arthur Barrett, GOC Northern Command and an officer of extensive frontier experience, closed the discussion by suggesting that Standing Orders
offered the best means of standardising tactics for specific operations and
then pointed out:

> I think there is no doubt that mountain warfare is a science. I have
> always regarded it as a thing very like a game of chess which wants a
> great deal of skill to avoid mistakes, but at the same time it is not a
> science that can be said at any one time to have reached its finality. We
> are always going on evolving new things and a great many of these
> points that have been raised have been evolved gradually from experi-
> ence. We must not assume that the stage we have reached now is the
> last stage of the process. I hope we shall go on evolving many more

new points and go on improving our skill in this particular science, and in that way I think it not at all a bad thing that there should be differences of opinion; that one officer should think one way and one another and that they should go on practising the things in different ways until, in course of time, we shall evolve more new methods ... We must remember that the increased armament of these tribes that we fight against will go on modifying our rules and systems. I think that any new expedition we might get into now will probably have to be conducted on very different lines from any we have had in the past.[7]

A series of disastrous skirmishes along the Derajat border during the spring of 1917 reinforced the importance of specialised training in mountain warfare for units in the NWFP. A totally unprecedented event occurred on 1st May, when 51 officers and men were killed with 59 wounded and missing primarily due to their inexperience and poor training, during an attack on a convoy between Nili Kach and Khajuri Kach.[8] On 2nd May 1917 the GOC Northern Command warned: 'If we employ troops inexperienced in hill warfare, it appears to me that incidents in the Gomal are likely to be repeated ... To frontier warfare the second reserve is quite untrained'.[9] It was now all too apparent, however, that now no real difference existed in experience and training between any of the troops left in India.[10]

The Mountain Warfare School had already begun work to improve standards of training after it re-opened at Abbottabad in March 1917, specifically to instruct officers and NCOs in the principles of war with special reference to mountain warfare. It was intended that its students would then return and teach their own units, thereby establishing for the first time a common doctrine throughout the Army in India. Under the command of Colonel William Villiers-Stuart, a highly experienced 5th Gurkha Rifles (Frontier Force) officer, innovative teaching methods were quickly developed to illustrate the principles and minor tactics of what he termed 'trans-border warfare'. Six three-week-long courses were held between March and October 1917, five of which consisted of 48 officers ranging in rank from Second Lieutenant to General, while the final class was reserved for 48 Warrant Officers and NCOs. A large part of the course, however, was devoted to studying the normal principles of war, as most officers were so inexperienced, before dealing with the specialised modifications required in trans-border warfare. Instruction was given by means of lectures, indoor and outdoor schemes and sand-table models which provided a theoretical idea of frontier tactics. An attached infantry company, cavalry squadron, machine-gun detachment and battery of mountain artillery, moreover, demonstrated ambushes, piqueting and other minor tactics in the surrounding hills, as well as providing manpower with which the students could practise while supervised by experienced officers. To add realism, the demonstration troops and students were opposed by Indian sepoys dressed and armed as a 'savage opponent'.[11] This practical system of training proved highly successful. After attending in July 1917, Colonel Harry Ross observed: 'Our course was run by Lt. Col. Villiers-Stuart who had spent practically the whole of his service on the frontier & was not only a keen & knowledgeable soldier, but a good & clear lecturer. Our work was very interesting – lectures, accompanied by practical examples in the hills. All were very well depicted.'[12] During 1917 524 officers, Warrant Officers and NCOs from units stationed throughout India attended the course before the school closed to prevent its interfering with the course of normal collective training. For other officers the service press continued during the war to provide a source of information in addition to *FSR* for officers interested in studying mountain warfare.[13]

The punitive expedition conducted in Waziristan during the summer and autumn of 1917 emphasised the continued importance of training in mountain warfare. It was fortunate that the poorly-trained imperial troops, accompanied by an unprecedented amount of supporting arms, services, and modern equipment to compensate for their low efficiency, encountered little serious opposition.[14] Despite the efforts of the Mountain Warfare School, a lack of uniformity in piqueting and other minor tactics was still evident during the fighting.[15] Although afterwards hostile activity in tribal territory was confined primarily to raiding, the conduct of mountain warfare remained of considerable importance for units serving in the border cantonments. To help improve standards of training, in April 1918 the Mountain Warfare School was again reopened at Abbottabad with an increased establishment of instructors and demonstration troops. Six courses were held between April and October, each having vacancies for 96 British officers. Two were held specifically for senior officers, while four were reserved for junior regimental officers, as a growing proportion of these temporary wartime officers required greater elementary instruction than prior students.[16] Junior officers were given even greater opportunities to practise the skills they had learnt by commanding the demonstration troops and carrying out practical exercises on the hill sides. As a former chief instructor later pointed out:

There is so much in this vitally important business that the average soldier in India gets no opportunity of learning. Theory and the sand table cannot teach the rapid tackling of situations unexpectedly sprung upon even the smallest body of men in a Frontier campaign. The School of Mountain Warfare supplied both the men for the students to handle, and a carefully trained enemy who did all that was least expected of them, on the rocky spurs out of Abbottabad.[17]

When the Mountain Warfare School closed down in October 1918, it had succeeded for the first time in teaching and disseminating a common doctrine of frontier warfare to a large number of officers serving in India. Moreover, it had also devised tentative guidelines for the use in frontier warfare of modern military equipment, developed during the First World War, although only small quantities as yet had arrived in India. As a result a new pamphlet was published in June 1918, as a supplement to *FSR*, addressing the conduct of operations against both Afghan troops and the trans-border tribes and containing information regarding the employment of hand and rifle grenades, Lewis guns, and Vickers machine guns in tribal territory.[18] However, although 988 officers and 204 NCOs had attended courses at Abbottabad during the war, the vast majority of units in India still remained below pre-war standards of training in mountain warfare by the end of hostilities in the Middle East and Europe.[19]

THE THIRD AFGHAN WAR AND THE 1919–20 WAZIRISTAN CAMPAIGN

The Army in India was given no real respite to demobilise and recover from the effects of the First World War. On 4th May 1919 the regular Afghan Army crossed the Durand Line and occupied Bagh at the head of the Khyber Pass. It was quickly apparent that their plan of campaign depended on the active participation of the Pathan tribes and strenuous efforts were made throughout the war to enlist tribal support by calls for *jihad* and gifts of money and arms.[20] The initial Afghan success in the Khyber area, however, proved short-lived as large numbers of imperial reinforcements were concentrated on the North-West Frontier, although most units were predominantly composed of new recruits and 'old soldiers' and far below pre-war standards of efficiency. On 11th May Afghan forces were forcibly ejected from Bagh to forestall a local tribal rising that posed a far more serious threat to British security. When the 1st (Peshawar) Division attacked and occupied Dakka in Afghanistan on 13th May it forcibly separated the Mohmands and Afridis and prevented them from fighting alongside Afghan troops. However, when Afghan regulars and tribesmen appeared in Mohmand country at Chitral, and Fort Spin Baldek in Baluchistan the situation worsened. The Afghan troops and tribesmen in the Gandab Valley, however, withdrew when they failed to induce the Mohmands to attack Shabkadr. A secondary Afghan operation at Chitral was also repulsed by local forces, while other Afghan troops were quickly defeated in Baluchistan and forced to withdraw. Throughout the rest of May the security of the Khyber Pass became of paramount importance and permanently occupied piquets were constructed between Dakka and Haft Chah to secure the road. Despite the deployment of an entire infantry brigade, Afridis still sniped the road, cut telegraph and telephone lines, ambushed convoys and constructed road blocks. On 15th–16th May the 6th Infantry Brigade carried out punitive operations against tribal settlements near Ali Musjid but, on several occasions, hostile *lashkars* gathered in the surrounding hills. Following the desertion of large numbers of its men with their arms and equipment, the Khyber Rifles – a tribal militia – was disbanded on 17th May. While ground operations were in progress the RAF was given an opportunity to demonstrate what it could do when BE2C aircraft attacked the Afghan line of communications near Dakka and then bombed Jalalabad on the 17th, 20th and 24th May 1919, destroying the military quarter and dispersing a parade of Afghan troops. During the ensuing confusion Afridi and Mohmand tribesmen looted arms, ammunition and equipment from their erstwhile allies and then dispersed into the surrounding mountains to await further developments. Kabul was also bombed on 24th May by a single four-engined Handley Page aircraft.[21]

The Afghan offensive from Khost, commencing on 23rd May 1919, was considerably more successful when troops advancing down the Kaitu Valley enlisted the active support of local Wazir sections. Isolated detachments of the North Waziristan Militia and regular troops in the Upper Tochi Valley quickly evacuated their posts and withdrew to within the administrative border. Those militiamen garrisoning Miranshah, however, mutinied, seizing weapons and ammunition from the fort, setting off several similar incidents by smaller detachments stationed in the lower Tochi Valley. At Wana and in the Gomal, Afridi and Wazir officers and men in the South Waziristan Militia followed suit, forcing their British officers and the remaining loyal sepoys to withdraw under heavy attack. Further desertions occurred en route and, after suffering serious casualties, the survivors finally reached safety at Mir Ali (see Figure 6).[22] The 1,100 deserters seized 1,190 rifles and over 700,000 rounds of ammunition from their posts which were then employed with deadly effect against imperial troops. Now emboldened Mahsud tribesmen attacked isolated

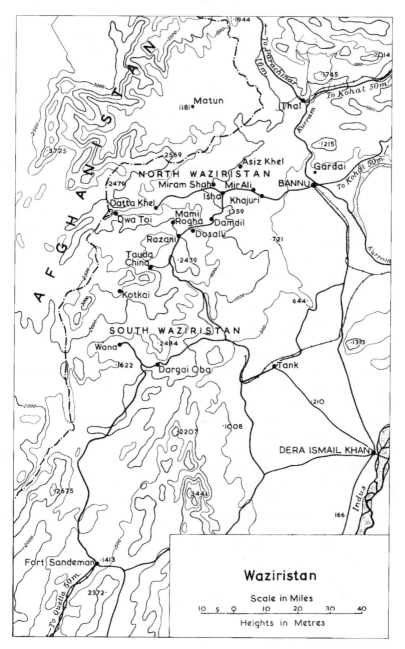

Fig. 6.   Waziristan and the Derajat

posts at Dardoni, Idak and Jandola and raided the Derajat. On 27th May 1919 Afghan troops and tribesmen surrounded the British garrison at Thal, but although artillery fire destroyed petrol dumps, rations, forage and the wireless station, all infantry assaults were successfully repulsed. Reinforcements, diverted from the Khyber under Brigadier General Reginald Dyer, relieved the garrison and buttressed the defences in the Kurram, forcing Nadir Shah to withdraw harassed by aircraft, armoured cars and cavalry after abandoning large quantities of equipment and supplies. This engagement effectively ended operations, and on 3rd June an armistice was agreed with the Afghan armed forces.

A general tribal rising, however, occurred during the summer between the Kabul River and Chaman despite the armistice that posed a far more serious threat than the Afghan Army. Troops carrying out reconnaissances, piquets and foraging parties at Dakka were repeatedly sniped at by Afghan tribesmen, while Afridis harassed the troops in the Khyber Pass and raided Peshawar District in strength. On 17th July 1919 the Khyber Pass was closed, when 10,000 tribesmen gathered in the Bazar Valley and attacked piquets between Bagiari and Ali Musjid. Barley Hill piquet was captured the following day by Afridi tribesmen and deserters still wearing khaki uniforms, who carried out a carefully implemented assault under the cover of intense rifle fire, demonstrating the growing sophistication of tribal tactics.[23] Normal conditions were gradually restored by imperial forces after sweeps were made in the Khajuri Plain for hostile *lashkars* and when many tribesmen returned home at the end of July to sow crops. The Derajat border remained the main source of concern as Waziristan Force struggled to relieve isolated posts and prevent raids committed by Mahsud and Wazir gangs containing a high proportion of ex-servicemen in their ranks. Although the Third Afghan War ended officially on 8th August 1919, settlements with the independent tribes were hindered by Afghan officials and raiding on an unprecedented scale. Afridi attacks in the Khyber Pass and across the border of Peshawar and Kohat Districts increased during the autumn. To avoid further fighting apart from the destruction of Chora Fort in the Bazar Valley, however, punitive operations against the Afridis were deliberately restricted, due to the serious fighting already under way in the Derajat and the acknowledged dangers inherent in invading Tirah. Instead, until a political settlement was arranged the following year Indian troops and local irregulars concentrated on intercepting raiders in Peshawar and Kohat Districts and blockading tribal territory.[24]

The situation in the Derajat steadily deteriorated during the late summer and autumn of 1919. Between 9th August and 18th November 1919

Mahsud and Wazir raiding gangs, varying between 70 and 600 tribesmen, committed 182 offences in Zhob, the Derajat and the Punjab, killing 225 British subjects, wounding 276 and kidnapping and ransoming a further 126 civilians; in the process large quantities of camels, cattle and private property were stolen and carried off into the hills.[25] To punish the Mahsuds and Wazirs, restore British prestige and maintain the security of the administrative border, punitive operations were judged essential. During the autumn military operations in Waziristan were delayed, however, by a lack of transport, extremely hot weather in the Derajat and because the majority of available Indian troops were war-weary and unready for further fighting. A chronic shortage of officers and a lack of training amongst the local Indian garrison resulted in many successful tribal attacks. In explanation the Viceroy pointed out in October 1919:

> We have roughly two experienced officers per battalion in the Indian Army. The rest are men of practically no military experience and certainly no frontier war experience. Moreover, the troops on the whole have very short service. The result is that *vis-à-vis* the Wazir and Mahsud our men are inferior, and the officers, through their inexperience, are unable to make up for deficiencies in the rank and file. It was because of this inexperience of our officers and troops that during the recent operations we had to mass such large forces on our frontier. And, as in the case of tribal operations the junior officers have to take responsibility for the work, we must expect these set-backs from time to time.[26]

The size of the force which assembled in the Derajat during the autumn of 1919 was unprecedented, reflecting the serious fighting that was anticipated against the heavily armed local tribesmen in Waziristan and the recognised poor quality of the available manpower. 29,256 raw, untrained Indian troops and 33,987 non-combatant followers were placed under the command of Major-General Skipton Climo, organised into six infantry brigades, four infantry battalions, four cavalry regiments, sappers and miners and two mountain batteries. The combatant troops were accompanied by large quantities of supporting units – field ambulances, hospitals, survey detachments, postal units, pigeon lofts and photographic sections – as well as large numbers of unarmed followers, greatly increasing the size of the force, the number of transport animals and the size of supply columns. A notable exception from the order of battle, despite appeals from Climo, were any troops belonging to the Machine Gun Corps equipped with Vickers heavy machine guns, as acclimatised British units were unavailable apart from No. 6 Mountain Battery.[27] While this large force assembled the RAF was given an opportunity to carry out independent bombing raids after modern Bristol fighters, DH9 and DH10 bombers augmented the small detachment of BE2Cs at Tank. During the autumn small-scale punitive air raids were mounted over Waziristan, but it proved difficult to obtain reliable information regarding the impact of bombing on the local inhabitants.[28]

On 18th November 1919 the Tochi Valley was re-occupied by two brigades without resistance, apart from one small tribal section which submitted the following day after being bombed by 17 aircraft. Throughout this operation, fighting was marked by its absence, but piqueting and the defence of perimeter camps provided some useful training in mountain warfare for the inexperienced troops.[29] While operations in the Tochi were under way RAF aircraft bombed the main Mahsud settlements at Kaniguram, Makin and Marobi in central Waziristan between 13th and 21st November after the tribesmen failed to comply with terms, dropping a daily average of 10,000 lbs of bombs. Intermittent air raids continued until the end of the month, destroying stocks of fodder and food and causing cultivation to cease, villages to be evacuated and a decline in raiding after livestock was dispersed into smaller flocks requiring more men for their concealment and protection. Aircraft then attacked houses belonging to influential maliks to force them to agree terms with the imperial authorities. Despite RAF claims to have inflicted severe damage, however, the Mahsuds did not submit, which made ground operations against them essential.[30]

The two brigades of the former Tochi Column regrouped at Jandola early in December in preparation for operations in central Waziristan. The decision to employ a single striking force, renamed the Derajat Column ('Deracol') on 27th November, under the command of Major-General Andrew Skeen, reflected the shortage of transport, the large winter scale of baggage and stores required, the recognised low fighting ability of the raw and untrained regiments available and the large numbers of breech-loading rifles in Mahsud hands. A single line of communication also required fewer troops, a smaller number of administrative units and reduced the demand for transport and supplies to a minimum. Moreover, it was hoped that an advance by a single column would encourage the tribesmen to mass, giving imperial troops an opportunity to inflict a decisive defeat at the outset of the campaign.[31]

'Deracol' met little resistance when it advanced up the Tank Zam Valley on 18th December 1919, but it soon halted at Palosina to build a perimeter camp and permanent piquets to secure its line of communication. An initial attempt to construct a camp piquet on Mandanna Hill the following day, however, ended in disaster when the 1/55th Rifles and the

1/103 Mahratta Light Infantry were repulsed, with 95 dead and 140 wounded, by a strong Mahsud *lashkar* that captured 131 rifles and 10 Lewis guns from the disorganised sepoys (see Figure 7).[32] 19th December 1919 was dubbed 'Derby Day' by those remaining in camp who watched as both battalions raced to the security of the perimeter camp below. This dramatic defeat caused considerable alarm, and the Derajat Column 'stood to' all night anticipating an assault by the tribesmen on the encampment.[33] Mandanna Hill was captured without opposition the following day when a full brigade supported by all the available artillery and aircraft was committed. A 110-man garrison belonging to the 2/19th Punjabis, occupying hastily constructed *sangars* on the hill top, was overrun and routed by 20–50 Mahsuds while consolidating its position. The demoralised survivors – abandoning rifles, Lewis guns, Mills bombs, and other equipment – frantically withdrew to the safety of the perimeter camp in the valley below pursued by a Mahsud force under half their strength.[34] This disaster forced the Derajat Column onto the defensive, although on 21st December 67th Brigade, under the command of Brigadier-General F.G. Lucas, attempted to construct a piquet at 'Black Hill' or Tarakai to the north of the perimeter camp to restore the column's badly shaken morale. A covering detachment, protecting a working party busily building *sangars*, was attacked and overrun by 800–1,000 Mahsud swordsmen, protected by intense rifle fire from ranges of 1,500 yards, who approached unseen through the broken terrain. Intense hand-to-hand fighting occurred around the position, but the 3–24th Sikh Pioneers were eventually forced to withdraw when their supply of ammunition and grenades was exhausted. A counterattack failed ignominiously, although heavy supporting artillery fire broke up the massed tribesmen – inflicting 250 dead and 300 wounded – while the covering troops withdrew to the safety of the perimeter camp below, having lost a further 66 dead and 250 wounded during the engagement.[35]

The heavy casualties inflicted on the Derajat Column between 19th and 21st December 1919 indicated that the majority of its infantry battalions were incapable of carrying out comparatively simple tactical operations against the tribesmen. A combination of poor leadership, lack of basic individual training and almost complete ignorance of the specialised principles and minor tactics of hill warfare had played directly into Mahsud and Wazir hands. Perhaps the most alarming feature was the wide disparity revealed between the fighting ability and morale of the tribesmen and that of the Indian infantry. Mahsud *lashkars* had demonstrated a degree of military skill and tactical effectiveness never before encountered. Their carefully organised attacks were unprecedented, with

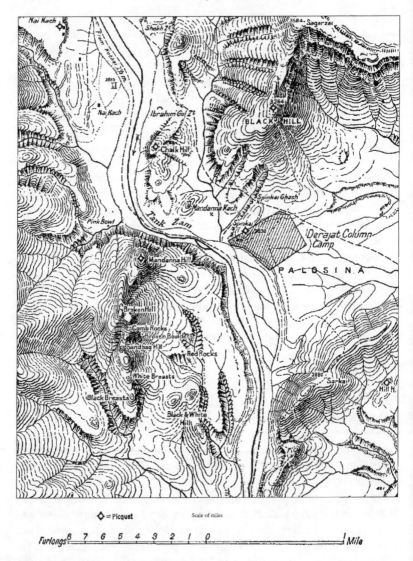

Fig. 7.   Map to illustrate operations in the area surrounding Palosina Perimeter
Camp, 19th/20th December 1919

well-concealed marksmen providing sufficient covering rifle fire to pin
down imperial troops, enabling swordsmen to close and engage in hand-
to-hand combat. It was strikingly apparent that the character of frontier
warfare had altered considerably, primarily as a result of tribal re-
armament with high velocity rifles and by their skilful combination of fire
and movement. This new-found tactical effectiveness was primarily attributable to the presence of large numbers of deserters and pensioners from
the militia and Indian Army in their ranks. Ex-servicemen formed
one-fifth to one-sixth of the Mahsud fighting strength – approximately
2,000 men – encountered during the initial phase of the campaign, providing *lashkars* with leadership, discipline and tactical training that they had
always lacked before in Waziristan.[36] Despite being highly effective,
however, these new tactics were vulnerable to artillery fire, Lewis guns
and aircraft, and dramatically increased tribal casualties. As a result the
lashkars dispersed on 21st December, in heavy rain, to replenish their
stores, bury their dead and remove their wounded from the fighting at
Tarakai which was occupied by imperial troops the following day without
resistance. The discovery of over 50 dead Mahsuds and, more
significantly, the uncharacteristic abandonment of large numbers of rifles
near the position provided an indication of tribal losses. This invaluable
breathing space was used by the column to build further permanent
piquets to safeguard the perimeter camp and the line of communications
without any serious opposition.[37]

Mahsud *lashkars* had nearly inflicted a decisive defeat on the Indian
Army in the hills around Palosina. Morale was badly shaken by the heavy
losses and the apparent inability of imperial troops to secure piquets in the
surrounding hills. After two days' operations the column had marched
only three miles and had suffered three serious defeats. As Sir John
Smyth, the Brigade Major of 43rd Brigade, later observed in his memoirs:
'We had realized that our troops were untrained in mountain warfare and
they would have to buy their experience, but we had hoped that the price
would not be so high. Only a few people ... realized how close we had
come to a real débâcle.'[38] On 21st December a seriously worried Climo
and Skeen met the CGS at Khirgi, where they requested immediate reinforcements to bolster their demoralised troops, as well as unsuccessfully
asking for permission to employ poison gas against the Mahsuds.[39] Two
Gurkha battalions were immediately sent to Waziristan as a result while
further reinforcements were organised in India. Major-General Climo
ordered Skeen to henceforth mount attacks with at least a full brigade and
to ensure that all piquets were thoroughly fortified before proceeding with
further operations.[40] As a result of poor weather, which limited air support,

the column halted until 28th December 1919 to reorganise and secure its line of communications. Despite no further repetition of the earlier disastrous incidents the fighting quality and morale of the troops at Palosina remained a serious source of concern. As a result two unreliable battalions were removed from the Derajat Column and relegated out of harm's way to the lines of communications below Khirgi. On 30th December 1919 the commander of Waziristan Force voiced his concerns:

> The actions last week have given some valuable lessons which will be of immediate interest and importance ... Those operations have shown the vital necessity of regaining some standard of musketry efficiency. Marksmanship and fire discipline are two of the first essentials in frontier fighting and the present Indian Army as a general rule has never learnt these two arts. The result is that as the men have no faith in their rifles, they have little self-confidence and look to auxiliaries, such as Artillery, aeroplanes and Lewis guns for their protection and to win the battle. In this connection, it may be remarked that practically none of the junior British officers have had experience of hill warfare and experience of warfare against a civilised and organised enemy is not necessarily good training for hill warfare against a savage enemy ... Nothing can replace these arts, and frontier warfare must remain expensive on lives and rich in unpleasant incidents until our infantry regain some of their ancient knowledge of musketry and fire discipline and so get renewed confidence in themselves and in their weapons.[41]

To compensate for the poor quality of his shaken troops, Skeen now relied heavily on superior numbers, heavy fire support from his sole highly effective battery of 3.7" howitzers and Lewis guns, and continuous close support from Bristol Fighters, which had proved a great success on the battlefield. Indeed, he was so convinced of the need for air support that no further advances were attempted until the weather permitted its use.[42] On several occasions during the fighting Lewis guns proved more of a liability than an asset, however, as poorly trained Indian troops expended vast quantities of ammunition to little effect. Many weapons were lost during December due to poor training, and as a result Lewis guns were withdrawn from platoons and massed to form battalion or brigade reserves under the direct supervision of British officers.[43]

Mahsud resistance, poor weather and the difficult terrain along the Tank Zam Valley forced Skeen to mount a slow, deliberate, and methodical advance during late December and early January, of only 2–4 miles a day, interspersed by frequent halts to construct permanent piquets to protect his lengthening line of communications and to amass stores.[44] An attack on

the 4–39th Garwhal Rifles on 2nd January gave some grounds for opti-
mism, when its comparatively well-trained, well-led and disciplined troops
defeated Mahsud tribesmen in hand-to-hand fighting.[45] The morale of the
Derajat Column slowly improved as the promised Gurkha and Frontier
Force battalions and drafts containing a large proportion of trained and
seasoned senior officers arrived, replacing a further three demoralised and
unreliable units that were relegated to the lines of communication.[46] To
provide experienced officers, units throughout India and the Middle East
were also combed, and 40 men were sent to bolster regiments already in
Waziristan.[47] Further fighting provided confirmation that major changes
had occurred in the nature of frontier warfare, with conditions altering
markedly in disfavour of imperial troops. On 6th January 1920 Major-
General Skipton Climo summarised the difficulties facing his troops:

> The factor which affects everything is the prevalence amongst the tribes
> of low-trajectory rifles with an adequate supply of smokeless ammuni-
> tion ... The tribesmen therefore have the arms and ammunition for cov-
> ering fire. This they employ, and under its cover they are able to
> concentrate for attack and carry out much of their approach after con-
> centration. It should be realised that the tribesman is now a more
> scientific fighter than he has been in the past ... Another obvious result
> of the improvement of armament is the increase in casualties. There has
> not been much sniping into camp so far ... the tribesmen are realising
> that unaimed fire is a waste of ammunition ... Day sniping in conse-
> quence has increased and is responsible for many casualties. It is most
> difficult to compete with in broken and hilly country such as the
> Column is operating in at present.[48]

The range, rate of fire and accuracy of .303 magazine rifles enabled
Mahsuds and Wazirs to deliver effective fire on Indian columns and
inflict casualties at ranges of 1,000–1,200 yards. As had been demonstrated on a small scale 21 years before in the Bara Valley, individual
snipers or small parties of tribesmen firing at long range could now seriously impede or halt the progress of an Indian column. Tribal marksmen
hidden on the broken hillsides and employing smokeless ammunition
were exceedingly difficult to locate, causing the advance to grind to a halt
until the snipers had been killed, suppressed or forced to move position.
Imperial troops resorted to heavy prophylactic fire in an endeavour to
silence tribal marksmen, but this usually proved ineffective and bad
for morale and consumed vast quantities of ammunition, further exacerbating transport and supply difficulties. To complicate matters *lashkars*
deliberately restricted the fire of older black-powder Enfield, Snider and

Martini-Henry rifles to the hours of darkness to prevent betraying tribal positions.[49]

The main task of the Derajat Column as it edged forwards towards Kaniguram became the construction and occupation of heavily fortified permanent piquets to protect the main body. All piquets had now to be built at distances of 1,000–1,500 yards at commanding points on either side of the route of march to keep snipers out of effective range. Their placement and withdrawal was frequently heavily contested by *lashkars* so that a full brigade had to be deployed. The strength of Mahsud resistance and their modern rifles meant carefully organised deliberate attacks had to be staged, requiring close co-operation between mountain artillery, machine guns and the RAF. In many ways this approximated to European conditions, but there remained important differences in methods due to the terrain and tribal tactics. The range of .303 rifles meant attempts to outflank Mahsud positions were more tiring and time-consuming, often ineffective, and had to cover longer distances than before. Indeed, the distinction between a deliberate attack and the seizure of piquet positions became blurred, as the advance resolved itself into a constant series of engagements to force the tribesmen back frontally and on both flanks, with continuous fighting to secure piquets and cover the movement of transport columns. Imperial troops fought a heavily-pressed rearguard action at the end of each day, as they withdrew to the security of a perimeter camp harassed relentlessly by Mahsud riflemen, who without hesitation engaged in hand-to-hand combat when an opportunity offered. It was now impossible to ensure that all commanding positions within effective rifle range of a column were occupied, and piquets had to employ their weapons to deny tribesmen use of all other potentially threatening terrain features and keep them at a respectable distance. Piquet positions themselves were now frequently overlooked from the surrounding hills and had to be heavily fortified with stone walls, traverses, and belts of barbed wire to protect their garrisons from both rifle fire or direct assault. This required large quantities of engineering stores and a considerable amount of time and labour. Each piquet took a day on average to construct, often involving heavy fighting. Between 29th December 1919 and 8th January 1920 42 dead, 163 wounded and 30 missing were lost during such operations, which often required the commitment of the full strength of the column until each piquet was consolidated.[50]

This heavy fighting and the number of troops deployed meant the Derajat Column was also completely dependent on a permanent fixed line of communications to service its logistical requirements. It was simply impossible for columns to operate further than three days' radius of action from its supply line without reducing medical services, ammunition and defence stores below an acceptable level. The vastly increased scale of supporting arms, equipment and medical services now required by imperial troops compounded the transport problem, causing a further decline in mobility and speed of movement. Imperial tactics further exacerbated transport and supply problems as expenditure of ammunition, in addition to food, clothing and engineering stores, spiralled to unprecedented levels. A lengthy halt was required after each stage of the advance to amass sufficient stores, causing as much delay as tribal resistance. It was vital to ensure the security of the line of communications and widen tracks, as convoys composed of pack animals were required on a daily basis to evacuate casualties and replenish supplies. 1,400 mules and 1,800 camels (excluding first-line animals carrying equipment with units) accompanied the advancing troops, while 2,000 camels worked on the lines of communication. The protection of these convoys necessitated the permanent retention of large heavily fortified piquets established by the main body as it advanced at half-mile intervals throughout the operations, replacing the small temporary detachments hitherto employed in frontier warfare each day to protect convoys. In the face of such strong tribal opposition, it was now simply too costly to piquet commanding features on a daily basis. Their construction further exacerbated the supply problem as they required large quantities of barbed wire, stakes and defence stores. In addition, moveable columns were required in each section of the line of communication to escort convoys and carry out punitive operations in the immediate vicinity.[51]

The cumulative effect of improvements in tribal armament and tactics on the conduct of mountain warfare and corresponding changes in imperial methods was to slow every phase of the operations in Waziristan. Climo concluded his appreciation of the situation on 6th January:

> I am of opinion that the days of lightning frontier campaigns, except against insignificant tribes, are over. Such campaigns must be more deliberate, will entail more troops for the defence of the communications, will require more transport and will be more expensive in lives, but the results to be obtained will probably be better and more lasting as we will take heavier toll of the enemy and will sensibly reduce his stock of fighting men.[52]

'Deracol' halted at Kotkai until 6th January, while preparations were made to advance through the precipitous 80-yard Ahnai Tangi gorge. As a precursor to the main attack, it was necessary to seize and consolidate positions on the heights along both flanks of the valley around the entrance of the gorge. Intense tribal resistance and difficult terrain made it impossible to complete the piquets before nightfall, when the first attempt was made on 7th January, so the 43rd and 67th Brigades returned to camp (see Figure 8). An attempt to construct a piquet near Zeriwam on 9th January was abandoned as darkness approached after heavy attacks. Fighting the following day was equally unsuccessful when the covering troops were forced to withdraw by heavy and accurate sniping. The casualties suffered on the 9th–10th January amounted to a further 170 killed and wounded, but the vital positions on the east flank of the valley remained in tribal hands. The continued strong opposition around the entrance to the gorge prompted Major-General Skeen to risk a highly dangerous night advance to secure positions overlooking the Ahnai Tangi, to prevent the hopefully surprised tribesmen organising an effective defence and to nullify the impact of their rifles. Despite the rank scepticism of many experienced officers, the attack carried out by 43rd and 67th Brigades on 11th January 1920, across difficult terrain, achieved complete surprise and captured the positions with the loss of only 5 dead and 28 wounded, as due to the cold weather the ill-disciplined opposing tribesmen had not occupied their defences overnight. Despite this victory it was still all too apparent, however, that Indian troops could not compete with the Mahsuds without full and close co-operation with aircraft and artillery. On 13th January 1920 Climo explained:

> I doubt if it is understood how desperate the fighting has been during these operations. It would have tried highly even the pre-war Frontier Force or similar regiments with long experience of the Frontier and years of training. It is, perhaps, to be expected that those who do not know India and the frontier, and even some who have fought on the frontier in pre-war days, but lack the knowledge and imagination to realise what conditions have altered with the great improvement of the armament of the tribesmen, cannot understand or believe the standard of training that is required for the Infantry in the conditions that prevail on the Frontier to-day. To such, the belief is natural that the mere frontier tribes cannot be formidable opponents to modern troops nor can they believe that the standard of training or method of tactics that succeeded in the great war can, in former cases, be insufficient for and, in the latter case, be inapplicable to a Frontier campaign … Here, however, matters are quite different.[53]

The attack on the Ahnai Tangi gorge on 14th January encountered strong resistance as Indian troops attempted to seize positions along the ridge flanking the Tank Zam Valley, leading to the heaviest fighting of the

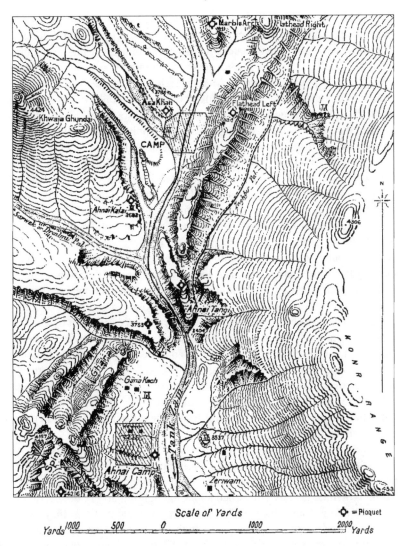

Fig. 8.   Map to illustrate operations in the area surrounding the Ahnai Tangi Gorge, 7th–14th January 1920

campaign. Intense rifle fire and concerted attacks by a large *lashkar*, which had anticipated the tactical importance of the position, greeted the 2/5th Gurkha Rifles as its men secured a permanent piquet on Flathead Left, while the main column was checked by accurate small arms fire from tribesmen occupying positions at Marble Arch and Flathead Right, making their capture also imperative before the advance could continue. The strength of the Mahsud counter-attacks, however, soon made it clear that any advance further along the ridge was impossible. As a result the hard-pressed Indian troops consolidated their position at Flathead Left, while heavy rifle fire made the column hastily construct a perimeter camp in the valley below at Asa Khan. Four determined attacks were made by Mahsud swordsmen under intense covering rifle fire against Flathead Left, who were beaten off with bayonets, stones, knives and grenades at a heavy cost to the defending troops. This position was finally consolidated overnight, but its capture and subsequent defence cost 17 officers and 365 other ranks dead or wounded, in the most stubbornly contested and decisive engagement of the entire campaign. Such losses were extremely serious in light of the dissipation of the column's strength in garrisoning permanent piquets, perimeter camps and escorting supply columns on its line of communications. However, bombing and strafing attacks carried out by Bristol Fighters, combined with the physical presence of several aircraft overhead which had exhausted their stores, prevented Mahsud attacks being pressed home to close quarters. Three aircraft were shot down, however, by small-arms fire from the ground. A large number of dead men and abandoned rifles were left in front of the piquet when the *lashkar* finally withdrew, but it had nearly captured a position from where the main column could have been decimated by rifle fire.[54]

'Deracol' remained at Asa Khan for three days to evacuate casualties, amass stores and await the arrival of reinforcements needed to continue the advance. Despite the steady progress now being made, Major-General Climo remained acutely concerned about the fighting ability of several of his units due to their ignorance of hill warfare or the fact that they were recruited from the Indian plains.[55] When the Inspector General of Infantry in Northern Command, Brigadier-General William Villiers-Stuart, visited the column, Skeen complained that the only troops under his command on which he could rely were the 1/55th Rifles and his Gurkha battalions; he once again requested experienced British officers and Gurkhas as reinforcements, with further aircraft, artillery, trench mortars and ammunition, as well as again asking for permission to employ mustard gas.[56] The Derajat Column's confidence and tactical skill steadily improved as the continued fighting provided practical experience of hill warfare and its men learnt basic infantry skills under active service conditions. Between 29th December and 20th January it fought over twenty major engagements involving the commitment of more than a brigade. Night operations were now regularly employed to seize piquets, jumping-off areas and important defensive positions during five of the larger operations. These avoided heavy casualties, extended operations outside daylight hours and often forestalled the tribesmen occupying and defending strong positions and thereby using their rifles to full effect. During January the column steadily advanced, as its strength was augmented by further Gurkha battalions accustomed to fighting in mountainous terrain, allowing three further units to be replaced.[57]

The back of Mahsud resistance had nearly been broken, however, as the relentless British advance and the heavy losses they had suffered during the earlier fighting had sapped tribal morale. On 28th January the formidable Barari Tangi gorge was captured when a night attack secured dominating positions on the heights at Barari Centre, the Barrier and Gibraltar, from the surprised defenders who offered little resistance.[58] Despite this setback, a large *lashkar* assembled once again the following day, emboldened by promises of support from an Afghan officer and two 9lb mountain guns. While imperial troops constructed piquets north of the gorge they opened fire, but they were almost immediately suppressed by British artillery, shattering tribal expectations that they would decisively affect the campaign. Another *lashkar* spotted ahead of the column was also successfully engaged by artillery and aircraft and forced to disperse. This sudden British advance, further heavy casualties and the inability of the Afghans to render effective support effectively shattered tribal morale. In comparison, the confidence of the column and its commander increased as it became evident that organised tribal resistance had ceased after the main *lashkars* dispersed into the hills.[59]

During February imperial troops only encountered sporadic resistance from tribesmen inhabiting the immediate area, with fighting confined to sniping, raids and attacks on rearguards.[60] As a result it was able to complete the further planned stages of the operation far quicker than had been anticipated, despite deteriorating weather. The protection of the increasingly vulnerable lengthening line of communication, however, was a particular concern and absorbed a large proportion of the available troops. Interference with convoys was fortunately considerably less than expected due to permanent piquets, and as the remaining Mahsuds still concentrated on attacking the head of the column. During February punitive operations were conducted for the first time in an endeavour to make the Mahsuds agree terms. Between 19th and 28th February 51 towers and 450 buildings were destroyed by 'Deracol' in the heart of Mahsud territory near Makin. Many casualties were caused by riflemen hidden on the steep scrub-covered hills and in gorges around Piazha Algad. Tribal disorganisation and demoralisation, however, was made apparent by such limited opposition in terrain otherwise ideally suited to tribal tactics.[61] On 1st March the Makin area was evacuated and the column proceeded to a new camp near Kaniguram, from where further punitive operations were carried out against the remaining hostile sections. A raid into the Upper Baddar Toi valley between 6th and 8th April demonstrated imperial troops' new-found confidence and proficiency in hill warfare, after which the Derajat Column occupied a permanent camp at Ladha and ended active operations.[62]

LESSONS OLD AND NEW: TRAINING AND NEW TECHNOLOGY

The Waziristan Campaign officially ended in May 1920, when the head-quarters of 'Deracol' was dissolved, although the inability of the divided Mahsud sections to make peace and the Wana Wazirs' continued hostility meant that imperial troops remained in the area. It was evident that a new era had begun in frontier warfare that had been foreseen by several observers before the First World War. 366 dead, 1,683 wounded and 237 missing had been suffered by Waziristan Force in fighting of unparalleled severity. This represented the highest 'butcher's bill' ever suffered during operations against the trans-border Pathan tribes. Tribal *lashkars* had fought with courage, determination and skill never encountered before. As a direct result of the dramatic improvements in tribal tactics, the large quantities of .303 rifles in their possession and the presence of a significant number of ex-servicemen, the Indian Army had nearly been defeated. The low level of basic individual infantry training and a lack of knowledge and experience of the principles and minor tactics of mountain warfare amongst imperial troops had been the most alarming feature of the fighting. It was directly responsible for the heavy losses at Mahsud hands. General Sir Charles Monro, the Commander-in-Chief in India, concluded the official despatch on the Waziristan campaign:

> [The operations] have merely borne out the principles of mountain warfare, which are well known from many former campaigns. It is, however, necessary here to lay emphasis upon the supreme importance of adequate training of troops prior to their employment in a mountain campaign. Nothing can take the place of careful individual training. If possible, it is more essential in mountain warfare then in any other class

of fighting that troops should have confidence in their weapons. This can only be obtained by systematic individual training, which must include instruction in making the best tactical use of ground, in the principles of fire and movement, and the mental development of the soldier to such a degree of alertness, that no target escapes from detection and appropriate action is immediately taken. At the beginning of these operations, a proportion of the troops were not fully masters of their weapons. This was due to ignorance of how to use them to the best advantage, as, owing to the demands made by the Great War, men had been somewhat hastily trained, and it is probable the severity of fighting in December was due, to a certain degree, to this lack of training.[63]

As during the earlier Tirah campaign, the learning curve had proved both steep and costly in lives as the tribesmen exploited the long list of mistakes committed by British officers and Indian troops. To counteract improving tribal military effectiveness the fighting in Waziristan had also led to the first widespread use of new tactics: permanent piquets and night operations. They had proved highly successful, and indicated that they would have to be employed again if heavy tribal resistance was encountered. It was also evident that imperial troops were now reliant on large amounts of supporting arms, services and equipment which exacerbated the transport and supply problems always inherent in frontier warfare. Despite the lessons learnt by the Derajat Column regarding the use of modern military equipment, it had been made all too abundantly clear that the post-war Army in India needed, once again, to train its officers and men in the specialised tactics of mountain warfare against a well-armed tribal adversary.

The fact that the Third Afghan War and ensuing fighting in Waziristan had ended with large numbers of imperial troops concentrated in the NWFP both reinforced the need for specialised training in frontier fighting and prompted a major re-evaluation of frontier policy. Intermittent fighting continued for the next three years in Waziristan under very different operational conditions from that during 1919–20, with three brigades tied down guarding the line of communication of a striking force based at Ladha. As the future Field Marshal Slim later observed: 'On every village green in England monuments were rising which proclaimed the war was over, yet here I had only to raise my eyes to see once more the piled sandbags, the rough stone parapet, and writhing strands of barbed wire.'[64] In March 1920 Lord Chelmsford, the Viceroy, sanctioned the temporary occupation of central Waziristan as the best means of pacifying the area and protecting the administrative border, and agreed to the construction of roads suitable for motor transport from the Derajat to forward perimeter camps.[65] In June 1920 those units permanently stationed in the NWFP and Baluchistan, comprising 12 Infantry brigades, were redesignated the Covering Troops while the rest of the army was divided between a Field Army, organised, trained and equipped primarily for operations in Afghanistan, and Internal Security troops intended to maintain order in India. 43 Indian infantry battalions, three pioneer battalions, six Indian cavalry regiments, four field and 12 1/2 pack artillery batteries, as well as two 1/2 companies of armoured cars were distributed between Peshawar, Kohat and the Derajat as well as in Waziristan. Unlike the rest of the Army in India, these units had a lower scale of transport, signals and wheeled artillery, and were maintained on a permanent war footing ready to take the field immediately in event of a tribal rising. The number of British units – five infantry battalions – was deliberately kept at a minimum, however, as the climate was regarded as inimical to their health and as Indian troops were thought to be better adapted to tribal warfare.[66]

The near disasters of the winter of 1919–20 ensured that immediate steps were taken by the General Staff in India to provide appropriate training for units in the NWFP while the Waziristan operations were still in their final stages. To provide sufficient trained instructors for the post-war Army in India Northern Command hurriedly reopened the Mountain Warfare School at Abbottabad on 1st February 1920. Colonel William Villiers-Stuart, assisted by four experienced officers, an attached infantry battalion, mountain artillery battery and a cavalry squadron as demonstration troops, once again assumed command.[67] A series of courses was held during the spring, summer and autumn to train British officers lacking any previous knowledge of mountain warfare, to refresh the minds of those with limited experience, and finally to provide students with notes, précis and examples of training schemes and demonstrations to assist in teaching their own units.[68] The curriculum followed the same practical and realistic system of instruction used before, beginning with an explanation of the basic principles of war – a deliberate attempt to avoid over-specialisation – before introducing various modifications required in their application to 'trans-border' warfare. As it was assumed that the comparatively well-trained students now at Abbottabad already possessed a detailed knowledge of the normal principles of war a far greater proportion of the curriculum was devoted to the principles and minor tactics of hill warfare. Examples from prior frontier campaigns were used to demonstrate principles and various points made during lectures, which were illustrated using sand-table models and demonstration troops. Members of the Directing Staff stressed the importance of individual skills in mountain warfare – skill-at-arms, self-reliance, vigilance and personal judgement – as it was impossible to employ all modern weapons because of the terrain and to overcome 'trans-border loneliness', resulting from employing small, widely dispersed detachments. Officers were urged to develop a 'spirit of suspicion' to defeat a tribal enemy at his own game. To prevent 'regrettable incidents', students were introduced to various types of ambushes that had been employed by the Pathans in the past and the correct means of countering them. The syllabus also covered: piqueting, examples of drill preparations, camp and bivouac routine, effective covering fire, *sangars*, cavalry, mountain artillery, notes on destroying a village, the use of Lewis and Vickers machine-guns in trans-border warfare, how to study a hill campaign, transport and supply, common mistakes in the field and lessons derived from recent fighting. Particular attention was directed towards the lessons learnt in Waziristan about modifications in tactics and the employment of modern equipment in hill warfare, which was particularly important given widespread confusion regarding the correct use of new weapons in tribal territory.[69] The school was able to effect important changes in imperial tactics. As Villiers-Stuart noted in his diary:

> We were able to revolutionise the methods of building *sangars*; show how very effective smoke candles can be when carried by riflemen and used sensibly; we taught a really sound method of attacking and destroying villages and retiring from them; the use of ambuscades; and a thousand matters of attack, defence, camp procedure, removal of wounded and much more which, though vaguely known and practised in the old Piffer regiments, had never been codified as standard practice.[70]

Despite its obvious success, the school was not retained by the Army in India as a permanent training establishment, as the principle was re-established that units would carry out training under the direction of the staff of the formations to which they belonged.[71]

The General Staff was well aware that it would take some time, however, before the level of basic individual military skills and proficiency of units had been restored to pre-war standards. On several occasions this was driven home during the early 1920s when Mahsud gangs secured embarrassing victories against imperial units still largely composed of raw, untrained troops. These incidents and other training difficulties were such that on several occasions during the early 1920s the resuscitation of a new PFF was discussed, as many officers recognised that specialised troops would be more effective than the regular army in frontier warfare.[72] To many officers the provision of an up-to-date training manual for units again became a concern as units periodically served a

tour of duty in the NWFP in the Covering Troops. Indeed, it was essential
following the closure of the Mountain Warfare School. However, the provisional post-war edition of *FSR* published in 1920 still referred to 'savage
warfare' solely in terms of fighting against opponents reliant on shock
tactics, and lacked the detail that the many inexperienced officers and
NCOs of the post-war army required.[73] Fighting in Waziristan had demonstrated that this was no longer the case. Indeed, a contradiction existed in
the declaration in *FSR* that the principles of war applied without any reservations to all forms of warfare, but that important modifications were
required in their application during operations in tribal territory. To
provide an up-to-date source of guidance, a small pamphlet on mountain
warfare was prepared at AHQ during 1920 to complement *FSR* pending
the publication of a larger volume. The Commandant of the Staff College
at Quetta, however, vigorously opposed the circulation of this manual,
believing it was misleading and would reduce mountain warfare to a set of
locally applied, specialised rules that would make officers forget that the
wider principles of war underlay all military operations. Particular criticism was reserved for the Standing Orders it included which, he feared,
officers would accept as 'gospel' rather than just as an example.[74] A
revised edition was published during January 1921, and 15,000 copies
were issued that laid down general principles to govern the conduct of
'uncivilized' warfare as well as general principles of mountain warfare
against the trans-border Pathan tribes for all three arms of service. It summarised the minor tactics of mountain warfare – piqueting, protection on
the march, protection of the lines of communication, camps and bivouacs
and night operations – and, moreover, provided outline guidance regarding
the use of new equipment such as Lewis guns.[75] Training was also facilitated by the publication of several text books during the early 1920s
written by experienced Indian Army officers which complemented official
sources of guidance.[76] The headquarters of Wazirforce also produced its
own tactical notes containing guidance for all three arms of service, compiled from memoranda it had periodically issued, which were distributed
to units under its command.[77]

Other training establishments also covered the conduct of frontier
warfare. The Royal Military College at Sandhurst, responsible for training
officers for both the British and Indian armies, covered the topic as experienced subalterns were in such short supply throughout the Army in India.
A small manual was specifically printed for use at the college to facilitate
instruction, including extracts from the official history of the Waziristan
campaign and *Small Wars: Their Principles and Practice*, and listing
various lessons derived from the Tirah campaign.[78] When the Staff

College at Quetta reopened after the First World War, frontier warfare once again featured in its curriculum.[79] In 1922 its syllabus included seven lectures, indoor exercises and student conferences devoted to the conduct of military operations on the North-West Frontier and the political problem posed by the tribes. The lessons learnt during the fighting in Waziristan formed the subject of three detailed lectures which discussed the operations of the Derajat Column in depth.[80] Frontier warfare once again formed part of the curriculum of the Staff College at Camberley, where training followed similar lines to those before the First World War, although visiting lecturers provided further information regarding the military and political problems associated with the frontier.[81]

Those lessons learnt regarding the capabilities and limitations of modern weapons in frontier fighting originally developed and employed on the battlefields of the First World War were also carefully evaluated by the General Staff in India following the Third Afghan War and tested during the ensuing protracted operations in Waziristan. To many British officers automatic weapons, modern artillery, gas, motor transport, armoured cars, tanks and aircraft offered the best means of reducing the frequency and duration of punitive expeditions, minimising casualties, increasing mobility and reducing the amount of manpower deployed on the frontier. Such interest was fostered by various proponents of new equipment, who believed their employment would revolutionise not only European warfare, but also operations carried out throughout the British Empire. Moreover, it appeared that the use of such equipment against a 'savage' opponent was particularly justified to counterbalance improving tribal armament and military effectiveness, and until the Indian Army regained its pre-war efficiency.[82] The Army Department, however, noted in June 1920: 'The only limiting factor we should accept in this respect is that of mobility, and we consider that our forces should be armed and equipped with all modern appliances to the highest degree compatible with mobility.'[83]

Imperial infantry battalions had a dramatically increased range of weapons following the First World War, although the rifle remained the most effective weapon in tribal territory. Hand and rifle grenades enabled soldiers to defend the immediate vicinity of piquets without being exposed to enemy rifle fire, and to clear dead ground and wooded terrain.[84] Automatic weapons appeared the best means to counter improved tribal armament and tactics. Lewis guns dramatically increased the number of automatic weapons in each battalion, but professional opinion was divided regarding their tactical employment in mountain warfare or whether they should be a platoon, company or battalion weapon.[85] 16 Lewis guns were

finally allocated to infantry units in India – one per platoon – to maintain
rifle strength and as difficulties in providing adequate ammunition were
anticipated in tribal territory. The weight of each weapon (28lbs per gun
and a 3lb bipod), however, was such that a mule was needed to carry each
weapon, ammunition and equipment, which was often unable to keep up
with the infantry and acted as a drag on cross-country mobility in the
hills.[86] Vickers machine guns were also added to the establishment of each
infantry battalion in 1921, following the disbandment of the Machine Gun
Corps, and quickly proved a valuable weapon at the disposal of infantry
commanders.[87] Their long range, accuracy and high sustained rate of fire
provided the infantry with its own echelon of supporting fire between their
small arms and mountain artillery. Vickers guns were utilised to protect
the placement of piquets, support attacks and withdrawals and to defend
perimeter camps and outlying defences. Their greatest drawback was the
additional pack transport required to carry the weapons, equipment and
ammunition, considerably increasing the length of columns on the march.
Moreover, their comparatively slow speed coming in and out of action
limited mobility, and it was difficult to direct their fire in broken terrain.[88]

The mountain artillery once again demonstrated it effectiveness during
the Third Afghan War and in Waziristan. Several important lessons were
evident both with regard to training and equipment. When opposed to
tribesmen armed with rifles, close co-operation between the infantry and
gunners proved essential, although the increased range of modern ordnance meant batteries no longer had to operate close to the forward troops.
A lack of a reliable means of communication between the infantry and
gun positions to direct artillery fire, however, indicated that a simple and
universal system as well as special training was needed by imperial troops
to ensure effective co-operation.[89] The 3.7″ QF pack howitzer represented
a distinct qualitative improvement over 10lb and 2.75″ guns currently in
service, with a range of 5,900 yards, an all-round traverse and high trajectory that enabled it to fire from positions located on the valley floor. It
was able to search dead ground and clear *sangars*, nullahs and positions
out of the direct line of sight of Indian troops with accurate, rapid indirect
shell fire, although the lack of a shrapnel round initially limited the
weapons' effectiveness. It also took longer to come into action, was
difficult to range accurately and was unable to land shells on ridges except
by chance, and additional mules were required to carry the weapon and its
heavy ammunition. During the early 1920s the relative tactical value of
guns and howitzers in mountain warfare remained a subject of controversy
amongst gunners in India, although it was generally accepted that both
types of ordnance needed to co-operate to obtain the best results.[90]

Apart from areas where roads existed or where the valleys were negotiable by draught animals, mountainous terrain and problems of transport and supply restricted the employment of heavier-calibre artillery in tribal territory. A section of 6" guns, capable of firing a 100lb shell over 10,000 yards, was manhandled to Ladha in June and shelled Makin at intervals until September 1921, destroying buildings and preventing crops from being harvested. Although the presence of the 6" guns and the threat of heavy bombardment proved effective in controlling a large area of central Waziristan, no other heavy artillery was deployed because of transport and supply difficulties apart from static 15lb and four 4.5" post-defence guns scattered in forts throughout the area.[91]

The potential use of chemical weapons in frontier warfare had already been evaluated during the autumn of 1919 when Major-General Charles Foulkes, the former Director of Gas Duties in France, visited the NWFP.[92] A detailed memorandum written by Foulkes advocating the use of mustard gas against the trans-border Pathan tribes was circulated by the CGS in November to senior political and military officers, many of whom supported its conclusions.[93] Following the 1919–20 Waziristan campaign Foulkes' proposals received even wider endorsement from British officers acquainted with recent changes in frontier warfare. On 10th January 1920 Brigadier Walter Leslie summed up the view of officers with the Derajat Column: 'Gas is the best means of reducing the casualty list (on our side) & here we are all strongly in favour of it.'[94] The heavy fighting in Waziristan added weight to Foulkes' views, and while lecturing at Delhi he stressed that gas would help redress many of the disadvantages that imperial troops worked under when operating in tribal territory.[95] After close consultation between the Commander-in-Chief, the General Staff in India and the political authorities, the Government of India finally decided in February 1920 that no distinction should be made between the use of gas and other modern equipment.[96] A decision regarding its employment, however, was deferred by the Secretary of State for India largely on moral grounds, until the wider implications of its use had been fully discussed in London; although pending a decision, reserves of gas-filled shells and aircraft bombs were stockpiled and research regarding gas warfare in India was conducted.[97] The matter was finally shelved when in July 1922 the Government of India was directed that chemical weapons could only be employed in retaliation for a gas attack on imperial troops.[98]

The use of motor transport for the movement and supply of imperial troops, hand-in-hand with road construction in tribal territory, attracted considerable thought and experiment as the best means of revolutionising the administrative conduct of frontier warfare, although pack transport remained essential to all operations in the hills. Lorries transported troops and supplies in the Khyber Pass during the Third Afghan War with some success.[99] During the 1919–20 operations five companies of Ford Vans were used on the line of communications of Waziristan Force as far as the road head at Khirgi from where pack transport carried supplies to the forward troops.[100] As roads were constructed in Waziristan in accordance with government policy, lorries slowly replaced pack transport animals, which had represented the 'Achilles heel' of Indian troops during prior frontier operations. Their speed, reliability, ease of protection and vastly increased load-carrying capacity made them a valuable asset. Motor transport added enormously to the mobility and striking power of fighting troops by increasing their radius of action and reducing the number of protective detachments required on the lines of communication, as well as by greatly simplifying the problems of supply and the evacuation of wounded.[101]

Armoured cars had demonstrated their versatility in India during the First World War, when their mobility, firepower and relative invulnerability to rifle fire had made them ideal in the NWFP for reconnaissance, patrolling, the pursuit of raiding gangs, escort duties and the support of beleaguered outposts in areas where roads or open ground existed.[102] Two and a half companies were allocated to the Covering Troops and provisional guidelines for their use on the frontier were issued in 1921.[103] A company of Jeffrey Quad Armoured cars was deployed in Waziristan in October 1921, to 'open roads', co-operate with moveable columns and escort convoys. Similar duties were carried out by No. 7 Company, equipped with Rolls-Royce armoured cars, in the Tochi valley and the Derajat. A reduction in the number of road protection troops resulted, as motor transport convoys were faster and shorter and therefore more difficult to attack.[104]

The employment of tracked armoured fighting vehicles, with greater protection, firepower and off-road mobility than armoured cars, was carefully investigated during the spring of 1920 when Colonel Philip Johnson, Superintendent of Tank Design and Experiment at the War Office, toured the frontier and visited Wazirforce at Kaniguram. In a detailed report discussing the employment of tanks in operations against Afghanistan, internal security and versus the trans-border Pathan tribes, he enthusiastically proposed that punitive columns consisting solely of tanks, personnel carriers, self-propelled artillery, engineer tenders and armoured ambulances, capable of traversing boulder-strewn river beds and invulnerable to rifle fire, could be employed in tribal territory in the future.[105] While acknowledging that steep and rocky terrain represented an insuperable obstacle to existing tanks, Johnson believed that tracked vehicles could be devised capable of operating on the frontier, thereby revolutionising hill warfare.

His 'visionary' proposals received a justifiably sceptical reception from experienced frontier soldiers in London.[106] Several officers serving in Waziristan, also familiar with the capabilities of tanks, spoke in more guarded terms, emphasising their importance on the lines of communication rather than just as fighting vehicles.[107] Despite believing that ultimately Johnson's views would be correct, Colonel J.F.C. Fuller at the War Office concurred:

> My own opinion is that as regards hill warfare we should not trouble too much about tanks as fighting weapons, but that we should concentrate in producing reliable cross-country tractors which will cut down the enormous number of transport animals and coolies which are required at present to supply the troops ... the great problem which now faces the military authorities in India in hill fighting is an administrative one and I am of opinion that a fairly reliable machine can be produced in the course of the next year or two which will go far to solve the present difficulties.[108]

During the early 1920s considerable interest was maintained in India in the capabilities of both fighting and supply tanks on the frontier to reduce casualties amongst troops and pack animals.[109] Two experimental tropical tanks arrived at Ahmednagar in January 1922, but irreparably broke down before they could be properly evaluated. Despite this setback Colonel E.B. Hankey, who had accompanied the vehicles, held further discussions regarding the use of carrier and fighting tanks in tribal territory; and after touring the frontier he added his support to the growing weight of opinion that tanks could be used effectively in frontier warfare.[110] An experimental (AT 2) 'Dragon' carrier tank was carefully tested in March–August 1923 at Ahmednagar and near Peshawar.[111] It was then evaluated by the 5th Indian Infantry Brigade, under the command of Colonel William Villiers-Stuart, near Asad Khel in Waziristan between 16th and 21st August 1923. The former commandant of the Mountain Warfare School recommended the use of tanks for trans-border fighting, in addition to other arms, following tests simulating different types of operation common in hill warfare.[112] Major-General James Charles, GOC Wazirforce, added his support: 'The very great assistance which they are capable of rendering, in my opinion, merits their inclusion in the establishments of our war formations.'[113] The now clearly convinced Indian military authorities finally placed orders early in 1924 for four Vickers MK I Light Tanks, armed with two Vickers guns, and four Citroen Kergresse half-track cars, for use as carrier vehicles, although their arrival was delayed by further modifications in their design.[114] A combination of serious mechanical faults when tested on the

North-West Frontier in 1925 and the cost of maintaining the vehicles, however, ultimately meant the Government of India finally declined to purchase further tanks at their current stage of development.[115]

The Third Afghan War and the Waziristan Campaign represented the most extensive use of airpower in the British Empire, giving the RAF and General Staff in India an opportunity to assess the capabilities of airpower in frontier warfare.[116] To most observers aircraft appeared the most significant technological weapon at the disposal of the imperial authorities, capable of quickly penetrating the deepest recesses of tribal territory while enjoying relative invulnerability from attack. However, after the promise displayed during the Third Afghan War, when raids on Jalalabad and Kabul directly contributed to a rapid end to the war, the results of independent bombing in Waziristan proved disappointing. Despite intensive air raids the Mahsuds did not submit and rapidly adapted to air attack, refuting claims that aircraft would demoralise the local population and make them surrender. The sparsely inhabited mountainous terrain, the small size of villages and the resilience of mud buildings, limited the effectiveness of attack from the air, although considerable casualties were inflicted on livestock. When the Derajat Column reached Kaniguram a special committee, appointed to investigate the damage inflicted by aircraft, discovered that most bombing had been inaccurate and that the majority of buildings had been only slightly damaged.[117]

On the other hand, Bristol Fighters had provided remarkably effective close-support to the Derajat Column. Aircraft inflicted heavy casualties on *lashkars* with bombs and machine-gun fire, providing heavy, flexible fire support that the infantry had long been denied on the frontier. They dramatically improved imperial morale while correspondingly reducing that of the opposing tribesmen, although several low-flying aircraft were shot down by rifle fire. The impact of close-support declined, however, when Mahsud *lashkars* learnt to utilise the rocky, steep terrain for concealment and to cease movement when aircraft were overhead. It was apparent that there were, however, important differences in providing tactical air support on the frontier when compared to conventional military operations. Pilots needed to be well acquainted with the tactics of mountain warfare and had to maintain close contact with troops on the ground. An effective means of intercommunication between ground and air other than Popham Panels was essential to allow troops to indicate targets otherwise hidden from pilots. The employment of aircraft to direct artillery fire was unsuccessful as few massed bodies of tribesmen, guns or forts were encountered that represented a worthwhile target. Aerial reconnaissance also proved generally unreliable as mountainous terrain afforded excellent cover and concealment, while the clothing of the tribesmen made them difficult to spot from the air. On the other hand, aerial photographs provided valuable tactical and topographical information that considerably aided planning.[118]

During the early 1920s the RAF squadrons deployed in the NWFP – under the control of the General Staff in India – were employed in close co-operation with of the army, supporting picquets, assisting withdrawals, directing artillery fire, communicating between advance and rear guards and supplying photographic intelligence.[119] Despite continued success in this role, the Air Staff in England were firmly convinced, however, that aircraft could be most effectively employed independently to control the trans-border Pathans by carrying out aerial demonstrations, punitive bombing, intercepting raiders and supporting locally recruited irregulars, in accordance with the doctrine of air control originally developed in the Middle East.[120] Aircraft carried out several independent raids on tribal sections implicated in raids on the lines of communication. Following an attack on the 4–39th Garwhal Rifles in March 1921, for example, Makin was bombed for three days and aircraft strafed tribesmen and livestock.[121] However, the small number of available aircraft, their limited reliability due to an embargo on purchase of spares, difficult climatic conditions and restrictions imposed by the political authorities meant that any lessons learnt were inconclusive at best.[122]

The Air Staff was finally given an opportunity to express their official views on the use of aircraft when a senior officer was despatched from England in 1922 to prepare a detailed report on the role, organisation and administration of the RAF in India. Air Vice Marshal John Salmond and his staff toured the North-West Frontier during the summer, gathering information from the civil and military authorities regarding the use of aircraft in operations against both the trans-border Pathan tribes and Afghanistan.[123] Salmond was convinced that aircraft could completely replace troops in tribal territory, based on experience gained by the RAF in Somaliland and the Middle East. In August 1922 he submitted a report to Lord Rawlinson, the Commander-in-Chief in India, proposing sweeping changes both in the conduct of frontier warfare and in policy towards the trans-border Pathan tribes. This envisaged the RAF as the primary instrument of tribal control, resting on the belief that sustained independent bombing could disrupt tribal life to such an extent that even the most stubborn tribes would accept terms with comparatively few casualties and without the legacy of hatred which he believed ground operations engendered. To test his views Salmond also proposed a practical experiment in Waziristan whereby six squadrons working in close co-operation with the political authorities would assume full responsibility for controlling its inhabitants.[124] Such sweeping proposals received a mixed reception from members of the General Staff and the Foreign and Political Department, who respectively feared cutbacks in the army and that bombing would provoke further hostilities in tribal territory and complicate relations with Afghanistan.[125] Despite strongly opposing various proposals for employing aircraft against Afghanistan and for maintaining internal security, Lord Rawlinson initially supported the idea about an experiment in Waziristan as long as a controversial General Staff scheme to permanently occupy the area was also put into effect; however, he refused to accept that a conclusive case had been presented sufficient to fundamentally change policy until air control had been tested in practice in Mesopotamia.[126]

THE MANUAL OF OPERATIONS ON THE NORTH-WEST FRONTIER OF INDIA

The Razmak operations during the autumn and winter of 1922–23 finally ended large-scale fighting in Waziristan, although minor operations dragged on until 1925. A mixed brigade, with two additional battalions for camp protection, was henceforth permanently stationed on the Razmak plateau in a new fortified cantonment to support the loose political administration and newly raised Civil Armed Forces – Scouts, Khassadars and Frontier Constabulary – recently raised to support the new 'Modified Forward Policy' adopted in the area.[127] This controversial decision meant that despite Rawlinson's earlier support the proposed RAF experiment in Waziristan was put on hold and later abandoned. A combination of the low efficiency of existing squadrons, insufficient aircraft and the fact that most senior army officers believed air control was incompatible with the new 'hearts and minds' policy adopted in Waziristan meant that henceforth the employment of the RAF on the frontier was restricted to army co-operation and occasional minor independent operations, conducted under detailed restrictions imposed by the Government of India.[128]

The cessation of hostilities prompted individual British officers and the General Staff to carefully assess the important lessons learnt by the Army in India during the extended fighting in 1920–23 (complementing those learnt in the winter of 1919–20), together with further information regarding the capabilities and limitations of modern equipment. Many new methods were now employed by imperial troops, whose standard of training and efficiency in frontier fighting by early 1924 had been restored to a semblance of pre-war standards, to counter improved tribal military effectiveness. As Colonel Donald Robertson remarked at the RUSI that year:

> One sometimes wonders what the spirits of our forbears, those wardens of these same marches, whose names inspired awe along the whole border, would have to say of our system of permanent piquets, of the numerical strength we now think necessary for a picquet, of the barbed wire, bombs and other impedimenta which are nowadays essentials. Perhaps they would remark that 'Safety First', however admirable a motto for the London streets, never led an army to victory; that, in war, achievement, and an avoidance of risk, do not go hand in hand, and that mobility is the handmaiden of success.[129]

The General Staff clearly recognised that improvements in tribal armament and tactical effectiveness meant henceforth that imperial columns had to operate in considerable strength in the face of even moderate opposition and any advance through tribal territory had to be deliberate, governed by the establishment of a permanent and carefully protected line of communication in its rear. Except in the face of light opposition, the radius of action of smaller self-contained columns was so limited by the large number of unwieldy pack animals now required by imperial troops that their employment was unfeasible in practice.[130]

Those lessons learnt at such cost during the recent fighting in Waziristan and appropriate training to counter improved tribal military effectiveness formed the subject of several articles in the military press, written by officers eager to ensure that they were not forgotten by the Army in India.[131] The impact of improved tribal armament on frontier fighting, for example, was discussed at length by Colonel Charles Kirkpatrick in a JUSII article, who complained that the section on mountain warfare in *FSR* was outdated and pointed out that the Mahsuds and Afridis could no longer be regarded as 'savages' in a purely military sense, either in terms of their armament or tactics. He warned that operations akin to those in Waziristan during 1919–20 would recur if serious resistance was encountered, and outlined the modifications in tactics evolved by experience during the fighting, emphasising the importance of increasing dispersion and supporting fire from machine guns, pack artillery and aircraft to facilitate operations.[132] Now that continuous road protection formed such a large part of military operations on the frontier, the different systems adopted to protect the lines of communication merited special attention, especially since the wide variety of terms currently used to describe piqueting caused dangerous confusion and uncertainty amongst units joining the Covering Troops from other commands in

India. Indeed, the relative merits of different systems of protection used on the march in mountain warfare formed the subject of a minor controversy amongst officers in Waziristan over the relative merits of the 'block' or 'battalion and company sector' systems of piqueting.[133] Writing on this subject in October 1925, however, Colonel Clement Milward warned: 'It is contended that it is a great mistake to make mountain warfare too specialised and too hidebound by rules in which only troops specially trained in this form of warfare can specially participate. The general tactics of the British Army as laid down in *FSR* should be applicable to all warfare.'[134] Until authoritative guidance was issued the only means of ensuring some degree of uniformity lay in the Standing Orders issued by units and formations serving in the NWFP.[135] Several books also appeared during the mid-1920s directed at British officers serving in India, discussing the conduct of frontier warfare under modern conditions that stressed the value of specialised training.[136] As Colonel Herman de Watteville observed in his detailed study of the operations in Waziristan – part of the Campaigns and their Lessons series – published in 1925: 'The soldier required for frontier must be trained for the end in view. This fact had already been proved in the Tirah Campaign of 1897–98.'[137]

A more realistic appreciation of the capabilities and limitations of modern equipment in mountain warfare had been formed as a result of the fighting in Waziristan. Trials and recent experience had demonstrated that the majority of new weapons and equipment developed in the First World War were largely ineffective, due to the terrain and associated transport and supply problems.[138] Lewis guns, Vickers machine guns and the 3.7″ howitzer were the only significant additions to the Indian arsenal capable of being effectively employed in tribal territory. They did not require any fundamental changes in tactics; but their cumulative effect was to increase the amount of heavy equipment carried in the field and the number of pack animals required to support imperial units, and to slow movement through the hills. Indeed, in many respects the advantages accrued from modern weapons did not counterbalance vastly improved tribal firepower and tactics and greater relative mobility. Moreover, modern military equipment had other important implications for policy towards the inhabitants of tribal territory. In the 1922–23 JUSII prize essay competition the winning author warned that the employment of modern military technology on the North-West Frontier must be tempered by the fact that the Pathans were British subjects and that the ultimate objective of British policy was to conciliate them and ensure lasting peace on the border.[139] After discussing at length the employment of the latest 'scientific and mechanical methods of warfare' on the North-West Frontier and recommending road building in tribal territory, Colonel Frederick Keen perceptively concluded:

> We must not allow ourselves to be led into the error of pinning our faith to revolutionary developments and superseding well tried arms and weapons by others which have not yet proved conclusively that they can perform all that is claimed for them. When such questions arise as the replacing of ground troops by aeroplanes we must 'hasten slowly'. For centuries past cavalry, infantry and artillery have been found essential for the winning battles. We know that our infantry as at present organised and equipped, if well trained, well led and adequately supported by artillery, can go anywhere and accomplish anything in reason on the Frontier. The day may dawn when we shall be able to dispense with these arms, but emphatically the time is not yet. Meanwhile there is ample scope to apply the developments of science, aerial warfare, wireless telegraphy and telephony, mechanical vehicles armed and unarmed, in co-operation with and as most useful auxiliaries to the more prosaic forces which will inevitably bear the brunt of the fight for generations to come ... Finally, when adopting new weapons and new methods we must be careful that in achieving the purely military object, they do not endanger the more important political object which we must always keep in view. Coercion must be used as a stepping stone to control.[140]

The drastic retrenchment of the military budget and lack of skilled Indian personnel, moreover, decided the issue and prevented the acquisition of large quantities of new arms and equipment. Most heavy weapons available were restricted to the immediate vicinity of the lines of communication due to transport and supply difficulties, although the construction of roads in tribal territory in Waziristan allowed MT to ease the supply problem that had dogged prior operations and clearly altered the tactical problem for troops operating off them. Even the limited quantities of new arms and equipment now used lowered the mobility of imperial troops when operating in the hills and increased the quantity of pack transport on which they depended, thereby lengthening columns and exacerbating problems of protection as well as reducing their rate of movement. The infantryman and pack mule still reigned supreme in frontier warfare. Writing in 1925, Captain Mervyn Gompertz concluded:

> One cardinal fact remains. The use of the Lewis gun enables a reduction in the strength of piquets and to increase fire effect: the motor vehicle and the tractor may speed up operations: wireless telegraphy may add

the personal touch: the glider may become the infantry of the air to assist the infantry of the ground: yet the age-long principle remains that it is the soldier who will win or lose the frontier.[141]

The fact that large numbers of imperial troops were deployed in close contact with the increasingly well-armed trans-border Pathan tribes as part of the Covering Troops had clearly confirmed the continued need for specialised instruction in mountain warfare for the Army in India. Although the revised 1924 edition of *FSR* still incorporated a chapter on warfare in 'undeveloped' and 'semi-civilized countries', it was clearly accepted by many officers and the military authorities that the general principles of war and a small section on mountain warfare that it contained was an insufficient basis for training. To provide a detailed and authoritative source of guidance for imperial troops about frontier fighting under modern conditions during 1924 the lessons of Waziristan were finally incorporated in a new manual compiled at AHQ, intended to complement *FSR* and the training manuals for the various arms of service.[142]

The contents of the *Manual of Operations on the North-West Frontier of India*, published in 1925, reflected the important changes that had occurred in frontier warfare since the First World War. No fewer than 35,000 copies were printed, and by October 1925 they had been issued to units serving throughout India. Its pages reflected the Indian Army's extensive experience of military operations against the trans-border Pathan tribes, and brought up to date the existing doctrine and system of training caused by improved tribal tactics, leadership and equipment and changes in the organisation, training and equipment of imperial troops. It represented a significant improvement over solely relying on *FSR* as the basis of all training, although it still discussed the conduct of mountain warfare with close reference to the principles of war. This manual included chapters describing the trans-border Pathans and tribal territory, fighting troops and their characteristics, protection on the march and when halted, the organisation and protection of the lines of communication, the conduct of the attack and withdrawal for all three arms, foraging and demolitions as well as administrative routine in camp and on the line of march. It emphasised the importance of appropriate training for all three arms of service, especially with regard to the development of individual skills of self-reliance, vigilance and initiative to overcome the peculiar difficulties encountered when fighting in tribal territory. Infantry units were urged to achieve a high standard of skill at arms and fieldcraft, as well as physical fitness and endurance to enable their men to move quickly across hillsides in pursuit of tribesmen. A section of the manual also discussed the use of the RAF in co-operation with troops, and it even went on to cover the employment of tanks in hill warfare even though they were as yet unavailable in India. Particular importance was attached to close co-operation between the infantry and mountain artillery to counter increasingly well-armed tribal *lashkars*. Imperial troops on duty in tribal territory were warned to stay alert despite prolonged periods without contact with hostile tribesmen. Officers were encouraged to read histories of past campaigns, and it was suggested that, wherever possible, training should take place in country approximating the frontier hills. It pointed out, however, that valuable instruction could be carried out using sand models, maps and cinema films.[143]

5 The Modernization of Mountain Warfare, November 1925–August 1939

The Army in India quickly settled down into the normal routine of peace-time service, with imperial troops stationed in the Khyber Pass, the Kurram Valley, Waziristan and the administered areas of the NWFP held in imme-diate readiness to support the Civil Armed Forces and local political admin-istration if required. Throughout the remainder of the inter-war period Indian regiments served a two-year tour of duty out of every six in the Covering Troops' Districts, allowing them to steadily accumulate a cadre of trained and experienced officers and men. In comparison, British infantry units only served an infrequent one-year tour of duty in the area.[1] Both British and Indian units normally had a year's notice before they joined formations stationed in the NWFP, allowing them to carry out pre-liminary mountain warfare training on the parade ground or nearby suitable terrain in preparation for their move to the frontier. An advance party of officers and NCOs was normally attached to a unit currently serving in a border garrison for three months to familiarise it with local conditions and to ensure a smooth tactical and administrative handover.[2] When a unit arrived these men provided a cadre of experienced instructors, and special 'nursery' columns gave troops an opportunity to learn about mountain warfare 'shepherded' by units already in the garrison under the close super-vision of experienced officers.[3] While stationed in the border cantonments, imperial troops trained intensively in mountain warfare, based on the *Manual of Operations on the North-West Frontier of India*, supervised by the staff and senior officers of the formations to which they belonged. Standing Orders periodically issued by the staff of those formations perma-nently stationed along the border provided further sources of tactical guid-ance for both peacetime training and active service, amplifying points laid down in the official manual and taking into account local conditions and requirements at each station.[4] To aid British officers a new experiment was tried in 1925 when Northern Command issued a cinema film demonstrating piqueting and staff duties required during operations in tribal territory.[5]

138

Tours of duty in the Covering Troops' districts were always regarded as providing imperial troops with particularly valuable and highly realistic training under 'semi-active service' conditions. Indeed the tribesmen were popularly regarded as the best tactical 'umpires' in the world, ready to exploit the slightest mistake committed by unwary troops.[6] As one officer observed:

> There was no pretence at all about our daily military training. Any fool could see the practical necessity of it, and examples were always occurring to show the penalty of neglect. There was not an atom of useless trimmings about our training on the frontier. Everything we did and learned fitted into the essential job of living among a wily and warlike enemy ... One bit of slackness, one violation of the 'golden rules' of frontier warfare, or one moment's relaxation of vigilance, and retribution would fall quickly upon the offending body of soldiers. For the 'enemy' never relaxed their vigilance. They were always round our camps and columns, well-armed and tough, just waiting for the moment · when the soldier would slip up.[7]

The Waziristan Military District, in particular, provided ideal opportunities for training during periodic 'flag marches' or 'columns' carried out from Razmak, Manzai and Bannu, during which imperial troops took full military precautions, as well as near continuous camp and road protection duties that now dominated all operations on the frontier as further roads were built in accordance with government policy. Former battle-grounds, like the Ahnai Tangi, Palosina or Makin, were close at hand for officers with an interest in studying frontier warfare, while local tribesmen willingly discussed recent operations from 'the other side of the hill'.[8] Troops deployed in the area, however, operated under detailed restrictions imposed by the political authorities governing the use of force and relations with the local inhabitants. Units serving in the settled areas also received instruction in mountain warfare in areas where suitable terrain existed. For example, in Kohat District training areas existed at Chichanna, Dhoda and Siab, Alizai, Khwaja Kizar and Chillibagh ideal for battalion training; while manoeuvres at brigade level were carried out by the local garrison and near Balyamn and Shinwari.[9]

British and Indian units serving in the Field Army concentrated on conventional 'open' warfare, primarily based on operations in Afghanistan or the Middle East against a 'second-class enemy', during individual and collective training into which each year was divided. A series of large manoeuvres were held during the mid-1920s to study conventional military operations using modern equipment, which demonstrated the conflicting and increasingly divergent requirements of 'open' and mountain warfare.[10] During the inter-war period the priority attached by the military authorities in India to training for fighting in mountainous terrain was a subject of considerable professional controversy between officers, whose attention focused on a likely conventional conflict, and those concerned with the day-to-day requirements of Indian defence. Most British service officers normally focused on conventional military operations and were often highly critical of the specialised doctrine employed for 'savage warfare' on the frontier, believing that the lesser was by default contained in the greater. To such soldiers frontier warfare often appeared increasingly stereotyped, anachronistic and diametrically opposed to European practice, as the first hesitant steps to mechanise and to absorb the lessons of the First World War were taken in England.[11] The emphasis placed by the Indian military authorities on training for 'savage warfare' and its apparent reluctance to adopt modern equipment was increasingly criticised as units in England began to adopt new equipment and training.[12] In comparison, the Indian Army lagged steadily behind, primarily as a result of budgetary constraints and the lack of equipment suitable for either frontier warfare or internal security.[13] Most Indian Army officers for whom frontier service formed such a large part of normal military experience, however, more readily appreciated the importance of mountain warfare training. As one officer noted in the JUSII in July 1930:

There are two forms of warfare to be taught in India, *viz*, open warfare and mountain warfare. Except for those stationed on the frontier the former of course requires the most attention, but mountain warfare should never be entirely neglected in view of the fact that wherever the Army in India fights in the future it is almost certain to be in mountainous country. In addition, about a third of our Army in India is presently stationed on the frontier and practically every unit takes a turn of duty there sooner or later. It has been argued and will continue to be argued to the end of all time, particularly by those whose knowledge of mountain warfare is limited, that such training is unnecessary and even detrimental, but the undoubted fact remains that troops unaccustomed to and untrained for warfare in mountainous country are at a very great disadvantage until they have learnt the 'tricks of the trade' and are physically fit to climb mountains, which they can never be so long as they confine themselves entirely to foot-slogging on the plains.[14]

THE SEARCH FOR MOBILITY

The criticism levelled at the Army in India about how it conducted mountain warfare redoubled during the summer of 1930 when civil disturbances in the NWFP sparked widespread unrest in tribal territory. To deal with a combination of widespread internal disorder, tribal incursions into Peshawar District and unrest in Waziristan elements of the Field Army hurriedly reinforced the Covering Troops Districts.[15] It appeared to many outside observers that army units had grown ponderous, over-cautious and their tactics too stereotyped, especially after Afridi *lashkars* raided Peshawar District in strength on two occasions and then escaped largely unscathed back across the administrative border. In comparison, the high mobility and effectiveness of the lightly equipped South Waziristan Militia, Kurram Militia and Frontier Constabulary enabled them to deal successfully with elusive tribal raiders, prompting accusations that the military was incapable of performing its allotted role in the watch and ward of tribal territory. The very fact that it had been found necessary to reinforce the garrison in Peshawar District with irregulars appeared to indicate that its effectiveness had declined, prompting several suggestions in the press for the re-establishment of a localised force organised, trained and equipped exclusively for operations against the trans-border Pathans.[16]

Most of the lessons the Indian Army learnt from the 1930 operations were mixed and contradictory. The mobility conferred by the road network in Waziristan and within the NWFP, together with the provision of MT, had altered the strategic, tactical and administrative conduct of frontier warfare, enabling reinforcements to be rushed to threatened points along the border. For example, two and a half infantry battalions and a company of sappers were transported 42 miles by lorry between 7th and 9th July 1930 from Bannu to reinforce Razmak. Armoured cars were used extensively in Peshawar District between 7th and 14th August to patrol the area, and in Waziristan to support isolated posts. The speed of MT convoys where roads existed also eased piqueting and lightened the task of the road protection troops. Lorries transported piqueting troops and their supporting machine guns in areas where light opposition was encountered, making it possible to employ each echelon on more than one task a day, without impeding a column's movement and ensuring that men remained fresh. Perhaps more significantly, MT greatly simplified the logistical and administrative problems encountered by troops operating in tribal territory. A convoy of 84 lorries carried $5\frac{1}{2}$ days' supplies, for example, for the Razmak Column on 23rd July 1930, a distance of $15\frac{1}{2}$ miles from Razmak to Ladha, along roads and the bed of the Baddar Toi river, before returning to camp later the same day. Indian columns utilising motor vehicles were tied, however, to advancing along predictable routes, enabling hostile tribesmen to anticipate their lines of approach, to concentrate and prepare defences. Furthermore, the cross-country mobility of most available motor vehicles was so limited that they were restricted to those areas where animal-drawn carts had previously been employed.[17]

The off-road mobility and tactical effectiveness of imperial columns operating in Waziristan had clearly undergone a marked decline due to the large numbers of troops now deemed necessary and changes in the organisation, equipment and training of units. As a result the pace of an advance and the distance a column could march in a single day were lower than 50 years earlier, as the number of mules on which they depended had dramatically increased due to the higher scales of arms, equipment, supplies and maintenance services now required in the field. This growing 'tail' of pack animals compounded the administrative and tactical problem faced by British commanders and acted as a brake on mobility, reducing the circuit of action of columns and slowing down every stage of operations, lengthening the line of march and exacerbating the already difficult problem of ensuring all-round protection.[18] To complicate matters a company of Vickers machine guns formed in each British and Indian infantry battalion in 1929 (in accordance with a new imperial establishment) meant additional mules were now needed to carry these comparatively immobile heavy weapons and their ammunition. This considerably reduced the rifle strength of Indian infantry battalions (now consisting of a machine gun and three infantry companies), despite restrictions being initially placed on the number of machine guns to maintain both numbers and mobility in the hills.[19] An infantry battalion was unable to provide the same number of piquets as before, lowering the distance it could protect from three to two miles, which effectively limited the distance a column could march in a single day.[20] Not only did this new organisation reduce manpower, but no guidance was issued about how to handle a reorganised battalion on the frontier, so that Commanding Officers had to devise new methods while fighting was in progress. The extra firepower conferred by the additional machine guns dramatically increased the expenditure of ammunition, making *lashkars* wary of engaging Indian columns or following up rearguards, thereby limiting opportunities to inflict heavy casualties.[21] Further problems and delays were caused by the strict observance of full military precautions and an obsession with the principle of security, slowing movement to a crawl and tying Indian columns to cautious and unimaginative advances along the valley floors. It now took longer to piquet a route, as periodic halts were necessary while covering machine-gun and artillery fire was carefully arranged to support the placement and withdrawal of piquets. Fear of casualties, the recovery of dead and wounded and efforts to prevent the theft of arms and ammunition also stultified efforts to bring hostile *lashkars* to battle or to achieve surprise. An inability to differentiate between the tactical requirements of conventional open warfare and those on the frontier further compounded the problem. On many occasions British commanders mounted ponderous, deliberate set-piece attacks backed with a full panoply of supporting arms, despite the fact that the *lashkars* seldom awaited the results.[22]

The events of the summer of 1930 led to a detailed investigation during the spring of 1931 of the Army in India's role on the North-West Frontier by a special committee appointed by the Government of India to examine the civil-military system developed to manage the inhabitants of independent territory. A series of witnesses interviewed by the Tribal Control and Defence Committee were highly critical of the army and called for the resuscitation of the PFF and the 'de-regularisation' of the units stationed in the NWFP. Its final report echoed earlier press criticisms and suggested that the military authorities should consider the merits of forming a new PFF and various measures to lighten the arms and equipment of regular units.[23] This view was quickly dismissed by General Staff in India, however, which strongly opposed the idea due to the inherent organisational difficulties that were involved. Indeed, such a drastic change ignored the other important roles of the Covering Troops which could not be carried out by lightly equipped troops and the reasons that had originally prompted the delocalisation of the PFF in 1903. Instead, the military authorities countered by arguing that a military organisation designed to fight the regular Afghan army, supported by foreign troops and the frontier tribes, was by default automatically suited to fighting the tribesmen alone. Moreover, as long as the North-West Frontier and Afghanistan remained the most likely theatre of operations of the Indian Army, it strongly believed that all imperial troops required experience of the terrain and similar tactics to those required in Afghanistan.[24] This view was also supported in the service press. Writing in response to criticisms of the army's current organisation, training and equipment in the JUSII one anonymous officer observed:

> Surely no-one wants an army trained on North-West Frontier mountain warfare lines only. This would be truly retrograde. Then indeed would it become a second-rate army. All the cost of higher military education, Staff College and modern equipment could be economised if we are to

limit our horizon to the hills of the Frontier. Even though it may be
years before it fights again outside Asia, there are plenty of potential
enemies in Asia, whom it will require all the inventions of the highest
form of military science, training, organization and equipment, to overcome. Any tendency for specialization for mountain warfare operations
on the North-West Frontier must be resisted ... The thinking soldier, if
he is to be any value to his profession, must avoid parochialism. The
'khaki' of the Frontier is undoubtedly fascinating, but it is not the only
topic of thought for the British officer.[25]

Rather than making any fundamental changes in current organisation, the
General Staff instead carefully assessed the 'sticky' performance of imperial units, with particular thought directed towards increasing the circuit of
action of mechanised Indian columns and the cross-country mobility of
Indian soldiers in the hills.

The strategic mobility and circuit of action of columns in the Covering
Troops Districts was increased with comparative ease by further road-
building in the NWFP and the gradual mechanisation of imperial units. A
network of roads constructed on the Khajuri Plain during 1930–31, to deny
access to an area from where tribesmen had attacked Peshawar District,
was the most immediate extension of the road-building policy, while
further roads were completed in Waziristan in accordance with the
Modified Forward Policy.[26] To pacify new areas of tribal territory, work
began on a further series of roads in 1934 when a crore of rupees was allocated, although it proved an expensive, time-consuming process and frequently provoked opposition from the local inhabitants.[27] Henceforth all
punitive operations in tribal territory were combined with road construction
to allow small, lightly-equipped columns to be supplied and operate in the
hills as well as extending political control.[28] Hand-in-hand with road building went the slow introduction into service in India of motor transport, trac-
tors and fully tracked vehicles – Carden Lloyd Mark VI Armoured
Machine Gun Carriers and Mark 1A Light Tanks – whose performance and
cross-country mobility greatly exceeded vehicles already in use.[29]

It proved a far more difficult problem to improve the off-road mobility
of imperial troops in mountainous terrain. This was addressed by reducing
or lightening personal clothing, arms and equipment, decreasing the scale
of supporting weapons, cutting down the number of pack animals required
to support imperial troops and changes in training. Many Indian battalions
replaced their heavy ammunition boots with *chaplis* and substituted
lightweight clothing in place of the normal issue. Amounts of ammunition
and equipment carried by each soldier were also reduced to cut down

weight while on frontier service. A considerably lighter and more reliable replacement for the cumbersome Lewis gun, with its attendant mule, and the Vickers machine gun (the Vickers-Berthier) was gradually introduced during the 1930s, increasing the mobility of imperial troops without loss of firepower.[30] Despite continued criticism of the new machine-gun company, however, the Vickers was retained in service and the number in each Indian battalion was increased during 1931 by two further weapons to maintain a uniform organisation with the rest of the British Army.[31] As it represented the main brake on the mobility of columns operating in tribal territory the reduction or complete replacement of the large quantity of pack transport used by the Covering Troops was carefully considered. This administrative tail of Indian columns was successfully docked by cutting down superfluous animals and the number of troops required for their care and protection. However, despite being regarded as anachronistic by many officers, pack mules and camels clearly still remained essential in all operations mounted beyond a road head.[32] Air supply was also carefully considered as an alternative means of maintaining troops and to reinforce isolated posts now that a flight of two Bomber Transport aircraft was available in India.[33] A wireless set and stores were parachuted into beleaguered Sorarogha post in Waziristan in 1930, and two days' rations were also dropped by aircraft later the same year to a column during the biennial relief of the garrison at Chitral.[34] Despite the potential demonstrated on both occasions, the General Staff remained sceptical because of the limited number of aircraft available, the expense and their inability to evacuate casualties.[35] A lack of adequate funding decided the issue by preventing the purchase of an additional squadron of Bomber Transport in 1930 needed to make air supply a practical proposition.[36]

Much thought was also devoted by the General Staff to improving of the tactical effectiveness and mobility of imperial units by changes in current tactical doctrine and training. Many officers acknowledged that continued improvements in tribal armament and tactics meant imperial troops needed a high standard of training in mountain warfare. As Captain D. McK. Kennelly argued in the *Journal of the Royal Artillery*:

> Training for mountain warfare cannot remain stationary. With each year the danger on the North-West Frontier of India increases; the tribesmen are becoming better armed and better acquainted with our manner of dealing with them. Every endeavour should be made to counter this increase in efficiency on their part by new methods of training.[37]

Northern Command suggested several revisions in the *Manual of Operations on the North-West Frontier of India* in 1930 taking into account recent changes in organisation, equipment and training, but the publication of a new volume was shelved by AHQ until further experience had been assimilated and other commands had submitted their views.[38] Instead, the employment of motor transport for the rapid despatch of re-inforcements to the Covering Troops and to increase the mobility of columns was discussed in the *A.H.Q. India Training Memorandum* issued in July 1931. The operations on the Khajuri and Aka Khel plains during the winter of 1930–31 also provided a considerable amount of valuable practical experience about large-and small-scale night operations and the use of armoured cars to carry out tactical reconnaissance, cover the advance of columns and establishing piquets, protecting perimeter camps and, finally to escort motor transport convoys. Following these operations further amendments to the *Manual of Operations on the North-West Frontier of India* were once again suggested by Northern Command, but until further experience of the new machine-gun organisation in infantry units, the mechanisation of the second-line transport, and the capabilities of light tanks in hill warfare had been gained the compilation of a revised manual was not sanctioned.[39]

No radical changes were made by the General Staff in the system of periodic relief of units stationed in the NWFP or training methods used by the Army in India, although the amount of time devoted to training in mountain warfare was increased. Particular attention was now paid to improving physical fitness, speed of cross-country movement and the individual skills required in tribal territory, with a resulting increase in the efficiency of most units. It was widely accepted that any British or Indian unit could quickly become proficient in mountain warfare. However, the system of reliefs meant that at any one time half the border garrisons consisted of units whose standard of training on arrival did not meet accepted standards, often resulting in too close adherence to the letter of the guidelines laid down in the training manuals, lack of confidence and an over-obsession with protection.[40] Most Indian Army battalions now contained a large cadre of officers, NCOs and other ranks with practical experience and training in frontier warfare. When the 2/14th Punjab Regiment was stationed at Mir Ali in Waziristan in November 1933, for example, all its officers, except newly joined subalterns, were 'old hands'. The frequent incidence of service in the NWFP kept most Indian battalions 'frontier-minded', allowing them to quickly achieve a high state of efficiency by intensive training when they returned to a border station. To supplement the official training manuals additional tactical guidance was issued to troops on the frontier, intended to acquaint them with local conditions. Northern Command issued notes that recommended units arriving in

Waziristan, for example, to read the official history and an unofficial text-book on the 1919–20 operations, and provided them with copies of various Standing Orders and tactical notes periodically issued by the staff of Waziristan District.[41]

British battalions serving on the frontier were generally unprepared for operations in tribal territory, with prior training and experience predicated on conventional 'open warfare' or internal security duties. The only guidance immediately available to them during the early 1930s about operations in tribal territory was a small section on 'Warfare in Undeveloped and Semi-Civilised Countries' in *FSR*, which recommended they look at the *Manual of Operations on the North-West Frontier* for further information.[42] An intermittent one-year tour of duty with the Covering Troops prevented them accumulating an experienced cadre of 'frontier hands', placing even greater reliance on 'on-the-job' training. While some became highly proficient during their tour of service, in general British units were seldom as effective as Indian in terms of cross-country mobility or familiarity with local tactical requirements. It also often proved more difficult to ensure that British troops maintained as high a standard of alertness as Indian troops over extended periods of time.[43] Much depended on whether officers were willing to adapt to local conditions. As Colonel Hugh Pettigrew later noted:

> How good or bad these regiments were on the frontier depended on just one thing, and that was how ready they were to learn. All the Indian and Gurkha regiments spent two years in every six on the frontier and had a large proportion of old men experienced in frontier warfare and the ways of the Pathan. Brigadier and Staff of Razmak, Bannu and Wana brigades had all spent many years in Waziristan or elsewhere on the frontier. They all said the same, and we all came to know it. If a British regiment arrived at Razmak, or better still at Bannu prior to its march up to Razmak, and said: 'We are new to this. You are not. Please teach us!' then it would soon be a regiment well able to look after itself and take a share of responsibility in mobile columns, piqueting and so on. But let a regiment think that it knew, and that it was too famous to have to learn, to think that the Highlands of Scotland bore any real resemblance to the mountains of Waziristan, and that regiment might have trouble. And during its year in Waziristan it would be of little use to anyone, and often a liability.[44]

A combination of cap-badge rivalry, a rapid changeover of personnel while serving in India, the comparative amateurism of British officers, and racism militated against the assimilation of the necessary skills required on the frontier from experienced Indian units. Professional arrogance also acted as a bar to learning. As Major-General Charles Gwynn observed in 1934, to many British officers trained to think solely in terms of the events of the Great War, internal security and frontier policing appeared of comparatively insignificant importance.[45]

Training of British officers, NCOs and men was facilitated by the publication of a new unofficial textbook in 1932 written by General Sir Andrew Skeen specifically directed at junior officers of the British service 'as he is less likely in his wider range of service to be trained for the local problem which all officer in India have to keep in mind.' *Passing it On: Short Talks on Tribal Fighting on the North-West Frontier of India* provided a detailed source of clear and comprehensive information in an easily readable form regarding the trans-border Pathan tribes, tactics and administration in hill warfare, based on the author's extensive experience.[46] It assumed an authoritative position, running to three editions, and was widely read in Britain and India. Two copies were specially issued to British Army officers' and sergeants' messes and one copy to other British and Indian combatant units in India at the orders of the Commander-in-Chief, Sir Philip Chetwode, to allow British soldiers to benefit from the tactical and administrative guidance provided by one of the Indian Army's most experienced frontier soldiers.[47]

The tactical handling of frontier operations remained a subject of controversy in the service press, despite those changes undertaken during the early 1930s and a further training directive issued in March 1933 by AHQ which emphasised the importance of light infantry training, lightening personal equipment, reducing the logistical tail of Indian columns and improving cross-country mobility not only for mountain warfare but also in conventional military operations.[48] The growing complexity of modern weapons, mechanisation and the increasing dependence of Indian columns on maintenance services in the field was explicitly linked to the declining effectiveness and relative mobility of the Indian Army in the question set for the 1933 JUSII prize-essay competition. 'Borderer' argued in the winning essay that military organisation, equipment, armament and training devised for 'civilised' European mass warfare were inappropriate for operations against lightly armed tribesmen. Indeed, a growing preoccupation with conventional warfare meant that the Indian Army was ignoring the immediate and pressing requirements of tribal control, in which it was becoming increasingly ineffective. In a telling critique, he identified the fundamental conflict between the requirements of tribal control and European warfare that had been made explicit with the initial hesitant attempts of the Army in India to modernise during the early 1930s.

'Borderer' noted that the military authorities needed to compromise between large scales of modern weaponry and mobility in the hills:

> Surely the answer is that for operations on the North-West Frontier, for the most likely *rôle* of a large majority of the Indian Army year in year out, they are unnecessary and worse than unnecessary, dangerous. Damaging because they destroy mobility, damaging because they sap *morale* and initiative, damaging because they lead to an inevitable downpeering contempt among friend and foe alike, politely veiled sometimes on the part of the Scout, jeeringly open on the countenance of the more ribald tribesman; damaging because the necessity for their study prevents officers from studying their more likely *rôle* and training fully their men in that *rôle* which two matters are in themselves a fully whole time task ... Let us teach the man in the ranks and the Platoon Commander to rely first on his own rifle with the addition of the grenade if necessary, backing it up with the light automatic which he must render more mobile than it is at present. In graver trouble let them call upon the bigger brother with the Vickers Gun and when things are really sticky let them ask for the final arbiter of frontier battle, the 3.7 How.[49]

'Borderer' believed that the growing divergence between the military requirements of 'savage' and 'civilised' warfare in terms of training, organisation and equipment could no longer be reconciled, and presented such an insuperable problem that he included a detailed scheme for the formation of a localised frontier force for service on the North-West Frontier.[50] Despite presenting such detailed and well-argued proposals, the localisation of a portion of the Indian Army on the North-West Frontier remained an anathema to the General Staff in India. Other articles critical of existing tactical doctrine appeared in the service press during 1934, questioning current British methods such as the continued use of perimeter camps, whose construction was so time-consuming that it entailed a serious loss of mobility, now that each battalion now possessed a large number of automatic weapons that greatly simplified protection at night.[51] Apart from those minor modifications introduced since the First World War, the doctrine of frontier warfare remained largely unchanged. Writing in 1934, Major-General Henry Rowan-Robinson, however, summed up an opinion shared by a growing number of officers in India:

> The normal methods employed in such operations are elaborately described in the training manuals and elsewhere. A considerable litera-ture has in fact grown up around them. They are, however, recognized

to be thoroughly unsatisfactory; and, with the multiplication of weapons, vast requirements in ammunition and insistence on luxuries, they are daily becoming more so.[52]

THE MOHMAND CAMPAIGN, AUGUST–SEPTEMBER 1935

The Mohmand operations, which eventually involved four brigades of imperial troops, provided a practical test of the various changes introduced during the 1930s.[53] A combination of lightened and reduced scales of personal equipment carried by Indian sepoys and special light infantry training succeeded in speeding up piqueting and improved cross-country mobility, but the machine-gun company in each battalion still acted as a serious brake on mobility. Nearly the entire strength of a support company was required to manhandle two Vickers machine guns and their ammunition to positions in the hills. The rifle strength of British and Indian infantry battalions was quickly absorbed in protective duties, especially guarding the growing quantity of supporting services used in the operation. To preclude tribal resistance, quicken the pace of the advance and extend the distance columns could march in a single day the hours of darkness were routinely exploited to seize important tactical features. Perhaps the most striking feature of the campaign was the willingness of Indian commanders and units to undertake large operations at night, enabling them to seize the initiative, disconcert tribal plans, and avoid the delay inherent in mounting deliberate attacks against strongly defended positions. As a result, columns were able to penetrate deeper into tribal territory before they had to return to the security of a perimeter camp each night. During the operations around Ghalani, for example, Indian troops operated in the distant Toriatigga Valley and could still return to the main perimeter camp. Similarly terrain features around the Nahakki gorge were occupied before dawn on 18th September enabling troops to seize the pass and then construct a new perimeter camp on the Kamalai Plain before nightfall.[54] Not all operations, however, were so one-sided. Despite these improvements in imperial tactics the Mohmands also demonstrated their own fighting skills on 29th September when two isolated platoons of 5/12th Frontier Force Regiment (Queen Victoria's Own Corps of Guides) were overwhelmed by a tribal attack that killed 33 and wounded a further 50 British and Indian officers and men.

New equipment made its debut during the Mohmand campaign, opening new possibilities for frontier warfare in the future. A single tractor-drawn battery of medium artillery supplemented the mountain batteries, whose longer-ranged and more powerful 18lb guns were able to support several Indian columns advancing on a broad front from a central position. Perhaps of greater significance was the use of a single company of Mk II light tanks which formed a component part of a force operating in tribal territory for the first time. Throughout the fighting they worked in close co-operation with the 18th King Edward's Own Cavalry as mobile troops. They proved highly effective, refuting earlier claims that tanks would be ineffectual in mountain warfare. Tribal opposition was materially reduced when light tanks acted as mobile machine-gun posts in support of infantry. Their invulnerability to rifle fire and cross-country mobility quickened the pace of operations, as tanks could easily advance through tribal positions and force the defenders to withdraw. During the advance to Dand on 23rd August they acted as advance guard troops, supporting the posting of piquets by advancing through tribal positions and delivering fire from the rear on occupied hills and ridges. Light tanks also successfully covered the withdrawal of Indian columns operating in the Toriatigga Valley on 14th September and on the Nahakki Plain, pinning down pursuing tribesmen until the infantry had rejoined the main body. Infantry officers also employed light tanks for reconnaissance purposes, carrying out personal examinations of routes used for larger operations. The terrain in the open valleys of Mohmand country did not present any serious obstacle, although cavalry was used to reconnoitre the ground and engineers had to construct tank-crossings over *nullahs* and improve the track across the Nahakki Pass. An attempt by the tribesmen to impede the movement of tanks by digging pits and strewing the roads with rocks and boulders had little effect.[55]

The combatant troops of 'Mohforce' were dependent on large quantities of support and ancillary units throughout the fighting which had both tactical and administrative implications for frontier warfare. A large number of non-combatant signals, field ambulances, engineer parks, ordnance depots and MT accompanied 'Mohforce', and each day motor vehicles carried ammunition, supplies and water to a roadhead from where pack transport carried it to the forward troops. A heavy consumption of small arms and artillery ammunition made it vital to maintain and protect a permanent line of communication along the Gandab Road to service growing logistical requirements, facilitate the movement of reinforcements and evacuate casualties. To maintain supplies engineers and contract tribal labour constructed a water pipeline and a track fit for motor transport along *nullah* beds from the main road, as Indian troops advanced deeper into tribal territory and later over the Nahakki Pass.[56] To encompass the large number of vulnerable vehicles and non-combatant troops perimeter camps grew in size and complexity. It often proved difficult to find a flat space large enough for all troops and equipment, and their construction was both time-consuming and required considerable labour. The number of troops now required to defend them, moreover, was considerable, but as the proportion of infantry to other arms had fallen it was often difficult to provide sufficient manpower.[57] However, such large encampments proved vulnerable to the carefully organised sniping employed with considerable success by the Mohmands to harass Indian troops during the campaign. Ambushes were successfully employed on several occasions to counter large parties of tribesmen operating in the surrounding hills at night. During the night of 18th September, for example, the 1/14th Punjab Regiment staged a series of ambushes around Wucha Jawar camp, which killed or wounded seven tribesmen and stopped further sniping.[58]

As a direct corollary of increasing dependence on support units the protection of the lines of communication assumed growing importance, leading to several important modifications in existing tactical methods and the deployment of large numbers of troops. Armoured cars regularly patrolled the Gandab road, but the burden of protection, as always, fell on the infantry. Permanent piquets were constructed in the Karappa Pass, but the intricate and relatively low-lying land between Kialgai and Karappa lacked terrain features that afforded a field of vision and fire. Nowshera Brigade and 3rd (Jhelum) Brigade adopted a system based on mobility and offensive defence which employed lightly equipped fighting patrols, with a strength of 1–2 platoons, who operated between strong posts constructed on either side of the road. A sweep of the complete sector was made each day before the road was opened to traffic, during which all positions from where rifle fire could be delivered on the column were carefully searched. This system proved highly successful, indicating that well-trained and lightly equipped troops could beat the tribesmen at their own game.[59]

The lessons learnt in Mohmand country clearly showed the General Staff in India and many other British officers that major changes had occurred in both the tactical and administrative conduct of frontier fighting. A detailed section discussing this campaign that appeared in the *A.H.Q. India Training Memorandum* for the 1935–36 collective training season began:

> The recent Mohmand operations showed marked advance in the conduct of operations of this nature and the methods employed. Apart from the advantages of a L. of C. with a road for M.T., which was effectively maintained, and of efficient administrative arrangements, the

rapid and complete success obtained in this campaign may be attributed to enterprising leadership, development of existing methods, and the introduction of innovations.

Units throughout India were ordered by the Commander-in-Chief to follow guidelines in this publication during training for frontier warfare which incorporated various important lessons learnt regarding the employment of night operations, light tanks, armoured cars and the protection of the lines of communication. Sufficient practical experience of the impact of changes in tactics, training, organisation and equipment on the conduct of hill warfare had now been gained to prompt the military authorities to begin preparation of a long awaited replacement for the *Manual of Operations on the North-West Frontier of India.*[60] Until this was available the increasingly outdated official manual was complemented by a further new unofficial text-book published during 1936 discussing training for mountain warfare. This addition to the already large body of unofficial literature on frontier fighting provided British officers with a series of sand table exercises, intended to teach elementary routine and tactics in mountain warfare, specifically aimed at units about to serve on the North-West Frontier for the first time.[61]

The improving state of relations between the RAF and the General Staff, following the appointment of Air Marshal Edgar Ludlow-Hewitt as AOC in India, meant the RAF also took a greater interest in tactical co-operation with the army in mountain warfare during 1936.[62] Under his command in April 1935 the Air Staff in India had issued instructions that all RAF training in the subcontinent should henceforth be directed solely towards efficiency in tribal warfare, although primarily employing air control methods that had been the cause of considerable inter-service rivalry since 1923.[63] This decision had strengthened Wing Commander John Slessor's – CO of No. 3 (Indian Wing) – growing conviction that it was time for a radical change in the system of army co-operation used in India, as the existing 'Aldershot model' in use (devised for conventional European warfare) was largely ineffective in mountainous terrain.[64] A series of exercises were carried out under his command in April 1935 by No. 3 (Indian) Wing at Quetta with the Fort Sandeman mobile column, to determine principles to guide future training and a suitable method of communication between ground and air, as most of the close-support methods developed in Waziristan in 1920–24 had been forgotten. However, the Quetta earthquake prevented further trials until the squadrons reformed at Chaklala in the northern Punjab.[65] In March 1936 the RAF and Northern Command began experimenting with close support methods in mountain warfare when No. 3 Indian Wing was given responsibility for overseeing the training of the two AC squadrons earmarked to support the Covering Troops.[66] Writing on 10th April 1936, Slessor urged that close support and air co-operation in mountain warfare should form part of the forthcoming training season with the army:

> The great cry now-a-days seems to be co-operation – the balanced use of all arms and Services in Frontier ... I should have thought there could be no better way of ensuring that good co-operation than by having a combined manual on which we all work, containing the description of all methods of Frontier warfare.[67]

During the summer TEWTs were held for officers under his command near Rawalpindi to demonstrate the effectiveness of close air support and study the inherent problems from the viewpoint of ground troops, while the Vickers-Bomb-Lewis (VBL) method of ground attack was developed by No. 20 (AC) Squadron at Peshawar. Several pilots were also attached to army units in Waziristan to gain an insight into their problems. Both the AOC in India and AHQ agreed that close air support in mountain warfare should form an element of collective training during the cold weather. 2nd (Rawalpindi) Brigade and aircraft from No. 3 (Indian) Wing took part in a large combined exercise at Khanpur staged by Northern Command between 17th and 25th November 1936, to both develop and test close air support tactics in mountain warfare, based on a provisional close-support manual written by Slessor and a draft of the new frontier warfare manual.[68] These manoeuvres, simulating tribal opposition to an Indian column engaged in road construction, provided valuable guidance regarding the practicalities of close support and indicated the importance of RAF liaison officers at column headquarters to observe and direct operations, as well as an effective means of intercommunication between the aircraft and forward troops and between columns and airfields. A further important lesson learnt during this exercise was that it was essential for the forward troops to indicate targets to pilots who otherwise were normally unable to locate tribesmen exploiting the scrub-covered mountainous terrain for cover. The final report on the exercise concluded: 'We consider that the experience of this training gives added reason to believe that, with further combined training of troops on the ground and aircraft in the air, close support in mountain warfare may be very effective in helping to overcome opposition, in reducing casualties to our own troops and in helping to speed up their movement. And the crux of the whole matter is effective communications.'[69]

THE 1936–37 WAZIRISTAN CAMPAIGN

The Waziristan Military District provided the army and RAF with an immediate opportunity to test the effectiveness of their new tactics and system of training, when in November 1936 the Tochi Column ('Tocol') and the Razmak Column ('Razcol') conducted 'flag marches' in the Khaisora Valley. 'Razcol' encountered unexpected resistance from Tori Khel Wazir tribesmen, incited by the Faqir of Ipi, as it advanced on 25th November, despite assurances from the political authorities that all was peaceful. It lost 14 dead and 43 wounded by the time it reached Bischhe Kaskai and constructed a perimeter camp. When the smaller 'Tocol' crossed the Katira River, supported by the Tochi Scouts, it was also held up by heavy sniping from marksmen hidden on both sides of the valley. A mounted cavalry charge by a single squadron of Probyn's Horse and close air support enabled it to reach the Jaler Algad River by dusk, after which Brigadier Francis Maynard decided to continue onwards during darkness to rendezvous with 'Razcol'. Heavy rifle fire stampeded its pack mules, forcing the column to halt, benighted, three and a half miles from Razcol, and construct a perimeter camp. Four tons of ammunition and supplies were dropped by parachute to the embattled troops which successfully joined the other column the following day after further fighting.[70] A combination of a lack of artillery, insufficient rifle strength and the excessive length of the day's march that 'Tocol' had attempted during the short November day had played directly into tribal hands. As a result of the hitherto comparatively peaceful conditions in the area, its commander had attempted a longer march than was compatible with the principle of security, without adequately piqueting the route or allowing sufficient time to construct a perimeter camp, and had also deliberately reduced the number of machine guns carried to provide more transport for supplies.[71] Moreover, as Colonel Hugh Pettigrew later pointed out:

> The main cause of the semi-disaster was nearly all the troops in Tocol were new to the Frontier, doing their first year in Bannu or Mir Ali. In this alone lay the fault, and the lesson. That with a column of only two battalions of infantry, with some horsed cavalry and mountain guns and the usual services, one of the two battalions should always be a seasoned one until the newcomers had been on at least two columns.[72]

The 3/7th Dogras in 'Tocol', for example, had only arrived in Waziristan from Burma in March 1936 and had been hurriedly introduced to frontier warfare at Kurramgarhi during the previous 'cold weather'.[73]

2nd (Rawalpindi) Brigade, 11th Light Tank Company, armoured cars, artillery and two additional infantry battalions ('Khaicol'), along with aircraft from No. 3 (Indian) Wing, immediately reinforced Waziristan Military District to prevent unrest spreading, to punish the Tori Khel Wazirs and to construct a road from Mir Ali through the Khaisora Valley to control of the area. General Sir John Coleridge, GOC Northern Command, was given full authority for the control of land operations, aided by the local Civil Armed Forces, and independent air operations. Tribal unrest was successfully localised by the rapid concentration of imperial troops in the area and the construction of a new road during December and January from Mir Ali into the Khaisora Valley under close military protection. Khaicol encountered little opposition during its slow and deliberate advance, apart from intermittent long-range sniping and during the withdrawal of 2nd (Rawalpindi) Brigade to camp on 22nd December. When the road had been completed, fortified buildings belonging to identified hostile tribesmen were then destroyed. Throughout the operation a senior RAF officer attached to the HQ of 'Khaicol' facilitated close co-operation between the two services, although offensive operations by aircraft were restricted to a proscribed area five miles in advance and on the flanks of the Indian column whose primary task was to protect technical troops engaged in road construction. In January hostile Afghan tribesmen aiding the insurgents were expelled across the Durand Line by imperial troops after the Faqir's headquarters at Arsal Kot was destroyed. On 15th January 1937 the Tori Khel Wazirs finally submitted and the area reverted to civil control, after operations that had cost the Indian Army 34 dead and 132 wounded.[74]

During the spring the situation deteriorated in Northern Waziristan after a series of offences were committed by hostile tribesmen, and villages in the Derajat were attacked by raiding gangs. A combination of political pressure, limited punitive bombing and air operations to deny tribesmen the use of certain areas failed to restore order. Piquets and posts throughout Waziristan were sniped and bridges, culverts and telephone lines damaged by small bands of hostile tribesmen. The HQ of 1st (Rawalpindi) Division, 1st (Abbottabad) Brigade and 3rd (Jhelum) Brigade reinforced the garrison, but these troops were immediately tied down in ensuring their own protection and in safeguarding the Bannu–Razmak road after local Khassadars (tribal policemen) became unreliable. This period of relative calm before the storm, however, allowed relatively inexperienced and untrained British units to be instructed before embarking on active operations. Prior instruction in mountain warfare given to the 1st Battalion Northamptonshire Regiment, for example, had been limited to six weeks at Hoshiapur each year, and its officers knew little of earlier campaigns in Waziristan or of their Pathan adversary when they were deployed.[75] When the 1st Battalion South Wales Borderers arrived at Mir Ali as part of 1st (Abbottabad) Infantry Brigade, Brigadier Roland Inskip personally supervised intensive instruction in advance guard duties, piqueting, and constructing perimeter camps, especially with regard to the training of junior leaders, complementing that received earlier at Abbottabad.[76] While permanent piquets were constructed to secure the roads on which they depended, the imperial troops remained on the defensive during the spring. A separate tiring and time-consuming road-opening operation was required each day to establish control along the lines of communication from perimeter camps located in each sector. Not all were unopposed. On the night of 20th/21st March a camp piquet at Damdil was attacked by Tori Khel Wazir tribesmen armed with swords, rifles and hand grenades. Hand-to-hand fighting occurred when the position was rushed by swordsmen, during which two Gurkhas were killed and eight wounded before the attack was repulsed. The advance guard of the 1st (Abbottabad) Brigade, guarding the Dosalli–Damdil road, was attacked on 29th March 1937 by an estimated 700–1,000 tribesmen who, hidden amongst scrub and nullahs alongside the road, opened heavy rifle fire while swordsmen closed and engaged in hand-to-hand combat. Armoured cars, artillery and aircraft soon supported the hard-pressed 1/6th Gurkha Rifles, inflicting an estimated 94 dead and 64 wounded on the withdrawing *lashkar*.[77] During the summer the strength of the 'hostile' *lashkar* steadily increased to over 4,000 men, consisting of Tori Khel Wazirs, a large number of Afghan tribesmen and a handful of individuals drawn from otherwise peaceful sections.[78] Frequent raids were carried out into the settled districts; camps and piquets were sniped and bridges, culverts and telephone lines were damaged by tribal gangs. However, only a small proportion of tribal fighting strength was involved, with the *lashkar* composed of a fluctuating collection of individuals from various tribes and sections rather than complete tribal units.[79]

The length of the lines of communication throughout Waziristan and the paucity of troops meant it was impossible to prevent successful small-scale tribal attacks against troops tied down in purely defensive duties. An ambush of a convoy moving through the Shahur Tangi gorge in Southern Waziristan on 9th April 1937, by a mixed Mahsud and Bhittani gang, provided a striking demonstration of the vulnerability of motor vehicles. After the soft-skinned lorries at the head and tail of the column were destroyed the convoy was penned in the defile, where its escort of four armoured cars were unable to elevate their machine guns sufficiently to engage the tribesmen on the heights above and the infantry escort was pinned down by intense rifle fire.[80] All Government convoys immediately ceased operation in Waziristan after the incident except on roads protected by troops. Between April and early December the Bannu–Wana road remained closed, and the isolated garrison at Wana was maintained by the Mahsud-owned Bagai Company, operating its lorries under tribal protection, and a flight of Bomber Transport Aircraft which flew in ammunition, supplies and relief troops. A 46-mile stretch of road between Bannu and Damdil was protected by the 1st (Rawalpindi) Division, whose troops were deployed in permanent piquets supplemented by daily patrols of infantry and armoured cars supported by artillery and aircraft. Although effective, these defensive arrangements reduced the number of troops free for offensive operations.[81] Armoured-car patrols replaced infantry detachments escorting convoys in May after it became apparent that their rifles offered too tempting and valuable a target for the tribesmen. Even so, movement of convoys and troops was restricted to specific 'Road Open Days' that required a major tactical operation by troops occupying a perimeter camp located in each sector of the line of communications. The hostile tribesmen, intermingled with the peaceful population, placed a constant strain on troops operating in Waziristan, and ensured that full military precautions had to be observed at all times by soldiers on monotonous 'Road Protection' (RP) duty. John Masters, serving with the 2/4th Prince of Wales's Own Gurkha Rifles, observed:

> This was the hardest task the Frontier offered, and we did it three times a week ... R.P. was hard because every day we had to cover the same stretch of road, and every day it became more difficult to obey the Cardinal Frontier principle of never doing the same thing in the same way twice running. We had to fight against fatigue and carelessness, because someone was watching. Someone was always watching – someone with an inborn tactical sense, someone who missed nothing.[82]

Those British or Indian regiments unwilling to maintain a high standard of vigilance paid the price in casualties from hostile tribesmen carefully watching their positions. Even more galling were the political restrictions imposed on engaging armed local tribesmen until they definitely committed a 'hostile' act. These were an unwelcome surprise to regimental officers unacquainted with the basis of British policy in Waziristan. Not surprisingly, some did not obey such restrictions and meted out exemplary punishment to tribesmen suspected of firing upon Indian columns or of having killed or mutilated imperial dead and wounded.[83]

On 22nd April 1936 the Waziristan Military District was placed once again under the direct control of General John Coleridge, when it became clear that political pressure and limited punitive and proscriptive bombing had failed to restore order, with orders to re-establish peaceful conditions throughout the area. 2nd (Rawalpindi) Brigade, 9th (Jhansi) Brigade and two battalions from 7th (Dehra Dunn) Brigade reinforced the garrison from the Field Army. 1st (Rawalpindi) Division quickly commenced offensive operations, intended to bring hostile tribesmen assembled in the Khaisora and Shaktu areas to battle over ground chosen to facilitate the use of all arms. To carry out this task 2nd (Rawalpindi) Brigade was augmented by four batteries of mountain artillery, light tanks and a RAF Army Co-operation squadron, along with additional troops for the protection of its lines of communication. It advanced from Mir Ali on 23rd April into the Khaisora Valley, but was unable to bring the elusive hostile *lashkar* to battle. The camp piquets surrounding Bische Kashkai perimeter camp in the Khaisora Valley, however, were heavily sniped and showered with hand grenades on the night of 27th April by Tori Khel tribesmen. A determined *lashkar* simultaneously attacked the main encampment, reaching within 20 yards of the perimeter wall before being repulsed with heavy losses by concentrated machine gun and rifle fire. As one officer observed:

> Thus ended an experience which in all recent history of frontier warfare is probably unique. Picquets and isolated detachments had often been attacked at night, and will probably continue to be on future occasions as long as the tribesman is what he is; but never before has an attack on so large a scale been made on a strongly defended camp bristling with automatic weapons and manned by some 3,000 men. One cannot believe that is ever likely again.[84]

Two days later the *lashkar* was lured out from the cover of rocks and bush, where aircraft, 3.7″ howitzers and machine-gun fire inflicted heavy casualties. Despite this heavy punishment the operations proved indecisive, as the Faqir of Ipi and the main body withdrew to the Shaktu Valley where it increased in strength during the summer.[85]

The newly formed Waziristan Division ('Wazdiv'), consisting of elements of the local garrison, concentrated near Dosalli during May to strike against hostile Tori Khel Wazir *lashkars* operating in the Shaktu area and open communications with the garrison at Razmak. In an endeavour to avoid the strongly fortified Sre Mela Gorge, which blocked an advance towards the Sham Plain, Bannu Brigade broke with the established doctrine of frontier warfare. During the night of 11th–12th May 1937 Bannu Brigade, led by eight platoons of Tochi Scouts, slowly advanced over the

2,000-foot knife-edged Iblanke Ridge bypassing the gorge, and reached the Sham Plain virtually unopposed. 1st (Abbottabad) Brigade simultaneously launched a converging attack which secured a foothold in the Sre Mela gorge with few losses, and the retreating *lashkar* suffered heavy casualties from aircraft as they withdrew across the Sham Plain. Many dispirited tribesmen dispersed, including most of an Afghan contingent, who had suffered heavy losses as they were not so well acquainted with Indian tactics as the local inhabitants.[86] To supply the advance troops 13,000lbs of hard rations and fodder were parachuted from Bomber Transport aircraft on 13th May until a secure permanent line of communication to Coronation Camp had been opened.[87] Wapiti and Audax aircraft provided tactical reconnaissance and close support to the 1st Division and the Razmak Brigade during these operations, while mounting daily sorties co-operating with convoys and road protection troops now scattered throughout Waziristan (see Figure 9). The destruction of the village of Arsal Kot, by troops based at Ghariom Camp, finally broke Tori Khel resistance and the majority of tribesmen dispersed to their homes, although the Faqir of Ipi evaded capture and took refuge on the Mahsud–Bhittani border, where he continued to stir up resistance.[88]

The fighting in the Khaisora Valley and on the Sham Plain ended large-scale tribal resistance in Northern Waziristan, but Razmak, Bannu and Wana brigades carried out further operations to restore peaceful conditions west of the Razmak–Jandola road and drive the Faqir of Ipi towards the frontier with Afghanistan. It proved difficult for the slow-moving converging columns, however, to bring the small and elusive bands of tribesmen that continued to resist. While these operations were in progress, 1st (Rawalpindi) Division remained in the Sham Plain and Shaktu River area, covering the construction of a 90-mile-long system of roads in the country enclosed by the Circular Road, previously only accessible to pack animals, which was inhabited by the hostile sections (see Figure 10). Four roads were built between May and October by troops, engineers and four specially enlisted Mahsud construction battalions from Dosalli, the lower Khaisora, Ahmedwam and Razmak that connected near Ghariom, making nearly all central Waziristan accessible to columns equipped on a pack basis.[89] Throughout the summer Wazdiv and Scouts carried out various minor operations in Southern Waziristan to disperse small bands of hostile tribesmen. The Razmak and Bannu brigades 'mopped up' the remaining hostile tribesmen gathered in the Upper Baddar and the Khaisora valleys during September and October, destroying villages belonging to those tribesmen implicated in raids. After a series of raids in the Derajat, a column operated in Bhittani

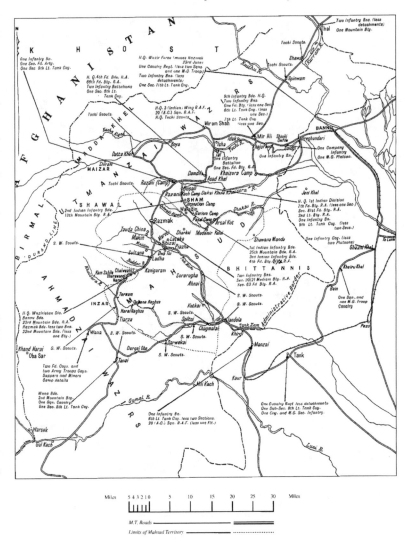

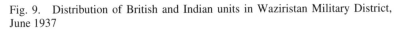

Fig. 9.   Distribution of British and Indian units in Waziristan Military District, June 1937

country in October and constructed a new road to the village at Kot. Imperial columns moved at will through tribal territory during the autumn, although small tribal gangs cut telegraph and telephone lines, destroyed bridges and culverts, and ambushed small parties of Indian

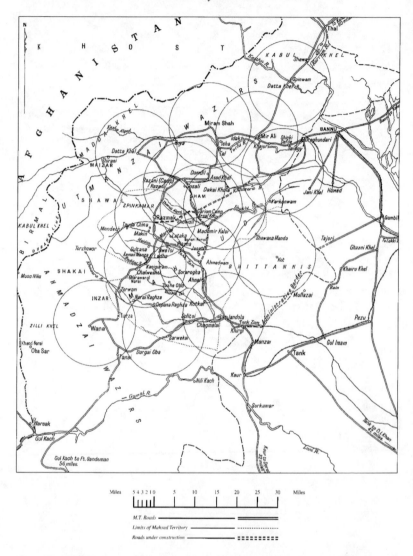

Fig. 10.   The road network in Waziristan Military District, October 1937

Note: Circles denote 10-mile (2-day) radius of action of Light Pack Transport columns operating from a roadhead

troops. When the new roads were completed at the end of October sufficient troops were freed for offensive operations in those parts of northern Waziristan harbouring the remaining hostile gangs. In

November, 1st (Abbottabad) Infantry Brigade swept the Khaisora and Lower Shaktu valleys. These operations represented the last of the campaign, after which the frequency of minor offences declined, raiding almost ceased and several hostile leaders submitted. Although the Faqir of Ipi remained at large, his influence was limited as he was forced to move his base repeatedly by columns and aircraft. During December the additional troops deployed in the area returned to their normal stations, with the exception of 3rd (Jhelum) Brigade, a mountain battery and light tank company which remained to support the garrison.[90]

THE LESSONS OF THE 1936–37 WAZIRISTAN CAMPAIGN

The 1936–37 Waziristan Campaign represented the largest-scale fighting carried out by the Army in India since the 1919–24 operations. Despite the fact that very few local tribesmen were actively engaged in the fighting, 61,000 regulars from the local garrison, the Field Army and irregulars had had to be deployed in the area. Despite the low intensity of the operations when compared to 1919–20, the Army in India had lost a total of 245 killed and 684 wounded, in addition to a further 73 deaths from disease.[91] The heavily armed Mahsuds and Wazirs had demonstrated once again their mastery of guerrilla warfare. The applicability of the existing doctrine studied by the Army in India and system of training had been demonstrated again during the fighting. Initial accusations in the press following the Khaisora operations, that the local garrison was untrained in frontier warfare, were simply unfounded as most Indian regiments contained officers and men with prior practical experience of the frontier, while instruction and practice in frontier warfare formed part of normal annual training of all units.[92] Nevertheless those units that neglected to obey the 'laws' or principles of frontier warfare, or were unwilling to maintain vigilance, suffered at the hands of the ever-present tribesmen. Many of the lessons learnt during the Mohmand operations were generally confirmed, indicating that the principles on which tactics and training for frontier warfare were based in India were generally sound and that there was no need for a major change in imperial tactics. It also provided further important practical experience regarding the use of light tanks, medium artillery and aircraft in frontier warfare, although infantry remained the predominant arm, especially during fighting in tribal territory, now divided into two main categories: operations by columns operating in rugged, mountainous areas and those associated with road protection along Wazirforce's extended lines of communication.

The infantryman and the pack mule still remained the key to all operations in difficult mountainous terrain impassable to wheeled transport and
where limited scope existed for tracked vehicles. The Khaisora operations
in November 1936 graphically demonstrated that the maximum distance a
fully equipped Indian column could march, taking full precautions and
allowing sufficient time to establish a perimeter camp before nightfall, was
limited to 8–10 miles in the face of active tribal opposition. Despite reduc-
tions in their number, the factor which dictated the speed of movement
and circuit of action of a column remained the protection of the large
quantity of pack transport required to carry supplies, fodder and ammunition. It was only possible to move greater distances, or at a faster rate, by
reducing piqueting below an acceptable margin of safety, or by neglecting
to provide sufficient supporting artillery and machine-gun fire. The high
price paid by Tocol in November 1936 for attempting a longer march
than was compatible with the principle of security was not forgotten by
other commanders. During November 1937 it had been impossible for the
1st (Abbottabad) Brigade to cover more than 5–6 miles each day during
operations carried out in the Lower Shaktu Valley, due to the short hours
of daylight available, the difficult terrain and the time required for piqueting and the construction of a perimeter camp. Even this distance was only
possible because the transport advanced on a broad front along a *nullah*
bed which meant that only two miles of the route had to be piqueted.[93] The
need to pay careful attention to security was driven home during the
fighting and was essential as hostile tribesmen continually harassed
advancing columns and attacked small detached parties of troops whenever an opportunity arose. It was still vitally necessary to piquet all commanding features up to 1,500 yards from the line of march of Indian
columns or from perimeter camps to protect them from sniping. A full
platoon had to be employed in piquets out of direct support in light of
growing tribal skill in attacking such positions, which were normally provided with a protective ring of barbed wire to prevent their being rushed.
Night operations were also thoroughly vindicated, reducing tribal resistance and increasing mobility in the border hills, but as the Khaisora operations had also demonstrated, they needed to be carefully planned and
possess surprise to prevent columns from falling into disarray. In other
respects imperial tactics generally conformed closely to existing methods.
The 3.7″ howitzer, now equipping all mountain batteries in India, had
demonstrated its versatility, mobility and firepower once again and was
the only type of heavy support weapon in imperial hands capable of
accompanying columns operating in the hills. As one infantry officer
observed: 'Of all the ubiques it is undoubtedly the most ubiquitous.'[94]

Two companies of Mk II and Mk IIb Light Tanks were employed when ground permitted in sections or sub-sections to carry out reconnaissance, protect flanks, cover withdrawals and directly attack *lashkars*, adding to the strength and quickening the pace of movement.[95] The weight of firepower provided by machine guns, artillery, light tanks and aircraft operating with Indian columns had proved highly effective against large concentrated *lashkars* in the opening phases of the operations, but conversely exacerbated the problem of bringing the elusive tribesmen to battle. Moreover, the unrestricted employment of superior firepower with little thought to its long-term impact was now a thing of the past, as the political restrictions associated with the 'hearts and minds' campaign in Waziristan exerted a powerful influence on the fighting.

The 5,000-strong British-officered Tochi and South Waziristan Scouts (belonging to the Civil Armed Forces) had proved a valuable adjunct to the Army in India, carrying out operations independently and in cooperation with regulars throughout Waziristan both with columns and on the lines of communication. Their speed, mobility, light equipment and local knowledge enabled them to carry out advance guard duties, protect the flanks of columns, threaten the flanks and rear of the enemy, and conduct raids with far greater ease than heavily encumbered regulars who were more tied to the roads. However, their organization and light scale of equipment meant they were unable to overcome serious opposition without support from regular troops.[96]

It was clear that the conduct of military operations by the Army in India was now more than ever dependent on roads, especially for units from the Field Army. Roads increased the mobility of units in Waziristan and facilitated the supply of imperial columns. Lorries were employed on an unprecedented scale, allowing the number of pack animals and non-combatants to be considerably reduced from those needed during prior operations. The circular road allowed lightly equipped imperial troops to quickly concentrate and operate off a secure line of communication, greatly simplifying the whole problem of transport and supply as well as reducing the size and unwieldiness of columns. MT delivered troops, pack animals and supplies to the point where columns left the roads, refilled supply echelons and dumped stores at roadheads and were, to that extent, able to increase the radius of action of accordingly lightly equipped Indian troops. Further roads constructed during the operations (see Figure 10) allowed motor vehicles to operate in new areas of Waziristan, completing a system whereby the whole of central Waziristan was made accessible to columns operating from a road on a pack basis with a two-days' radius of action. Roads also allowed heavy weapons to be deployed in Waziristan. Five batteries of mechanised field artillery, as well as a section of the 20/21st Medium Battery, equipped with a mixture of 18lb, 4.5″ and 6″ guns firing a heavier weight of shell than normally used in frontier warfare, were employed to support columns within range and road protection troops. Harassing fire at unexpected intervals – directed by aircraft or registered silently – exerted a powerful moral impact and prevented tribesmen from sheltering in villages at night. However, it proved difficult to maintain communications between the Forward Observation Officers and batteries since the infantry, accustomed to working with only mountain batteries, found it difficult to work alongside and direct their fire.[97]

Road Protection along the extended lines of communication was the main task carried out by the majority of imperial troops deployed in Waziristan as a direct corollary of greater reliance on MT.[98] To piquet 10–12 miles of road a full infantry brigade was normally still required, with mobile reserves held in each sector ready to respond to tribal raids. The stereotyped procedure that most units employed for 'Road Open Days' – normally held three days a week – allowed little opportunity for personal initiative or any variation in minor tactics when positions of tactical importance had to be repeatedly occupied. Most Road Protection schemes employed in Waziristan surrendered the initiative and provided hostile tribesmen with an idea of the time, direction, method and destination of each detachment, as they piqueted a road each day, making them vulnerable to attack. In Road Protection considerable scope existed for the use of tanks and armoured cars, as well as motorised infantry battalions, which had considerably simplified protection of fast-moving convoys of motor transport. Armoured cars proved an effective and economical means of protecting roads, allowing the number of infantry deployed on such exacting duties to be reduced. They escorted convoys, patrolled long stretches of the lines of communications and provided fire support when necessary to road protection troops. On occasion they were supplemented by Light Tanks and improvised home-made armoured lorries. Infantry battalions embussed in lorries also proved a useful means of quickly reinforcing units in areas threatened by tribal *lashkars*. A clear lesson of the campaign was that, despite the employment of armoured cars, light tanks and lorry-borne infantry escorts, motor transport was highly vulnerable to sniping and ambush in hilly areas outside the security of static protective piquets.[99]

The close co-operation now developed between the RAF and the Army in India at tactical level, after long years of acrimonious disagreement over air control, was an outstanding feature of the operations in Waziristan.

Six squadrons – equipped with Westland Wapiti, Hawker Audax and Hawker Hart aircraft – were used in the largest air operation ever undertaken in India, as well as a flight of the newly-formed Indian Air Force. A combination of independent and operations in support of the army were employed. No. 1 and No. 2 (Indian) Wings, operating under the detailed restrictions imposed by the Government of India intended to prevent the death of women or children and attacks on friendly tribal sections, carried out independent bombing operations throughout the fighting. Aircraft carried out punitive bombing raids on houses belonging to those individuals directly implicated in attacks and villages belonging to hostile tribal sections. After warning notices were distributed warning the local inhabitants to evacuate an area large parts of Waziristan were 'proscribed' to disperse hostile tribesmen, stop a *lashkar* moving through an area, prevent access to an area of unrest, end interference with a line of communication or to reduce opposition to an advancing column.[100] Daily reconnaissance sorties throughout Waziristan provided photographic intelligence that enabled column commanders to locate hostile *lashkars*, determine the number and location of piquets and perimeter camps in advance, and to direct long-range artillery fire. A particularly notable feature of the operations was the frequent use of Bomber Transport Aircraft to drop supplies to imperial columns and to maintain isolated posts. It increased the administrative mobility and hence the tactical mobility of imperial troops. After four tons of supplies and ammunition were successfully dropped during the Khaisora operations it was proposed that henceforth supply drops of food, fodder and ammunition should form a normal component of military operations in tribal territory to reduce the amount of pack transport required, remove the need for a permanent line of communication, extend the circuit of action of ground columns and to increase both their speed and mobility. A flight of Vickers Valentia aircraft from No. 70 (Bomber Transport) Squadron in Iraq augmented the flight already in India, carrying military personnel and stores and evacuating seriously wounded to base hospitals in India throughout the campaign.[101]

Those close-support tactics developed at Khanpur by No. 3 (Indian) Wing and 2nd (Rawalpindi) Brigade in November 1936 were thoroughly vindicated during the Khaisora operations, adding a new dimension to the tactical conduct of frontier warfare.[102] They formed an integral part of most of the fighting in Waziristan during 1937 with aircraft from Army Co-operation squadrons using the VBL system of ground attack to engage hostile tribesmen in contact with imperial troops and those advancing or retiring in 'proscribed' areas in advance or along the flanks of columns. Writing in March 1937 General Sir John Coleridge acknowledged: 'These operations have definitely proved the great value which close support by aircraft in mountain warfare can afford, and that this can best be obtained by a column commander having at his side an Air Force commander with whom he can easily and quickly collaborate.'[103] Aircraft constantly patrolled the sides and rear of columns during daylight hours ready to take immediate offensive action and, in the process, restricted hostile movement in the area. On several occasions close-support aircraft acted as flank guards or 'high piquets' when columns moved through steep and difficult country that otherwise would have entailed lengthy delays using infantry, despite the fact that it was recognised they could not provide complete security. Such aircraft increased the pace of Indian columns and inflicted heavy casualties on tribesmen concentrated to oppose advancing troops.[104] A senior RAF officer accompanied each column HQ to advise brigade commanders, liaise with units and ensure pilots received all necessary information. As had been anticipated, close communication between pilots and the forward troops was essential. R/T between aircraft and RAF mule-pack sets with column HQ formed the basis of communication, while a simple 'XVT' 'Close Support Intercommunication Code' developed during the autumn of 1936 supplemented Popham Panels, enabling troops to indicate their position and targets to supporting aircraft.[105] As the CO of No. 20 (A.C.) Squadron later explained:

> If any trouble was suspected, the RAF would keep one or more aircraft over the area throughout the hours of daylight. The support was based on the principle of keeping picket positions under general surveillance, and giving them direct assistance if they needed it. All pickets carried two white ground strips, and whenever they halted they would put these out in the form of an 'X' where it could be seen from the air. This showed their exact position. If the picket was under fire, it would put a 'V' with the view pointing in the direction of the enemy and there were many times we found the enemy through this help. If the picket were in danger of being overrun, it would use the emergency 'T' sign, the short arm being nearest the enemy. There are times when we bombed and shot up the enemy within thirty yards of a picket position. The pilot would mark the picket positions on his map and periodically drop a message on the column headquarters, giving pinpoint map references and stating which were in action.[106]

Despite RAF critics who still regarded such operations as a misuse of aircraft, close air support had now established itself as a valuable adjunct to all ground operations in tribal territory.

To a new generation of officers the Waziristan campaign demonstrated the necessity of a high standard of specialised training in the principles and minor tactics of frontier warfare for British and Indian units stationed in the Covering Troops' districts and for those elements of the Field Army in Northern Command detailed as immediate reinforcements. During 1937 the recent lessons learnt in tribal territory were included in reports issued by Northern Command and the *A.H.Q. India Training Memorandum* for the 1936–37 collective training season.[107] Training in frontier warfare was extended to form part of the individual and collective training period of every unit and brigade in India. Units of 1st (Rawalpindi) Division and those stationed in Lahore District, tasked to reinforce the Covering Troops on mobilisation, were also temporarily attached to columns operating in tribal territory to gain practical experience. Such training had immediate relevance as an estimated 200 'irreconcilable' tribesmen organised in small bands sniped troops, sabotaged roads, held up traffic and cut telegraph lines in Waziristan and occasionally raided villages in the Derajat during 1938 and 1939. As a result special defensive arrangements were necessary during 1938–39 on the line of communication to Razmak employing khassadars, Scouts, aircraft and the retention of 3rd (Jhelum) Brigade and other units from the Field Army to supplement the normal garrison.[108]

The planned replacement for the *Manual of Operations on the North-West Frontier of India* was not immediately available to these troops and others deployed elsewhere in the NWFP, despite agreement between the General Staff, Air Staff in India and the Foreign and Political Department regarding its contents. When the first draft was submitted to the India Office for approval in February 1936, General Sir William Bartholomew, the CGS, observed:

> It is most comprehensive and much larger than the old manual, but I think that it is right that this should be so. It is intended primarily for the use of officers of both services at Home and in India who have no knowledge of the Frontier or of Frontier fighting. I do not think there is anything controversial in the book so far as matters of principle are concerned. As regards the details of tactical methods, one can never please everybody and I daresay some experienced frontiers men will disagree with several things in the book with which others, equally experienced, will be in full agreement![109]

Controversy over the politically sensitive sections dealing with aircraft, however, prevented publication when the Secretary of State for India decided that they should be published separately classified for 'Official

Use Only' and only be given a limited circulation.[110] This decision bitterly disappointed Major-General Claude Auchinleck, who had spent a
considerable amount of time drafting the manual and securing agreement
between the RAF, army and political authorities in India. General Sir
Robert Cassels, the Commander-in-Chief in India, personally intervened
in May 1937 to prevent what he regarded as the 'emasculation' of the
manual. Writing to the Military Secretary at the India Office he explained:

> The whole object of the book is to present a comprehensive picture of
> modern frontier warfare, as at present in progress to all concerned with
> the idea of emphasising need of co-operation between land and air
> forces and their dependence on each other, which have been unfortu-
> nately been lacking in the past. I have done everything possible to put
> this right, and it is not too much to say that present operations have
> proved that this object has been achieved.[111]

This request and support from both the Air Ministry and War Office meant
the entire manual was finally reclassified as 'For Official Use Only',
although it was now too late for it to be printed during 1937.[112] Its arrival
was eagerly awaited in India by both services as a means to improve inter-
service relations and to provide guidelines regarding the conduct of operations under modern conditions.[113] Further differences regarding types of
air operations used by the RAF on the frontier during 1938, however,
meant that it was not until November 1938 that a final draft was approved
for publication.[114]

While this controversy was in progress the *Manual of Operations on
the North-West Frontier of India* was supplemented by further sources of
information outlining the lessons derived from recent frontier fighting.
Although a section on frontier warfare was specifically excluded from the
A.H.Q. India Training Memorandum issued in July 1938 (pending the
publication of the new manual) references to the use of aircraft and
artillery in Waziristan were included elsewhere in the text.[115] The service
press provided the most important means of disseminating information
regarding the recent fighting. A series of articles appeared in the JUSII
during 1938 ranging from accounts of the operations to detailed tactical
proposals regarding the conduct of frontier warfare in the future.[116] Many
officers were eager to record their experiences and discern lessons from
the recent operations, although not all were satisfied with the current
tactics or system of training employed in India. At the direct request of the
Deputy CGS, Colonel Francis Tuker prepared a paper for the JUSII based
on the innovative method of road protection used by the 1/2nd Gurkha
Rifles on the Razani sector of the lines of communication, where a system

of aggressive day and night patrolling, based on perimeter camps and permanent piquets throughout the sector, replaced the system of static road protection used elsewhere in Waziristan.[117] Writing under the pseudonym 'Auspex', he once again took the opportunity to condemn the current doctrine of frontier warfare, observing that the immense value of armoured and mechanised forces supplied from the air and supported by close support aircraft had not been fully exploited. Particular criticism was reserved for brigade columns and the system of piqueting on the move:

> The mountain warfare doctrinaires must be stopped from propounding it as a normal and good method. The Pathan's small-bore weapons killed it thirty years ago; it only suited the *jezail*. The nearer a commander can bring mountain warfare into line with modern warfare, the nearer he comes to success, for he will bring his superior firepower to bear to its maximum extent and at the right time.[118]

Despite such strong condemnation of orthodox wisdom, the official doctrine of frontier warfare remained largely unchanged although units and formations stationed on the frontier still experimented with new tactical methods. For example, during the Kharre operations in July 1938, two brigades and the Tochi Scouts stayed out in mutually supporting laagers overnight instead of employing an orthodox perimeter camp.[119]

The new manual – *Frontier Warfare (Army and Royal Air Force) 1939* – was issued to British and Indian units and RAF squadrons during March 1939, after hurried revisions were made taking into account the recent changes in infantry organisation. It provided the Army in India with a comprehensive and up-to-date formal written doctrine of frontier warfare upon which a comprehensive system of training was based. 20,000 copies were printed and circulated in England and India where it formed the basis of training for companies and higher formations for the remainder of British rule. It was considerably larger than its predecessor and codified the existing doctrine of frontier warfare currently in use in India modernised to the extent of discussing the use of aircraft, light tanks, and heavy artillery in tribal territory. The greater degree of understanding and co-operation between the Indian Army and the RAF was reflected in its contents, despite continued differences regarding the higher direction of tribal control, and it provided a comprehensive picture of frontier warfare that emphasised the need for co-operation of land and air forces and their dependence on each other. It described, in considerable detail, how aircraft could perform air blockades, proscriptive air action, destructive air action and ground/air co-operation in mountain warfare. Despite growing criticism doctrine, the manual still emphasised the continued importance of the established orthodox methods of frontier warfare, with columns, protective piquets and perimeter camps. It warned officers, however, against the dangers of operations becoming too stereotyped, as well as dismissing a growing belief in the fighting ability of Pathan *lashkars*. The Army in India's long historical experience of operations on the frontier was reflected in footnotes throughout the manual which contained references to prior operations. Officers were encouraged to read histories of military operations and it also included a bibliography of books dealing with both the frontier and frontier warfare.[120] Other sources of unofficial guidance complemented the new manual, such as articles in the service press that discussed the conduct of frontier warfare under modern conditions or the development of light infantry skills in the border hills.[121] Perhaps the most significant addition to this unofficial literature was a 4th revised edition of *Passing it On: Short Talks on Tribal Fighting on the North-West Frontier of India of India* published in 1939, which contained an additional chapter written by several Indian Army officers discussing the 1936–37 Waziristan operations.[122]

Conclusion
Frontier Warfare in Retrospect and Prospect, September 1939–August 1947

When the Second World War broke out in September 1939 the Army in India had had 90 years of sustained extensive experience of conducting military operations in tribal territory. Despite repeated punitive campaigns and various attempts to pacify tribal territory the now heavily armed trans-border Pathans still remained fiercely independent and an insistent threat to the security of the settled areas. Apart from where roads had penetrated the hills, the main distinguishing characteristics and tactics of frontier warfare still remained essentially unchanged from those initially encountered in 1849 with large mobile columns reliant on pack transport moving protected by a ring of piquets. Yet Indian Army officers were not dyed-in-the-wool reactionary conservatives clinging to outmoded methods long past their usefulness. The minor tactics employed to counter elusive guerrillas on the frontier remained essentially those originally developed by the PFF, and later disseminated to the rest of the Army in India after the 1897–98 Tirah Campaign, as they were more dependent on the terrain and tribal military characteristics than any other factors. Despite criticism in some quarters for being anachronistic, they still remained effective. As other modern supporting weapons could not be effectively exploited in the hills of tribal territory, frontier warfare still remained primarily the preserve of the infantryman and the pack mule, who conducted operations that still displayed all the characteristics of a traditional 'small war' rather than an internal security operation. Imperial troops still had to move and fight in remote mountainous areas, with all the attendant problems of transport and supply, against elusive lightly armed tribesmen that were, in comparison, inured to local conditions and experts in guerrilla warfare. Although frequently termed mountain warfare, the operations carried out in tribal territory were very different from those practised in Europe, representing a specialised form of 'savage warfare' tailored to local military requirements in India.

The need for a coherent formal written doctrine of frontier warfare for imperial troops remained as pressing as ever. Most Indian Army regiments were now highly proficient in the 'art' of frontier warfare as a result of a system of specialised training combined with frequent opportunities for active service. Although troops stationed in the NWFP still had to be warned repeatedly to maintain alertness, the vast majority of Indian Army units, especially Gurkha and Frontier Force regiments, by tradition, training and experience were now highly skilled in the intricacies of frontier warfare.[1] A comprehensive range of official training manuals, incorporating lessons painfully learned and a wealth of frontier fighting experience, were available to British officers that described in elaborate detail the specialised principles and minor tactics of frontier warfare, as well as official histories, handbooks and gazetteers containing detailed information regarding tribal territory and its inhabitants. Standing Orders issued by higher formations and brigades complemented the official manuals and laid down local variations in minor tactics and details that took into account the local terrain. Training at both the Staff Colleges at Camberley and at Quetta also provided senior officers with instruction in the specialised staff duties required when conducting operations in tribal territory. When the 2/2nd Gurkha Rifles arrived in Waziristan, for example, in October 1939 the CO and all company officers had prior frontier experience while the rest of the battalion had already received intensive instruction. As Adrian Hayter later observed:

> We had already heard many lectures, read many pamphlets, and carried out many TEWTS (Tactical Exercise Without Troops) on Frontier Warfare, to teach us the chain of command, administrative planning, evacuation of casualties, the tactical situations to be expected and their solution.[2]

Unlike in other parts of the British Empire, the Indian military authorities accepted it as axiomatic that untrained troops were a danger to themselves and formations to which they belonged and that pragmatic ad-hoc adaptation to local military requirements, 'making it up as you went along' or common sense was simply inappropriate for officers and men deployed in the NWFP. Thomas Mockaitis is simply incorrect to assert that: 'In the bump and shove of military life on the Northwest Frontier … soldiers were left to the time-honoured method of "making it up as they went along."'[3] The frequent recurrence of so-called 'regrettable incidents' forcibly underscored and repeatedly reminded the General Staff aware that the provision of a formal written doctrine and system of training was imperative, perhaps more so than in any other part of the Empire, to prevent British and Indian units suffering unnecessary casualties that might otherwise cause a minor incident to escalate into a major conflict. Nevertheless, losses were still regularly suffered at Pathan hands, although normally these occurred as a result of either a lack of any previous experience or a failure to obey the accepted 'laws' of frontier fighting which had to be taught and 'passed on' to new generations of officers and men.

The series of manuals promulgated by the General Staff in India represented a clearly thought-out, formal written doctrine upon which was based a comprehensive and progressive training programme to ensure its acceptance throughout the Army in India. They helped improve readiness, provided the same military language and ensured uniformity of knowledge and training amongst units throughout India, guaranteeing that regiments from various commands could operate together at short notice. As a result of the ongoing commitment to tribal control and offensive military strategies in event of war in Afghanistan, the General Staff devoted serious attention to systematically collating, preserving, and transmitting information relating to the conduct of frontier warfare as it represented a definite local, immediate and long-term military problem. This was an important reflection of military professionalism directed towards imperial requirements rather than in imitation of European practice. It was able to do so as it enjoyed almost complete independence from the War Office that directed training elsewhere in the British Empire. New military problems that might be encountered on the North-West Frontier and how they could be solved were actively considered by individual officers and the staffs of formations stationed in the NWFP. Training manuals were periodically revised and annual instructions issued to direct training, incorporating new ideas and experience gained during recent operations and modifications to existing tactics caused by changes in military organisation and equipment and improvements in tribal armament and fighting methods. In many respects, as Raffi Gregorian has observed, a combination of near-constant active service and a generally more professional attitude meant the Indian Army was more reflective and responsive to changes on the colonial battlefield than its British counterpart.[4] In comparison, the British Army at home concentrated on the tactics of a conventional European conflict against relatively similarly armed, trained and equipped opponents. Those British regiments without experienced officers and men that served in India arrived with training based on *FSR* and without any specific prior instruction for local Indian requirements. While in India they trained in accordance with local directives, but normally never acquired the same degree of efficiency in the specialised tactics of hill warfare as Indian units. A combination of short and infrequent tours of duty in tribal territory and the reluctance of professionally arrogant British service officers to acknowledge that special training was required meant that their units often suffered unnecessary casualties at tribal hands.

Other important means of communication existed by which the tactics of mountain warfare were 'passed on' outside official channels complementing the system of manuals and training. A considerable number of books, pamphlets and unofficial text-books were available to British officers written by their predecessors which provided further sources of information and guidance regarding operations against the trans-border Pathans. These amplified the necessarily condensed and often cryptic language of the drill books and training manuals often presented in a too indigestible form for junior officers and NCOs. Charles Callwell's now rather dated *Small Wars: Their Principles and Practice* remained the most easily available and most comprehensive treatment of colonial warfare available to officers in England. It is only possible to speculate, however, how widely it was read and to what extent training was based on its guidelines, although the book was used at both the Staff College at Camberley and the RAF Staff College at Andover during the inter-war period.[5] In India General Sir Andrew Skeen's *Passing it On: Short Talks on Tribal Fighting on the North-West Frontier* assumed an authoritative position and gained almost official acceptance when it was issued to British and Indian units. Several editions were published before the outbreak of the Second World War, revised and updated to reflect changes in imperial equipment and tribal tactics. Other sources of information and reference were available to officers in the form of regimental histories and various published personal accounts of operations against the trans-border Pathan tribes.

The military press and professional service institutions represented an important means of 'passing on' information to British officers. Debate about frontier fighting was primarily centred in the United Service Institution and its in-house periodical during the nineteenth and twentieth centuries. At lectures held at Simla the perceived 'lessons' of frontier warfare were regularly discussed by serving Indian Army officers, while the influential RUSI and other professional military organisations in England periodically deliberated upon the subject in contributions that later appeared in print. The sheer number of articles published in the JUSII – ranging from general discussions of frontier policy and the role of the army, to accounts of operations, potential new tactics and training, and detailed technical discussions of tactics and equipment for each arm – indicate the considerable professional interest maintained amongst British officers about frontier fighting. These represented an important means of broadening professional knowledge amongst British officers regarding tactics, training and the use of new equipment against the trans-border tribes. The service press also provided an important medium where officers dissatisfied with the methods employed on the frontier could present arguments for the adoption of new equipment and methods of instruction.

Finally, the uninterrupted sequence of military operations in tribal territory meant the ranks of Indian regiments contained a large permanent cadre of long-serving British and Indian officers, NCOs and other ranks who provided the final means of 'passing on' information relating to hill warfare. The comparatively short intervening period of time between tours of duty in the NWFP meant that nearly all Indian units now contained officers and men who had personal knowledge and recent experience of tribal territory and its inhabitants. Information regarding the conduct of operations was passed on to new subalterns and recruits by these men during training. Nearly all Indian Army officers above the rank of Major during the inter-war period had served on the North-West Frontier as subalterns and knew by personal experience what was involved in military operations against the trans-border tribes. As long as the continuity of training and experience was not interrupted this system worked effectively, but the transmission of information by word of mouth was haphazard at best and frequent omissions and errors often occurred.

The effectiveness of units of the Army in India, however, on the North-West Frontier is open to question. It must always be remembered that frontier warfare was not the sole task performed by the Army in India and the training, organisation and equipment intended for its other roles directly affected both its military effectiveness during operations in tribal territory and its approach to training. As has been demonstrated, the creation of a tactical doctrine suited to frontier fighting had been complicated and delayed by the two-way split between conventional military methods and those of colonial warfare. For both British and Indian units serving in the Army in India, the immediate military demands and experience of frontier warfare could not be regarded as the sole determinant of military organisation, equipment and training. Instead, they were always primarily trained and organised for conventional military operations, either in Asia or as part of an imperial expedition. Training emphasis at the Staff College and elsewhere was firmly fixed on the type of warfare anticipated in Europe. Most British officers always perceived themselves as training first and foremost for a conventional conflict, although this was tempered by a recognition of India's local military requirements of frontier warfare and internal security (the latter always came a poor third). As a result it proved

difficult to achieve the correct balance between the time devoted to training for conventional operations and that for frontier warfare, especially
during peacetime when local day-to-day military requirements always
loomed larger in the minds of Indian Army officers. In this respect frontier
warfare did encourage a degree of parochialism amongst some officers
unwilling to look beyond the local requirements of Indian defence. During
the twentieth century the pendulum swung from one extreme to another
regarding the importance attached to specialised training in hill warfare, as
preparations for a conventional conflict waxed and waned or when the
frequency of operations in tribal territory declined.

Following the First World War, the conflicting requirements of the two
types of operation became more explicit when it became apparent that the
two systems of training were almost contradictory in many respects.
Training and equipment for conventional warfare directly affected the military effectiveness of imperial troops during operations in tribal territory as
arms and heavy equipment, intended for 'civilised warfare', were adopted.
As a result of increasing dependence on supporting arms and services, the
relative mobility of Indian columns operating in the hills progressively
declined and they were tied to fixed lines of communication. Although the
construction of roads in tribal territory allowed the use of armoured cars,
light tanks, lorries, field and medium artillery in their immediate vicinity,
as well as units with higher scales of equipment, and considerably eased
supply and administrative difficulties, they did not remove the essential
problem encountered by imperial troops when they moved away from
them. The mountainous terrain in tribal territory afforded little further
scope for mechanisation, however, apart from some tracked vehicles,
making pack mules and infantry essential when columns operated in the
hills. Tactical flexibility and mobility evident in prior frontier campaigns
progressively declined, as it was simply impossible to reconcile the heavy
scale of equipment carried by regular troops and the attendant first-line
mule transport with rapid cross-country movement. Despite endeavours to
improve their speed and mobility, Indian columns could not match that of
lashkars as increasing quantities of heavy equipment, supplies and maintenance services exacerbated transport and supply problems that had always
dogged operations on the frontier. In many respects the Indian Army's
deployment on the frontier mirrored the paradox encountered by the
United States army during the nineteenth century when fighting against
native American Indians.[6] The commitment to tribal control reduced its
effectiveness in conventional military operations, while at the same time
the army's normal preoccupation with conventional war made it less fit for
its frontier mission. The various discussions regarding the relative merits

of resuscitating the PFF in the 1920s and 1930s reflected widespread recognition that specially trained, organised and lightly equipped troops would be much more efficient and mobile than regulars on periodic tours of duty. However, such proposals were unacceptable to the military authorities as long as Afghanistan and the North-West Frontier remained the most likely theatre of operations for the Army in India, as the area provided invaluable practical experience of the terrain and tribal tactics likely to be encountered across the Durand Line. In any event, the Scouts and various militias now performed the policing and, to a lesser degree, many of the military tasks previously carried out by the frontier force when it had been under civil control.

THE SECOND WORLD WAR AND TRIBAL TERRITORY

The watch and ward of tribal territory remained an insistent problem for the Army in India during the Second World War that tied down large numbers of imperial units. In 1943 57 British and Indian infantry battalions, for example, as well as four armoured car regiments were deployed in the NWFP.[7] Throughout the war the conduct of mountain warfare was closely studied by British and Indian troops stationed in Northern Command, although elsewhere in India attention was directed first towards training for operations against a 'modern' opponent either in mountains or deserts and then in a jungle environment following the Japanese invasion of Malaya and Burma.[8] Intermittent fighting occurred in Waziristan against elusive tribal gangs led by the Faqir of Ipi who inflicted a steady trickle of casualties on the garrison. As the CO of Razmak Brigade wryly observed on 24th November 1939: 'Last week we had 16 more casualties on one day, in fact we are losing more men here than the Army is in France!'[9] Between 1939 and 1945 regiments stationed in Northern Command were given intensive training in frontier warfare, as well as in the modifications required if the tribesmen were assisted by foreign troops.[10] *Frontier Warfare – India (Army and R.A.F.)* remained the main source of official guidance throughout the war, although amendments were added as further combat experience was collated.[11] The time-honoured doctrine of tribal warfare had immediate relevance for the garrison in Waziristan when, in February–May 1940, two brigades and supporting troops covered the construction of Frontier Constabulary posts in the Ahmadzai salient, used as a jumping-off point for tribesmen raiding the Derajat.[12] On the night of 7th/8th December 1940 the importance of specialised training in frontier warfare was driven home, when the 5/8th

Punjabis lost 58 dead and 55 wounded near Razmak after a demoralised piquet opened itself to attack by unwisely attempting to retire to a nearby perimeter camp.[13] Further large-scale operations and minor skirmishes continued against elusive *lashkars* led by the Faqir of Ipi throughout the rest of the war, although by 1944 the situation had considerably improved.[14]

Those general military skills learnt on the frontier were also deemed to have significance during the Second World War in other theatres of operations, although the specialised minor tactics of frontier warfare were generally conflict-specific. For example, at the request of the War Office twenty officers were provided by the Indian Army in April 1940 to act as advisers in mountain warfare to British units preparing for service in Norway.[15] In the mountains of East Africa, the skills learnt in tribal territory also had immediate relevance to imperial troops fighting against Italian troops.[16] Regarding units that had served on the frontier, an *Army in India Training Memorandum* issued in July 1941 noted: 'They may not have learnt all about modern warfare, but they had learnt the basic lessons, leadership, discipline, endurance, speed, fieldcraft; all these against a critical teacher – the Pathan.'[17] When German units advanced towards the Caucasus and posed a potential threat to Persia, Afghanistan and the subcontinent, it appeared that such training and experience had immediate relevance to units remaining in India. A pamphlet produced in India in 1941, describing tactics required against European troops in mountainous terrain, noted:

> The Army in India starts with having studied the Pathan and his ways and having acquaintance with conditions, tactical and administrative, of fighting in the mountains. It should, therefore, not only be more mobile than its prospective enemy, but should also be able to adapt the Pathan's harassing tactic to worrying a more stereotyped opponent both near the battle front and on the L. of C.[18]

As the war progressed and units of the battle-hardened Imperial Japanese Army threatened eastern India, the training and skills learnt in frontier warfare were also deemed of value for jungle warfare, as long as training was complemented by a period of intensive instruction to develop 'jungle sense' and to overcome initial 'jungle phobia'. A report prepared by the Infantry Committee in June 1943, that in part discussed the readiness of troops stationed in the NWFP for use against the Japanese, judged that: 'Troops trained in frontier warfare should quickly assimilate the technique of jungle warfare, owing to its similarity in principle to mountain warfare, and to the fact that so much jungle country is also mountainous.'[19]

British and Indian units serving in the border garrisons in the NWFP were once again 'milked' of experienced officers, NCOs and men as the war proceeded, to be replaced by an influx of inexperienced and untrained Emergency Commissioned Officers (ECOs) and new recruits. To provide trained instructors for units capable of teaching their own men and thereby avoid a repetition of the events of 1919–20 a series of mountain warfare courses were run for new units initially by Northern Command, using instructors and demonstration troops from 1st (Abbottabad) Infantry Brigade, on an *ad hoc* basis.[20] An Army School of Frontier Warfare opened at Kakul in March 1941, under the command of Colonel Frank Le Marchand, to instruct British and Indian NCOs, regimental officers and formation commanders in Northern Command and Western (Independent) District.[21] Eleven month-long courses were held annually, each having vacancies for 100 students selected from regular British and Indian battalions, Indian States Forces and the Nepalese Contingent, and with a smaller proportion allotted to personnel from armoured, engineer, artillery, RAF and IAF units. Particular attention was given to officers from British units, the majority of whom lacked any knowledge of frontier warfare or the Pathan tribes. Senior officers of new units, or those about to move to the frontier for the first time on a tour of duty, were given preference on each course. An ability to 'pass it on' also acted as the main guide in selecting candidates for the school, who were tested and ranked in their ability as instructors at the end of each course before returning to their units.[22] Its syllabus covered basic tactics, battle procedure, fire and movement, piqueting, advance and rearguard duty, patrolling and administration. Its instructors also taught various techniques employed for individual, platoon, company and battalion training and culminated by examining the duties required of a frontier brigade operating in tribal territory. An attached demonstration battalion gave presentations of piqueting, covering fire, ambushes, and organisation for the benefit of students and a large sand-table model of the local area facilitated training.[23] By 1943 the demand for trained instructors for the increasing number of newly raised Indian units in the North Western Army was such that an increase in the output of the Frontier Warfare School had to be sanctioned.[24] Instruction in mountain warfare was also studied elsewhere in India during the war. It formed part of the syllabus at the Poona Tactical School, the Officers' Training Schools at Bangalore and Mhow and an element of the tactical syllabus of the six-month-long War Course held between 1939 and 1945 at the Staff College at Quetta.[25] A series of new Military Training Pamphlets were also prepared for both army and RAF units to facilitate training of new 'hostilities-only' officers and men.[26] Perhaps the most important of these was a detailed manual, based on *Frontier Warfare – India (Army and Royal Air Force)*, specifically for platoon commanders explaining in some detail minor tactics on the frontier and how to go about training their men.[27]

Despite the authoritative guidance issued by the Frontier Warfare School and the existing official manuals and pamphlets, the conduct of frontier warfare was still discussed in the service press by officers serving in the NWFP throughout the war, especially regarding the employment of modern methods, training and equipment now in use elsewhere by imperial troops. In an article published in the JUSII in 1943, critical of the existing stereotyped tactical methods, Lt.-Colonel Francis Simpson pointed out:

> It may be said with some justification that the present is scarcely the time for such a study of Frontier Warfare, when the attention of all soldiers is being directed to other and more pressing forms of warfare, which are of immediate and pressing concern to all the armies of the Allied nations. At the same time Frontier Warfare, and all that it implies, is one of the unpleasant things – like many others – which we have always with us, and it can never be neglected, either now or in the future ... nothing is certain except that we must always be prepared to fight on the N.W. frontier, and so we must continually be thinking of how we shall fight there when the next time comes.[28]

Opinion clearly remained divided amongst Indian Army officers as to the respective merits of the traditional principles and minor tactics employed on the frontier. Several officers remained sceptical of proposals to introduce modern equipment and tactics devised primarily for other theatres of war. As Lt.-Colonel Paul Meade pointed out in the JUSII: 'Certain frontier procedures evolved through many years of careful thought and experience cannot be lightly discarded as too slow and cumbersome, even with the aid of most modern weapons, and anyone who, fresh from the speed of modern war, tries to take too short a cut may possibly as a result find himself very badly bogged.'[29] Perhaps the leading critic of frontier warfare added his voice to this wartime debate in 1944, reiterating his deeply held criticism of the 'die-hard' school of frontiersmen he had so long attacked. Writing under the pseudonym 'Auspex', Major-General Sir Francis Tuker, who had served as Director of Military Training in India at the beginning of the war, argued that the frontier had exerted a baleful influence on the Army in India and that in terms of training the lesser was contained in the greater. Indeed, if modern methods of warfare were adopted the need for traditional forms of 'frontier warfare' had now vanished:

The less is contained in the greater: that is, that training and methods employed for fighting a modern enemy will fit us, for example, to destroy quickly a N.W. Frontier enemy and that there is no need for such a thing as old 'Frontier Warfare' that some have come so much to love ... In fact, the most modern methods of getting mobility will do away with most of the troublesome things in 'Passing it On'. Dear as their perpetuation may be to some whose whole claim to military learning is that they can retail them to the layman, their continuance is just simply not soldiering.[30]

Such highly critical views were given wider currency when Tuker chaired a committee appointed in September 1944 to examine the defence of the North-West Frontier and reduce the size of the regular garrison. Its final report was submitted during the spring of 1945 and in part criticised the 'cumbersome' and 'unimaginative' tactics used on the frontier and condemned the neglect of modern equipment or techniques such as air supply. Moreover, it went on to make a searing indictment of the value of training derived from operations in tribal territory and its influence on the organisation, training and equipment of the army as a whole which, during the inter-war period, it was argued, had been predicated primarily on conducting small wars against the trans-border Pathans.[31]

THE LASTING LESSONS OF FRONTIER WARFARE

The Army in India returned to its normal peacetime duties of frontier policing and internal security following the Japanese surrender in August 1945. A Training Directive issued by the Commander-in-Chief later that month ordered that troops allotted to the role of frontier defence in North Western Army should concentrate solely on instruction in frontier warfare which once again became the responsibility of unit and formation commanders.[32] Until the end of the year, however, the Frontier Warfare School remained open at Kakul due to a shortage of trained instructors capable of teaching inexperienced British and Indian units.[33] The military authorities clearly realised that studying prior operations in tribal territory could provide valuable guidance for British officers serving in the NWFP. As the preface of the official history of military operations on the North-West Frontier between 1920–35, published in 1945, concluded:

Wars between 1st class Modern powers come and go. Armaments and battle grounds change with each upheaval. The tribes of the North-West Frontier of India however remain as heretofore an unsolved problem.

The Indian Army of the future will still have to deal with Mohmands and Afridis, Mahsuds and Wazirs. The Tangis and Kandaos of the past will again be contested. History repeats itself. Let it be read profitably.[34]

As comparatively few changes had occurred in either the tactics or the weapons employed on either side, perhaps in no other theatre of war could such a statement have had such a strong basis of fact. Opinion amongst British officers as to the value of the training derived from operations in tribal territory and the effectiveness of the methods employed by the Army in India, however, remained as divided as ever following the end of the war.[35]

The conduct of mountain warfare also attracted considerable official interest in the immediate aftermath of the war, with regard to applying modern tactics and equipment to operations in tribal territory.[36] Endeavours were also made to assimilate lessons from experience gained fighting against Axis troops in Europe, when training teams from 8th and 10th Indian divisions in Italy were sent to the North-West Frontier to lecture about fighting with modern equipment in mountainous terrain.[37] To specifically study those problems involved in conducting operations against elusive guerrilla opponents in a 'quick and decisive manner' an experimental brigade, with an attached Operational Research Section, was formed at the request of Field Marshal Claude Auchinleck, the Commander-in-Chief in India, in Northern Command during the autumn of 1946. After close consultation with experienced frontier officers, extensive trials were conducted by No. 47 (Experimental) Infantry Brigade in the NWFP and northern Punjab between October 1946–March 1947. These experiments aimed to provide the three Frontier Brigade Groups then stationed along the border with tactical guidance, to determine the principles underlying the employment of Indian troops in different circum-stances and the different tasks to be allotted to their commanders and, finally, to modify and develop modern methods of fighting for all types of operations especially with regard to increasing mobility. British officers clearly had an eye on the future as its brief also included operations against guerrillas in areas other than India.[38] Despite experiments with armour, airborne troops, close support and transport aircraft, and other modern equipment, the trials revealed that little had changed in the conduct of mountain warfare. It appeared that the normal precautions and tactical drills laid down in *Frontier Warfare – India (Army and Royal Air Force)*, evolved by the Indian Army as the result of a century of practical experience, remained relevant as the basis of operations against a tribal opponent.[39] As Brigadier T.N. Miller explained:

It may appear that the final recommendations are not as revolutionary as the original directive demands. The reasons for this is that nothing has yet changed either in the characteristics of mountainous country or of guerrilla opposition ... On the other hand modern developments make possible a great reduction of the administrative tail of columns, so increasing their mobility, and enabling bolder action against a guerrilla enemy, this in turn leading to the infliction of the necessary casualties to bring them to terms in a shorter time than heretofore.[40]

When the Raj ended in August 1947 and the Indian Army was divided between India and Pakistan the conduct of frontier warfare finally became irrelevant to the British Army. Following independence the thorny problem of controlling the trans-border Pathans was inherited by the Government of Pakistan, but its attention was firmly directed towards the disputed border with India. In accordance with a scheme originally discussed by the Government of India that involved the substitution of irregulars for the military garrison, it sanctioned the withdrawal of troops from tribal territory.[41] Between November and December 1947 the four Brigade Groups still remaining in Waziristan were withdrawn largely without incident, following which the policing of tribal territory was left to political officers backed by various reorganised and expanded Civil Armed Forces.[42]

The British Army, engaged in a succession of post-war emergencies scattered around the remainder of the far-flung empire, quickly forgot the specialised principles and minor tactics of frontier warfare, although its ranks contained a large number of ex-Indian Army officers, who had transferred in 1947, with considerable experience of conducting operations in mountainous terrain against lightly armed guerrilla opponents. Most of the guidelines laid down in manuals of frontier warfare published in India were now only of academic interest and these manuals were soon relegated to shelves in military libraries in England and India to gather dust. Despite this the minor tactics learnt in tribal territory proved of longer-term importance for the British Army. When a SAS company was deployed in Oman for operations against rebels operating on the Jebel Akhdar in the late 1950s, one officer who had been brought up in the NWFP brought with him the 'traditional wisdom' of mountain warfare learnt from his father who had fought against the trans-border Pathans.[43] Another frontier soldier – Major Tony Gibb – was also present serving with the Trucial Oman Scouts who had learnt the hard lessons of mountain warfare against a guerrilla opponent leading irregulars in Waziristan.[44] Both David Charters and Thomas Mockaitis have also noted similarities between frontier operations and those conducted by British troops in Southern Arabia in 1963–64.[45] In many respects the fighting that ensued when British troops were sent into the Radfan mountains in May–June 1964 was very reminiscent of that on the North-West Frontier and generally confirmed the tactical lessons learnt regarding mountain warfare in India.[46] As Major J.M. Slater observed:

> British troops ... were fighting a campaign the like of which ... had not been conducted on the same scale since before the Second World War, on the North West Frontier of India. Tactics were similar: mountain routes were picqueted, camps defended from a series of stone *sangars* and the troops were ever prey to the sniper's bullet. However, the technology of war had brought its sophistications; helicopters lifted the pickets and re-supplied isolated outposts. The firepower from guns, mortars and machine guns was impressive and air support from supersonic fighters was a far cry from the ancient Wapitis of the Frontier.[47]

It was fortunate that, once again, several senior ex-Indian or British Army officers were present who had prior experience of service in tribal territory that was equally applicable in operations against similarly lightly armed tribal opponents in the Middle East. It is difficult to discern, however, any other use of such specialised minor tactics in other post-1945 campaigns, although it is perhaps in more general terms that the frontier made a lasting contribution to military science. Several historians have noted that the lessons learnt by imperial troops while fighting tribal *lashkars* had wider implications for counter-insurgency during several post-war campaigns that bore a similarity to operations on the frontier.[48] In many respects frontier warfare during the inter-war period was a 'hybrid' form of conflict involving elements of both a counter-insurgency and a more traditional 'small war', during which imperial troops learnt to work in close co-operation with the civil authorities and to employ limited force. Thomas Mockaitis has also argued that a combination of military experience gained in fighting lightly equipped and highly mobile guerrillas and that gained administering tribal territory, had a wider impact on later colonial campaigns. It is difficult to disagree with his conclusion that it was the general administrative, policing and military skills learnt on the frontier in a form of warfare not unlike insurgency that proved invaluable in fighting guerrillas during a variety of post-war campaigns.[49] It is regrettable that the significance of the lessons learnt by British and Indian troops of the Army in India on the North-West Frontier have until now been generally forgotten or ignored by the British Army and military historians.

Notes

INTRODUCTION

1. B. Bond, *Victorian Military Campaigns* (London: Hutchinson and Company, 1967), App.1. pp.309–11.
2. Maj.-Gen. G. Wolseley, 'The Negro as Soldier', *Fortnightly Review*, 44/264 (1888), p.703.
3. Lt.-Col. C.E. Vickery, 'Small Wars', *AQ*, 6/2 (1923), p.307.
4. D.C. Gordon, 'Colonial Warfare', in R. Higham (ed.), *A Guide to the Sources of British Military History* (London, 1975), p.302, R.N. Buckley, 'Colonial Military History: A Research Note', *Iternario*, 5 (1981), p.69, H. Strachan, *European Armies and the Conduct of War* (London, 1983), p.76 and P. Burroughs, 'Imperial Defence and the late Victorian Army', *JICH*, 15/1 (1986), p.55.
5. See C. Townshend, *Britain's Civil Wars: Counterinsurgency in the Twentieth Century* (London, 1986), J. Pimlott, 'The British Experience', in I.F.W. Beckett (ed.) *The Roots of Counterinsurgency: Armies and guerrilla warfare, 1900–1945* (London, 1988), T.R. Mockaitis, *British Counterinsurgency, 1919–1960* (London, 1990) and I.F.W. Beckett, 'The Study of Counter-insurgency: A British Perspective', S*mall Wars and Insurgencies*, 1/1 (1990), pp.47–53.
6. I.F.W. Beckett, 'Low-Intensity Conflict: Its Place in the Study of War', in D.A. Charters, M. Milner and J.B. Wilson (eds.) *Military History and the Military Profession* (London, 1993), p.121.
7. Col. L. Hale, 'The Spirit of Tactical Operations Today', *Proc. R.A.I.*, 16 (1889), p.45.
8. K. Jeffery, 'Colonial Warfare', in C. McInnes and G.D. Sheffield, *Warfare in the Twentieth Century* (London, 1988), p.31.
9. See D.R. Headrick, 'The Tools of Empire: Technology and the Expansion of European Colonial Empires in the Nineteenth Century', *Journal of Modern History*, 51/2 (1979), pp.231–63 and D.R. Headrick, *Tools of Empire: Technology and European Imperialism* (New York, 1981).
10. D.E. Omissi, *Air Power and Colonial Control* (Manchester, 1991).
11. Burroughs, *op. cit.*, p.56.
12. See M. Crowder, 'Many Questions – Some Answers: African Resistance in West Africa – A General View', in R.E. Robinson, W. Mommsen and S. Forster (eds.) *Bismarck, Europe and Africa* (Oxford: 1988), J. Belich, *The New Zealand Wars and the Victorian Interpretation of Racial Conflict* (Auckland, 1986) and J. Laband, *Kingdom in Crisis: The Zulu Response to the British invasion of 1879* (Manchester, 1991).
13. H.R. Bailes, *The Influence of Continental Examples and Colonial Warfare upon the Reform of the Late Victorian Army* (University of London, Ph.D., 1980).
14. Capt. C. Callwell, *Small Wars: Their Principles and Practice* (London, 1896), 2nd ed. 1899 and 3rd ed. 1906.

15. Strachan, *op. cit.*, p.76 and I.F.W. Beckett, 'The Pen and the Sword: Reflections on Military Thought in the British Army, 1854–1914', *Soldiers of the Queen*, 68 (1992), p.6.

16. M. Howard, 'Colonial Wars and European Wars', in J.A. de Moor and H.L. Wesseling (eds.), *Imperialism and War: Essays on Colonial Wars in Asia and Africa* (Leiden, 1989), p.233.

17. R. Haycock, 'British Arms in India', in G. Jordan (ed.) *British Military History. A Supplement to Robin Higham's Guide to the Sources* (London, 1988), p.457 and Gordon, *op. cit.*, p.307.

18. See T.A. Heathcote, *The Indian Army: The Garrison of British Imperial India* (London, 1974), D.E. Omissi, *The Sepoy and the Raj: The Indian Army 1860–1940* (London, 1994) and T.A. Heathcote, *The Military in British India The Development of British Land Forces in South Asia 1600–1947* (Manchester, 1995).

19. Bond, *op. cit.*, p.7.

20. D.M. Peers, 'Stocktaking the New Military History of India: Militarism, Orientalism and Explanatory Models for the Company Raj' (Unpublished paper presented to the New Military History of South Asia Conference, Cambridge, 15–17th July 1997), pp.1–2, 4 and 8.

21. D.M. Anderson and D. Killingray, 'Consent, coercion and colonial control: policing the empire, 1830–1940', in D.M. Anderson and D. Killingray (eds.) *Policing the Empire. Government, Authority and Control, 1830–1940* (Manchester, 1991), 6–7.

22. For general background see Maj.-Gen. J.G. Elliot, *The Frontier 1839–1947* (London, 1968), A. Swinson, The North-West Frontier: People and Events 1839–1947 (London, 1967) and S. Chandra, *The Development of Mountain Warfare in the 19th Century* (London, M.Phil, 1968).

23. P. Mason, *A Matter of Honour, An Account of the Indian Army, its Officers and Men* (London, 1974), p.337.

24. Callwell, *op. cit.*, p.286.

CHAPTER 1

1.   Sir W. Barton, *India's North-West Frontier* (London, 1939), p.8. See Lt. C.M. Enriquez, *The Pathan Borderland* (Calcutta and Simla, 1910) and Col. H.C. Wylly, *From the Black Mountain to Waziristan* (London, 1912).

2.   *Military Report and Gazetteer on Chitral* (Simla, 1928), pp.20–8.

3.   *Military Report and Gazetteer on Dir, Swat and Bajaur* (Calcutta, 1928), p.55 and p.66.

4.   *Military Report on the Mohmand Country* (Calcutta, 1926), 3rd ed. pp.10–13 (Hereafter *Military Report on Mohmand Country*).

5.   *Military Report on Tribal country between Khyber and Kurram 1930* (Simla, 1930), 5th ed. pp.11–16 (Hereafter *Military Report on Tribal Country*).

6.   *Military Report on the Kohat District* (Simla, 1928), 3rd Ed. pp.18–20 and pp.35–6 (Hereafter *Military Report on Kohat District*) and Maj. C.H. Villiers-Stuart, 'The Kurram and Surrounding Country', *AR*, 7 (1914), pp.13–22.

7. *Military Report on Waziristan 1935* (Simla, 1936), pp.104–118 L/MIL/17/13/102 (Hereafter *Military Report on Waziristan*).

8. *A Dictionary of the Pathan Tribes on the North West Frontier of India* (Calcutta, 1910) L/MIL/17/13/6 See O. Caroe, *The Pathans 550 B.C.–A.D. 1957* (London, 1958).

9. A.S. Ahmed, 'Tribes and States in Central and South Asia', *Asian Affairs*, 11 (1980), p.156.

10. See A.S. Ahmed, *Pukhtun Economy and Society* (London, 1980) and R.O. Christiansen, *Conflict and Change Among the Khyber Afridis: a Study of British Policy and Tribal Society on the North-West Frontier 1839–1947* (University of Leicester, Ph.D., 1987).

11. Capt. C.C. Davies, *The Problem of the North West Frontier 1890–1908* (Cambridge, 1932), pp.18–36, W.K. Fraser-Tytler, *Afghanistan: A Study of Political Developments in Central Asia* (London, 1950), p.183 and J.W. Spain, *The Pathan Borderland* (The Hague, 1963), pp.104–109.

12. H. Elliot, the Secretary to the Government of India with the Governor General to the Board of Administration for the affairs of the Punjab, 16th May 1849 and General Order by the Right Honorable the Governor General of India, 18th May 1849, H/761.

13. *General Report on the Administration of the Punjab, for the years 1849–50 and 1850–51* (London, 1854), pp.24–32 and Lt.-Gen. H. Daly, 'The Punjab Frontier Force', *JRUSI*, 28/77 (1884), pp.907–24.

14 Cited in Col. S. Black, Secretary to Government Punjab Military Dept, to the President Army Organization Commission, 8th Sept. 1879, L/P&S/18/A134.

15 Maj. H.P. Burn, Deputy Secretary to the Board of Administration to Sir H. Elliot, Secretary to Government of India with the Governor General, 17th Dec. 1850, P/42/55.

16. Col. J.G. Medley, 'Defence of the North West Frontier', *JUSII*, 9/45 (1880), p.288.

17. Gen. Sir P.S. Lumsden and G.R. Elsmie, *Lumsden of the Guides: A Sketch of the Life of General Sir Henry Burnett Lumsden* (London, 1899), p.98 and Maj.-Gen. J.G. Elliot, *The Frontier 1839–1947* (London, 1968), p.100.

18. *Report Showing the Relations of the British Government with the Tribes, Independent and Dependent, on the North-West Frontier of the Punjab from Annexation in 1849 to the close of 1855* (Calcutta, 1855), p.54 and p.62 V/23/3 (Hereafter *Report Showing Relations 1849–1855*).

19. H.W. Bellew, *Our Punjab Frontier: Being a Concise Account of the various tribes by which the North-West Frontier of British India is Inhabited; shewing its present unprotected and unsatisfactory state, and the urgent necessity that exists for immediate reconstruction. Also, brief remarks on Afghanistan and our policy in reference to that country by a Punjab Official* (Calcutta, 1868), p.12 and *Report showing Relations 1849–1855*, pp.56–7.

20. Ibid., pp.59–60.

21. *Military Report on Waziristan*, pp.119–21, *Military Report on Tribal Country*, pp.17–18 and *Military Report on Mohmand Country*, pp.13–14.

22. Spain, *op. cit.*, pp.76–7, and A.S. Ahmed, 'Pukhtun Tribes in the Great Game', *Asian Affairs*, 11 (1980), pp.139–40.

23. Lt.-Col. W. Gordon, Chief Inspector of Musketry, to the Adj.-Gen., 4th Dec. 1867, L/MIL/3/784, Christiansen, *op. cit.*, pp.286–7 and Elliot, *op. cit.*, p.111.
24. Maj. W. MacKinnon, 'Jezail Experiments', *Proc. USII*, 4/20 (1875), pp.201–3.
25. Elliot, *op. cit.*, p.27.
26. Maj. J. Nicholson, Deputy Commissioner, to Maj. J.D. Macpherson, Military Secretary to the Chief Commissioner, 4th Sept. 1853, F/4/2549.
27. *Selections from the Records of the Government of India. (Foreign Department). No. VI Report on the Administration of the Punjab, Territories, comprising the Punjab Proper and the Cis and Trans-Sutlej States, for the Years 1851–52 and 1852–53* (Calcutta, 1853), pp.36–7 V/23/1 (Hereafter *Selections from Records No. VI*).
28. Brig. J.S. Hodgson, Commanding Punjab Irregular Force, to Maj. H.D. Macpherson, Military Secretary to the Commissioner, 29th April 1853, P/200/36.
29. Lt.-Col. Mackeson, Commissioner & Superintendent Peshawar Division, to Maj. J.D. Macpherson, Military Secretary to the Chief Commissioner, 2nd Sept. 1853 and Capt. J. Coke, Commanding 1st Punjab Infantry to Maj. J.D. Macpherson, 22nd Dec. 1853, F/4/2549.
30. Maj. J.D. Macpherson, Offg. Military Secretary Chief Commissioner Punjab, to Lt.-Col R.J. Birch, Offg. Secretary to the Govt. of India in the Military Department, 11th Oct. 1853, F/4/2549.
31. Minute by the Governor General, 3rd Nov. 1853, Lt.-Col. R.J. Birch, Off. Secretary to the Government of India in the Military Dept. to J. Lawrence, Chief Commissioner Punjab, 9th Nov. 1853, F/4/2549.
32. *Selections from Records No. VI*, p.37 and *Records of the Government of India Report on the Administration of Public Affairs in the Punjaub Territories from 1854–55 to 1855–56 Inclusive* (Calcutta, 1856), pp.94–5 V/10/2.
33. Maj.-Gen. F.W. Stubbs, *History of the Organization, Equipment, and War Services of the Regiment of Bengal Artillery, compiled from published works, official records, and various private sources* (London, 1895), p.571; Brig.-Gen. C.A. Graham, *A History of the Indian Mountain Artillery* (Aldershot, 1957), pp.4–6.
34. Brig. J.S. Hodgson, Commanding Punjaub Irregular Force, to Maj. N. Chamberlain, Military Secretary to the Board of Administration, 5th Oct. 1852, and C. Allen, Offg. Secretary to the Government of India to the Board of Administration for the affairs of the Punjab, 10th Nov. 1852, P/43/63.
35. R.H. Scales, *Artillery in Small Wars: The Evolution of British Army Doctrine 1860–1914* (Ph.D., Duke University, 1976), p.80.
36. See *History of the 1st Punjab Cavalry* (Lahore, 1887), *History of the Second Panjab Cavalry* (London, 1888) and *History of the 23rd Cavalry (Frontier Force), late 3rd Regiment, Punjab Cavalry (*No imprint, c.1910).
37. Brig.-Gen. J.S. Hodgson to Maj. H.D. Macpherson, Offg. Military Secretary to the Chief Commissioner, 10th March 1853, P/200/25.
38. S.S. Thorburn, *The Punjab in Peace and War* (Edinburgh and London, 1904), p.294.
39. *Report on the Administration of Public Affairs in the Punjaub Territories from 1854–55 to 1855–56 Inclusive* (Calcutta, 1856), p.97 V/10/2.
40. A.H. Shibly, *The Reorganisation of the Indian Armies, 1858–79* (London Ph.D., 1969) p.124.

41. Maj. R.C. Lawrence, Secretary to Government, Punjaub, Military Department, to Maj.-Gen. R.J. Birch. Secretary to the Government of India Military Department, with the Governor General, 25th Oct. 1859, P/191/144.
42. Maj. G. Hutchinson, Offg. Secretary to Government Punjab, Military Department, to Maj.-Gen. Sir R.G. Birch, Secretary to the Government of India in the Military Department, 1st Oct. 1860, P/191/44.
43. Maj.-Gen. R.J. Birch, Secretary to the Government of India Military Department, to the Secretary to Government, Punjab, Military Department, 19th Nov. 1860, and Memorandum by Sir John Lawrence, 8th Dec. 1860, *Lawrence Mss*, Mss.Eur.F.90/23.
44. *General Report on the Administration of the Punjab and its Dependencies, for 1859–60* (Calcutta, 1860), pp.40–1 V/10/13.
45. *Annual Report on the Administration of the Punjab Territories, for the year 1861–62* (Calcutta, 1862), p.17 V/10/17.
46. Brigade Standing Orders issued by the Brigadier General Commanding Punjab Frontier Force, 6th July 1867, P/436/42.
47. Gen. Sir J.L. Vaughan, *My Service in the Indian Army – and After* (London, 1904), p.33 and p.46 and G.W. Forrest, *Life of Field Marshal Sir Neville Chamberlain* (London, 1909), p.409.
48. Col. E. Hawthorne to the Secretary Government of India Military Department, 26th Sept. 1863, L/MIL/7/10631 and Forrest, *op. cit.*, p.419.
49. Thorburn, *op. cit.*, p.176.
50. Anon., 'Notes on the Late Campaign on the Punjab Frontier', *Cornhill Magazine*, 9/51 (1864), p.860 and Col. C.E. Stewart, *Through Persia in Disguise with Reminiscences of the Umbeylah Campaign* (London, 1911), p.52.
51. Field Marshal Lord Roberts, *Forty-One Years in India* (London, 1897), Vol. II pp.9–10 and Gen. J. Adye, *Recollections of a Military Life* (London, 1895), pp.207–20.
52. Nevill, *op. cit.*, p.62.
53. Lt. C.M. MacGregor, *Mountain Warfare: An Essay on the Conduct of Hill Operations in Mountainous Countries* (London, 1866), p.19 2nd Ed.
54. Col. J. Adye, *Sitana: A Mountain Campaign on the Borders of Afghanistan in 1863* (London, 1867), pp.34–5.
55. Ibid., p.85 and p.92.
56. Maj. G.V. Fosbery, 'The Umbeyla Expedition', *JRUSI*, 11/46 (1868), p.549.
57. Brig.-Gen. A. Wilde, Commanding Punjaub Irregular Force, to Major S. Black, Secretary to Government, Punjab Military Department, 17th June 1865, P/192/39.
58. Military Department Letter No. 485 of 1865: General, 7th Nov. 1865, and Col. H.W. Norman, Secretary to the Government of India, Military Department, to the Secretary to Government, Punjaub, Simla, 19th Sept. 1865, L/MIL/3/761.
59. Brigade Standing Orders issued by the Brigadier General Commanding Punjab Frontier Force, 6th July 1867, P/436/42.
60. Brig.-Gen. Commanding Punjab Frontier Force, to the Secretary to Government, Punjab, Military Department, 25th Sept. 1867, P/435/44.
61. Brig.-Gen. A. Wilde, Commanding Punjab Frontier Force, to the Secretary to Government, Punjab, Military Department, 24th June 1868, P/435/55.

62. Maj.-Gen. A. Wilde, Commanding Hazara Field Force, to the Q.M.G., 16th Sept. 1868, P/235/57.
63. Maj.-Gen. A. Wilde, Commanding Hazara Field Force, to the Adj.-Gen., 11th Oct. 1868, P/235/57, and Brig.-Gen. A.T. Wilde, 'Circular Memorandum for the information and guidance of Officers Commanding Batteries and Regiments', Huzarah Field Force, Sept. 1868, P/615.
64. To Brigadier-Generals Bright and Vaughan, Commanding Nos. 1 & 2 Brigades, 28th Sept. 1868, P/615.
65. Maj.-Gen. A. Wilde, Commanding Hazara Field Force, to the Adj.-Gen., 26th Oct. 1868, P/435/58.
66. Lt.-Col. P.S. Lumsden, Q.M.G. of the Army, to the Offg. Secretary to the Government of India, Military Department, 5th Nov. 1868, P/435/58.
67. Brig.-Gen. A.T. Wilde, Offg. Military Secretary to the Government Madras, to the Adj.-Gen., 5th May 1869, P/615.
68. Minute by His Excellency General Sir W. Mansfield, 25th Aug. 1869, *Keyes Mss*, Mss.Eur.D.1048/8.
69. Memorandum by Brigadier-General A.T. Wilde, 17th April 1869, and Major S. Black, Secretary to Government, Punjab, to Maj.-Gen. H.W. Norman, Secretary to Government of India, Military Department, 19th March 1870, *Keyes Mss*, Mss.Eur.D.1048/8.
70. Executive Commissariat Officer, Peshawur, to Lt.-Col. T.H. Sibley, Deputy Commissary General, Upper Circle, 2nd April 1872, P/620 and Military Department Despatch No. 434 of 1868: Decision to maintain two Mountain Batteries in the Bengal Presidency, 7th Nov. 1868, L/MIL/3/788.
71. Brig.-Gen. C.H. Brownlow, 'Notes on the Native Army of Bengal: Its present material and organisation, as compared with the past', Sept. 1875, L/MIL/17/2/468.
72. By an Adjutant, *An Essay on Tactics* (London, 1872), p.4.
73. Maj.-Gen. H.W. Norman, 'Memorandum on the Native Army,' 13th Jan. 1875, L/MIL/17/5/1670.
74. Vaughan, *op. cit.*, p.46.
75. See *Field Exercises and Evolutions of Infantry* (London, 1874), E.B. Hamley, *Operations of War* (London, 1866), and Capt. C. Clery, *Minor Tactics* (London, 1875).
76. See Lt. A. Gaselee, 'On the Carriage of Ammunition in Mountain Warfare', *Proc. USII*, 1/3 (1871), p.102, and Maj.-Gen. L. Shadwell, *Mountain Warfare: Illustrated by the Campaign of 1799 in Switzerland* (London, 1875).
77. Brig.-Gen. C.P. Keyes, Commanding Punjab Frontier Force, to Lt.-Col. S. Black, Secretary to Government, Punjab, Military Department, 7th Nov. 1870, P/620.
78. Military Department Separate Letter No. 183 of 1870: Reporting the arming of certain Native Regiments with the Enfield Rifles, 15th July 1870, L/MIL/3/104 and Memorandum from Brig.-Gen. C.P. Keyes, Commanding Punjab Frontier Force, to Captain C.S. McLean, Offg. Secretary to Government, Punjab, Military Department, 22nd Sept. 1871, P/608.
79. Military Department Separate Letter No. 349 of 1869: On the subject of army reduction, 4th Oct. 1869, L/MIL/3/102, and Maj.-Gen. F. Turner, Inspector General of Ordnance & Magazines, to the Secretary to the Government of India, Military Department, 9th Oct. 1868, L/MIL/3/833.

80. J.M. Ewart and E. Howell, *Story of the North-West Frontier Province* (Peshawar, 1930), p.13.

81. Brig.-Gen. C.P. Keyes, Commanding Punjab Frontier Force, to the Secretary to Government, Punjab, Military Department, 19th Oct. 1872, L/MIL/3/831.

82. Brig.-Gen. C.P. Keyes, Commanding Punjab Frontier Force, to Offg. Secretary to Government, Punjab, Military Department, 17th Feb. 1873, P/958, and Lepel Griffin, Offg. Secretary to Government, Punjab, to the Secretary to the Government of India, Foreign Department, 28th Feb. 1873, P/958.

83. Maj. G.A. Furse, *Studies on Military Transport* (Bombay, 1877), p.38.

84. *The Historical records, the 3rd Sikh Infantry, Punjab Frontier Force* (No Imprint: 1903), p.33, *History of the 1st Sikh Infantry, 1846–1886* (Calcutta, 1903), pp.90–1 and *History of the Second Panjab Cavalry* (London, 1888), p.26.

85. Lt.-Col. W.H. Paget, *Expeditions versus the North West Frontier Tribes* (Calcutta, 1874), pp.451–3.

86. Col. S. Black, Secretary to Government, Punjab, Military Department, to Col. H.K. Burne, Secretary to the Government of India, Military Department, 15th Sept. 1876, P/951.

87. Col. S. Black, Secretary to Government, Punjab, Military Department, to Col. H.K. Burne, Secretary to the Government of India, Military Department, 3rd Aug. 1877 L/MIL/3/876 and Brig.-Gen. C.P. Keyes, Commanding Punjab Frontier Force, to Col. S. Black, Secretary to Government, Punjab, Military Department, 13th Nov. 1876, P/951.

88. Lytton to Haines, 27th Sept. 1877, *Haines Mss*, NAM 8108–9–5.

89. *Report on the Administration of the Punjab and its Dependencies for the year 1877–78* (Lahore, 1878), pp.13–14 V/10/335.

90. Capt. E. Walsh, 'Mountain Guns for Indian Frontier Service', *Proc. R.A.I.*, 11 (1881), p.34 and Maj.-Gen. F. Howard, *Reminiscences 1848–1890* (London, 1924), p.254.

91. Brig.-Gen. C.C. Ross, Commanding Field Force Peshawar District, to Q.M.G., 21st Dec. 1877, L/MIL/7/15379.

92. Maj.-Gen. F. Roberts, 'A short account of the operations carried out against the Jowaki section of the Adam Kheyl Afridis' 8th Feb. 1878, L/MIL/7/15378.

93. Col. S. Black, Secretary to Government, Punjab, Military Department to Col. H.K. Burne, Secretary to the Government of India, Military Department, 25th April 1878, L/MIL/7/15379.

94. Capt. J.M. Trotter, 'Narrative of the Jawaki Campaign', *Proc. USII*, 7/31 (1878), p.49.

95. H. Strachan, *From Waterloo to Balaclava: Tactics, Technology and the British Army 1815–1854* (Cambridge, 1985), p.54.

CHAPTER 2

1. See *The Second Afghan War: Compiled and collated under the orders of Major-Genl. Sir C.M. MacGregor* (Simla, 1885), 6 vols.

2. See B. Robson, *The Road to Kabul: The Second Afghan War, 1878–1881* (London, 1986), p.66. See also B. Robson, *Roberts in India The Military Papers of Field Marshal Lord Roberts 1876–1893* (London, 1993) p.4.
3. Surgeon-Major J.H. Evatt, 'Personal Recollections of the Afghan Campaigns of 1878–79–80', *JUSII*, 19/82 (1890), p.305.
4. Col. H.B. Hanna, *The Second Afghan War, 1878–79–80: Its Causes, Its Conduct, and Its Consequences* (Westminster, 1899), Vol. 1 pp.271–8.
5. Memoranda for the Guidance of the Peshawar Field Force by order of Lieut.-General Sir Sam Browne, Commanding 1st Division, 17th Nov. 1878, *Browne Mss*, NAM 7703–49–5.
6. R. Gillham-Thomsett, *Kohât, Kuram, and Khost; or, Experiences and Adventures in the Late Afghan War* (London, 1884), pp.96–7.
7. Lt. M. Martin, 'Tactics in the Afghan Campaign', *JUSII*, 10/47 (1882), p.1.
8. Maj. J.H. Crowe, *An Epitome of the Afghan War, 1878–9 and 1879–80* (Woolwich, 1905), p.26.
9. Lt.-Col. G.T. Pretyman, 'Rough Notes on the Kabul-Kandahar March of August, 1880', *Proc. RAI*, 12 (1884), p.5.
10. Lt. C.G. Robertson, *Kurum, Kabul & Kandahar Being a Brief Account Record of Impressions in Three Campaigns under General Roberts* (Edinburgh, 1881), p.170.
11. Maj. J.A. Colquhoun, *With the Kurrum Field Force* (London, 1881), p.110.
12. Capt. C.B. Mayne, *Infantry Fire Tactics* (Chatham, 1885), pp.390–1.
13. Col. T.L. Bell, 'The Offensive-Defensive by Infantry in Extended Order', *JRUSI* 25/109 (1881), p.157 and Martin *op. cit.*, p.2.
14. Capt. C. Hoskyns, 'A Short Narrative of the Afghan Campaigns of 1879–80–81 from an Engineer's Point of View', *JRUSI*, 26/116 (1882), p.442.
15. Capt. R. Elias, 'A Streak of the Afghan War – Lieutenant General Sir Donald Stewart's March from Kandahar to Ghazni: with actions of Ahmed Khel and Urzu,' *JRUSI* 24/107 (1880), pp.670–1 and Maj. E.S. May, *Achievements of Field Artillery* (Woolwich, 1893), pp.144–51.
16. B. Robson, 'Maiwand, 27th July 1880', *JSAHR*, 51 (1973), pp.194–221.
17. *Report on the Administration of the Punjab and its Dependencies for 1878–79* (Lahore, 1879), pp.22–3 V/10/336.
18. Lt.-Col. E.F. Chapman, 'The March from Kabul to Kandahar in August and the Battle of the 1st September,' *JRUSI* 25/111 (1881), p.286 and Pretyman, *op. cit.*, p.6.
19. Military Department Despatch No. 141 of 1881: Recommendations in regard to the strength of the European troops in India, with reference to the proposals of the Indian Army Commission, 24th April 1881, L/MIL/7/10100 and Maj.-Gen. C.E. Callwell and Maj.-Gen. J. Headlam, *A History of the Royal Artillery from the Indian Mutiny to the Great War* (Woolwich, 1937), pp.263–4.
20. *Manual of Mountain Artillery Drill* (Simla, 1882).
21. Bell, *op. cit.*, pp.157–8.
22. Lt. M. Martin, 'Notes on the Operations in the Kurrum Valley, 1878–79', *JUSII*, 10/47 (1881), p.7.
23. Gen. Sir O. Cavenagh, 'Our Indian Army', *JRUSI*, 26/48 (1882), p.763.

24. Lt. R. de C. Porter, 'Warfare against Uncivilised Races; or, How to fight Greatly Superior Forces of an Uncivilised and Badly-Armed Enemy', *PPRE*, 15 (1881), pp.305–60.
25. Col. W.H. Goodenough, 'General Gordon on the Employment of Artillery in Irregular Warfare', *Proc. RAI*, 8 (1885), pp.121–25, Lt. C.E. Callwell, 'Notes on the Tactics of our Small Wars', *Proc. RAI*, 12 (1884), pp.531–52 and Lt. C.E. Callwell, 'Notes on the Strategy of our Small Wars', *Proc. RAI*, 13 (1885), pp.403–20.
26. See Sir P.L. MacDougall, 'The Late Battles in Soudan and Modern Tactics', *Blackwood's*, 135 (1884), pp.54–60, Maj. C. Cooper King, 'Soudan Warfare', *JRUSI*, 29/81 (1885), pp.887–908 and Lt.-Gen. G. Graham, 'Fire Tactics: Attack Formations and Squares', *JRUSI*, 30/83 (1886), pp.233–74.
27. Col. H.H. Knollys, 'The Present Position of Tactics in England, *USM*, 2 (1884), p.467.
28. Capt. C.E. Callwell, 'Lessons to be Learnt from the Campaigns in which British Forces have been employed since the year 1865', *JRUSI*, 31/139 (1887), p.412.
29. *Short Report on Important Questions dealt with during the tenure of Command of the Army in India by General Lord Roberts 1885–1893* (Simla, 1893), pp.76–8. See *Report of the Camp of Exercise held in the Neighbourhood of Delhi and Umballa 1885–86* (Calcutta, 1886).
30. Military Department Despatch No. 135 of 1885: Proposals for an increase to the Indian Army, 14th Aug. 1885, and Military Despatch No. 275 of 1885, 29th Oct. 1885, L/MIL/7/5446.
31. Military Department Despatch No. 111 of 1886: Transfer of the Punjab Frontier Force under the orders of the Commander-in-Chief India, 6th Aug. 1886, L/MIL/3/136 and Extract from General Order by His Excellency the Governor General In Council, 23rd July 1886, L/MIL/3/961.
32. See L. Harris, *British Policy on the North-West Frontier of India, 1889–1901* (University of London, Ph.D., 1960), pp.1–41.
33. *Standing Orders of the Punjab Frontier Force* (Simla, 1889), p.10 L/MIL/17/5/4310 and *Memoirs of Brigadier-General E.W.S.K. Maconchy 1860–1920* (Unpublished T.S. Memoir), Vol. 1, p.59 NAM 7908–62–1.
34. Capt. W.L. White, 'Mountain Artillery: Its Organisation, Equipment and Tactics', *Proc. RAI*, 15 (1887), pp. 403–17.
35. H.C. Simpson, 'Tactical Employment of Mountain Artillery' *USM* 1 (1888), pp.712–22.
36. Maj. E.J. de Latour, 'Mountain Artillery', *Proc. R.A.I*, 16 (1889), p. 519.
37. See Capt. A.H. Mason, *Expedition against the Black Mountain tribes by a force under Major-General Sir J.W. McQueen in 1888* (Simla, 1889). L/MIL/17/13/52.
38. Roberts to Galbraith, 21st Sept. 1888, L/MIL/17/5/1615/11.
39. Circular Memorandum for the information and guidance of Officers Commanding Batteries and Regiments, Hazara Field Force, 30th Sept. 1888, L/MIL/17/5/1615/11.
40. Maj.-Gen. J.W. McQueen, Commanding Hazara Field Force, to Adj.-Gen. in India, 19th Nov. 1888, P/3484.
41. E.M. Spiers, *The Late Victorian Army 1868–1902* (Manchester, 1992), p.250.

42. Capt. A.H. Mason, 'The Miranzai Expedition of 1891', *JRUSI*, 36/168 (1892), p.123.
43. E.P. Oliver, 'Punitive Operations on the North-West Frontier of India', *Fortnightly Review*, 50 (1891), p.93.
44. E.F. Knight, *Where Three Empires Meet: A Narrative of Recent Travel in Kashmir, Western Tibet, Gilgit, and the adjoining Countries* (London, 1893), p.373 and Capt. H.L. Nevill, *Campaigns on the North-West Frontier* (London, 1912), p.365.
45. *Infantry Drill* (London, 1889), pp.207–8.
46. Lt.-Col. E. Paquie, 'Warfare in Mountainous Countries', *JUSII*, 21/98 (1892), pp.525–43.
47. Capt. H.V. Cox, 'Jungle Fighting', *JUSII*, 21/97 (1892), pp.443–7.
48. *Infantry Drill (Provisional)* (London, 1892), p.185.
49. Lt.-Col. E. Gunter, *Outlines of Modern Tactics* (London, 1893) and Capt. J. Sherston, *Tactics as Applied to Schemes* (London, 1894), pp.49–50.
50. Maj. G.M. Bullock, 'Mountain Warfare as Applied to India', *JUSII*, 22/107 (1893), p.330.
51. Capt. F.C. Carter, 'Mountain Warfare as Applied to India', *JUSII*, 22/110 (1893), pp.414–66.
52. *Infantry Drill* (London, 1893).
53. Maj. H.C. Simpson, 'Notes on Mountain Artillery Establishments, their Training, and Personal Equipment,' *Proc. RAI* 21 (1894), p.265.
54. See *Report on the Mountain Artillery Practice Camps at Dhagul and Rajpur, 1892–93* (Simla, 1893) and *Report on the Mountain Artillery Practice Camps held at Rajpur, Dhagul, and Paniala in 1893–94* (Simla, 1894). L/MIL/7/10831.
55. Capt. F.C. Carter, 'On the Tactical training in District Concentrations, Best Prepared for Preparing the Army in India for War:- (a) Against a Civilised Enemy. (b) Against Savage Tribes in Mountain or Jungle Warfare', *JUSII*, 23/117 (1894), p.146.
56. Ibid., p.175.
57. Capt. W.G. Hamilton, 'On the Tactical Training in District Concentrations best fitted for Preparing the Army in India for War', *JUSII*, 23/119 (1894), pp.103–4.
58. Ibid., pp.105–7.
59. Maj. O.C. Radford, *Notes for Panjab Probationers on 1. Castes 2. Hill Tactics 3. Customs 4. Idiomatic Sentences* (Lahore, 1894), pp.25–31.
60. Brig.-Gen. A.H. Turner to Adj.-Gen. in India, 16th Nov. 1894, L/MIL/7/15362.
61. See Lt.-Col. A.H. Mason and Lt. G.K. Cockerill, *Operations against the Mahsud Waziris by a force under the command of Lieutenant-General Sir William Stephen Alexander Lockhart in 1894–95, with a short account of the events which led up to the expedition* (Simla, 1897) L/MIL/17/13/108.
62. See Capt. W.R. Robertson, *An Official Account of the Chitral Expedition 1895* (Calcutta, 1898) and Capt. G.J. Younghusband and Capt. F.E. Younghusband, *The Relief of Chitral* (London, 1895).
63. Field Marshal Sir W. Robertson, *From Private to Field Marshal* (London, 1921), p.71.

64. *The Chitral Expedition 1895 containing an account of the adventures and captivity of Lieutenants Fowler and Edwards together with full details of the operations of General Low's force* (Allahabad, 1895), p.29.

65. GOC Chitral Relief Force. to the Adj.-Gen. in India, 5th April 1895, *White Mss*, Mss.Eur.F.108/35.

66. Townshend to Durand, 25th April 1895, *White Mss*, Mss.Eur.F.108/37 and Lt. C.G. Stewart, 'An Account of the Relief of Chitral Fort from Gilgit and the Siege of Chitral', *Proc. RAI*, 22 (1895), pp.399–404.

67. T.R. Moreman, 'The Arms Trade and the North-West Frontier Pathan Tribes, 1890–1914', *JICH*, 22/2 (1994), pp.191–2.

68. See H.C. Thomson, *The Chitral Campaign: A Narrative of Events in Chitral, Swat and Bajour* (London, 1895), Capt. F.E. Younghusband, 'The Chitral Campaign', *JRUSI*, 40/215 (1895), pp.5–23, Capt. G.F. Herbert, 'The Artillery in Chitral, *Proc. RAI,* 22 (1895), pp.501–10 and Maj. A.W. Radcliffe, 'Convoy Escort Duties in Mountain Warfare', *JUSII*, 24/121 (1895), pp.226–8.

69. Maj. F.C. Carter, 'Mountain Warfare in India', *JRUSI*, 39/213 (1895), pp.1071–1100.

70. A Frontier Soldier, 'Notes on Mountain Warfare', *JUSII*, 25/124 (1896), pp.19–43.

71. Lt.-Col. E. Gunter, *Outlines of Modern Tactics* (London, 1895), p.239.

72. T. Miller Maguire, 'Our Art of War as Made in Germany,' *USM* 13 (1896), p.126.

73. Maj.-Gen. E.A. Wood, comments on Maj. W.D. Conner, 'Incidents of Bush Warfare', *Proc. RAI*, 23 (1896), p.92.

74. Capt. C.E. Callwell, *Small Wars: Their Principles and Practice* (London, 1896).

75. 'Small Wars: Their Principles and Practice by Captain C.E. Callwell, R.A.', *JUSII*, 25/125 (1896), pp.228–9.

76. See Maj. G.V. Kemball, *Operations of the Tochi Field Force in 1897–98* (Simla, 1900) L/MIL/17/13/101.

77. Capt. H.F. Walters, *The Operations of the Malakand Field Force and the Buner Field Force 1897–98* (Simla, 1900), pp.15–20 L/MIL/17/13/55.

78. Maj.-Gen. Sir B. Blood, Commanding the Malakand Force, to the Adj.-Gen. in India, 14th Aug. 1897, P/5477.

79. B. Blood, *Four Score Years and Ten: Sir Bindon Blood's Reminiscences* (London, 1933), p.302.

80. Lt. Viscount Fincastle and lt. P.C. Elliot-Lockhart, *A Frontier Campaign: A Narrative of the Malakand and Buner Field Forces on the North West Frontiers of India* (London, 1898), pp.133–4 and GOC Malakand Field Force to Adj.-Gen. in India, 18th Sept. 1897, L/P&S/7/97.

81. Jefferys to White, 21st Sept. 1897, *White Mss*, Mss.Eur.F.108/38.

82. Maj.-Gen. Sir Bindon Blood to Adj.-Gen. 20th and 21st Sept. 1897, L/P&S/7/96.

83. GOC Malakand Field Force to Adj.-Gen. in India, 2nd Oct. 1897, L/P&S/7/97.

84. Maj.-Gen. Sir B. Blood, Commanding the Malakand Field Force, to the Adj.-Gen. in India, 27th Oct. 1897, P/5477.

85. Blood to White, 7th Oct. 1897, *White Mss*, Mss.Eur.F.108/38.

86. Foreign Department Despatch No. 143 of 1897 (Frontier): Disturbances on the North-Western Frontier, 14th Oct. 1897, L/P&S/7/96.
87. White to Elgin, 1st Sept. 1897, *Elgin Mss*, Mss.Eur.F.84/71 and Capt. H.F. Walters, *Operations of the Tirah Expeditionary Force 1897–98, under the command of General Sir William Stephen Alexander Lockhart* (Simla, 1900), p.3 L/MIL/17/13/99.
88. Revised Scheme for an Expeditionary Force against the Afridi and Orakzai Tribes on the Peshawar and Kohat Borders, L/MIL/7/15867 and *Report on the Working of the Army Veterinary Department with the Tirah Expeditionary Force 1897–98* (Calcutta, 1898), p.1.
89. *Report on the Commissariat-Transport Arrangements of the Tirah Expeditionary Force, 1897–98* (Calcutta, 1899), p.54 L/MIL/17/5/1856.
90. H.W. Mills, *The Tirah Campaign – being the Sequel of the Pathan Revolt in North-West India* (Lahore, 1898), pp.40–2.
91. Wylly, *op. cit.*, p.vii.
92. Standing Orders by General Sir. W.S.A. Lockhart, Commanding Tirah Expeditionary Force, 9th Oct. 1897, NAM '1997–98' (549.14).
93. Capt. A.K. Slessor, *The Second Battalion Derbyshire Regiment in Tirah* (London, 1900) p.44 and p.95.
94. General Officer Commanding, Tirah Expeditionary Force, Fort Lockhart, to the Adj.-Gen. in India, 18th Oct. 1897, L/P&S/7/96.
95. GOC TEF to Adj.-Gen. in India, 20th Oct. 1897, L/P&S/7/97, Yeatman Biggs to White, 23rd Oct. 1897, *White Mss*, Mss.Eur.F.108/38 and Lt.-Gen. Sir G.F. MacMunn, 'The Storming of Dargai (20th December 1897)', *A.Q.*, 17, 2 (1928), pp.370–9.
96. Foreign Department Despatch No. 158 of 1897 (Frontier): Correspondence regarding the Tirah Afridis and the Orakzai tribe, and the punitive expedition sent against them under General Sir W. Lockhart, 11th Nov. 1897, L/P&S/7/97.
97. Gen. Sir W.S. Lockhart, Commanding Officer TEF, to Adj.-Gen. in India, 9th Dec. 1897, P/5477.
98. Col. C.E. Callwell, *Tirah 1897* (London, 1911), p.64 and Field Marshal Lord Birdwood, *Khaki and Gown: An Autobiography* (London, 1942), p.85.
99. Col. L. James, *High Pressure: Being Some Record of Activities in the Service of the Times Newspaper* (London, 1929), p.34.
100. Lt.-Col. Sir F. O'Connor, *On the Frontier and Beyond: A Record of Thirty Years' Service* (London, 1931), p.11.
101. Gen. Sir A. Haldane, *A Soldier's Saga: The Autobiography of General Sir Alymer Haldane* (Edinburgh and London, 1948), pp.107–8.
102. GOC Tirah Expeditionary Force to Adj.-Gen. in India, 30th Oct. 1897, L/MIL/7/15867.
103. Gen. Sir W.S.A. Lockhart, Commanding T.E.F. to the Adj.-Gen. in India, 9th Dec. 1897, L/MIL/7/15887 and Capt. L.J. Shadwell, *Lockhart's Advance Through Tirah* (London, 1898), pp.11–12.
104. GOC TEF to Adj.-Gen. in India, 31st Oct./1st Nov. 1897, L/MIL/7/15867.
105. GOC TEF to Adj.-Gen. in India, 3rd Nov. 1897, L/MIL/7/15867.
106. GOC TEF to Adj.-Gen. in India, 16th Nov. 1897, L/MIL/7/15867.
107. Col. T.H. Holdich, *The Indian Borderland* (London, 1901), p.362.
108. Mills, *op cit.* pp.119–20 and Birdwood, *op. cit.*, p.86.

109. Lt.-Col. R.G. Thomsett, *With the Peshawar Column, Tirah Expeditionary Force* (London, 1899), pp.212–13.
110. GOC TEF to Foreign Secretary, 5th Nov. 1897, L/P&S/7/97.
111. A.H. Atteridge, *The Wars of the 'Nineties. A History of Warfare in the Last Ten Years of the Nineteenth Century* (London, 1899), p.511.
112. Lt.-Col. G.F.R. Henderson, *Technical Training of Infantry* (Dublin, 1899), pp.9–10.
113. Maconchy, *op. cit.*, pp.239–40.
114. GOC TEF to Adj.-Gen. in India, 10th Nov. 1897, L/P&S/7/97.
115. Maconchy, *op. cit.*, p.225.
116. Military Department Despatch No. 4 of 1898: Enquiry into the circumstances attending the losses sustained by the Northamptonshire Regiment in Tirah, on the 9th November 1897, 4th Jan. 1898, L/MIL/7/15882 and Lockhart to Adj.-Gen. in India, 26th Jan. 1898, L/MIL/7/15887.
117. Lockhart to White, 16th Nov. 1897, *White Mss*, Mss.Eur.F.108/38.
118. Gen. Sir W.S. Lockhart to Adj.-Gen. in India, 14th Nov. 1897. L/MIL/7/15882.
119. Col. H.D. Hutchinson, *The Campaign in Tirah, 1897–1898* (London, 1898), p.124.
120. Gough, *op. cit.*, p.58.
1201. GOC TEF to Foreign Secretary, 17th Nov. 1897, L/P&S/7/99.
122. GOC TEF to Adj.-Gen. in India, 20th Nov. 1897, *White Mss*, Mss.Eur.F.108/43.
123. Gen. E.G. Barrow, 'Campaign Diaries', *Barrow Mss*, Mss.Eur.E.420/27, p.21, G.R. de H. Smith, 'Personal Diary during Malakand Expedition and Operations of Tirah Expeditionary Force, 1897, pp.116–7 *Smith Mss* Mss.Eur.B.203/6 and Hutchinson, *op. cit.*, pp.146–7.
124. 'Field Force Memorandum', 18th Nov. 1897, *White Mss*, Mss.Eur.F.108/38.
125. Callwell 1911, *op. cit.*, p.105.
126. Col. Sir R. Warburton, *Eighteen Years on the Khyber, 1879–1898* (London, 1900), p.307.
127. GOC TEF to Adj.-Gen. in India, 12th Dec. 1897, L/P&S/7/99.
128. James, *op. cit.*, p.43.
129. Thomsett, *op. cit.*, pp.146–7.
130. Gen. Sir W.S.A. Lockhart, Commanding the Tirah Expeditionary Force, to the Adj.-Gen. in India, 4th April 1898, L/MIL/7/15887.
131. Lt.-Gen. Sir A.P. Palmer to Chief of Staff, TEF, 31st Jan. 1898, L/MIL/7/15899.
132. Foreign Department Despatch No. 69 of 1898 (Frontier): Settlement with the Afridis and the opening of the Khyber Pass, 5th May 1898, L/P&S/7/103.

CHAPTER 3

1. K.M. Saxena, *The Military System of India (1850–1900)* (New Delhi, 1974), pp.268–9.
2. *Summary of Measures considered or carried out in the Military Department of the Government of India during the Viceroyalty of the Earl of Elgin and Kincardine, January 1895 to December 1899* (Calcutta, 1899), p.55.

3. Government General Order publishing numerical and amended nominal returns of killed, wounded, and missing in the Tirah Expeditionary Force from the 12th October 1897 to the 6th April 1898, 3rd June 1898, L/MIL/3/1082.
4. Adj.-Gen. in India to the Secretary to the Government of India Military Department, 24th Feb. 1898, L/MIL/7/15887.
5. Foreign Department Despatch No. 120 of 1899 (Frontier): Returns showing in detail the results of the examination of rifled arms surrendered by tribes on the North-West Frontier, 22nd June 1898, L/P&S/7/114.
6. Lockhart to Elgin, 16th Dec. 1897, *Elgin Mss*, Mss.Eur.F.84/71.
7. Haughton to Gough, 16th Jan. 1898, *Gough Mss*, NAM 8304–32–404.
8. North-Western Frontier Arms Trade Committee to the Secretary to the Government of India Foreign Department, 18th April 1899, L/P&S/7/114.
9. Col. Sir T.H. Holdich, 'Tirah', *Geographic Journal*, 12/4 (1898), p.357.
10. See Foreign Department Despatch No. 147 of 1901 (Frontier): Measures adopted in view to stopping the illicit trade in arms and ammunition on the North-West Frontier, 29th Aug. 1901, L/P&S/7/136.
11 Curzon to Hamilton, 4th Sept. 1901, *Curzon Mss*, Mss.Eur.F.111/160.
12. Hamilton to Elgin, 21st Jan. 1897 and 11th Feb. *Elgin Mss*, Mss.Eur.F.84/16, Elgin to Brackenbury, 23rd Jan. 1898, *Elgin Mss*, Mss.Eur.F.84/33a and A.H. Atteridge, *The Wars of the 'Nineties. A History of Warfare in the Last Ten Years of the Nineteenth Century* (London, 1899), p.533.
13. 'Guerrilla', 'The North-West Frontier', *Imperial and Asiatic Quarterly Review*, 8, 15 (1899), pp.42–3.
14. L. Oppenheim, 'The Tirah and Khartoum Expeditions', *Nineteenth Century*, 44/262 (1898), pp.1041–7 and L. James, *The Indian Frontier War – Being an Account of the Mohmund and Tirah Expeditions 1897* (London, 1898), p.vii.
15. Capt. F.M. Edwards, 'Recent Frontier Warfare', *JUSII*, 27/132 (1898), p.335.
16. Maj.-Gen. C.E. Callwell and Maj.-Gen. J. Headlam, *A History of the Royal Artillery from the Indian Mutiny to the Great War* (Woolwich, 1937), p.266.
17. 'The North-West Frontier: By a Frontier Political Officer', *Imperial and Asiatic Quarterly Review*, 5/9 (1898), pp.5–6.
18. Nicholson to Spenser Wilkinson, 2nd March 1898, *Spenser Wilkinson Mss*, NAM 9011–42–13.
19. Atteridge, *op. cit.*, pp.533–4.
20. *Memoirs of Brigadier-General E.W.S.K. Maconchy 1860–1920* (Unpublished T.S. Memoir), Vol. I, p.222 NAM 7908–62–1.
21 Maj. A.C. Yate, 'North-West Frontier Warfare', *JRUSI*, 42/248 (1898), pp.1191–2.
22. Col. H.D. Hutchinson, 'The Story of Tirah and the Lessons of the Campaign', *JUSII*, 27/132 (1898), p.243.
23. Collen, comments on Ibid., pp.255–6.
24. Morton, comments on Ibid., pp.256–7.
25. Lt.-Col. J.A. Pollock, 'Notes on Hill Warfare', *JUSII*, 27/131 (1898), pp.131–47, R.C., 'Proposal for Infantry Attack in Mountain Warfare', *JUSII*, 27/132 (1898), pp.479–80, and Capt. H.T. Kenny, 'A German

Account of the North-West Frontier Campaign', *JUSII*, 27/132 (1898), pp.481–98.

26. Lt.-Col. J.A. Pollock, *Notes on Hill Warfare* (Simla, 1898).

27. Col. J.P.C. Neville, 'The Tactical Principles and Details Best Suited to Warfare on the Frontiers of India', *JUSII*, 28/136 (1899), pp.191–223, Lt.-Col. H.H. Hart, 'The Tactical Principles and Details Best Suited to Warfare on the Frontiers of India', *JUSII*, 28/136 (1899), pp.244–72, Capt. E. Peach, 'The Tactical Principles and Details Best Suited to Warfare on the Frontiers of India', *JUSII*, 28/137 (1899), pp.329–60 and Lt.-Col. J.G. Ramsey, 'The Tactical principles and Details Best Suited to Warfare on the Frontiers of India', *JUSII*, 29/138 (1900), pp.85–110.

28. Lt. W.L. Churchill, *Story of the Malakand Field Force. An Epitome of Frontier Warfare* (London, 1898), pp.283–301 and Col. H.D. Hutchinson, *The Campaign in Tirah, 1897–98* (London, 1898), pp.224–46.

29. Capt. L.J. Shadwell, *Lockhart's Advance Through Tirah* (London, 1898).

30. Capt. and Brevet Maj. G.J. Younghusband, *Indian Frontier Warfare* (London, 1898).

31 Brig.-Gen. C.E. Egerton, *Hill Warfare on the North West Frontier of India* (Allahabad, 1899), p.1.

32. Lt.-Col. A.R. Martin, *Mountain and Savage Warfare* (Allahabad, 1898), 2nd ed. 1899.

33. Maj. E. Peach, *Handbook of Tactics for Savage Warfare* (Allahabad, 1898). 2nd ed.

34. Maj. E.H. Rodwell, *Four Bangalore Lectures* (Lahore, 1899).

35. Lt.-Col. F.H. Plowden, *The Battalion on the Frontier* (Lahore, 1899).

36. Peach 1899, *op. cit.*, p.344.

37. Capt. A.A. Campbell, 'The Limitations of Infantry Fire Control and Discipline', *JUSII*, 330/143 (1901), p.120.

38. Neville, *op. cit.*, pp.219–20.

39. Gen. Sir W.S. Lockhart to the Adj.-Gen. in India, 26th Jan. 1898, L/MIL/7/15887.

40. Lockhart to White, 16th Nov. 1897, *White Mss*, Mss.Eur.F.108/38, and Deputy Secretary to the Government of India, Military Department to the Adj.-Gen. in India, 7th Feb. 1898, L/MIL/7/15886.

41 'The Gurkha Scouts', *Blackwood's*, 165/502 (1899), pp.802–15, Peach 1899, *op. cit.*, pp.332–4, and Ramsey, *op. cit.*, p.109.

42. Capt. R.G. Burton, 'Shikar as Training for Scouts', 28/134, *JUSII*, 28/134 (1899), pp.88–90 and Lt. R.D. Alexander, 'A System of Training Scouts for Hill Warfare', *JUSII*, 33/157 (1904), pp.397–406.

43. See E.M. Spiers, 'The Use of the Dum Dum Bullet in Colonial Warfare', *JICH*, 4/1 (1975), pp.3–14.

44. Principal Medical Officer, Tirah Expeditionary Force, to the Principal Medical Officer, Her Majesty's Forces in India, 10th March 1898, L/MIL/7/12026.

45. Military Department Despatch No. 149 of 1900: Reserves of ammunition to be maintained in India. Proportion of bullets of Indian pattern, 11th Oct. 1900 and Military Department Despatch No. 81 of 1901: Retention in regimental charge of ammunition with Mk II, I.P bullets at certain stations near the North-West Frontier of India, 13th June 1901 L/MIL/7/12030.

46. Maj. F.W. Cardew, Deputy Secretary to Government of India Military Dept. to Adj.-Gen. in India, 5th Aug. 1902 L/MIL/7/12030.

47. Capt. M.E. Carthew Yorstoun, 'Machine Guns', *JUSII*, 27/131 (1898), pp.208–19, and Lt. H.P. de la Bere, 'With Machine Guns in Tirah', *USM*, 19 (1899–1900), pp.165–72.

48. Capt. G.F. MacMunn, 'The Artillery at Dargai', *Proc. RAI*, 25 (1898), pp.173–78.

49. Military Department Despatch No. 31 of 1898: Addition of another Battery of Native Mountain Artillery to the Establishment of the Army in India, 24th Feb. 1898, L/MIL/7/10133 and Military Department Despatch No. 194 of 1899: Improvements in the organisation of the horse, field, and mountain, batteries on India, 2nd Nov. 1899, L/MIL/7/10139.

50. QMG in India, to the Secretary to the Government of India, Military Department, L/MIL/7/15867.

51 GOC TEF to the Inspector General of Artillery in India, 27th Nov. 1897, L/MIL/7/15886.

52. Maj.-Gen. Sir B. Blood, Commanding the Malakand Force, to the Adj.-Gen. in India, 27th Oct. 1897, P/5477 and Lt. C.B. Ballard, 'The Diary of the 10th Field Battery R.A., with the Malakand Field Force', *Proc. RAI*, 25 (1898), pp.419–38.

53. Inspector-General of Artillery to the Lt.-Gen. Commanding the Forces, Punjab, 27th Oct. 1897, L/MIL/7/15867 and Capt. G.F. MacMunn, 'The Artillery in the Indian Campaigns of 1897–8', *Proc. R.A.I.*, 26 (1899), pp.229–42.

54. Capt. W.B. James, 'The Training and Equipment of Cavalry and Mounted Infantry in India and their Respective Roles in War', *JUSII*, 32/150 (1903), pp.34–76 and Capt. D.C. Crombie, 'Cavalry in Frontier Warfare', *JUSII*, 39/178 (1910), pp.109–18.

55. Yate, *op. cit.*, pp.1171–93.

56. Ibid., p.1191.

57. Lt.-Col. G.F.R. Henderson, *Technical Training of Infantry* (Dublin, 1899), p.18.

58. Maj.-Gen. W.F. Gatacre, 'A Few Notes on the Characteristics of Hill-Fighting in India, and Training of Infantry Necessary for same Possible in England', *JRUSI*, 43/260 (1899), p.1066.

59. Ibid., pp.1080–1.

60. Maj. C.E. Callwell, *Small Wars: Their Principles and Practice* (London, 1899), pp.346–7.

61 'Life on the Punjab frontier', *Navy & Army Illustrated*, 7 (1898), p.45.

62. Maj. A. Keene, 'The British Soldier in India', *JUSII*, 27/132 (1898), pp.406–7.

63. Hart, *op. cit.*, p.268, Peach, *op. cit.*, pp.357–8 and Maj. A.C. Yate, 'Sixty Years of Frontier Warfare', *JRUSI*, 44/286 (1900), pp.223–4.

64. Anon., 'Lessons in Hill Fighting', *Navy & Army Illustrated*, 7 (1899), p.415, Atteridge, *op. cit.*, pp.533–4, and Henderson, *op. cit.*, pp.12–3.

65. From QMG in India, 20th Oct. 1898, P/5475 and Command Order by the Lieutenant-General Commanding the Forces in Bengal, 18th Oct. 1898, L/MIL/17/5/356.

66. *Report on the Attock Manoeuvres March 1899* (Simla, 1899), p.23, *Dening Mss* NAM 7810–106–40.

67. *Report on the Attock Manoeuvres February 1900* (Simla, 1900), p.63 L/MIL/17/5/1807.
68. Lt.-Gen. R. Baden-Powell, *Indian Memories; Recollections of Soldiering, Sport, Etc.* (London, 1915), pp.272–5.
69. Yate 1900, *op. cit.*, p.243.
70. *Mountain Warfare* (Simla, 1900), Preface.
71 *Frontier Warfare 1901* (Calcutta, 1901).
72. *Infantry Drill (Provisional)* (London, 1902).
73. See Lt.-Col. E. Gunter, *Outlines of Modern Tactics* (London, 1899), pp.259–69, Maj.-Gen. Sir R.C. Hart, *Reflections on the Art of War* (London, 1901), 3rd Ed. pp.342a–342l and Maj. L.J. Shadwell, *North-West Frontier Warfare: Being an Appendix to Sherston's 'Tactics as Applied to Schemes'* (Calcutta, 1902).
74. Hamilton to Elgin, 21st Jan. 1898, *Elgin Mss*, Mss.Eur.F.84/16, and Anon., 'The Tirah Campaign – An Eye Witness', *Fortnightly Review*, 63/375 (1898), p.393.
75. Hamilton to Elgin, 4th March 1898, *Elgin Mss*, Mss.Eur.F.84/16.
76. See Military Department Despatch No. 30 of 1898: Manner in which Brigadier-General Kempster exercised his command during the operations in Tirah, 24th Feb. 1898 L/MIL/7/15892.
77. Lt.-Gen. Sir G.F. MacMunn, *The Romance of the Indian Frontiers* (London, 1931), p.239.
78. Lt.-Col. J.E. Nixon, *Notes for Staff Officers on Field Service* (Lahore, 1897) 2nd Ed. 1898.
79. Hart, *op. cit.*, p.269 and Shadwell 1902, *op. cit.*, p.vii and pp.93–6.
80. T. Miller-Maguire, *Strategy and Tactics in Mountain Ranges* (London, 1904), p.5. See also T. Miller-Maguire, *Analysis of Callwell's Small Wars* (London, 1902).
81 Maj. F.G. Marsh, 'The Afridi and Orakzai Country', *A.R.*, 7 (1914), p.29.
82. Gen. Sir G. de S. Barrow, *The Fire of Life* (London, 1941), p.116.
83. *Notes on Staff Duties in Hill Warfare in India for the use of Officers attending Staff Rides* (London, 1906).
84. *Records of the Staff College, Quetta. (Established 1905)* (Simla, 1908), pp. 4 and 10.
85. Brig.-Gen. W. Braithwaite, 'The Staff College, Quetta', *AR* 3 (1912), p.418.
86. Brevet.-Maj. W.D. Bird, *Some Principles of Frontier Mountain Warfare* (London, 1909).
87. Maj.-Gen. E. Collen and A.C. Yate, 'Our Position on the North-West Frontier', *Empire Review*, 2/10 (1901), p.388.
88. Military Department Despatch No. 186 of 1902: Proposed reconstitution of the commands and staff of the military districts on the North-West Frontier, 2nd Oct. 1902, L/MIL/7/7455.
89. R.S. Dey, *A Brief Account of the Punjab Frontier Force* (Calcutta, 1905), p.3.
90. Manoeuvres held at Bannu on 3rd November 1903, under Brig-General J.B. Woon, Commanding Bannu Tochi Force, Nov. 1903, *Dening Mss*, NAM 7810–106–44.
91 Lt.-Gen. Sir G.F. MacMunn, *Behind the Scenes in Many Wars* (London, 1930), p.82.

92. Maj.-Gen. L. Dening, Commanding Vth (Mhow) Division to Brig.-Gen. T. Capper, 14th July 1906, *Dening Mss*, NAM 7810–106–55.

93. Capt. A.W. Taylor, *Jungle Warfare: the conduct of small expeditions in the jungles and hilly tracts of Burma, and a system of drill and musketry instruction connected therewith, for the use of officers of the Burma Military Police* (Rangoon, 1902).

94. Maj. C.B. Morgan, *Hints on Bush Fighting* (London, 1899) and Lt.-Col. A.F. Montanaro, *Hints for a Bush Campaign* (London, 1901).

95. *Bush Fighting. (An Appendix to 'Frontier Warfare')* (Calcutta, 1903).

96. *Frontier Warfare and Bush Fighting* (Calcutta, 1906).

97. GOC Bazar Valley Force to Foreign Secretary, 21st Feb. and 25th Feb. 1908, L/P&S/10/46.

98. Lt.-Col. G.O. Roos-Keppel, 'Political Report of the Bazar Valley Expedition, 4th March 1908, L/P&S/10/46.

99. Minto to Morley, 23rd March 1908, *Morley Mss*, Mss.Eur.D.573/14.

100. C.W. Miles, *The Zakka Khel and Mohmand Expedition* (Rawalpindi, 1909), p.13, and Maj. G.F. MacMunn, 'The Old Frontier Story', *Fortnightly Review*, 27/158 (1909), p.251.

101   Gen. Sir J. Willcocks, *The Romance of Soldiering and Sport* (London, 1925), pp.234–5, and Lt. A.H. Burn, 'The Mohmand Expedition. Some Reminiscences', *USM*, 38 (1909), pp.317–8.

102. *Report on Brigade Training, Bannu Brigade, under the orders of Major-General C.G.M. Fasken, Commanding Bannu Brigade. February 1908* (Allahabad, 1908).

103. Birdwood, *op. cit.*, pp.206–7. See also *Field Service Standing Orders for the Kohat Brigade by Brigadier-General W.R. Birdwood Commanding Kohat Brigade* (Roorkee, 1911).

104. 'The General Staff in India', *AR*, 2 (1912), p.22.

105. Gen. Sir O. Creagh, 'The Army in India and the New Field Service Regulations', *AR*, 4 (1913), pp.31–9.

106. Ibid., pp.34–5.

107. *Field Service Regulations, Part I Operations 1909 (Reprinted with Amendments 1912)* (London, 1912), pp.191–212.

108. Maj. E.J. Wood, 'Specialisation in Training', *JUSII*, 40/183 (1911), pp.165–69.

109. By a C.O., 'Reflections on the Training of the Infantry Officer', *JUSII*, 40/183 (1911), p.147.

110. Col. C.E. Callwell, *Tirah 1897* (London, 1911).

111   Capt. H.L. Nevill, *Campaigns on the North-West Frontier* (London, 1912).

112. Col. H.C. Wylly, *From the Black Mountain to Waziristan* (London, 1912).

113. Col. W.E. Venour, 'Training for Frontier Warfare', *JUSII*, 42/193 (1913), p.381.

114. Ibid., pp.382–9.

115. Sir. P. Lake, comment on Ibid. p.389–90.

116. *Proceedings of the Army in India Committee, 1912. Vol. II Minutes of Evidence* (Simla, 1913), p.163 L/MIL/17/5/1751/3.

117. *Notes on the Indian Frontiers* (Simla, 1912), pp.43–4 and Nevill, *op. cit.*, pp.365–81.

118. Annual Return showing the Class Composition, Countries and Establishments of the Indian Army, Imperial Service Troops, Military Police and Militia on 1st January 1908, L/MIL/7/17084.
119. Moreman, *op. cit.*, pp.204–10.
120. Statement of Fighting Strengths and Armament of Independent Tribes on the North-West frontier (Cis-Durand Line), 27th June 1910, L/P&S/7/242.
121 *Report on the Arms Traffic. 1st July 1911 to 30th June 1913. (Including a Note on the Operations of the Makran Field Force in April and May 1911)* (Simla, 1913) L/MIL/7/168641.
122. F. Lovat, *Arms Traffic* (London, 1911), p.43.

CHAPTER 4

1. L. Baha. *N.-W.F.P. Administration under British Rule 1901–1919* (Islamabad, 1978), pp.81–3.
2. Despatch by His Excellency General Sir C.C. Monro, Commander-in-Chief in India, on the part played by India, including the Indian States, in the prosecution of the war, 9th April 1919, L/MIL/7/18779 and *Summary of the Administration of Lord Hardinge of Penshurst November 1910–March 1916* (Delhi, 1916), p.92 V/27/230/72.
3. *Report on the Principal Measures taken in India during the War to Maintain Training at the Standard required in Modern War* (Calcutta, 1919), p.2 and App. A L/MIL/7/5466 (Hereafter *Report on Principal Measures*).
4. Ibid., App. B.
5. See *Despatch by His Excellency General Sir Charles Carmichael Monro, C-in-C India, on the minor military operations undertaken from March 1916 to March 1917 on the North-West Frontier of India, and elsewhere in the Indian Empire, including Aden, also in South and South-East Persia* (Simla, 1917), pp.3–4 L/MIL/3/1116.
6. *Report of a Conference of General Officers held at Delhi 22nd to 24th February 1917 under the direction of His Excellency the Commander-in-Chief in India* (Delhi, 1917), pp.21–5 L/MIL/17/5/1759.
7. Ibid., pp.25–6.
8. *Report of the Attack by Mahsuds on a Convoy Proceeding from Nili Kach to Khajuri Kach 1st May 1917* (Simla, 1917), L/MIL/7/15933.
9. GOC Northern Command to CGS, 2nd May 1917, L/P&S/10/373.
10. CGS to GOC Northern Army, 3rd May 1917, L/P&S/10/373.
11. R.M. Maxwell (ed.), *Villiers-Stuart goes to War* (Edinburgh, 1990), pp.192–200 and Government of India Army Department to CGS, 3rd May 1917, L/MIL/7/18930.
12. *The Diaries of Harry Ross* (Unpublished T.S. Memoir, 1929), p.71, *Ross Mss*, Mss.Eur.B.235/3.
13. See Lt.-Col. G.M. Baldwin, 'Some Experiences of Indian Cavalry in Frontier Warfare', *JUSII*, 44/199 (1915), pp.179–88, Capt. A.H. Beaman, 'Mohmand Shows', *JUSII*, 45/205 (1916), pp.405–23 and Maj. I. Battye,'Frontier Mountain Warfare', *JUSII*, 46/206 (1917), pp.91–126.

14. See *Despatch by Lieutenant-General Sir Arthur Arnold Barrett, commanding the Northern Army, on the operations against the Mahsuds, March-August 1917* (Simla, 1917), L/MIL/17/13/112.
15. Maj. F.O. Wyatt, 'Mountain Guns for Mountain Warfare', *JUSII*, 47/210 (1918), p.103.
16. Government of India Army Department to CGS, 15th May 1918, L/MIL/7/18930.
17. G. Dunbar, *Frontiers* (London, 1932), pp.301–2.
18. See *Notes on Trans-Border Warfare with special reference to the Combination of Various Arms and Weapons* (Calcutta, 1918) 2nd Ed. 1919.
19. *Report on Principal Measures*, p.18.
20. See *Despatch by His Excellency General Sir Charles Carmichael Monro on the Third Afghan War* (Simla, 1919) L/MIL/17/14/68 (hereafter *Despatch on Third Afghan War)* and *The Third Afghan War 1919. Official History* (Calcutta, 1926) (hereafter *Official History 1919*).
21. *Despatch on Third Afghan War*, p.10 and *Official History 1919*, p.49.
22. Major G.H. Russell, Commandant South Waziristan Militia, to Inspecting Officer Frontier Corps, 15th June 1919, L/P&S/11/155 and C.C. Trench, *The Frontier Scouts* (London, 1986), pp.38–45.
23. *Official History 1919*, pp.76–8.
24. Viceroy, Foreign and Political Dept, to SSI, 22nd Dec. 1919, L/MIL/7/15939 and *Summary of Chief Events in North-West Frontier Tribal Territory from 8th August 1919 to 31st December 1920* (Delhi, 1921), pp.8–9 L/MIL/7/16944.
25. Chief Commissioner NWFP, to Foreign Secretary to the Government of India in the Foreign and Political Department, 3rd Dec. 1919, L/P&S/11/167.
26. Chelmsford to Montagu, 8th Oct. 1919, *Montagu Mss* Mss.Eur.D.523/9.
27. *Despatch by His Excellency General Sir Charles Monro on the Operations in Waziristan* (Simla, 1920), p.3 L/MIL/7/16930 (Hereafter *Despatch on Waziristan*).
28. Waziristan Force Weekly Appreciation for week ending 18th October 1919, PRO WO 106/56 and Royal Air Force, India. Summary of Operations 28th September to 8th October (inclusive), 7th Nov. 1919, L/MIL/17/5/4118.
29. *Despatch on Waziristan*, p.3 and Waziristan Force Weekly Appreciation for week ending 22nd November 1919, PRO WP 106/56.
30. Waziristan Force Weekly Appreciation for week ending 22nd November 1919 and week ending 6th December 1919, PRO WO 106/56 and Royal Air Force India. Summary of Operations from 9th November to 15th December 1919 (inclusive), 11th Jan. 1920, L/MIL/15/5/4120.
31. *Operations in Waziristan 1919–20* (Calcutta, 1921), pp.92–3 (hereafter *Waziristan 1919–20*).
32. GOC Waziristan Force to War Section, Delhi, 20th Dec. 1920, L/P&S/10/870 and *Waziristan 1919–20*, p.102.
33. D. Rees, *Indian General Service Medal* (Unpublished TS Memoir, 1955), Vol. 4 pp.181–9 NAM 6706–21 and Ross, *op. cit.*, pp.47–9 *Ross Mss*, Mss.Eur.B.235/4.
34. *Despatch on Waziristan*, p.8.

35. GOC Waziristan Force to War Section, Delhi, 22nd Dec. 1919, L/MIL/17/5/4119, *Waziristan 1919–20*, pp.102–6, and Capt. D. Rees, *Pioneer Piquet. 21st December 1919* (London, 1954).

36. *Despatch on Waziristan*, p.10, *Waziristan 1919–20*, p.108 and Maj.-Gen. A. Le G. Jacob, 'Waziristan', *REJ*, 42 (1928), p.227.

37. GOC Advanced Waziristan Force to War Section, Delhi, 23rd Dec. 1919, L/P&S/10/870 and *Despatch on Waziristan*, p.10.

38. Sir J. Smyth, *Milestones* (London, 1979), p.70.

39. GOC Waziristan Force to War Section, 21st Dec. 1919, L/P&S/10/870 and GOC Waziristan Force to War Section, Delhi, 22nd Dec. 1919, L/MIL/17/5/4119.

40. Viceroy (Army Department), to SSI, 22nd Dec. 1919 and GOC Waziristan Force to the War Section, Delhi, 22nd Dec. 1919, L/MIL/17/5/4119.

41. Waziristan Force Weekly Appreciation for week ending 30th December 1919, PRO WO 106/56.

42. GOC Advanced Waziristan Force to War Section, Delhi, 24th Dec. 1919, L/P&S/10/870 and Royal Air Force, India, Summary of Operations from 16th December to 31st December 1919 (inclusive), 4th Feb. 1920, L/MIL/17/5/4119.

43. Waziristan Force Weekly Appreciation for the week ending 30th December 1919, PRO WO 106/56.

44. GOC Advanced Waziristan Force to Foreign Secretary, 27th Dec. 1919, L/P&S/10/870.

45. *Waziristan 1919–20*, pp.109–10.

46. R.A. Curties, '7 (Bengal) Indian Mountain Battery, 1919–20', in C.H. MacFetridge and J.P. Warren (eds.), *Tales of the Mountain Gunners* (Edinburgh, 1973), p.101.

47. Commander-in-Chief in India, to the GOC Egyptian Expeditionary Force, 23rd Dec. 1919, L/MIL/17/5/4119.

48. Waziristan Force Weekly Appreciation for week ending 6th January 1920, PRO WO 106/56 (hereafter Weekly Appreciation for 6th January 1920).

49. *Waziristan 1919–20*, p.97.

50. Notes from War Diaries, Part DCL Waziristan Force, May 1920, L/MIL/7/18853.

51. Weekly Appreciation for 6th January 1920.

52. Ibid.

53. Waziristan Force Weekly Appreciation for week ending 13th January 1920, PRO WO 106/56.

54. *Despatch on Waziristan*, pp.13–14 and *Waziristan 1919–20*, pp.115–9.

55. Waziristan Force Weekly Appreciation for week ending 20th January 1920, PRO WO 106/56.

56. Maxwell, *op. cit.*, pp.241–3.

57. *Despatch on Waziristan*, p.14.

58. Viceroy, Army Department, to SSI, 9th Feb. 1920, L/MIL/3/2512.

59. *Despatch on Waziristan*, p.15 and Waziristan Force Weekly Appreciation for week ending 3rd February 1920, L/MIL/17/5/4119.

60. Waziristan Force Weekly Appreciation for weeks ending 3rd and 10th February 1920, PRO WO 106/56.

61. Waziristan Force Weekly Appreciation for week ending 24th February 1920, PRO WO 106/56.
62. Waziristan Force Weekly Appreciation for week ending 31st March 1920, PRO WO 106/56.
63. *Despatch on Waziristan*, pp.18–19.
64. Field Marshal Sir W. Slim, *Unofficial History* (London, 1959), p.101.
65. Viceroy, Foreign and Political Dept. to SSI, 23rd March 1920, L/MIL/7/15939.
66. Army Department Despatch No. 2 (Special): The size, composition and organisation of the military forces in India, L/MIL/7/13315 and Review of important military events in India No. 1 of 1920, 28th June 1920, L/MIL/7/12491.
67. To General Officer Commanding Northern Command, 18th Jan. 1920, 29th Jan. 1920, and To Chief of the General Staff in India, 23rd Feb. 1920. P/10875.
68. To General Officer Commanding Northern Command, 24th Jan. 1920, P/10875, Graham, *op. cit.*, p.202 and Maxwell, *op. cit.*, pp.254–6.
69. *Mountain Warfare School. Abbottabad, Synopsis of Lectures 1920 (Revised 1921)* (Rawalpindi, 1921) and Capt. A.D. Simmons, 'Notes on Mountain Warfare Course at Abbottabad 1920, 19th July 1920', *Symons Mss*, DMM 62/1687/297.
70. Maxwell, *op. cit.*, p.259.
71. Army Department Despatch No. 101 of 1920: Policy to be adopted in future in connection with the military training establishments of the Army in India, 25th Nov. 1920, L/MIL/7/7223.
72. See *Proceedings of the Military Requirements Committee 1921. Report. (Lord Rawlinson's Committee)* (Simla, 1921), p.6, Montgomery to Marshall, 12th Aug. 1921, *Montgomery-Massingberd Mss*, LHCMA 128 and Rawlinson to Montgomery, 6th Dec. 1922, *Montgomery-Massingberd Mss*, LHCMA 135.
73. *Field Service Regulations Vol. II Operations (Provisional)* (London, 1920), pp.261–89.
74. Vaughan to Montgomery, 28th July 1920, *Montgomery-Massingberd Mss*, LHCMA 116.
75. *Notes on Mountain Warfare* (Calcutta, 1920).
76. 'Frontier', *Frontier Warfare* (Bombay, 1921) and S.H.C., *Mountain Warfare Notes* (Poona, 1921).
77. *Wazirforce Tactical Notes* (Dera Ismail Khan, 1921).
78. *Notes on Frontier Warfare* (Aldershot, 1922).
79. Vaughan to Montgomery, 28th July 1920, *Montgomery-Massingberd Mss*, LHCMA 116.
80. See Staff College Quetta 1922, North-West Frontier Warfare. *Ismay Mss* III/2/14–27 LHCMA.
81. Anderson to Montgomery, 19th July 1921, *Montgomery-Massingberd Mss*, LHCMA 128.
82. *The Army in India and its Evolution* (Calcutta, 1924), p.38 and p.43.
83. Army Department Despatch No. 2 (Special) of 1920: The size, composition and organization of the military forces in India, 24th June 1920, L/MIL/3/1118.

84. Maj.-Gen. S.H. Climo, Commanding Waziristan Force, to CGS, 19th April 1920, L/MIL/7/18853.
85. See Maj. J.G. Lecky, 'Notes on the Tactical Use of Lewis Guns in Mountain Warfare', *JUSII*, 49/219 (1920), pp.170–188a and Ishmael, 'Tactical use of Lewis Guns (A Criticism)', *JUSII*, 50/223 (1922), pp.260–9.
86. *The Army in India and its Evolution* (Calcutta, 1924), p.44.
87. Army Department Despatch No. 12 of 1921: Proposed organization and establishments of the fighting units of the post-war Army in India, 3rd Feb. 1921, L/MIL/7/13315.
88. Capt. H.J. Davis, 'The Employment of Machine Guns with a Battalion of Infantry: With Special Reference to the Indian Frontier', *JRUSI*, 67/468 (1922), pp.688–96.
89. Capt. J.A Deane, 'Notes on the Co-operation of Artillery and Infantry in Mountain Warfare', *JRA*, 46/11 (1919–20), pp.510–13 and Maj. and Bvt Lt.-Col. A.F. Jarrett, 'Co-operation in Mountain Warfare', *JRA*, 47/3 (1920–21), pp.21–2.
90. *Despatch on Waziristan,* p.18, *Reports by the Inspector General of Communications and Directors of Services Waziristan Force 1919–20* (Simla, 1920), p.19 and Maj. and Lt.-Col. A.J. Farfan, 'Mountain Artillery in Waziristan 1919–20', *JUSII*, 50/222 (1921), pp.187–97.
91. Precis of important military events in India from 1st March 1920 to 28th June 1921, 18th July 1921, p.2 PRO WO 106/157, *Despatch by H.E. General Lord Rawlinson of Trent, C-in-C in India, on the operations of the Waziristan Force for the period 1st April 1921 to 31st December 1921* (Delhi, 1921), p.3 L/MIL/17/13/122 and Graham, *op. cit.*, pp.218 and 221.
92. See E.M. Spiers, 'Gas and the North-West Frontier', *JSS*, 6/4 (1983), pp.99–102.
93. Maj.-Gen. C.H. Foulkes, 'Memorandum on the use of Gas in Frontier Warfare', 3rd Nov. 1919, *Foulkes Mss*, LHCMA 6/105.
94. Leslie to Foulkes, 10th Jan. 1921, *Foulkes Mss.*, LHCMA 6/106.
95. Lecture at Delhi to the Viceroy, C-in-C and Members of the Supreme Council and Lecture at Delhi on 22.1.20 to Army H.Q. Officers, *Foulkes Mss*, LHCMA 6/106.
96. Viceroy, Army Dept. to SSI, 6th Feb. 1920 and Army Department Despatch No. 12 of 1920: The use of gas in Warfare, 12th Feb. 1920, L/MIL/7/19238.
97. Memorandum Circulated by the Secretary of State for India, 12th May 1920, L/MIL/7/19238.
98. Military Despatch No. 39 to Governor-General in Council, 20th July 1922, L/MIL/7/19238.
99. *Despatch on Third Afghan War*, p.3.
100. *Report on the Working of the Lines of Communication Waziristan Force by Brigadier-General H.C. Tytler, Inspector General of Communications, Waziristan Force, together with certain Notes and Appendices collected for the information of the Staff College Camberley* (Delhi, 1920), p.21.
101. *The Army in India and its Evolution* (Calcutta, 1924), pp.42–3.
102. See *Notes on Armoured Cars* (Simla, 1915), p.4 and Brig.-Gen. Montagu, *Report on Mechanical Transport and Armoured Cars in India* (Simla, 1917), p.12.

103. *Armoured Car Training. Training and War (Provisional)* (London, 1921), pp.263–9.
104. Col. E.B. Hankey, 'Report on visit to India', 1st Feb. 1922, L/MIL/7/17132.
105. Report on the Possible use of Tanks in India by Lieut.-Colonel P. Johnson, Tank Corps, 9th April 1920, pp.8–40 L/MIL/7/17133.
106. Lt.-Gen. H.V. Cox, 'Notes on Colonel Johnson's Report on the use of Tanks in India', 6th Aug. 1920, L/MIL/7/17133. See also comments during discussion following Lt.-Col. P. Johnson, 'The Use of Tanks in Undeveloped Country', *JRUSI*, 66/462 (1921), pp.191–204.
107. Matthew-Lannowe to Fuller, 1st April 1921 and Note by Colonel W.S. Leslie, 8th May 1921, L/MIL/7/17133.
108. Fuller to Cobbe, 20th May 1921, L/MIL/7/17133.
109. Montgomery to Chetwode, 27th Sept. and 16th Nov. 1921, *Montgomery-Massingberd Mss*, LHCMA 133 and Rawlinson to Wilson, 27th Sept. 1921, *Wilson Mss*, IWM 2/13F/1.
110. Col. E.B. Hankey, 'Report on visit to India', 1st Feb. 1922, L/MIL/7/17132.
111. Government of India, Army Department, to Secretary, Military Department, 24th May 1923, L/MIL/7/17132.
112. Report by Colonel W.D. Villiers-Stuart, Aug. 1923, L/MIL/7/1115.
113. Report by Major-General J.R.E. Charles, 30th Aug. 1923, L/MIL/7/ 11159.
114. Viceroy, Army Department, to High Commissioner for India, 10th March 1924 and Birch to Cobbe, 17th March 1924, L/MIL/7/11159.
115. Review of Important Military Events in India No. 4 of 1925, 21st Jan. 1925, L/MIL/7/12491 and Maj. E.W. Sheppard, 'The Royal Tank Corps in India between the Wars', in B.H. Liddell Hart (ed.) *The Tanks* (London, 1959), Vol. 1 p.408.
116. See D.E. Omissi, *Air Power and Colonial Control.* (Manchester, 1991) for a detailed account of the RAF in policing the British Empire.
117. Waziristan Force Weekly Appreciation for week ending 16th March 1920, PRO WO 106/56.
118. Maj.-Gen. S.H. Climo, Commanding Waziristan Force, to CGS, 24th Jan. 1920, SCL 954.914 IND, *Despatch on Waziristan*, p.18 and *Waziristan 1919–20*, pp.150–1.
119. See *Despatch by His Excellency General Lord Rawlinson of Trent on the Operations of the Waziristan Force for the period 8th May 1920 to 31st March 1921* (Delhi, 1921), p.9 L/MIL/7/16930 (Hereafter *Despatch on Operations May 1920–March 1921*).
120. Trenchard to Rawlinson, 14th Feb. 1921, *Trenchard Mss*, MFC 76/1/136.
121. *Despatch on Operations May 1920–March 1921*, p.8.
122. S.E. Pears, Resident in Waziristan, to GOC Waziristan Force, *Salmond Mss*, B2599.
123. Omissi, *op. cit.*, p.47.
124. Report by Air Vice Marshal Sir John Salmond on the Royal Air Force in India, Aug. 1922, L/MIL/7/7765.
125. Note by Mr Denys Bray, 23rd Aug. 1922, and Lt.-Col. F.H. Humphrys, H.M. Minister Kabul, to Secretary to the GOI in the Foreign and Political Dept., 2nd June 1923, L/MIL/7/7765.

126. Lord Rawlinson, 'Memorandum on Air Vice-Marshal Sir John Salmond's Report, c. Aug. 1922, L/MIL/7/7765, Rawlinson to Trenchard, 22nd Aug. 1922, *Trenchard Mss*, MFC 76/1/136/2, and Rawlinson to Salmond, 21st/22nd Aug. 1922, *Salmond Mss*, B2608.

127. See Army Department Despatch No. 42 of 1922: Control of Waziristan, 27th July 1922, L/MIL/7/16951 and Army Department Despatch No. 68 of 1923: Policy in regard to Waziristan, 15th Nov. 1923, L/MIL/3/1119.

128. See Army Department Despatch No. 22 of 1925: Report by Air Vice-Marshal Sir Edward Ellington on the Royal Air Force Operations in Waziristan for the period 9th March 1925 to the 1st May 1925, 9th July 1925, L/MIL/7/16950.

129. Col. D.E. Robertson, 'The Organisation and Training of the Army in India', *JRUSI*, 69/474 (1924), p.326.

130. General Staff Note on Waziristan, 17th Sept. 1923, *Montgomery-Massingberd Mss*, LHCMA 140.

131. See Maj. M. Everett, 'The Destruction of Makin – February 1923', *JUSII*, 55/238 (1925), pp.15–29, Col. F.S. Keen, 'Lewis Guns in Frontier Warfare', *JUSII*, 54/234 (1924), pp.81–97 and Capt. C.W. Toovey, 'The Engagement of Black Hill Piquet on the 21st December 1919', *JUSII*, 55/241 (1925), pp.54–64.

132. Col. C. Kirkpatrick, 'Some Thoughts on Frontier Fighting', *JUSII*, 54/236 (1924), pp.325–38.

133. Col. C. Kirkpatrick, 'Some Thoughts on Frontier Fighting, II', *JUSII*, 54/237 (1924), pp.510–24 and Capt. B. Bradshaw-Smith, 'Protection on the March in Mountain Warfare', *JUSII*, 55/240 (1925), pp.49–54. See also Wazirforce Training Memorandum No. 2 Mountain Warfare – Protection on the March, 10th Feb. 1924, *Matheson Mss*.

134. Col. C.A. Milward, 'Protection on the March, Mountain Warfare', *JUSII*, 55/238 (1925), p.45.

135. See *Standing Orders for Frontier Warfare. 16th Infantry Brigade 1924* (Ahmednagar, 1924).

136. See Lt.-Col. H. de Watteville, *Waziristan 1919–20* (London, 1925) and Col. J.P. Villiers-Stuart, *Letters of a Once Punjab Frontier Force Officer to his Nephew giving his Ideas on Fighting on the North West Frontier and in Afghanistan* (London, 1925).

137. de Watteville, *op. cit.*,, p.209.

138. M. Jacobson, *The Modernization of the Indian Army, 1925–39* (University of California, Irvine, Ph.D. 1979), p.2.

139. Col. F.S. Keen, 'To what extent would the use of the latest scientific and mechanical methods of warfare affect operations on the North-West Frontier of India?', *JUSII*, 53/233 (1923), pp.393–415.

140. Ibid., p.415.

141. Capt. M.C. Gompertz, 'The Application of Science to Indian Frontier Warfare', *AQ*, 10 (1925), p.133.

142. *Field Service Regulations Vol. II (Operations)* (London, 1924), p.215.

143. *Manual of Operations on the North-West Frontier of India* (Calcutta, 1925).

CHAPTER 5

1. Lt.-Col. H.B. Hudson, *Those Blue Remembered Hills* (unpublished T.S. Memoir, 1980), p.70, *Hudson Mss*, Photo.Eur.179, and Col. H.R. Pettigrew, *'It Seemed Very Ordinary': Memoirs of Sixteen Years Service in the Indian Army 1932–47* (unpublished T.S. Memoir, 1980), p.65 IWM 84/29/1.
2. Brig. W.J. Jervois, *The History of the Northamptonshire Regiment: 1934–1948* (London, 1953), pp.2–3 and Lt.-Col. W.E. Maxwell, *Capital Campaigners: The History of the 3rd Battalion (Queen Mary's Own) The Baluch Regiment* (Aldershot, 1948), p.88.
3. Lt.-Gen. G.N. Molesworth, *Curfew on Olympus* (London, 1965), p.85 and Brig. J.H. Prendergast, *Prender's Progress: A Soldier in India, 1931–47* (London, 1979).
4. See *Kohat District Standing Orders for War and for Local Columns* (Lahore, 1927), *Landi Kotal Standing Orders for War 1936* (Landi Kotal, 1936) and *Standing Orders for Hill Warfare for 1st (Abbottabad) Infantry Brigade, May 1939* (Abbottabad, 1939).
5. Review of Important Military Events in India No. 2 of 1925, 4th July 1925, L/MIL/7/12491.
6. J. Smyth, *Milestones* (London, 1979), p.63, Lt.-Gen. Sir P. Neame, *Playing with Strife. The Autobiography of a Soldier* (London, 1947), p.134 and Maj. J. Croft, 'North West Frontier: Training Ground Supreme', *AQ*, 122/1 (1992), pp.51–60.
7. R. Hilton, *Nine Lives: The Autobiography of an Old Soldier* (London, 1955), pp.104–5.
8. Capt. R.E. Wood, 'Life on the Frontier', *REJ*, 42 (1928), p.243. See also "W", 'Mahsud Waziristan 1919–20', *JUSII*, 60/259 (1930), pp.193–200 and Pettigrew, *op. cit.*, p.54.
9. *Military Report on the Kohat District* (Simla, 1928), p.65.
10. See *Eastern Command Manoeuvres* (Simla, 1925) and *Report on the Staff Exercise and Manoeuvres held under the orders of the G.O.C.-in-C Northern Command, India 22nd November to 30th November 1925* (Calcutta, 1926).
11. Lt.-Gen. Sir F. Morgan, *Peace and War: A Soldier's Life* (London, 1961), pp.90–1.
12. Bvt. Maj. B.C. Dening, *The Future of the British Army: The Problem of Duties, Cost and Composition* (London, 1928), pp.60–2 and M. Jacobson, *The Modernization of the Indian Army, 1925–39* (University of California, Irvine, Ph.D., 1979), pp.27–8.
13. T.A. Heathcote, *The Military in British India The Development of British Land Forces in South Asia 1600–1947* (Manchester, 1995), p.242.
14. 'An Infantry Officer', 'Collective Training in a Battalion', *JUSII*, 60/259 (1930), p.128.
15. See *Despatch by H.E. Field Marshal Sir W.R. Birdwood on the Disturbances on the North-West Frontier of India from 23rd April to 12th September, 1930* (Delhi, 1930), L/MIL/7/16956 (Hereafter *Despatch on Disturbances*).
16. 'Editorial', *JUSII*, 61/262 (1931), pp.1–9 and Mauser, 'A Forgotten Frontier Force', *English Review*, 52 (1931), pp.69–72.

17. Ibid., p.17, Review of Important Military Events in India No. 3 of 1930, 28th Oct. 1930, L/MIL/7/12491.
18. 'Editorial', *JUSII*, 61/262 (1931), p.8.
19. Kirke to Bethell, 1st June 1928, *Kirke Mss*, Mss.Eur.E.396/7 and Army Department Despatch No. 20 of 1928: Reorganisation of Cavalry and Infantry units in India, 29th Nov. 1928, and Memorandum Explaining the Proposed Reorganisation of Cavalry and Infantry Units in India, L/MIL/7/13317.
20. *Memorandum on Army Training (India) Collective Training Period 1929–30* (Simla, 1930), p.4 L/MIL/17/5/2199.
21. *Despatch on Disturbances*, p.18 and Review of Important Military Events in India No. 3 of 1930, 28th Oct. 1930, L/MIL/7/12491.
22. 'Mouse', 'Babu Tactics', *JUSII*, 61/262 (1931), pp.60–65.
23. *Report of the Tribal Control and Defence Committee 1931* (Delhi, 1931), pp.38–9 L/MIL/17/13/34.
24. General Staff Criticism of the Tribal Control and Defence Committee, 19th May 1931, L/P&S/12/3171 and Jacobson, *op. cit.*, p.92.
25. Light Infantry, 'Mobility', *JUSII*, 62/266 (1932), p.11.
26. Review of Important Military Events in India No. 4 of 1931, 21st Jan. 1932, L/MIL/7/12492 and Col. C.V. Jackson, 'The Wana–Ladha Road', *REJ*, 50 (1936), pp.27–37.
27. Willingdon to Hoare, 9th Sept. 1934, *Templewood Mss*, Mss.Eur.E.240/7, GOI, Foreign and Political Dept., to SSI, 26th Nov. 1934., L/P&S/12/3202, and Marshal Sir P. Chetwode, 'The Army in India', *JRUSI*, 82/525 (1937), pp.7–8 and p.12.
28. Gen. Sir K. Wigram, 'Defence in the North–West Frontier Province', *JRCAS*, 24/1 (1937), pp.77–8.
29. Review of Important Military Events in India No. 2 of 1929, 11th July 1929, Review of Important Military Events in India No. 2 of 1930, 12th July 1930, L/MIL/7/12491 and Review of Important Military Events in India No. 1 of 1932, 22nd April 1932, L/MIL/7/12492.
30. Review of Important Military Events in India No. 3 of 1932, 9th Nov. 1932, L/MIL/7/12492, Review of Important Military Events in India No. 2 of 1934, 21st July 1934, L/MIL/7/12492 and Jacobson, *op. cit.*, p.320.
31. AHQ to Headquarters Northern Command, Southern Command, Eastern Command, Western Command and Burma Independent District, 1st June 1931, L/MIL/7/5505.
32. Field Marshal W.R. Birdwood, 'Recent Indian Military Experience', *United Empire*, 22 (1931), p.246.
33. Field Marshal Sir W. Slim, *Defeat into Victory* (London, 1956), p.544.
34. *Despatch on Disturbances*, p.17 and *Summary of Administration of Field Marshal Sir W.R. Birdwood as Commander-in-Chief India* (Simla, 1931), p.39 L/MIL/17/5/1619.
35. General Staff Criticism of the Tribal Control and Defence Committee, 1931, 9th May 1931, pp.3–4 L/P&S/12/3171.
36. Army Department Despatch No. 20 of 1930: Proposal to increase the strength of the Royal Air Force in India by an Air Transport Squadron, 25th Sept. 1930, and G.M. Young, Secretary to the Government of India, Army

Department, to the Secretary Military Department, India Office, 18th Aug. 1931, L/MIL/7/7769.

37. Capt. D. Mc. Kennelly, 'Artillery Support of Pickets in Mountain Warfare', *JRA*, 57/2 (1930–1), p.253.

38. *Memorandum on Army Training (India) Collective Training Period 1929–30* (Simla, 1930), p.13 L/MIL/17/5/2199.

39. *A.H.Q. India Training Memorandum No. 2 Collective Training period 1930–31* (Simla, 1931), pp.3–6 L/MIL/17/5/2199.

40. Maj.-Gen. J.G. Elliot, *The Frontier 1839–1947* (London, 1968), pp.117–8.

41. *Waziristan Relief Notes* (Northern Command, 1933).

42. *Field Service Regulations Vol. II (Operations)* (London, 1929), p.207.

43. Prendergast, *op. cit.*, p.57, J. Morris, *Hired to Kill. Some Chapters of Autobiography* (London, 1960), p.127 and 'The Looker-On', 'The North-West Frontier in the Thirties', *AQDJ*, 97 (1969), p.249.

44. Pettigrew, *op. cit.*, p.65. See also pp.88–9.

45. Maj.-Gen. Sir C.W. Gwynn, *Imperial Policing* (London, 1934), p.7.

46. Gen. Sir A. Skeen, *Passing it On: Short talks on Tribal Fighting on the North-West Frontier of India* (Aldershot, 1932), and J.G.S., 'Reviews', *JUSII*, 62/269 (1932), pp.589–91.

47. Indian Army Order 80. Books – 'Passing it On' by General Sir Andrew Skeen, 22nd Dec. 1932, L/MIL/17/5/274.

48. AHQ India to GOC-inC. Northern, Western, Eastern and Southern Commands, 31st March 1933, L/MIL/7/12492. See 'Auspex', 'A Matrimonial Tangle (or Mountains and Machine Guns)', *JUSII*, 63/272 (1933), pp.367–74 and Lt.-Col. O.D. Bennett, 'Some Regrettable Incidents on the N.-W.F.', *JUSII*, 63/271 (1933), pp.193–203.

49. 'Borderer', 'With the Tendency of Modern Military Organisation towards Mechanisation, the increasing complexity of modern weapons and the dependency of troops on the maintenance services, it is asserted by many that Regular troops are losing the degree of mobility necessary for the successful performance of their role on the North-West Frontier. Discuss how this can be overcome so that freedom of action and tactical mobility are assured in the Army of India.', *JUSII*, 64/274 (1934), pp.14–5.

50. Ibid., pp.15–26.

51. See 'Jamshed', 'The Legend of Baridzai', *JUSII*, 64/274 (1934), pp.123–9 and Lt.-Col. H.S. Pearson, 'The Perimeter Wall', *JUSII*, 64/274 (1934), pp.119–22.

52. Maj.-Gen. H. Rowan-Robinson, *The Infantry Experiment* (London, 1934), p.10.

53. See Report on Mohmand Operations, 28th Nov. 1935, L/MIL/7/16968 and *Official History of Operations on the N.W Frontier of India 1920–35* (Delhi, 1945) (hereafter *Official History 1920–35*), pp.189–244.

54. Ibid., pp.240–1.

55. Lt.-Col. L. Lawrence-Smith, 'Cavalry and Tanks with Mohforce, 1935', *CJ*, 26 (1936), pp.552–61, *Official History 1920–1935*, pp.243–4 and Jacobson, *op. cit.*, p.80.

56. 'Commenger', 'Engineer Work in the Mohmand Operations', *REJ*, 51, pp.507–22.

57. 'Shpagwishtama', 'The Changing Aspect of Operations on the North-West Frontier', *JUSII*, 66/283 (1936), pp.102–10.
58. Maj. J.D. Shapland, 'North-West Frontier Operations – Sept/Oct, 1935', *JRA*, 64/2 (1937–8), pp.209–10 and Col. P. Morison, 'Service Milestones', n.d., *Morison Mss*, Mss.Eur.D.1175/2.
59. Shapland, *op. cit.*, p.208 and *Official History, 1920–1935,* p.244.
60. *A.H.Q. India Training Memorandum No. 12 Collective Training period 1935–36* (Delhi, 1936), pp.2–8 L/MIL/17/5/2199.
61. Maj. D.B. Mackenzie, *Mountain Warfare on the Sand Model* (Aldershot, 1936) and R.L.G., 'Reviews', *JUSII*, 66/284 (1936), p.307.
62. D.J. Waldie, *Relations between the Army and the Royal Air Force* (London, D.Phil., 1980), pp.210–11.
63. See Air Staff (India) Memo No. 1 April 1935: Tactical Methods of Conducting Air Operations against Tribes on the North-West Frontier of India, 17th May 1935, *Bottomley Mss*, B22.
64. Slessor to Sutton 15th April 1935, *Slessor Mss*, PRO AIR 75/29, Air Chief Marshal Sir J. Slessor, *The Central Blue: Recollections and Reflections* (London, 1956), pp.121–3 and Sir J. Slessor, *These Remain. A Personal Anthology* (London, 1969), pp.118–20.
65. HQ No. 3 (Indian) Wing, to HQ, RAF India, 17th May 1935, *Slessor Mss*, PRO AIR 75/29.
66. Secretary to the Government of India (Army Department Air Force Branch) to the Secretary, Military Department, 10th March 1936, L/MIL/7/19307.
67. Slessor to Peck, 10th April 1936, *Slessor Mss*, PRO AIR 75/31.
68. 'Close Support Tactics. Provisional', 1936, *Slessor Mss*, PRO AIR 75/31.
69. Combined Report on Air Co-operation Training 2 (Rawalpindi) Infantry Brigade and 3 (Indian) Wing, RAF, Khanpur Area 17–25 November 1936', *Slessor Mss*, PRO AIR 75/31.
70. *Official History of the Operations on the N.W. Frontier of India, 1936–7* (Delhi, 1943), pp.5–16. L/MIL/17/13/42 (Hereafter *Official History 1936–37*) and Report on the Operations in Waziristan 25th November 1936 to 16th January, 1937 (First Phase), 21st June 1937, L/MIL/7/16971.
71. Prendergast, *op. cit.*, p.86.
72. Pettigrew, *op. cit.*, p.89.
73. C.T. Atkinson, *A History of the 1st (P.W.O.) Battalion the Dogra Regiment* (Southampton, 1950), pp.123–5, and Trench, *op. cit.*, pp.126–7.
74. Report on the Operations in Waziristan 25th November 1936 to 16th January, 1937 (First Phase), 21st June 1937, L/MIL/7/16971, Operations in Waziristan, 24th November 1936 to 15th January 1937, Jan. 1937, *Slessor Mss*, PRO AIR 75/31 and Col. R.L. Bond, 'The Khaisora Road,' *REJ*, 52 (1938), pp.190–203.
75. G. Moore, *'Just as Good as the Rest': A British Battalion in the Faqir of Ipi's War Indian N.W.F. 1936–37* (Huntingdon, 1979), p.10 and p.42.
76. Lt.-Col. G.A. Brett, *History of the South Wales Borderers and the Monmouthshire Regiment, 1937–1952 Part 1* (Pontypool, 1953), p.13 and Maj.-Gen. A.E. Williams, 'Waziristan 1937', n.d. *Williams Mss*, I.W.M. 88/56/1.

77. 'Action of the 1st (Abbottabad) Infantry Brigade Near Damdil, 29th March 1937', *JUSII*, 68/290 (1938), pp.33–8.
78. *M.O.3 Unofficial Letter on Afghanistan and the North–West Frontier of India, 1st April 1936–March 31st 1937* (Simla, 1937), p.19 L/WS/1/192.
79. *Report on the Administration of the Border of the North-West Frontier Province for the Year 1936–37* (Delhi, 1937), pp.1–2 L/P&S/12/3148.
80. Anon., 'Attack on the Convoy at Shahur Tangi on the 9th April 1937', *JUSII*, 67/288 (1937), pp.261–65, and Lt.-Col. J.A. Bolam, 'The Shahur Tangi Affair', n.d., *Bolam Mss*, Mss.Eur.C.308.
81. Report by the Commander-in-Chief in India on the operations carried out in Waziristan between 16th January 1937 and the 15th September 1937 (Second Phase), 24th Nov. 1937, L/MIL/7/16971.
82. J. Masters, *Bugles and a Tiger* (London, 1956), p.222.
83. Ibid., pp.208–9 and Lt.-Gen. F.I.S. Tuker, 'Frontier 1937', n.d., p.7 *Tuker Mss*, IWM 71/21/5/10.
84. Maj. D.A. Mackenzie, 'Operations in the Lower Khaisora Valley, Waziristan, in 1937', *JRUSI*, 82/528 (1937), p.814.
85. *M.I. Unofficial Letter on Afghanistan and the North–West Frontier of India, April 1937 to March 1938* (Simla, 1938), pp.20–1 L/WS/1/192.
86. Maj. W.D. Lentaigne, '"Iblanke" – The Advance to the Sham Plains 11/12th May 1937', *JUSII*, 68/291 (1938), pp.131–52 and Masters, *op. cit.*, pp.234–41.
87. Supplement No. 3 to Monthly Intelligence Summary No. 5 on Events in Waziristan from 12th to 19th May 1937, 22nd May 1937, App. A L/MIL/5/1065 and M.F. Kemmis Betty, 'Waziristan, 1937', in C.H.T. MacFetridge and J.P. Warren (ed.), *Tales of the Mountain Gunners: An Anthology* (Edinburgh, 1973), p.118.
88. Report by His Excellency the Commander-in-Chief in India on the operations carried out in Waziristan between the 16th January 1937 and the 15th September 1937 (Second Phase), 24th Nov. 1937, L/MIL/7/16971.
89. Maj. A.E. Armstrong, 'More Roads (Waziristan, 1937)', *REJ*, 53 (1939), pp.1–16 and Lt.-Col. W.R. Penny, 'Waziristan 1937', *RSQJ*, 7 (1939–40), pp.43–62.
90. 'Report by His Excellency the Commander-in-Chief in India on the operations carried out in Waziristan (Final Phase) between the 16th September 1937 and the 15th December 1937', 14th April 1938, L/MIL/7/16971.
91. *Official History 1936–37*, p.229.
92. 'Editorial', *JUSII*, 67/288 (1937), pp.238–40.
93. Maj. T.H. Angus, 'Operations in the Lower Shaktu Valley, 16th/18th November 1937', *JUSII* 68/292 (1938), pp.335–42.
94. Mackenzie, *op. cit.*, p.821.
95. Gort to Inskip, 29th Dec. 1937, *Inskip Mss*, IWM INP 1/2 and Slessor 1956, *op. cit.*, p.131.
96. *Report on the Administration of the Border of the North-West Frontier Province for the Year 1936–37* (Delhi, 1937), p.31, R. Bromhead, 'Trust Begets Trust. The Problem of Waziristan', *JUSII*, 69/297 (1939), pp.470–1 and Pettigrew, *op. cit.*, p.88.
97. 'Chimariot','Mountain Artillery in Frontier Warfare', *JRA*, 65 (1938–39), pp.90–5 and Graham, *op. cit.*, p.249.

98. Lt.-Col. F.C. Simpson, 'Review of Frontier Policy from 1849–1939', *JUSII*, 74/16 (1944), p.307.

99. C.G. Ogilvie, Secretary to GOI to Secretary Military Department, India Office, 4th Feb. 1938, L/MIL/7/7235 and Jacobson, *op. cit.*, pp.81–2.

100. Report on Air operations in Waziristan No. 1 (Indian) Group, 17th February to 7th December 1937, 22nd Dec. 1937, *Bottomley Mss*, B2304.

101. Capt. A.V. Brooke-Webb, 'Relief by Air', *JRA*, 66 (1939–40), pp.225–8 and Review of Important Military Events in India No. 4 of 1937, 30th Oct. 1937, L/MIL/7/12492.

102 Report on the Operations in the Khaisora-Shaktu area of Waziristan, 25th November 1936 to 25th January 1937, 25th Feb. 1937, *Bottomley Mss*, B2300 and Mackenzie *op. cit.*, p.822.

103. Coleridge to CGS, 12th March 1937, *Rees Mss*, Mss.Eur.F.274/4.

104. Air Commodore N.H. Bottomley, 'The Work of the Royal Air Force on the North-West Frontier', *JRUSI*, 84/535 (1939), pp.775–8.

105. A.I.L.O., 'Close Support by Aircraft on the North West Frontier', *JUSII*, 70/298 (1940), p.16.

106. Air Marshal Sir B. Embry, *Mission Completed* (London, 1957), p.80.

107. Comments and Deductions on the Khaisora Operations, Waziristan, 8th June 1937, *Rees Mss*, Mss.Eur.F.274/4 and *A.H.Q. India Training Memorandum No. 14 Collective Training Period 1936–37* (Delhi, 1937), pp.8–12 L/MIL/17/5/2199.

108. See Report by His Excellency the Commander-in-Chief in India on the operations carried out in Waziristan between the 16th December 1937 and the 31st December 1938 and Report by His Excellency the Commander-in-Chief in India on the operations carried out in Waziristan between the 1st January 1939 and the 31st December 1939, 6th June 1940, L/MIL/7/16971.

109. Bartholomew to Wilson, Feb. 1937, L/WS/1/257.

110. Wilson to Auchinleck, 18th May 1937, and Auchinleck to Wilson, 27th May 1937, L/WS/1/257.

111. Commander-in-Chief to Wilson, 28th May 1937, L/WS/1/257.

112. Wilson to Auchinleck, 2nd July 1937, L/WS/1/257.

113. Newall to Deverell, 20th Sept. 1937, PRO AIR 8/529.

114. Waldie, *op. cit.*, p.216, Under Secretary to the Government of India Defence Department, to the Secretary Military Dept, India Office, 28th June 1938, and SSI to Government of India Army Department, 3rd Nov. 1938, L/WS/1/257.

115. *A.H.Q. India Training Memorandum No. 16 Collective Training period 1937–38* (Delhi, 1938), p.1 L/MIL/17/5/2199.

116. See Lt.-Col. C.J. Wood, 'An Operation in the Vicinity of Spinwam – 20th October 1937', *JUSII*, 68/292 (1938), pp.255–66, Maj. M. Glover, 'Ordnance Service in Waziristan', *JUSII*, 68/292 (1938), pp.311–15 and Maj. J.E. Hirst, 'Second Echelon in Frontier Operations', *JUSII*, 68/293 (1938), pp.431–447.

117. Lt.-Col. G.R. Stevens, *History of the 2nd King Edward VII's Own Goorkha Rifles (The Sirmoor Rifles)* (Aldershot, 1952), Vol. III pp.33–4.

118. Auspex, 'The Dream Sector, L. of C.', *JUSII*, 68/291 (1938), p.209.

119. Lt.-Col. F.C. Simpson, 'Review of Frontier Policy from 1849–1939', *JUSII*, 74/317 (1944), p.484.

120. *Frontier Warfare – India (Army and Royal Air Force)* (Delhi, 1939).
121. See Anon, 'Cooperation between Light Tanks and Infantry (With special Application to Mountain Warfare vis-a-vis Infantry Battalion Officers), *JUSII*, 69/296 (1939), pp.309–23 and Maj. C.M. Wingfield, 'Mountain Warfare', *JUSII*, 69/297 (1939), pp.493–505.
122. Gen. Sir A. Skeen, *Passing it On: Short Talks on Tribal Fighting on the North-West Frontier of India* (London, 1939), 4th ed.

CONCLUSION

1. Maj.-Gen. J.G. Elliot, *The Frontier 1839–1947* (London, 1968), p.1.
2. A. Hayter, *The Second Step* (London, 1962), p.98.
3. T.R. Mockaitis, *British Counterinsurgency in the post-imperial era* (Manchester, 1995), p.133.
4. R. Gregorian, 'Jungle Bashing' in Malaya: Towards a Formal Tactical Doctrine', *Small Wars and Insurgencies*, 5/3 (1994), p.342.
5. A.D. English, 'The RAF Staff College and the Evolution of British Strategic Bombing Policy', *JSS*, 16/3, p.420.
6. R.M. Utley, 'The Contribution of the Frontier to the American Military Tradition', in H.R. Borowski (ed.), *The Harmon Memorial Lectures in Military History, 1959–1987* (Washington, 1988), p.58.
7. Maj.-Gen. S. Woodburn-Kirby, *The War against Japan, volume III: The Decisive Battles* (London, 1962), p.27.
8. *Army in India Training Memorandum, No. 2 War Series* (Simla, 1940), p.1 L/MIL/17/5/2240.
9. Lewis to Wife, 24th Nov. 1939, *Lewis Mss*, IWM 74/48/1.
10. W.H. Alston, '*My Day and Age'*, *The Memoirs of William Lowry Alston at one time a British Officer in H.M. Indian Army 1917–1947* (Unpublished T.S. Memoir), Vol. VI, p.2, Vol. VII, pp.33–4 and Vol. VIII, pp.32–3 NAM 8005–151.
11. *Army in India Training Memorandum No. 14 War Series January–February 1942* (Simla, 1942), App. F.
12. Defence Department Despatch No. 2 of 1941: Operations in Waziristan from the 1st January 1940 to the 24th May 1940, 15th Feb. 1941, L/WS/1/1526.
13. Brig. L.E. Dennys, 'Report of Action on Tabe Zangai on the Night of 7/8th Dec. 1940', L/MIL/7/16971.
14. See War Department Despatch No. 1 of 1942: Report by His Excellency the Commander-in-Chief India on the operations in Waziristan between 25th May 1940 and 30th September 1941, 25th Sept. 1942 and War Department Despatch No. 1 of 1943: Report by His Excellency the Commander-in-Chief in India on the operations carried out in Waziristan between the 1st October 1941 and 31st December 1942, 2nd Aug. 1943, L/WS/1/1526.
15. GOI Defence to Department to SSI, 24th April 1940, L/WS/1/377 and Brig. J.H. Prendergast, *Prender's Progress: A Soldier in India, 1931–47* (London, 1979), p.114.
16. Brig. W.E. Condon, *The Frontier Force Rifles* (Aldershot, 1953), p.290.

17. *Army in India Training Memorandum No. 9 War Series July 1941* (Delhi, 1941) L/MIL/17/5/2240.
18. *Military Training Pamphlet No. 7 (India) Extensive Warfare (Notes on warfare in mountainous country between modern forces in Eastern theatres)* (Simla, 1941), p.3, 2nd ed. L/MIL/17/5/2248.
19. Report of the Infantry Committee 1943, 1st–14th June 1943, L/WS/1/1371.
20. Capt. B.J. Donlea, 'Notes on Mountain Warfare Course Abbottabad,' April 1940, *Donlea Mss*, LHCMA, Col. W.N. Nicholson, *The Suffolk Regiment 1928 to 1946* (Ipswich, 1947), p.151 and Lt.-Col. R.M. Maxwell to Author, 14th Sept. 1994.
21. Under Secretary to the Government of India, Defence Department (Army Branch), to Chief of the General Staff, 7th March 1941, L/WS/1/529.
22. *Courses of Instruction, India No. 11 Frontier Warfare School, India, Kakul 1941* (Delhi, 1941) L/MIL/17/5/2201.
23. Lt.-Col. R.M. Maxwell to Author, 14th Sept. 1994, and Interview with Major F. Delens, 11th Oct. 1994.
24. DMT, GHQ India, DMT, War Office, 18th June 1943, L/WS/1/1302.
25. E.D. Smith, *Battle for Burma* (London, 1979), p.10, Lt.-Col. H.B. Hudson, *Those Blue Remembered Hills* (Unpublished TS Memoir, 1980), p.225 *Hudson Mss* Photo.Eur.179 and Director of Military Training, General Headquarters India, to Director of Military Training, War Office, 18th June 1943, 1st Aug. 1942, App. G. L/WS/1/1364.
26. See *Military Training Pamphlet No. 6 (India) The Support of Land forces in Tribal Warfare on the Western Frontier of India, 1940* (Simla, 1941) *Army/Air Operations Pamphlet No. 8 (India) Air Forces in Support of the Army in Tribal Warfare on the Western Frontier of India 1944* (Delhi, 1944).
27. *Military Training Pamphlet No. 16 (India) Platoon Leading in Frontier Warfare* (Simla, 1942) 2nd Ed. 1945.
28. Lt.-Col. F.C. Simpson, 'Frontier Warfare in Retrospect and Prospect', *JUSII*, 73/313 (1943), p.378.
29. Lt.-Col. P.A. Meade, 'Frontier Tactics Defended', *JUSII*, 74/314 (1944), p.65.
30. 'Auspex', 'Reflections on Mobility in land Forces', *JUSII*, 74/315 (1944), pp.155–9.
31. Lt.-Gen. Sir F. Tuker, *While Memory Serves* (London, 1956), p.360 and *Frontier Committee 1945* (Calcutta, 1945), p.4.
32. GOC in Chief to North Western Army, Southern Army, Eastern Command and Central Command, 28th Aug. 1945, L/WS/1/767.
33. CGS to HQ North Western Army, Southern Army, Eastern Command and Central Command, 5th Sept. 1945, L/WS/1/789.
34. *Official History of Operations on the N.W Frontier of India 1920–35* (Delhi, 1945), p.vii.
35. See Maj. W.J. Spaight, 'The Frontier Myth', *JUSII*, 75/320 (1945), pp.374–6, Brig. M.R. Roberts, 'Frontier Realities', *JUSII*, 76/322 (1946), pp.53–9 and 'The Admiral', 'Further Thoughts on Frontier Myths', *JUSII*, 76/323 (1946), pp.225–9.
36. Record of a Conference held at Government House, 24th April 1946, L/P&S/12/3266.

37. Report by General Sir Claude J.E. Auchinleck, Commander-in-Chief in India covering the period 1st January to 31st December 1945, 30th June 1947, p.22 PRO WO 203/2670 and DMT India to the DMT, War Office, 1st Aug. 1945, L/WS/1/767.

38. Brig. M.C. Frye, Director of Weapons & Equipment, to Brig. J.R. Reynolds, 6th May 1946, and Directive – The Experimental Frontier Bde, 6th May 1946, L/WS/1/1485.

39. Mountain Warfare against Guerrilla Enemy Final Report on Trials by 25 (Experimental) Infantry Brigade, April 1947, PRO WO 231/34.

40. Brig. T.L. Miller to GHQ (I) DMT Branch, 20th April 1947, PRO WO 231/34.

41. M. Ayub Khan, *Friends not Masters. A Political Autobiography* (Lahore, 1967), p.18.

42. Lt.-Col. H.E. Cotton, 'Operation Curzon – The Evacuation of Waziristan', *REJ*, 62 (1948), pp.183–200 and G. Curtis, 'North-West Frontier of Pakistan – An Old Problem in a New Setting', *AQ*, 56/2 (1948), pp.185–6.

43. Gen. Sir P. de la Billière, *Looking for Trouble. From SAS to Gulf Command: The Autobiography* (London, 1995), pp.28–9.

44. M. Mann, *The Trucial Oman Scouts: The Story of a Bedouin Force* (Norwich, 1994), pp.102–3.

45. D. Charters, 'From Palestine to Northern Ireland: British adaptation to low-intensity operations', in D. Charters and M. Tugwell (eds.), *Armies in Low-Intensity Conflict: A Comparative Analysis* (London, 1989), p.190 and Mockaitis, *op. cit.*, pp.2, 8 and 52–3.

46. See Lt.-Col. T.M. Stevens, 'Operations in the Radfan, 1964' *JRUSI*, 110/640 (1965), pp.335–46 and Brig. G.S. Heathcote, 'Operations in the Radfan', *JRUSI*, 111/641 (1966), pp.30–40,.

47. Maj. S.M. Slater, 'Radfan', *British Army Review* (Dec. 1981), p.16.

48. C. Townshend, *Britain's Civil Wars: Counterinsurgency in the Twentieth Century* (London, 1986), p.150, T. Jones, 'The British Army, and Counter-Guerrilla Warfare in Transition, 1944–52', *Small Wars and Insurgencies*, 7/3 (1996), p.273 and James, *op. cit.*, p.53.

49. T.R. Mockaitis, *British Counterinsurgency, 1919–1960* (London, 1990), p.87.

Select Bibliography

A. PRIMARY SOURCES (UNPUBLISHED)

(i) Private Papers

Oriental and India Office Library and Records

Barrow Mss. Papers of General Sir Edmund Barrow, Mss.Eur.E.420.
Birdwood Mss. Papers of Field Marshal Sir W.R. Birdwood, Mss.Eur.D.686.
Bolam Mss. Papers of Lt.-Col. J.V. Bolam, Mss.Eur.C.308.
Bruce Mss. Papers of R.I. Bruce and Lt.-Col. C.E. Bruce, Mss.Eur.F.163.
Cunningham Mss. Papers of Sir George Cunningham, Mss.Eur.D.670.
Curzon Mss. Papers of George Curzon, Mss.Eur.F111/F112.
Elgin Mss. Papers of the Ninth Earl of Elgin and 13th Earl of Kincardine, Mss.Eur.F.84.
Grey Mss. Papers of Brigadier C.E. Gray, Mss.Eur.D.1037.
Keyes Mss. Papers of General Sir Charles Keyes, Mss.Eur.D.1048.
Kirke Mss. Papers of General Sir Walter Mervyn St George Kirke, Mss.Eur.E.396.
Lawrence Mss. Papers of Sir Henry Lawrence, Mss.Eur.F.90.
Monro Mss. Papers of General Sir Charles Carmichael Monro, Mss.Eur.D.783.
Morison Mss. Papers of Colonel O. Morison, Mss.Eur.D.1175.
Morley Mss. Papers of John, Viscount Morley of Blackburn, Mss.Eur.D.573.
Muspratt Mss. Papers of Major-General Sydney Muspratt, Mss.Eur.F.223.
Parsons Mss. Papers of Major-General Sir Arthur Parsons, Mss.Eur.D.696.
Phillips Mss. Papers of Major T.J. Phillips, Mss.Eur.C.393.
Rees Mss. Papers of Major-General Thomas Wynford Rees, Mss.Eur.F.277.
Roos-Keppel Mss. Papers of Lt.-Col. George Roos-Keppel, Mss.Eur.D.613.
White Mss. Papers of Field Marshal Sir George White Mss, Mss.Eur.F.108.

Public Record Office

Ardagh Mss. Papers of Lt.-Gen. Sir John Ardagh, PRO WO 30/40.
Kitchener Mss. Papers of Field Marshal Earl Kitchener of Khartoum, PRO WO 30/57.
Roberts Mss. Papers of Sir Frederick Roberts, PRO WO 105.
Slessor Mss. Papers of Air Marshal J.C. Slessor, PRO AIR 75.

Liddell Hart Centre for Military Archives

Bartholomew Mss. Papers of General Sir W. Bartholomew.
Donlea Mss. Papers of Captain B.J. Donlea.
Foulkes Mss. Papers of Major-General C.H. Foulkes.
Howell Mss. Papers of E. Howell.
Ismay Mss. Papers of General H.I. Ismay.

Liddell Hart Mss. Papers of Captain B.H. Liddell Hart.
Montgomery-Massingberd Mss. Papers of Field Marshal Sir A. Montgomery-
Massingberd.

Aviation Records Department, Royal Air Force Museum

Bottomley Mss. Papers of Air Chief Marshal Sir N.H. Bottomley, B2234–B2312
and A790–A803.
Salmond Mss. Papers of Air Vice-Marshal J. Salmond, B2580–B2662.
Trenchard Mss. Papers of Marshal of the R.A.F. Viscount Sir H. Trenchard, MFC
76/1.

National Army Museum

Browne Mss. Papers of General Sir S. Browne, NAM 7703-49.
Dening Mss. Papers of Lt.-General Sir L. Dening, NAM 7810-106.
Egerton Mss. Papers of Major-General C.C. Egerton, NAM 6502-104.
Haines Mss. Papers of General Sir P. Haines, NAM 8108-9.
Kempster Mss. Papers of Brigadier-General F.J. Kempster, NAM 7607-37.
Mason Mss. Papers of Lt.-Colonel A.H. Mason, NAM 7809-32.
Molesworth Mss. Papers of Lt.-General G.N. Molesworth, NAM 6509-56.
Rawlinson Mss. Papers of Lord Rawlinson of Trent, NAM 5201-33.
Roberts Mss. Papers of Sir Frederick Roberts, NAM 7101-23.
Spenser Wilkinson Mss. Papers of H. Spenser Wilkinson, NAM.
Tighe Mss. Papers of Lt.-Colonel S.C. Tighe, NAM 8206-83.
Gough Mss. Papers of Field Marshal Gough, NAM 8304-32-404.

Imperial War Museum

Inskip Mss. Papers of Major-General R.D. Inskip, IWM INP 1/1.
Lewis Mss. Papers of Major-General H.V. Lewis, IWM 74/48/1.
Maynard Mss. Papers of Brigadier F.H. Maynard, IWM 76/183/1.
Tuker Mss. Papers of Major-General F.I.S. Tuker, IWM 17/21/1-8.
Wilson Mss. Papers of Field Marshal Sir H. Wilson, IWM HHW 2/13/.
Williams Mss. Papers of Major-General A.E. Williams, IWM 88/56/1.

The Gurkha Museum, Winchester

Villiers-Stuart Mss. Papers of Brigadier-General W.D. Villiers-Stuart, V1-5.

Dorset Military Museum, the Keep, Dorchester

Symons Mss. Papers of Captain A.D. Symons. DMM 62/1687/297.

Collections in private hands

Matheson Mss. Standerwick Court, Frome, Somerset.

Unpublished Memoirs

W.H. Alston, *'My Day and Age': The Memoirs of William Lowry Alston at one time a British Officer in H.M. Indian Army 1917–1947* (Unpublished T.S. Memoir, 1961–2) NAM 8005-151.

Lt.-Col. H.B. Hudson, *Those Blue Remembered Hills* (Unpublished T.S. Memoir, 1980) Photo.Eur.179.

Brig.-Gen. E.W. Maconchy, *Memoirs of Brigadier-General E.W.S.K. Maconchy 1860–1920* (Unpublished T.S. Memoir, nd) NAM 7908-62-1.

Col. H.R.C. Pettigrew, *'It Seemed Very Ordinary': Memoirs of Sixteen Years Service in the Indian Army 1932–47* (Unpublished T.S. Memoir, 1980) IWM 84/29/1.

D. Rees, *Indian General Service Medal* (Unpublished T.S. Memoir, 1955) NAM 6706-21.

Col. H.R. Ross, *The Diaries of Harry Ross* (Unpublished T.S. Memoir, 1929) Mss.Eur.B.235.

Interviews

Col. A. Gibb, Colonel A.A. Mains, Major T. Matheson, Major A. Delens.

(ii) Official Documents

Public Record Office

War Office Papers

War Office General Correspondence	WO 32
Miscellaneous Reports and Memoranda	WO 33
Directorate of Military Operations and Intelligence	WO 106
Director of Military Intelligence Papers, 1917–1948	WO 208

Air Ministry Papers

Air Historical Branch Records	AIR 5
Papers of the Chief of the Air Staff	AIR 8
Directorate of Plans	AIR 9
R.A.F. Overseas Commands	AIR 23

India Office Library and Records

Home Miscellaneous Series	H/761

Military Department Records

Official Correspondence from India	L/MIL/3
Compilations and Miscellaneous	L/MIL/5
Military Collections	L/MIL/7
Military Department Library	L/MIL/17
Registers and Indexes	Z/L/MIL
War Staff Series Files 1921–50	L/WS/1

Political and Secret Department Records

Political and Secret Home Correspondence	L/P&S/7
Political and Secret Subject Files	L/P&S/10
Political and Secret Annual Files	L/P&S/11
Political and Secret Collections	L/P&S/12
Political and Secret Memoranda	L/P&S/18
Political and Secret Library	L/P&S/20

Proceedings

Punjab Foreign Proceedings (Frontier) 1889–1901	P/141-6079
Foreign Department Proceedings (Frontier) 1890–1921	P/3737-11085
India Military Proceedings 1849–1937	P/41/32-P/12099

B. PRIMARY SOURCES (PUBLISHED)

(i) Parliamentary Command Papers

Kandahar and Khyber Pass, HC [2811], *BPP* (1881), LXX.

Black Mountain, HC [5561], *BPP* (1888), LXXVII.

Orakzai and Black Mountain, HC [6526] *BPP* (1891), LIX.

Hunza-Nagar, HC [6621], *BPP* (1892), LVIII.

Chitral: 1895, HC [7864], *BPP* (1896), LXXII.

Military Operations on the North-West Frontiers of India. Papers regarding British relations with the Neighbouring tribes on the North-West Frontier of India and the Military Operations undertaken against them during the year 1897–98, HC [8713-4], *BPP* (1898), 2 Vols., LXIII.

Return setting out Wars and Military Operations on or beyond the Borders of British India in which the Government of India has been engaged since 1849, in chronological order; the causes of such Wars and Operations; the locality in which troops operated; the results obtained; the number of troops employed; the cost of such Wars and Operations; and the amount of any contributions towards such costs from the British Treasury, HC [13], *BPP* (1900), LVII.

Papers regarding British relations with the neighbouring tribes on the North-West Frontier of India and the Punjab Frontier Administration, HC [496], *BPP* (1901), XLIX.

Mahsud-Waziri operations, HC [1177], *BPP* (1902), LXXI.

Papers regarding, I, Orakzais: requests of certain clans to be taken under British administration, II, Zakka Khel Afridis: operations, III, Mohmands: operations, HC [4201], *BPP* (1908), LXXIV.

East India (Afghanistan) Papers regarding Hostilities with Afghanistan, 1919, HC [324], *BPP* (1919), XXXVII.

Tribal Disturbances in Waziristan (25th November–14th June, 1937), HC [5495], *BPP* (1937).

(ii) Official Publications

Official Histories (listed chronologically)

Lt.-Col. W.H. Paget, *Expeditions versus the North West Frontier tribes* (Calcutta: Office of Superintendent of Government Printing, 1874).

The Anglo-Afghan War of 1879–80 compiled at the Intelligence Branch of the Quartermaster-General's Department, Horse Guards (London: War Office, 1881).

The Second Afghan War: Compiled and collated by and under the orders of Major-Genl. Sir C.M. MacGregor (Simla: Government Central Branch Press, 1885) 6 vols.

Lt.-Col. W.H. Paget and Lt. A.H. Mason, *Expeditions versus the North West Frontier Tribes* (London: Published by Authority, 1884).

The Mahsud-Waziri Expedition 1881 (Simla: Government Central Branch Press, 1884).

Capt. A.H. Mason, *Expedition against the Black Mountain tribes by a force under Major-General Sir Withers McQueen in 1888* (Simla: Intelligence Branch, 1889).

Capt. A.H. Mason, *Operations against the Orakzai Tribes on the Miranzai Frontier under the command of Brigadier-General Sir William Alexander Lockhart in 1891* (Simla: Intelligence Department, 1891).

Capt. A.H. Mason, *Operations of the Zhob Field Force under Major-General Sir George Stuart White in 1890* (Simla: Intelligence Branch, Q.M.G.'s Dept, 1892).

Capt. A.H. Mason, *Expedition against the Isazai Clans on the Hazara Border by a force under the command of Major-General Sir William Stephen Alexander Lockhart in 1892* (Simla: Intelligence Branch, Q.M.G.'s Dept, 1894).

Capt. A.H. Mason, *Expedition against the Hasanzai and Akazai tribes of the Black Mountain by a force under the command of Major-General William Kidston Elles in 1891* (Simla: Intelligence Branch, Q.M.G.'s Dept, 1894).

Lt. F.G. Cardew, *The Second Afghan War. Abridged and Re-edited* (Calcutta: Office of the Superintendent of Government Printing, 1897).

Lt.-Col. A.H. Mason and Lt. G.K. Cockerill, *Operations against the Mahsud Waziris by a force under the command of Lieutenant-General Sir William Stephen Alexander Lockhart in 1894–95, with a short account of the events which led up to the expedition* (Simla: Intelligence Branch, Q.M.G.'s Dept, 1897).

Capt. W.R. Robertson, *An Official Account of the Chitral Expedition 1895* (Calcutta: Intelligence Branch, Q.M.G.'s Dept, 1898).

Capt. F.A. Hoghton, *Operations of the Mohmand Field Force in 1897* (Simla: Intelligence Branch, Q.M.G.'s Department, 1899).

Maj. G.V. Kemball, *Operations of the Tochi Field Force in 1897–98* (Simla: Intelligence Branch, Q.M.G.'s Dept, 1900).

Capt. G.H. Walters, *Operations of the Tirah Expeditionary Force 1897–98, under the command of General Sir William Stephen Alexander Lockhart* (Simla: Intelligence Branch, Q.M.G.'s Dept, 1900).

Capt. H.F. Walters, *The Operations of the Malakand Field Force and the Buner Field Force 1897–98* (Simla: Intelligence Branch, Q.M.G.'s Dept, 1900).

Major G.B. Unwin, *History of the blockade of the Mahsud Waziris in 1900–1901* (Simla: Intelligence Branch, 1904).

Frontier and Overseas Expeditions from India (Simla: Published by Authority, 1907–13).

Vol. I. *Tribes North of the Kabul River* (Simla: 1907).

Vol. II. *North-West Frontier Tribes between the Kabul and Gumal Rivers* (Simla: 1908).

Vol. I Supplement A. *Operations against the Mohmands 1908* (Calcutta: 1910).

Vol. II. Supplement A. *Operations against the Zakka Khel Afridis* (Calcutta: 1908).

Operations in Waziristan 1919–1920 (Calcutta: G.S.I., 1921).

The Third Afghan War 1919. Official History (Calcutta: G.S.I., 1926).

Official History of Operations on the N.W Frontier of India 1920–35 (Delhi: Manager of Publications, Delhi, 1945).

Official History of the Operations on the N.W. Frontier of India, 1936–7 (Delhi: Army Department, 1943).

Reports and Government of India Publications (listed chronologically)

General Report on the Administration of the Punjab, for the years 1849–50 and 1850–51 (London: Printed for the Court of Directors 1854).

Selections from the Records of the Government of India. (Foreign Department). No. VI General Report on the Administration of the Punjab Territories, comprising the Punjab Proper and the Cis and Trans-Sutlej States, for the Years 1851–52 and 1852–53 (Calcutta: Thos. Jones, Calcutta Gazette Office, 1854).

Report on the Administration of Public Affairs in the Punjaub Territories from 1854–55 to 1855–56 Inclusive (Calcutta: Official, 1856).

Report Showing the Relations of the British Government with the Tribes, Independent and Dependent, on the North-West Frontier of the Punjab from Annexation in 1849 to the close of 1855 (Calcutta, 1855).

General Report on the Administration of the Punjab and its Dependencies, for 1859–60 (Calcutta: Bengal Printing Company Limited, 1860). Through to 1866–67.

Report Showing the Relations of the British Government with the tribes on the North-West Frontier of the Punjab, from annexation in 1849 to the close of 1855; and continuation of the same to August 1864 (Lahore: Punjab Government, 1865).

Report on the Administration of the Punjab and its Dependencies for the year 1874–75 (Lahore: Government Civil Secretariat Press, 1875) through to 1885–86.

Short Report on Important Questions dealt with during the tenure of Command of the Army in India by General Lord Roberts 1885–1893 (Simla: Government Central Printing Office, 1893).

Report on the Mountain Artillery Practice Camps at Dhagul and Rajpur, 1892–93 (Simla: Government Central Printing Office, 1893).

Report on the Mountain Artillery Practice Camps held at Rajpur, Dhagul, and Paniala in 1893–94 (Simla: Government Central Printing Office, 1894).

Report on the Mountain Artillery Practice Camps held at Rajpur and Dhagul in 1894–95 (Simla: Government Central Printing Office, 1895).

Report on the Commissariat-Transport Arrangements of the Tirah Expeditionary Force, 1897–98 (Calcutta: Office of the Superintendent of Government Printing, 1899).

A Dictionary of the Pathan Tribes on the North West Frontier of India (Calcutta: Office of the Superintendent of Army Printing, 1899), 2nd ed., 1910.

Report on the Attock Manoeuvres March 1899 (Simla: Government Central Branch Press, 1899).

Summary of the Measures considered or carried out in the Military Department of the Government of India during the Viceroyalty of the Earls of Elgin and Kincardine, January 1895 to December 1899 (Calcutta: Office of Superintendent of Government Printing, 1899).

Administration Report on the North-West Frontier Province from 9th November 1901 to 31st March 1903 (Peshawar: N.W.F.P. Government Press, 1903).

Administration Report of the North-West Frontier Province (Peshawar: Government Press 1901–40).

Report on Brigade Training, Bannu Brigade, under the orders of Major-General C.G.M. Fasken, commanding Bannu Brigade. February 1908 (Allahabad: Pioneer Press 1908).

Records of the Staff College, Quetta. (Established 1905) (Simla: Government Central Printing Office, 1908) 2 vols.

Report of a Conference of Staff Officers held at Agra under the direction of Lieutenant-General Sir Beauchamp Duff January 1909 (Simla: Government Monotype Press, 1909).

Maj. R.T. Ridgeway, *Pathans* (Calcutta: Government of India, 1910).

Record of Lord Kitchener's Administration of the Army in India 1902–1909 (Simla: Government Central Branch Press, 1909).

Proceedings of the Committee on the Obligations devolving on the Army in India, its Strength and Cost (Army in India Committee, 1912) (Simla: Government Central Press, 1913), 6 vols.

North-West Frontier 1914. Report of Punitive Operation against the Bunerwals on 23rd February 1914 (Delhi: G.S.I., 1914).

Report by Major-General Hugh O'Donnell on an attack on Spina Khaisora on the 7th January 1915 (Simla: G.S.I., 1915).

Report on the operations in the vicinity of Miranshah, 25th and 26th March 1915 (Simla: G.S.I., 1915).

Report of a Conference of General Officers held at Delhi 22nd to 24th February 1917 under the direction of His Excellency the Commander-in-Chief in India (Delhi: G.S.I., 1917).

Report by His Excellency General Sir Charles Carmichael Monro, C-in-C India, on the minor military operations undertaken from March 1916 to March 1917 on the North-West Frontier of India, and elsewhere in the Indian Empire, including Aden, also in South and South-East Persia (Simla: G.S.I., 1917).

Despatch by Brigadier-General G.M. Baldwin, Commanding Derajat Brigade, on the Action of the Derajat Column near Sarwekai (Simla: Government of India, 1917).

Report by Lieutenant-General Sir Arthur Arnold Barrett, commanding the Northern Army, on the operations against the Mahsuds, March–August 1917 (Simla: G.S.I., 1917).

Report of the Attack by Mahsuds on a Convoy Proceeding from Nili Kach to Khajuri Kach 1st May 1917 (Simla: Government of India, 1917).

Report on the Action near Sarwekai 10th May 1917 (Simla: Government of India Press, 1917).

Report on the action of the Derajat Movable Column near Karab Kot 21st April 1917 (Simla: Government of India Press, 1917).

Report on the Operations of the 45th Brigade, Waziristan Field Force at Nanu 21st June 1917 (Simla: Government of India, 1917).

Reports of the Attack by Mahsuds on Tut Narai Post 31st May 1917 (Simla: Government of India, 1917).

Report by Major-General Sir Richard Wapshare, commanding 4th (Quetta) Division, on the operations undertaken against the Marri and Khetran tribes during the period March to May 1918 (Simla: G.S.I., 1919).

Report on the Principal Measures taken in India during the War to Maintain Training at the Standard required in Modern War (Calcutta: G.S.I., 1919).

Reports by G.O.C. Baluchistan Force on the Operations in the vicinity of Lakaband, Kapip and Fort Sandeman 13th–18th July 1919 (Simla: G.S.I., 1919).

Report on the Action at Spin Baldek (Simla: G.S.I., 1919).

Recruiting in India, before and during the war of 1914–18 (Delhi: A.H.Q. in India, 1919).

Report by Major General S.H. Climo on the Operations of the Waziristan Field Force from the 10th to 23rd June 1919 (Simla: G.S.I., 1919).

Short narrative of events forwarded by Major-General Skipton Hill Climo, commanding Waziristan Field Force, from 27th May to 9th June 1919 when the relief of Jandola was effected (Simla: G.S.I., 1919).

Despatch by His Excellency General Sir Charles Carmichael Monro on the Third Afghan War (Simla: Government Central Press, 1919).

Despatch by His Excellency General Sir Charles Carmichael Monro on the Operations in Waziristan 1919–1920 (Simla: A.H.Q. India, 1920).

North-West Frontier Policy (Simla: G.S.I., 1920).

Report on the Working of the Lines of Communication Waziristan Force by Brigadier-General H.C. Tytler, Inspector General of Communications, Waziristan Force, together with certain Notes and Appendices collected for the information of the Staff College Camberley (Delhi: Superintendent of Government Printing, 1920).

Reports by the Inspector General of Communications and Directors of Services Waziristan Force. 1919–20 (Simla: Superintendent Government Printing, 1920).

Proceedings of the Military Requirements Committee 1921. Report. (Lord Rawlinson's Committee) (Simla: Superintendent, Government Central Press, 1921).

Proceedings of the Military Requirements Committee 1921. Minutes of Meetings and Record of Evidence including written Memoranda and Index to Evidence (Simla: Superintendent, Government Central Press, 1921).

Waziristan and the Lessons of the last 60 years (Simla: Government Central Press, 1921).

Report of a Committee Assembled under Order in Council, dated January 6th, 1922, to consider future policy in Waziristan (Delhi: Superintendent Government Printing, India, 1922).

The Army in India and its Evolution (Calcutta: Superintendent of Government Printing, 1924).

Despatch by His Excellency General Lord Rawlinson of Trent on the Operations of the Waziristan Force for the period 8th May 1920 to 31st March 1921 (Delhi: G.S.I., 1921).

Despatch by H.E. General Lord Rawlinson of Trent, C-in-C in India, on the operations of the Waziristan Force for the period 1st April 1921 to 31st December 1921 (Delhi: G.S.I., 1921).

Report on the Administration of the Border of the North-West Frontier Province (Peshawar: Government Press, 1921–38).

Despatch by His Excellency General Lord Rawlinson of Trent on the Operations of the Waziristan Force for the period 1st January 1922 to the 20th April 1923 (Simla: G.S.I., 1923).

Proceedings of the Military Requirements Committee 1921. Minutes of Meetings and Record of Evidence including written Memoranda and Index to Evidence (Simla: Superintendent, Government Central Press, 1921).

Eastern Command Manoeuvres (Simla: G.S.I., 1925).

Summary of Chief Events in North-West Frontier Tribal Territory from 1st January to 31st December 1922 (Delhi: General Staff Branch, 1923) 1922–1928, 1930–1933.

Report of the Committee on the Armed Civil Forces of the North West Frontier Province (Simla: Government of India Press, 1926).

Lt.-Col. J. Keen, *The North-West Frontier Province and the War* (Peshawar: N.W.F.P. Government 1928).

Report on the Staff Exercise and Manoeuvres held under the orders of the G.O.C.-in-C Northern Command, India 22nd November to 30th November 1925 (Calcutta: Government of India Central Publication Branch, 1926).

Report on Northern Command Manoeuvres (India) 1928 (Delhi: Government of India Press, 1929).

Memorandum on Army Training (India) Individual Training Period 1929 (Delhi: Government of India Press, 1929) 1929–38.

J.M. Ewart and E. Howell, *Story of the North-West Frontier Province* (Peshawar: Government Printing and Stationary Office, 1930).

Memorandum on Army Training (India) Collective Training Period 1929–30 (Simla: Government of India Press, 1930).

A.H.Q. India Training Memorandum No. 2 Collective Training period 1930–31 (Simla: Government of India Press, 1931) 1931–38.

Despatch by H.E. Field Marshal Sir W.R. Birdwood on the Disturbances on the North-West Frontier of India from 23rd April to 12th September, 1930 (Delhi: Printed by the Manager, Government of India Press, 1930).

Summary of Administration of Field Marshal Sir W.R. Birdwood as Commander-in-Chief India (Simla: Government of India Press, 1931).

Report of the Tribal Control and Defence Committee 1931 (Delhi: Government of India, 1931).

Expert investigation of the strength, composition and functions of the Army in India, 1931 (Simla: G.S.I., 1931).

Report of the Frontier Watch and Ward Committee (New Delhi: Government of India Press, 1936).

Lt.-Col. F.M. Matthews, *Pathans* (New Delhi: Government of India, 1938).

Report of the Modernization Committee (Simla: Army Headquarters, India, 1938).
'Report of the Expert Committee on the Defence of India 1938–39 (Chatfield Committee)', Delhi, 30th Jan. 1939, L/MIL/17/5/1802.
Report of the Frontier Committee 1945 (Calcutta: Government of India, 1945).

Military Reports, Tribal Tables, and Gazetteers

Capt. A.H. Mason, *Report on the Black Mountain and adjacent independent territory* (Simla: Government Central Press, 1888).
Capt. A.H. Mason, *Notes on Spin and Wano and the Adjacent Country* (Simla: Government Central Press, 1892).
Capt. A.H. Mason, *Report on the Mahsud-Waziri Tribe* (Simla: Intelligence Branch Q.M.G.'s Department, 1894).
Lt.-Col. A.H. Mason, *Report on the Hindustani Fanatics* (Simla: Intelligence Branch Q.M.G.'s Department, 1895).
Capt. E.J. Swayne, *Tribal tables of the Bunerwals and neighbouring tribes* (Simla: Intelligence Branch, Q.M.G.'s Dept, 1897).
Capt. A.S. Hamilton, *Military Report of Southern Waziristan* (Simla, 1900).
Military Report on the Country between the Kabul and Kurram Rivers (Calcutta: Division of the of Chief of Staff, 1908).
Notes on the Indian Frontiers (Simla: G.S.I., 1912).
Military Report on the Derajat Brigade Area (Simla: G.S.I., 1913).
Military Report on the Bannu Brigade Area (Simla: G.S.I., 1915).
Military Report on Khost and the Country between the Kurram and Tochi Rivers (Simla: G.S.I., 1919).
North-West Frontier Tribal Tables (Simla: Government Central Press, 1921).
Military Report on Rawalpindi District (Simla: G.S.I., 1922).
Military Report on United Provinces District (Simla: G.S.I., 1923).
Military Report on Central Provinces District (Simla: G.S.I., 1923).
Military Report on Waziristan (Simla: G.S.I., 1924).
Military Report on the Madras District, 1924 (Simla: G.S.I., 1925).
Military Report on the Mohmand Country (Calcutta: G.S.I., 1926).
Military Report and Gazetteer on Buner and adjacent Independent Territory (Delhi: G.S.I., 1926).
Military Report and Gazetteer on Dir, Swat and Bajaur (Calcutta: G.S.I., 1928) 2nd Ed.
Military Report and Gazetteer on Chitral (Calcutta: G.S.I., 1928).
Military Report on the Kohat District (Simla, G.S.I., 1928) 3rd Ed.
Mobilization. Tribal Tables of the Mahsuds, Wazirs (Darwesh Khel) and Daurs (Simla: G.S.I., 1928).
Military Report on Lucknow District (Simla, G.S.I., 1928).
Military Report on the Sind Independent Brigade Area (Calcutta: G.S.I., 1928).
Military Report on the Peshawar District 1928 (Delhi, 1928).
Military Report on the Meerut District, 1928 (Calcutta, 1929).
Military Report (including railway appendix) on the Mhow District 1929 (Simla, 1930).
Military Report on Tribal country between Khyber and Kurram (Simla: G.S.I., 1930).
Military Report on the Bombay District 1931 (Simla: G.S.I., 1931).

Military Report on the Deccan District 1930 (Calcutta: G.S.I., 1931).
Military Report on the Poona (Independent) Brigade Area (Calcutta: G.S.I., 1932).
Military Report on Waziristan (Calcutta: G.S.I., 1936).
Military Report and Gazetteer on Dir, Swat and Bajour (Calcutta: Political Department, 1937).
Military Report and Gazetteer on the Peshawar District (Calcutta: G.S.I., 1939).
Routes in Waziristan, Bannu and Derajat (New Delhi: G.S.I., 1939).
Military Report and Gazetteer of Indus Kohistan, Black Mountain and adjacent territory (Simla: G.S.I., 1941).
Routes in Chitral, Gilgit & Kohistan (Simla: G.S.I., 1942).
Mobilization. Air Force objectives, Afridis & Orakzais Country (Simla: G.S.I., 1928).
Mobilization. Tribal Tables of the Mahsuds, Wazirs (Darwesh Khel) and Daurs (Simla: G.S.I., 1928).
Instructions Governing the employment of Armed Forces in the Maintenance of Tribal Control on the North-West Frontier of India and Baluchistan (Simla: Defence Department, 1940).

Training Manuals

Field Exercises and Evolutions of Infantry (London: H.M.S.O., 1867) Eds. of 1874, 1877 and 1884.
Manual of Mountain Artillery Drill (Simla: Government Press, 1882).
Infantry Drill (London: H.M.S.O., 1889).
Infantry Drill (Provisional) (London: H.M.S.O., 1892).
Mountain Artillery Drill (London: H.M.S.O., 1891).
Infantry Drill (London: H.M.S.O., 1893).
Infantry Drill (Provisional) (London: H.M.S.O., 1902).
Mountain Artillery Drill 1897 (Calcutta: Government of India Central Printing Office, 1897).
Mountain Artillery Training (Calcutta: Office of Superintendent of Government Printing, India, 1902).
Mountain Warfare (Simla: Adjutant-General in India, 1900).
Frontier Warfare 1901 (Simla: Superintendent of Government. Printing, 1901).
Bush Fighting. (An Appendix to 'Frontier Warfare') (Calcutta: Superintendent of Govt. Printing, India, 1903).
Frontier Warfare and Bush Fighting (Calcutta: Government Printing, 1906).
Notes on Staff Duties in Hill Warfare in India (London: General Staff, War Office, 1906).
Training and Manoeuvre Regulations, 1909 (London: War Office, 1909).
Field Service Regulations, Part I Operations (London: War Office, 1909).
Field Service Regulations, Part I Operations. 1909 (Reprinted with Amendments, 1912) (London: War Office, 1912).
Notes on Warfare on and across the North West Frontier of India, with special reference to the Combination of the Various Arms and Weapons (Calcutta: Superintendent of Govt. Printing, 1918).
Notes on Warfare on and across the North West Frontier of India, with special reference to the Combination of the Various Arms and Weapons (Calcutta: Superintendent of Government Printing, 1919).

Field Service Regulations Vol. II Operations (Provisional) (London: War Office, 1920).

Training Instructions. Mountain Warfare. Peshawar District (Peshawar: Anand, 1920).

Notes on Mountain Warfare (Calcutta: Superintendent of Government Printing, 1920).

Mountain Warfare School. Abbottabad, Synopsis of Lectures 1920 (Revised 1921) (Rawalpindi: Fazal Elahi for General Staff Northern Command, 1921).

Wazirforce Tactical Notes (Dera Ismail Khan: New Commercial Press, Headquarters. Waziristan Force, 1921).

Training and Manoeuvre Regulations 1923 (With additions for India) (Calcutta: Superintendent of Government Printing, 1924).

Field Service Regulations Vol. II (Operations) (London: War Office, 1924).

Manual of Operations on the North-West Frontier of India (Calcutta: Army H.Q. India, 1925).

Manual of Jungle Warfare for Officers of the Burma Military Police (Rangoon: Deputy Inspector-General of Military Police, 1928).

Field Service Regulations Vol. II (Operations) (London: H.M.S.O., 1929).

Waziristan Relief Notes (Northern Command, 1933).

Notes on Imperial Policing 1934 (London: War Office, 1934).

Training Regulations 1934 (London: H.M.S.O., 1934).

Field Service Pocket Book, India (Delhi: Manager of Publications, 1935).

Field Service Regulations, Vol. II Operations – General (London: H.M.S.O., 1935).

Frontier Warfare – India (Army and Royal Air Force) (Delhi: Defence Department, 1939).

Courses of Instruction, India No. 11 Frontier Warfare School, India, Kakul 1941 (Delhi: G.S.I., 1941).

Military Training Pamphlet No. 6 (India) The Support of Land forces in Tribal Warfare on the Western Frontier of India, 1940 (Simla: G.S.I., 1941).

Military Training Pamphlet No. 7 (India) Extensive Warfare (notes on warfare in mountainous country between modern forces in Eastern theatres.) (Simla: G.S.I., 1941).

Military Training Pamphlet No. 16 (India) Platoon Leading in Frontier Warfare (Simla: G.S.I., 1942).

Army/Air Operations Pamphlet No. 8 (India) Air Forces in Support of the Army in tribal Warfare on the Western Frontier of India 1944 (Delhi: G.S.I., 1944).

Standing Orders

Standing Orders of the Punjab Frontier Force (Simla: Government Central Press, 1889).

Standing Orders of the 2nd Punjab Infantry (Calcutta: Thacker Spink, 1895).

Part II. Standing Orders of the 56th Punjabi Rifles F.F. (Bangalore: Higginsbotham & Co., 1910).

Field Service Standing Orders for the Kohat Brigade by Brigadier-General W.R. Birdwood Commanding Kohat Brigade (Roorkee: 1st K.G.O.s Sappers and Miners' Press, 1911).

Standing Orders (War) for the Waziristan Field Force June 1919 (Dera Ismail Khan: New Commercial Press, 1919).

Standing Orders for Frontier Warfare. 16th Infantry Brigade 1924 (Ahmednagar, 1924).
Kohat District Standing Orders for War and for Local Columns (Lahore: The Model Electric Press, 1927).
Standing Orders of the 2nd Battalion 13th Frontier Force Rifles (Agra: Dayalbagh Press, 1934).
Landi Kotal Standing Orders for War 1936 (Landi Kotal: Risalpur Press, 1936).
Standing Orders for Hill Warfare for 1st (Abbottabad) Infantry Brigade, May 1939 (Abbottabad, 1939).

(iii) Periodicals

Military

Proceedings of the United Service Institution of India	(Proc. U.S.I.)
Journal of the United Services Institution of India	(J.U.S.I.I.)
Journal of the Royal United Services Institute	(J.R.U.S.I.)
Proceedings of the Royal Artillery Institution	(Proc.R.A.I.)
United Service Magazine	(U.S.M.)
Journal of the Royal Artillery	(J.R.A.)
Navy & Army Illustrated	
Professional Papers of the Corps of Royal Engineers	(P.P.R.E.)
Royal Engineers Journal	(R.E.J.)
Army Review	(A.R.)
Army Quarterly	(A.Q.)
Cavalry Journal	(C.J.)
Royal Signals Quarterly Journal	(R.S.Q.J.)

Civilian

Blackwood's Edinburgh Magazine	(Blackwood's)
Cornhill Magazine.	
Contemporary Review	
Edinburgh Review	(E.R.)
Fortnightly Review	(F.R.)
Geographic Journal	
Nineteenth Century	(Nineteenth)
The Asiatic Review	
Journal of the Central Asian Society 1914–1939	(J.R.C.A.S.)
Imperial and Asiatic Quarterly Review	(I.A.Q.R.)

(iv) Published Memoirs

Gen. J. Adye, *Recollections of a Military Life* (London: Smith Elder, 1895).
Maj.-Gen. Sir J. Adye, *Soldiers and Others I Have Known* (London: Herbert Jenkins, 1925).
Maj. W. Ashe, *Personal Records of the Kandahar Campaign by Officers engaged therein* (London: David Bogue, 1881).

Brig.-Gen. H.H. Austin, *Some Rambles of a Sapper* (London: Edward Arnold, 1928).

Lt.-Gen. R. Baden-Powell, *Indian Memories: Recollections of Soldiering, Sport, Etc.* (London: Herbert Jenkins, 1915).

Gen. Sir G. de. S. Barrow, *The Life of General Sir Charles Carmichael Monro* (London: Hutchinson, 1931).

Gen. Sir G. de S. Barrow, *The Fire of Life* (London: Hutchinson, 1941).

Field Marshal Lord Birdwood, *Khaki and Gown: An Autobiography* (London: Ward Lock, 1942).

Field Marshal Lord Birdwood, *In My Time* (London: Skeffington, 1946).

Lt.-Col. L.V. Blacker, *Pathans, Planes and Petards* (Bournemouth: privately printed, 1972).

Sir B. Blood, *Four Score Years and Ten: Sir Bindon Blood's Reminiscences* (London: G. Bell, 1933).

Brig. R.C. Bristow, *Memories of the British Raj. A Soldier in India* (London: Johnson, 1974).

R.I. Bruce, *The Forward Policy and its Results: or, Thirty-Five Years Work amongst the Tribes on our North-Western Frontier of India* (London: Longmans, Green, 1900).

Maj.-Gen. C.E. Callwell, *The Memoirs of Major General Sir Hugh MacCalmont* (London: Hutchinson, 1924).

Lord Chatfield, *It Might Happen Again* (London: Heinemann, 1947).

Maj. J.A. Colquhoun, *With the Kurram Field Force* (London: W.H. Allen, 1881).

Gen. G. O'Moore Creah, *The Autobiography of General Sir O'Moore Creah* (London: Hutchinson, 1924).

Maj. H. Daly, *Memoirs of General Sir Henry Dermot Daly* (London: John Murray, 1905).

G. Dunbar, *Frontiers* (London: Ivor Nicholson & Watson, 1932).

Col. A. Durand, *The Making of a Frontier: Five Years' Experience and Adventures in Gilgit, Hunza, Nagar, Chitral and the Eastern Hindu Kush* (London: John Murray, 1899).

E. Edwardes, *Memorials of the Life and Letters of Major-General Sir Herbert B. Edwardes* (London: Kegan Paul, Trench, 1886).

Maj. H.B. Edwardes, *A Year on the Punjab Frontier* (London: Richard Bentley, 1851).

G.R. Elsmie, *Field Marshal Sir Donald Stewart, An Account of His Life, Mainly in his Own Words* (London: 1903).

Air Chief Marshal B. Embry, *Mission Completed* (London: Methuen, 1957).

Air Chief Marshal P. Joubert de la Ferté, *The Fated Sky* (London: Hutchinson, 1952).

Maj.-Gen. J.F.C. Fuller, *Memoirs of an Unconventional Soldier* (London: Ivor Nicholson and Watson, 1936).

Surgeon R. Gillham-Thomsett, *Kohât, Kuram, and Khost; or, Experiences and Adventures in the Late Afghan War* (London: Remington, 1884).

Lt.-Col. R.G. Thomsett, *With the Peshawar Column, Tirah Expeditionary Force* (London: Digby, Long, 1899).

Gen. Sir H. Gough, *Soldiering On* (London: Arthur Baker, 1954).

B.J. Gould, *The Jewel in the Lotus: recollections of an Indian political* (London: Chatto and Windus, 1957).

Capt. F. Guest, *Indian Cavalryman* (London: Jarrolds, 1959).

Gen. Sir A. Haldane, *A Soldier's Saga: The Autobiography of General Sir Aylmer Haldane* (Edinburgh and London: William Blackwood, 1948).

A. Hayter, *The Second Step* (London: Hodder and Stoughton, 1962).

Lt.-Col. M.C.A. Henniker, *Memoirs of a Junior Officer* (Edinburgh and London: William Blackwood, 1951).

R. Hilton, *Nine Lives: The Autobiography of an Old Soldier* (London: Hollis and Carter, 1955).

Maj.-Gen. Sir F. Howard, *Reminiscences 1848–1890* (London: John Murray, 1924).

Brig. F. Ingall, *The Last of the Bengal Lancers* (London: Leo Cooper, 1988).

General Lord Ismay, *The Memoirs of General the Lord Ismay* (London: Heinemann, 1960).

P. N. Kaul, *Frontier Callings* (Delhi: Vikas Publishing House, 1976).

J. Laffin, *Swifter than Eagles* (London: Blackwood, 1964).

D. Lee, *Never Stop the Engine* (London: Thomas Harmsworth, 1983).

Sir P.S. Lumsden and Gen. G.R. Elsmie, *Lumsden of the Guides: A Sketch of the Life of General Sir Henry Burnett Lumsden* (London: John Murray, 1899).

E. Lydall, *Enough of Action* (London: Jonathan Cape, 1949).

Gen. N. Lyttleton, *Eighty Years: Soldiering, Politics and Games* (London: Hodder and Staughton, 1927).

Lt.-Gen. Sir G.F. MacMunn, *Behind the Scenes in Many Wars* (London: John Murray, 1930).

L. Mallam and D. Day, *A Pair of Chaplis and a Cassock* (London: privately printed, n.d.).

J. Masters, *Bugles and a Tiger* (London: Michael Joseph, 1956).

Maj.-Gen. E.S. May, *Changes and Chances of a Soldiers Life* (London: Phillip Allen, 1925).

Maj. R.C. Mitford, *To Cabul with the Cavalry Brigade* (London: W.H. Allen, 1881).

Lt.-Gen. G.N. Molesworth, *Curfew on Olympus* (London: Asia Publishing House, 1965).

Lt.-Gen. Sir F. Morgan, *Peace and War: A Soldier's Life* (London: Hodder and Stoughton, 1961).

J. Morris, *Hired to Kill: Some Chapters of Autobiography* (London: Rupert Hart-Davis, 1960).

Lt.-Gen. Sir P. Neame, *Playing with Strife: The Autobiography of a Soldier* (London: Harrap, 1947).

Lt.-Col. Sir F. O'Connor, *On the Frontier and Beyond: A Record of Thirty Years' Service* (London: John Murray, 1931).

Gen. Sir N. Poett, *Pure Poett* (London: Leo Cooper, 1991).

Brig. J.H. Prendergast, *Prender's Progress: A Soldier in India, 1931–47* (London: Cassell, 1979).

Lord F. Roberts, Field Marshal, *Forty-One Years in India* (London: Richard Bentley, 1897).

Lt. C.G. Robertson, *Kurum, Kabul and Kandahar Being a Brief Record of Impressions in Three Campaigns* (Edinburgh: David Charles, 1881).

Sir W. Robertson, Field Marshal, *From Private to Field Marshal* (London: Constable, 1921).

G.B. Scott, *Twenty Years on the North-West Frontier* (Allahabad: Pioneer, 1906).

Air Marshal Sir J. Slessor, *The Central Blue: Recollections and Reflections* (London: Cassell, 1956).

Sir J. Slessor, *These Remain. A Personal Anthology* (London: Michael Joseph, 1969).

Field Marshal Sir W. Slim, *Defeat into Victory* (London: Cassell, 1956).

Gen. H. Smith-Dorrien, *Memories of Forty-Eight Years Service* (London: John Murray, 1925).

Sir J. Smyth, *Milestones* (London: Sidgewick and Jackson, 1979).

Col. C.E. Stewart, *Through Persia in Disguise with Reminiscences of the Umbeylah Campaign* (London: George Routledge & Sons, 1911).

F.T. Stockdale, *Walk Warily in Waziristan* (Ilfracombe: A.H. Stockwell, 1982).

Lt.-Col. E.A. Stotherd, *Sabre and Saddle* (London: Seeley Service, 1933).

Brig.-Gen. T. Ternan, *Some Experiences of an Old Bromsgrovian: Soldiering in Afghanistan, Egypt and Uganda* (Birmingham: Cornish Brother, 1930).

J.H. Thornton, *Memoirs of Seven Campaigns: A Record of Thirty-Five Years in the Indian Medical Department in India, China, and the Sudan* (Westminster: Archibald Constable, 1895).

Lt.-Gen. Sir F.I. Tuker, *While Memory Serves* (London: Cassell, 1956).

Gen. Sir J.L. Vaughan, *My Service in the Indian Army – and After* (London: Archibald Constable, 1904).

Col. Sir R. Warburton, *Eighteen Years on the Khyber, 1879–1898* (London: John Murray, 1900).

Col. J.S. Western, *Reminiscences of an Indian Cavalry Officer* (London: Allen & Unwin, 1922).

Brig.-Gen. Sir J. Willcocks, *From Kabul to Kumassi: Twenty-Four Years of Soldiering and Sport* (London: John Murray, 1904).

Gen. Sir J. Willcocks, *The Romance of Soldiering and Sport* (London: Cassell, 1925).

Lt.-Col. A. Wilson, *Sport and Service in Assam and Elsewhere* (London: Hutchinson, 1924).

Maj.-Gen. N. Woodyatt, *Under Ten Viceroys: The Reminiscences of a Gurkha* (London: Herbert Jenkins, 1922).

Major A.C. Yate, *Lieutenant Colonel John Haughton, Commandant of the 36th Sikhs: A Hero of Tirah* (London: John Murray, 1900).

Maj.-Gen. G. Younghusband, *A Soldier's Memories in Peace and War* (London: Herbert Jenkins, 1917).

Maj.-Gen. Sir G. Younghusband, *Forty Years a Soldier* (London: Herbert Jenkins, 1923).

(v) Other Contemporary Published Works

Col. J. Adye, *Sitana: A Mountain Campaign on the Borders of Afghanistan in 1863* (London: Richard Bentley, 1867).

Gen. Sir J. Adye, *Indian Frontier Policy* (London: Smith Eldar, 1897).

C.F. Andrews, *The Challenge of the North-West Frontier: A Contribution to World Peace* (London: Allen & Unwin, 1937).

Anon. War Correspondents of the 'Pioneer', *The Risings on the North-West Frontier. Being a complete narrative with specially prepared maps of the various risings of the frontier tribes in the Tochi Valley, the Swat valley, the country of the Mohmands and the Momunds, and the country of the Afridis and Orakzais; and of the several punitive campaigns undertaken against these tribes, as well as the two minor expeditions sent against the Utman Khels and the Bunerwals; the whole covering a period extending from the middle of June, 1897, to the end of January, 1898* (Allahabad: Pioneer, 1898).

The Chitral Expedition 1895 containing an account of the adventures and captivity of Lieutenants Fowler and Edwards together with full details of the operations of General Low's Force (Allahabad: Pioneer, 1895).

Indian Frontier Organisation (Allahabad: Pioneer, 1920).

Mountain Warfare Camp and Bivouac Routine (Ferozepore: 1/9th Bn Hampshire Regiment, 1917).

Notes on Frontier Warfare (Aldershot: Gale and Polden, 1922).

A.H. Atteridge, *The Wars of the 'Nineties. A History of Warfare in the Last Ten Years of the Nineteenth Century* (London: Cassell, 1899).

E. Bartlett, *Battalion and Brigade Drill for Savage Warfare* (London: W. Clowes, 1904).

Sir W. Barton, *India's North-West Frontier* (London: John Murray, 1939).

'Beechwood', *My Diary of the Punjab Camp of Exercise, 1872–73 (Being a series of letters to The Englishman)* (Bombay: Thacker Vining, 1873).

H.W. Bellew, *Our Punjab Frontier: Being a Concise Account of the various tribes by which the North-West Frontier of British India is Inhabited; shewing its present unprotected and unsatisfactory state, and the urgent necessity that exists for immediate reconstruction. Also, brief remarks on Afghanistan and our policy in reference to that country by a Punjab Official* (Calcutta: Wyman, 1868).

Lt. W.G.L. Beynon, *With Kelly to Chitral* (London: Edward Arnold, 1896).

Capt. A.H. Bingley, *Notes on the Warlike Races of India and its Frontiers compiled to accompany Bremner's Types of the Indian Army* (London: War Office, 1897).

Bvt.-Maj. W.D. Bird, *Some Principles of Frontier Mountain Warfare* (London: Hugh Rees, 1909).

Field Marshal Sir C.H. Brownlow, *Stray Notes on Military Training and Khaki Warfare* (London: 1909).

Lt.-Col. C.E. Bruce, *Waziristan, 1936–37: The problems of the North-West Frontier of India and their Solutions* (Aldershot: Gale and Polden, 1938).

R.I. Bruce, *The Forward Policy and its Results: or, Thirty-Five Years Work amongst the Tribes on our North-Western Frontier of India* (London: Longmans, Green, 1900).

By an Adjutant, *An Essay on Tactics* (London, W. Mitchell, 1872).

Capt. C.E. Callwell, *Hints on Reconnaissance in Little Known Countries* (London: Intelligence Division, 1892).

Capt. C.E. Callwell, *Small Wars: Their Principles and Practice* (London: H.M.S.O., 1896) 2nd ed. 1899, 3rd ed. 1906.

Maj. C.E. Callwell, *The Tactics of Today* (Edinburgh and London: William Blackwood and Sons, 1900).

Col. C.E. Callwell, *Tirah 1911* (London: Constable, 1911).

Maj.-Gen. Sir C.E. Callwell, and Maj.-Gen. Sir J. Headlam, *A History of the Royal Artillery from the Indian Mutiny to the Great War* (Woolwich: Royal Artillery Institution, 1937).

G. Casserly, *Manual of Training for Jungle and River Warfare* (London: T. Werner Laurie, 1915).

Lt. W.L.S. Churchill, *The Story of the Malakand Field Force* (London: Mandarin, 1990).

Capt. C. Clery, *Minor Tactics* (London: H.S. King, 1875).

Lt.-Gen. S.H. Climo, *Mountain Warfare Notes* (Poona: Scottish Mission Press, 1921).

Capt. S.M. Congreve-Schneider, *The Zhob Valley Expedition* (London: Dawson & Sons, 1889).

S. Cotton, *Nine Years on the North West Frontier, 1854–1863* (London: Richard Bentley, 1868).

M. Coxe, *The Punjaub and North-West Frontier of India by an Old Punjaubee* (London: C. Kegan Paul, 1878).

Maj. J.H.V. Crowe, *An Epitome of the Afghan War, 1878–9 and 1879–80* (Woolwich: Royal Artillery Institution, 1905).

J. Dacosta, *A Scientific Frontier* (London: W.H. Allen, 1891).

R.S. Dey, *A Brief Account of the Punjab Frontier Force* (Calcutta: W. Newman, 1905).

Brevet Major B.C. Dening, *The Future of the British Army: The Problem of Duties, Cost and Composition* (London: Witherby, 1928).

K. Dunnoley, *Drill Made Easy: Savage Warfare* (London: 1900).

M. Durand, *The Life of Field Marshal Sir George White VC* (Edinburgh and London: William Blackwood and Sons, 1915).

Brig.-Gen. C.C. Egerton, *Hill Warfare on the North West Frontier of India* (Allahabad: Pioneer, 1899).

Lt. C.M. Enriquez, *The Pathan Borderland* (Calcutta and Simla: Thacker, Spink, 1910).

Lt. Viscount Fincastle, and Lt. P.C. Elliot-Lockhart, *A Frontier Campaign: A Narrative of the Malakand and Buner Field Forces on the North West Frontiers of India* (London: Methuen, 1898).

G.W. Forrest, *Life of Field Marshal Sir Neville Chamberlain* (London: William Blackwood, 1909).

Maj. G.A. Furse, *Studies on Military Transport* (Bombay: Education Society Press, 1877).

'Frontier', *Frontier Warfare* (Bombay: Thacker, n.d.) (*c*.1920s).

Col. J.C. Gawler, *Sikhim: With Hints on Mountain and Savage Warfare* (London: Edward Stanford, 1873).

Lt.-Col. E. Gunter, *Outlines of Modern Tactics* (London: William Clowes, 1893) 2nd Ed. 1895, 3rd Ed. 1899.

Maj.-Gen. Sir C.W. Gwynn, *Imperial Policing* (London: Macmillan, 1936).

E.B. Hamley, *Operations of War* (London: 1866).

Col. H.B. Hanna, *The Second Afghan War, 1878–79–80: Its Causes, Its Conduct, and Its Consequences* (Westminster: Archibald Constable), 3 Vols.

Maj.-Gen. Sir R.C. Hart, *Reflections on the Art of War* (London: William Clowes, 1901).

Lt.-Col. G.F.R. Henderson, *Technical Training of Infantry* (Dublin: Sibly, 1899).

Col. G.F.R. Henderson, *The Science of War* (London: Longmans, Green, 1905).

G.Y.J. [George Younghusband], *Two Lectures to the Guides* (Poona: Scottish Mission Industries, 1908).

Lt.-Col. P. Hehir, *Prevention of Disease and Inefficiency with Special Reference to Indian Frontier Warfare* (Allahabad: Pioneer, 1911), 2nd ed.

Lt.-Col. W.C.G. Heneker, *Bush Warfare* (London: Hugh Rees, 1907).

Col T.H. Holdich, *The Indian Borderland* (London: Methuen, 1901).

Col. H.D. Hutchinson, *The Campaign in Tirah, 1897–1898* (London: Macmillan, 1898).

L. James, *'With the Chitral Relief Force'* (Calcutta: 'Englishman' Press, 1895).

L. James, *The Indian Frontier War – Being an Account of the Mohmund and Tirah Expeditions 1897* (London: Heinemann, 1898).

Col. L. James, *High Pressure: Being Some Record of Activities in the Service of the Times Newspaper* (London: John Murray, 1929).

Hon. A. Keppel, *Gun-Running and the Indian North-West Frontier* (London: John Murray, 1911).

Brig. A.A. Kinloch, *Forms of Attack* (Allahabad: Pioneer, 1892).

E.F. Knight, *Where Three Empires Meet* (London: Longmans, Green, 1893).

Lt.-Col. C.J. McCartie, *A New System of Field Hospitals and Ambulances in Hill Warfare* (Calcutta: Thacker, Spink, 1899).

Lt. C.M. MacGregor, *Mountain Warfare: An Essay on the Conduct of Hill Operations in Mountainous Countries* (London: Nissan and Parker, 1866).

Maj. G.F. MacMunn and Maj. A.C. Lovett, *The Armies of India* (London: Adam and Charles Black, 1911).

Lt.-Gen. Sir G.F. MacMunn, *The Romance of the Indian Frontiers* (London: Jonathan Cape, 1931).

Lt.-Gen. Sir G.F. MacMunn, *The Martial Races of India* (London: Sampson Low, Marston, n.d.).

T. Miller-Maguire, *Analysis of Callwell's Small Wars* (London: Harmsworth, 1902).

T. Miller-Maguire, *Guerrilla or Partisan Warfare* (London: William Clowes and Sons, 1904).

T. Miller-Maguire, *Strategy and Tactics in Mountain Ranges* (London: William Clowes and Sons, 1904).

Maj. D.B. Mackenzie, *Mountain Warfare on the Sand Model* (Aldershot: Gale and Polden, 1936).

Lt.-Col. A.R. Martin, *Mountain and Savage Warfare* (Allahabad: Pioneer, 1899).

Maj. E.S. May, *Achievements of Field Artillery* (Woolwich, Royal Artillery Institution, 1893).

Lt.-Col. E.S. May, *A Retrospect on the South African War* (London: Sampson Low, Marston, 1901).

Capt. C.B. Mayne, *Infantry Fire Tactics* (Chatham: Gale and Polden, 1885).

Capt. C.B. Mayne, *The Late Battles in the Soudan and Modern Tactics* (Chatham: Gale and Polden, 1885).

Capt. C. McFall, *With The Zhob Field Force 1890* (London: Heinemann, 1895).

C.W. Miles, *The Zakka Khel and Mohmand Expedition* (Rawalpindi: J.R. Thapur and Sons, 1909).

Lt.-Col. A.F. Montanaro, *Hints for a Bush Campaign* (London: Sands, 1901).

Maj. C.B. Morgan, *Hints on Bush Fighting* (London: William Clowes & Sons, 1899).

240   *Select Bibliography*

H. Woosnam Mills, *The Pathan Revolt in North-West India* (Lahore: Civil and Military Gazette, 1897).

H. Woosnam Mills, *The Tirah Campaign – being the Sequel of the Pathan Revolt in North West India Enlarged and Revised* (Lahore: Civil and Military Gazette, 1898).

Capt. H.L. Nevill, *Campaigns on the North-West Frontier* (London: John Murray, 1912).

H. Newman, *Umra Khan and the Chitral Campaign* (Lahore: Civil and Military Gazette, 1897).

Lt.-Col. J.E. Nixon, *Notes for Staff Officers on Field Service* (Lahore: Civil and Military Gazette, 1897), 2nd ed. 1898.

R. North, *The Punjab Frontier Force. A Brief Record of their Services 1846–1924* (Dera Ismail Khan: Commercial Steam Press, 1934).

E.E. Oliver, *Across the Border: or Pathan and Biloch* (London: Chapman and Hall, 1890).

Maj. E. Peach, *Handbook of Tactics for Savage Warfare* (Allahabad: Pioneer, 1898).

Col. H.R. Pettigrew, *Frontier Scouts* (Selsey: privately printed, 1965).

Lt.-Col. F.H. Plowden, *The Battalion on the Frontier* (Lahore: Civil and Military Gazette, 1899).

Lt.-Col. J.A. Pollock, *Notes on Hill Warfare* (Simla: U.S.I.I., 1899).

Maj. O.C. Radford, *Notes for Panjab Probationers on 1. Castes 2. Hill Tactics 3. Customs 4. Idiomatic Sentences* (Lahore: Civil and Military Gazette, 1894).

Capt. D. Rees, *Pioneer Piquet. 21st December 1919* (London: privately printed, 1954).

Sir G.S. Robertson, *Chitral – the Story of a Minor Siege* (London: Methuen, 1898).

Maj. E.H. Rodwell, *Four Bangalore Lectures* (Lahore: Civil and Military Gazette, 1899.

Lt.-Col. E.H. Rodwell, *Tactical lectures* (Lahore: Civil and Military Gazette, 1903).

Maj.-Gen. H. Rowan-Robinson, *The Infantry Experiment* (London: William Clowes and Sons, 1934).

Maj.-Gen. L. Shadwell, *Mountain Warfare: Illustrated by the Campaign of 1799 in Switzerland* (London: H.S. King, 1875).

Lt.-Gen. Shadwell, *The Life of Colin Campbell, Lord Clyde* (Edinburgh and London: Blackwood, 1881).

Capt. L.J. Shadwell, *Lockhart's Advance Through Tirah* (London: W. Thacker Spink, 1898).

Maj. L.J. Shadwell, *North-West Frontier Warfare: Being an Appendix to Sherston's 'Tactics as Applied to Schemes'* (Calcutta: Thacker, Spink, 1902).

Capt. J. Sherston, *Tactics as Applied to Schemes* (London: Gale and Polden, 1894).

Capt. J. Sherston and Maj. L.J. Shadwell, *Tactics as Applied to Schemes* (London: W. Thacker, 1897).

Gen. Sir A. Skeen, *Passing it On: Short talks on Tribal Fighting on the North-West Frontier of India* (London: Gale and Polden, 1932), 2nd ed. 1932, 3rd ed. 1934, 4th ed. 1939.

Capt. A.K. Slessor, *The 2nd Battalion Derbyshire Regiment in Tirah* (London: Swan Sonnenschein, 1900).

Maj.-Gen. F.W. Stubbs, *History of the Organization, Equipment, and War Services of the Regiment of Bengal Artillery, compiled from published works, official records, and various private sources* (London: W.H. Allen, 1895).

Capt. A.W.N. Taylor, *Jungle Warfare: the conduct of small expeditions in the jungles and hilly tracts of Burma, and a system of drill and musketry instruction connected therewith, for the use of officers of the Burma Military Police* (Rangoon: Superintendent of Government Printing Rangoon, 1902).

S.S. Thornburn, *The Punjab in Peace and War* (Edinburgh and London: William Blackwood and Sons, 1904).

H.C. Thomson, *The Chitral Campaign: A Narrative of Events in Chitral, Swat and Bajour* (London: William Heinemann, 1895).

Col. J.P. Villiers-Stuart, *Letters of a Once Punjab Frontier Force Officer to his Nephew giving his Ideas on Fighting on the North West Frontier and in Afghanistan* (London: Sifton Praed, 1925).

'Arthur Vincent', *The Defence of India* (London: Oxford University Press, 1922).

Lt.-Col. H. de Watteville, *Waziristan 1919–20* (London: Constable, 1925).

C.B. Wallis, *West African Warfare* (London: Harrison & Sons, 1905).

Col. H.C. Wylly, *From the Black Mountain to Waziristan* (London: Macmillan, 1912).

Maj. A.C. Yate, *Lieutenant Colonel John Haughton, Commandant of the 36th Sikhs: A Hero of Tirah* (London: John Murray, 1900).

Capt. G.J. Younghusband and Capt. F.E. Younghusband, *The Relief of Chitral* (London: Macmillan, 1895).

Capt. and Brevet Major G.J. Younghusband, *Indian Frontier Warfare* (London: Kegan Paul, Trench, Trübner, 1898).

(vi) Regimental Histories

The Historical Records of the (Queen's Own) Corps of Guides, raised 14th December 1846 (Lahore: Punjab Military Dept, 1877).

Regimental Records. 5th Regiment, Punjab Cavalry (Lahore: W. Ball, 1886).

No. 3 (Peshawar) Mountain Battery, P.F.F., Battery History (Lahore: New Albion Press, 1886).

Historical Record of No. 1 (Kohat) Mountain Battery, Punjab Frontier Force (Lahore: Punjab Government Press, 1886).

Historical Records of the Services of the Queen's Own Corps of Guides (Lahore: Civil and Military Gazette, 1886).

History of the 1st Sikh Infantry, 1846–1886 (Calcutta: Thacker, Spink, 1887).

History of the 1st Punjab Cavalry (Lahore: Civil and Military Gazette, 1887).

The Historical Record of the 4th Sikh Infantry, Punjab Frontier Force (Lahore: Punjab Government Press, 1887).

The Historical Record of the 2nd (or Hill) Sikh Infantry, Punjab Frontier Force (Lahore: Punjab Government Press, 1887).

History of the Second Panjáb Cavalry (London: Kegan Paul, Trench, 1888).

The Historical Record of No. 4 (Hazara) Mountain Battery, Punjab Frontier Force (Lahore: Punjab Government Press, 1888).

History of the 2nd Punjab Infantry 1849–1888 (Calcutta: 1889).

History of the 4th Regiment, Punjab Infantry (Calcutta: Thacker, Spink, 1894).

History of the 2nd Punjab Infantry (Calcutta: no imprint, 1902).

History of the 1st Sikh Infantry, 1846–1886 (Calcutta: Thacker Spink, 1903).

The Historical Records The 3rd Sikh Infantry, Punjab Frontier Force (no imprint, 1903).

Historical Record of the 22nd Derajat Mountain Battery (Frontier Force) (Lahore: Albion, 1905).

32nd Sikh Pioneers Regimental History (Calcutta: Thacker and Spink, 1906).

A Short History of the 3rd (Queen's Own) Gurkha Rifles (London: Hugh Rees, 1907).

History of the 23rd Cavalry (Frontier Force), late 3rd Regiment, Punjab Cavalry (Lahore: no imprint, 1910).

Records of the 1/XXI Punjabis (Aldershot: Gale and Polden, 1919).

The 101st Grenadiers Historical Record of the Regiment, 1778–1923 (Aldershot: Gale and Polden, 1928).

History of the 5th Royal Gurkha Rifles (Frontier Force) 1858–1928 (Aldershot: Gale and Polden, 1930).

History of the 1st Battalion 5th Mahratta Light Infantry (Jangi Paltan) (Calcutta: Government of India Press, 1930).

Historical Records of the 3rd Sikhs 1847–1930 (Bournemouth: 1931).

History of the Guides 1846–1922 (Aldershot: Gale and Polden, 1938).

History of the 5th Royal Gurkha Rifles (Frontier Force) Vol. II 1929–1947 (Aldershot: Gale and Polden, 1956).

C.T. Atkinson, *A History of the 1st (P.W.O.) Battalion the Dogra Regiment* (Southampton: Camelot Press, 1950).

C.T. Atkinson, *The Dorsetshire Regiment Vol. II* (Oxford: Oxford University Press, 1947).

Lt.-Col. P.G. Bamford, *1st King George V's Own Battalion the Sikh Regiment 1846–1946* (Aldershot: Gale and Polden, 1948).

Brig. C.N. Barclay, *The History of the Sherwood Foresters (Nottinghamshire and Derbyshire Regiment) 1919–1957* (London: William Clowes and Sons, 1959).

Brig. C.N. Barclay, *The History of the Duke of Wellington's Regiment 1919–1952* (London: William Clowes and Sons, 1953).

Brig. C.N. Barclay, *The Regimental History of the 3rd Queen Alexandra's Own Gurkha Rifles Vol. II (1927 to 1947)* (London: William Clowes and Sons, 1953).

Brig. E.V. Bellers, *The History of the 1st King George V's Own Gurkha Rifles (The Malaun Regiment) Vol. II 1920–1947* (Aldershot: Gale and Polden, 1956).

Lt.-Col. G. Betham and Maj. H.V. Geary, *The Golden Galley: The Story of the Second Punjab Regiment 1761–1947* (Oxford: Oxford University Press, 1956).

Lt.-Col. Birdwood, *The Worcestershire Regiment 1922–1950* (Aldershot: Gale and Polden, 1952).

Brig. G. Blight, *The History of the Royal Berkshire Regiment (Prince Charlotte of Wales) 1920–1947* (London: Staples, 1953).

Lt.-Col. G.A. Brett, *History of the South Wales Borderers and the Monmouthshire Regiment, 1937–1952 Part 1* (Pontypool: Griffin, 1953).

Brig. W.E. Condon, *The Frontier Force Rifles* (Aldershot: Gale and Polden, 1953).

Brig. W.E. Condon, *The Frontier Force Regiment* (Aldershot: Gale and Polden, 1962).

J. de L. Conry, *Regimental History of the 2/19th Hyderabad Regiment (Berar)* (Aldershot: Gale and Polden, 1927).

Lt.-Col. M.J. Corbally, *The Royal Ulster Rifles 1793–1960* (Glasgow: 1960).

D. S. Daniell, *The Royal Hampshire Regiment 1918–1954* (Aldershot: Gale and Polden, 1955).

Capt. C.G. Dean, *The Loyal Regiment (North Lancashire) 1919–1953* (Preston: Regimental Headquarters, 1955).

Brig.-Gen. J. Evatt, *Historical Record of the 39th Royal Garwhal Rifles Vol. 1 1887–1922* (Aldershot: Gale and Polden, 1922).

Maj. J.T. Gorman, *2nd Battalion 4th Bombay Grenadiers (King Edward's Own) Historical Record of the Regiment, 1796–1933* (Western-super-Mare: Lawrence, 1933).

Lt.-Col. W.L. Hailes, *War Services of the 9th Jat Regiment* (Aldershot: Gale and Polden, 1938).

Lt.-Col W.L. Hailes and Maj. J. Ross, *The Jat Regiment: A History of the Regiment 1803–1947* (Bareilly: Jat Regimental Centre, 1967).

Col. T. Higginson, *Digest of Services of the 1st (Coke's) Regiment Punjab Infantry* (Simla: Chronicle, 1888).

Lt.-Col. F.H. James, *History of the 1st Battalion 6th Rajputana Rifles (Wellesley's)* (Aldershot: Gale and Polden, 1938).

Brig. W.J. Jervois, *The History of the Northamptonshire Regiment: 1934–1948* (London: Regimental History Committee, 1953).

Lt.-Commander P K. Kemp, *History of the Royal Norfolk Regiment 1919–1951* (Norwich: Regimental Association of the Royal Norfolk Regiment, 1953).

Lt.-Col. J.A. Kitson, *The Story of the 4th Battalion 2nd King Edward VII's Own Gurkha Rifles* (Aldershot: Gale and Polden, 1949).

Lt.-Col J.P. Lawford and Maj. W.E. Catto, *Solah Punjab The History of the 16th Punjab Regiment* (Aldershot: Gale and Polden, 1967).

D.M. Lindsay, *Regimental History of the 6th Royal Battalion 13th Frontier Force Rifles (Scinde), 1843–1923* (Aldershot: Gale and Polden, 1926).

D.M. Lindsay, *Regimental History of the 6th Royal Battalion (Scinde) 13th Frontier Force Rifles, 1843–1934* (Aldershot: Gale and Polden, 1935).

R. Macdonnell and M. Macaulay, *A History of the 4th Prince of Wales's Own Gurkha Rifles 1857–1937 Vol. I.* (Edinburgh and London: William Blackwood & Sons, 1940).

Lt.-Gen. G.F. MacMunn, *History of the Guides Part II 1922–1947* (Aldershot: Gale and Polden, 1950).

Lt.-Gen. G.F. MacMunn, *The History of the Sikh Pioneers (23rd, 32nd, 34th)* (London: Sampson, Low, Marston, 1936).

Lt.-Col. W.E. Maxwell, *Capital Campaigners The History of the 3rd Battalion (Queen Mary's Own) The Baluch Regiment* (Aldershot: Gale and Polden, 1948).

Col. H.S. McRae, *Regimental History of the 45th Rattray's Sikhs* (Glasgow: Robert Maclehose, 1933).

Capt. B.R. Mullaly, *History of the 10th Gurkha Rifles The First Battalion 1890–1921* (Aldershot: Gale and Polden, 1924).

Col. B.R. Mullaly, *Bugle and Kukri The Story of The 10th Prince Mary's Own Gurkha Rifles* (Edinburgh and London: William Blackwood & Sons, 1957).

Col. W.N. Nicholson, *The Suffolk Regiment 1928 to 1946* (Ipswich: East Anglian Magazine, 1947).

F.L. Petre, *The 1st King George's Own Gurkha Rifles. The Malaun Regiment 1815–1921* (London: R.U.S.I., 1925).

Lt.-Col. F.S. Poynder, *The 9th Gurkha Rifles 1817–1936* (London: R.U.S.I., 1937).

Maj. M.I. Quereshi, *History of the First Punjab Regiment 1759–1956* (Aldershot: Gale and Polden, 1958).

H.G. Rawlinson, *Napier's Rifles The History of the 5th Battalion 6th Rajputana Rifles* (Oxford University Press, 1929).

H.G. Rawlinson, *The History of the 3rd Battalion 7th Rajput Regiment (Duke of Connaught's Own)* (London: Oxford University Press, 1941).

By Officers of the Regiment, *The Historical Records of the 127th Baluch Light Infantry compiled from the Official Records from 1844 to 1905* (London: William Clowes and Sons, 1905).

Lt.-Col. J.E. Shearer, *A History of the 1st Battalion 15th Punjab Regiment* (Aldershot: Gale and Polden, 1937).

Capt. A.R. Solly, *Historical Records of the 4–5th Mahratta Light Infantry* (Lahore: Civil and Military Gazette, 1924).

J. Taylor, *The Devon's; A History of the Devonshire Regiment, 1685–1945* (Bristol: White Swan, 1951).

W.S. Thatcher, *The Fourth Battalion Duke of Connaught's Own Tenth Baluch Regiment in the Great War* (Cambridge: Cambridge University Press, 1932).

Capt. J.P. Villiers-Stuart, *History of the 55th Coke's Rifles Frontier Force formerly known as the 1st Punjab Infantry Panjab Frontier Force* (Waterford: N. Harvey, 1908).

Maj. R.S. Waters, *History of the 5th Battalion (Pathans) 14th Punjab Regiment formerly 40th Pathans ('The Forty Thieves')* (London: James Bain, 1936).

Maj. R.S. Waters, *Continuation of the History of the 5th Battalion (Pathans) 14th Punjab Regiment from 1937 to its disbandment subsequent to the conclusion of the campaign in Malaya on February 15th, 1942* (London: n.d.).

Maj.-Gen. N.G. Woodyatt, *The Regimental History of the 3rd Queen Alexandra's Own Gurkha Rifles* (London: Philip Allen, 1929).

Col. H.C. Wylly, *History of the 5th Battalion 13th Frontier Force Rifles 1849–1926* (Aldershot: Gale and Polden, 1929).

Col. H.C. Wylly, *History of the 3rd Battalion the 2nd Punjab Regiment* (Aldershot: Gale and Polden, 1927).

Col. H.C. Wylly, *The History of Coke's Rifles* (Aldershot: Gale and Polden, 1930).

Col. H.C. Wylly, *History of the Queen's Royal Regiment* (Aldershot: Gale and Polden, 1925).

Col. G.J. Younghusband, *The Story of the Guides* (London: Macmillan, 1908).

C. SECONDARY SOURCES

(i) Bibliographical Aids

A.S. Ahmed, *Bibliography of the North-West Frontier Province* (Peshawar: Tribal Affairs Research Cell, Government of NWFP, 1979).

A. Bruce, *An Annotated Bibliography of the British Army 1660–1914* (London, 1975).

A. Bruce, *A Bibliography of the British Army 1660–1914* (London, 1985).

F. Campbell, *Bibliography of Sources in the Departments of Documents, Photographs, Printed Books and Sound Records at the Imperial War Museum on Military operations in Waziristan on the North-West Frontier of India 1917–1937* (London: Imperial War Museum, 1979).

M.J. Cockle, *A Catalogue of Books Relating to the Military History of India* (Simla: Government Printing Office, 1901).

A. Farrington, *Guide to the records of the India Office Military Department IOR L/MIL & L/WS* (London: India Office Records, 1982).

R. Higham, *A Guide to the Sources of British Military History* (London, 1972).

G. Jordan (ed.), *British Military History. A Supplement to Robin Higham's Guide to the Sources* (London: Garland Publishing, 1988).

R.E. North, Lt.-Col., *The Literature of the North-West Frontier of India: A Select Bibliography* (Peshawar: 1945).

S.N. Prasad, *A Survey of the Work done on the Military History of India* (Calcutta, 1976).

(ii) Articles and Chapters

A.S. Ahmed, 'An Aspect of The Colonial Encounter on the North-West Frontier', *Asian Affairs*, 9 (1978), pp.319–27.

A.S. Ahmed, 'The Colonial Encounter on the North-West Frontier', *Journal of the Anthropological Society of Oxford*, 9/3 (1978), pp.167–74.

L. Baha, 'The North-West Frontier in the First World War', *Asian Affairs*, 20/2 (1970), pp.29–37.

H.R. Bailes, 'Technology and Imperialism: A Case Study of the Victorian Army in Africa', *Victorian Studies*, 24/1 (1980), pp.82–104.

H.R. Bailes, 'Patterns of Thought in the Late Victorian Army', *Journal of Strategic Studies*, 4/1 (1981), pp.29–46.

H.R. Bailes, 'Technology and Tactics in the British Army, 1866–1900', in *Men, Machines and War*, K. Neilson (ed.) (Toronto: Wilfred Laurier University Press, 1988).

M. Barthorp, 'Northamptons on the Frontier 1897 and 1937', *Journal of the Society of Army Historical Research*, 57 (1979), pp.111–14.

B. Bond, 'Colonial Wars and Primitive Expeditions', in *History of the British Army*, P. Young and J.P. Lawford (ed.) (London: A. Barker, 1970).

I.F.W. Beckett, 'The Study of Counter-insurgency: A British Perspective', *Small Wars and Insurgencies*, 1/1 (1990), pp.47–53.

I.F.W. Beckett, 'The Pen and the Sword: Reflections on Military Thought in the British Army, 1854–1914', *Soldiers of the Queen*, 68 (1992), pp.3–7.

I.F.W. Beckett, 'Low-Intensity Conflict: Its Place in the Study of War', in D.A. Charters, M. Milner and J.B. Wilson (eds.), *Military History and the Military Profession* (London: Praeger, 1993), pp.121–29.

J. Belich, 'The Victorian Interpretation of Racial Conflict and the New Zealand War: An Approach to the Problem of One-Sided Evidence', *Journal of Imperial and Commonwealth History*, 15 (1987), pp.123–47.

Group Captain O.C. Bryson, 'North-West Frontier Vignettes', *Army Quarterly and Defence Journal*, 102/3 (1972), pp.377–58.

P. Burroughs, 'Imperial Defence and the Victorian Army', *Journal of Imperial and Commonwealth History,* 15/1 (1986), pp.55–72.

Maj. J. Croft. 'North-West Frontier: Training Ground Supreme', *Army Quarterly,* 122/1 (1922), pp.51–60.

M. Crowder, 'Many Questions – Some Answers': African Resistance in West Africa – A General View', in R.E. Robinson, W. Mommsen and S. Forster (eds.), *Bismarck, Europe and Africa* (Oxford, 1988).

L. Crowell, 'Military Professionalism in a Colonial Context: The Madras Army circa 1832', *Modern Asian Studies,* 24/2 (1990), pp.225–73.

A.D. English, 'The RAF Staff College and the Evolution of British Strategic Bombing Policy', *Journal of Strategic Studies,* 16/3 (1993), pp.408–431.

T.D. Farrell, 'The Founding of the North-West Frontier Militias', *Asian Affairs,* 59/2 (1972), pp.168–75.

D.C. Gordon, 'Colonial Warfare 1815–1970', in R. Higham (ed.), *A Guide to the Sources of British Military History* (London: Routledge and Keegan Paul, 1972).

J. Greenhut, 'The Imperial Reserve: the Indian Corps on the Western Front, 1914–15', *Journal of Imperial and Commonwealth History,* 12/1 (1983), pp.54–73.

R. Gregorian, '"Jungle Bashing" in Malaya: Towards a Formal Tactical Doctrine', *Small Wars and Insurgencies,* 5/3 (1995), pp.338–59.

J. Harris, 'A Scientific Frontier for India: Background to the Forward Policy of the Nineties', *Canadian Journal of History,* 1 (1966), pp.46–71.

R. Haycock, 'British Arms in India', in G. Jordan (ed.), *British Military History. A Supplement to Robin Higham's Guide to the Sources* (London: Garland, 1988).

M. Hauner, 'One Man against the Empire: The Faqir of Ipi and the British in Central Asia on the Eve of and during the Second World War', in *The Second World War, essays in military and political history,* ed. W. Laqueur (London: 1982).

D.R. Headrick, 'The Tools of Empire: Technology and the Expansion of European Colonial Empires in the Nineteenth Century', *Journal of Modern History,* 51/2 (1979), pp.231–63.

K. Jeffery, 'An English Barrack in the Oriental Seas'? India in the Aftermath of the First World War', *Modern Asian Studies,* 15/3 (1981), pp.369–86.

K. Jeffery, 'The Eastern Arc of Empire: A Strategic View, 1850–1950', *Journal of Strategic Studies,* 5/4, pp. 531–45.

K. Jeffery, 'Colonial Warfare 1900–1939', in *Warfare in the Twentieth Century,* C. McInnes and G. D. Sheffield (eds.) (London: Unwin Hyman, 1988).

'The Looker-On', 'The North-West Frontier in the Thirties', *Army Quarterly and Defence Journal,* 97 (1969), pp.247–254 and 98 (1969), pp.38–47.

T.R. Moreman, 'The Indian Army and North-West Frontier Warfare, 1849–1914', *Journal of Imperial and Commonwealth History,* 20/1 (1992), pp.35–64.

T.R. Moreman, 'The Arms Trade and the North-West Frontier Pathan Tribes, 1890–1914', *Journal of Imperial and Commonwealth History,* 22/2 (1994) pp. 187–216.

T.R. Moreman and M. Navias, 'War in the Developing World', in L. Freedman (ed.), *War: A Reader* (Oxford: Oxford University Press, 1994).

T.R. Moreman, '"Small Wars and Imperial Policing": The British Army and the Theory and Practice of Land Warfare in the British Empire, 1919–1939', *Journal of Strategic Studies,* 19/4 (1996), pp.105–28.

D.E. Omissi, '"Martial Races": Ethnicity and Security in Colonial India 1858–1939', *War and Society*, 9/2 (1991), pp.1–27.

A.W. Preston, 'Sir Charles Macgregor and the Defence of India', *The Historical Journal*, 12/1 (1969), pp.58–77.

T.R. Mockaitis, 'The Origins of British Counterinsurgency', *Small Wars and Insurgencies*, 1/3 (1990), pp.209–225.

W. Murray Hogben, 'British Civil-Military Relations on the North West Frontier of India', in *Swords and Convenants*, A. Preston and P. Davies (eds.) (London: Croom Helm, Rowman and Littlefield, 1976).

D. Porch, 'Bugeaud, Gallieni and Lyautey', in *Makers of Modern Strategy from Machiavelli to the Nuclear Age*, P. Paret (ed.) (Oxford: Clarendon Press, 1986).

B. Robson, 'Maiwand, 27th July 1880', *Journal of the Society for Army Historical Research*, 51 (1973), pp.194–221.

B. Robson, 'The Eden Commission and the Reform of the Indian Army', *Journal of the Society for Army Historical Research*, 60 (1982), pp.4–13.

A. Preston, 'British Military Thought', *Army Quarterly*, 89/1 (1964), pp.57–64.

Maj. E.W. Sheppard, 'The Royal Tank Corps in India between the Wars', in B.H. Liddell Hart (ed.), *The Tanks* (London: Cassell, 1959) Vol. I.

E.M. Spiers, 'The Use of the Dum Dum Bullet in Colonial Warfare', *Journal of Imperial and Commonwealth History* 4/1 (1975), pp.3–14.

E.M. Spiers, 'Gas and the North-West Frontier', *Journal of Strategic Studies*, 6/4 (1983), pp.94–112.

C. Townshend, 'Civilisation and "Frightfulness": Air Control in the Middle East Between the Wars', in *Warfare, Diplomacy and Politics: Essays in Honour of A.J.P. Taylor*, C. Weighly (ed.) (London: Hamish Hamilton, 1986).

M.A. Yapp, 'British Perceptions of the Russian Threat to India', *Modern Asian Studies*, 21/4 (1987), pp.647–65.

Squadron Leader A.J. Young, 'Royal Air Force North-West Frontier, India, 1915–39', *Journal of the Royal United Services Institute*, 127/1 (1982), pp.59–64.

(iii) **Books**

A.S. Ahmed, *Millennium and Charisma* (London: Routledge and Kegan Paul, 1976).

A.S. Ahmed, *Pukhtun Economy and Society: Traditional Structure and Economic Development in a Tribal Society* (London: Routledge and Kegan Paul, 1980.

A.S. Ahmed, *Resistance and Control in Pakistan* (London and New York: Routledge, 1991).

G.J. Alder, *British India's Northern Frontier 1865–95* (London: Longmans, 1983).

C. Allen (ed.), *Plain Tales from the Raj* (London: Century, 1985).

D.M. Anderson and D. Killingray (eds.), *Policing the Empire: Government, Authority and Control, 1830–1940* (Manchester: Manchester University Press, 1991).

L. Baha, *N.-W.F.P. Administration under British Rule, 1901–1919* (Islamabad: National Commission on Historical and Cultural Research, 1978).

M. Barthorp, *The North-West Frontier: British India and Afghanistan, a pictorial history, 1839–1947* (Poole: Blandford, 1982).

I.F.W. Beckett, *The Roots of Counter-Insurgency: Armies and Guerrilla Warfare* (London: Blandford, 1988).

I.F.W. Beckett, *Johnnie Gough V.C.* (London: Tom Donovan, 1989).

J. Belich, *The New Zealand Wars and the Victorian Interpretation of Racial Conflict* (Auckland: Auckland University Press, 1986).

B. Bond, *Victorian Military Campaigns* (London: Hutchinson, 1967).

B. Bond, *The Victorian Army and the Staff College* (London: Eyre Methuen, 1972).

B. Bond, *British Military Policy between the Two World Wars* (Oxford: Clarendon Press, 1980).

O. Caroe, *The Pathans 550 B.C.-A.D. 1957* (London: Macmillan, 1958).

A. Clayton, *The British Empire as a Superpower, 1919–1939* (London: Macmillan, 1986).

T.C. Coen, *The Indian Political Service* (London: Chatto and Windus, 1971).

S.P. Cohen, *The Indian Army: Its Contribution to the Development of a Nation* (Delhi: Oxford University Press, 1991), 1st ed., 1971.

M. Crowder (ed.), *West African Resistance: The Military Response to Colonial Occupation* (London: Hutchinson, 1971).

Capt. C.C. Davies, *The Problem of the North West Frontier 1890–1908* (Cambridge: Cambridge University Press, 1932).

Maj.-Gen. J.G. Elliot, *The Frontier 1839–1947* (London: Cassell, 1968).

W.K. Fraser-Tytler, *Afghanistan: A Study of Political Developments in Central Asia* (London: Oxford University Press, 1950).

Brig.-Gen. C.A.L. Graham, *A History of the Indian Mountain Artillery* (Aldershot: Gale and Polden, 1957).

P. Griffith, *Forward into Battle: Fighting Tactics from Waterloo to the Near Future* (London: Crowood Press, 1990).

P. Griffith, *Battle Tactics of the Western Front: The British Army's Art of Attack, 1916–18* (London: Yale University Press, 1994).

D.M. Hart, *Guardians of the Khyber Pass: the Social Organisation and History of the Afridis of Pakistan* (Lahore: Vanguard, 1985).

M. Hauner, *India in Axis Strategy* (London: German Historical Institute, 1981).

D.R. Headrick, *Tools of Empire* (New York: Oxford University Press, 1981).

D.R. Headrick, *The Tentacles of Progress: Technology Transfer in the Age of Imperialism* (New York: Oxford University Press, 1988).

T.A. Heathcote, *The Indian Army: The Garrison of British Imperial India* (London: David and Charles, 1974).

T.A. Heathcote, *The Afghan Wars, 1839–1919* (London: Osprey, 1980).

T.A. Heathcote, *The Military in British India The Development of British Land Forces in South Asia 1600–1946* (Manchester: Manchester University Press, 1995).

L. James, *Imperial Rearguard: Wars of Empire, 1919–1985* (London: Brassey's Defence Publishers, 1988).

K. Jeffery, *The British Army and the Crisis of Empire* (London: Manchester University Press, 1984).

V.G. Kiernan, *European Empires from Conquest to Collapse* (London: Fontana, 1982).

J. Laband, *Kingdom in Crisis: The Zulu response to the British invasion of 1879* (Manchester: Manchester University Press, 1991).

J. Luvaas, *The Education of an Army: British Military Thought* (London: Cassell, 1965).

C.H.T. MacFetridge and J.P. Warren (eds.), *Tales of the Mountain Gunners: An Anthology* (Edinburgh: William Blackwood, 1973).

J.M. MacKenzie (ed.), *Popular Imperialism and the Military* (Manchester: Manchester University Press, 1991).

P. Mason, *A Matter of Honour: An Account of the Indian Army, Its Officers and Men* (London: Papermac, 1974).

R.M. Maxwell (ed.), *Villiers-Stuart on the Frontier* (Edinburgh: Pentland, 1989).

R.M. Maxwell (ed.), *Villiers-Stuart goes to War* (Edinburgh: Pentland, 1990).

C. Miller, *Khyber. British India's North West Frontier* (London: Macdonald and Jane's, 1977).

J.A. de Moor and H.L. Wesseling (eds.), *Imperialism and War: Essays on Colonial War in Asia and Africa* (Leiden: Universitaire pers Leiden, 1989).

G. Moore, *'Just as Good as the Rest': A British Battalion in the Faqir of Ipi's War Indian N.W.F. 1936–37* (Huntingdon: privately printed, 1979).

T.R. Mockaitis, *British Counterinsurgency, 1919–1960* (London: Macmillan, 1990).

T.R. Mockaitis, *British counterinsurgency in the post-imperial period* (Manchester: Manchester University Press, 1995).

D.E. Omissi, *Air Power and Colonial Control* (Manchester: Manchester University Press, 1991).

D.E. Omissi, *The Sepoy and the Raj: The Indian Army 1860–1940* (London: Macmillan, 1994).

T. Pocock, *Fighting General. The Public and Private Campaigns of General Sir Walter Walker* (London: Collins, 1973).

D.M. Peers, *Between Mars and Mammon. Colonial Armies and the Garrison State in India 1819–1835* (London: I.B. Tauris, 1995).

B. Robson, *The Road to Kabul: The Second Afghan War, 1878–1881* (London: Arms and Armour, 1986).

B. Robson, *Roberts in India. The Military Papers of Field Marshal Lord Roberts 1876–1893* (London: Alan Sutton, 1993).

K.M.L. Saxena, *A History of the Departments of the Indian Army, their Organisation and Administration from 1850–1900* (New Delhi: India Publishing House, 1974).

K.M.L. Saxena, *The Military System of India (1850–1900)* (New Delhi: Sterling Publishers, 1974).

A. Singer, *Lords of the Khyber: The Story of the North-West Frontier* (London: Faber and Faber, 1974).

J.W. Spain, *The Way of the Pathans* (London: Robert Hale, 1962).

J.W. Spain, *The Pathan Borderland* (The Hague, 1963).

E.M. Spiers, *The Army and Society* (London: Longmans, 1980).

E.M. Spiers, *The Late Victorian Army* (Manchester: Manchester University Press, 1992).

H. Strachan, *European Armies and the Conduct of War* (London: Unwin Hyman, 1983).

H. Strachan, *Wellington's Legacy: The Reform of the British Army 1830–1854* (Manchester: Manchester University Press, 1984).

H. Strachan, *From Waterloo to Balaclava: Tactics, Technology and the British Army 1815–1854* (Cambridge: Cambridge University Press, 1985).

A. Swinson, *The North-West Frontier: People and Events 1839–1947* (London: Hutchinson, 1967).

C. Townshend, *Britain's Civil Wars: Counterinsurgency in the Twentieth Century* (London: Faber and Faber, 1986).

C. Chevenix Trench, *The Frontier Scouts* (Oxford: Oxford University Press, 1986).

C. Chevenix Trench, *The Indian Army and the King's Enemies 1900–1947* (London: Thames and Hudson, 1988).

R. Wilkinson-Latham, *North-West Frontier, 1837–1947* (London: Osprey, 1977).

P. Woodruff, *The Men who Ruled India* (London: Jonathan Cape, 1953–4), 2 Vols.

(iv) Unpublished Theses and Papers

H.R. Bailes, *The Influence of Continental Examples and Colonial Warfare upon the Reform of the Late Victorian Army* (University of London, Ph.D., 1980).

D. Brief, *The Punjab and Recruitment of the Indian Army 1846–1918* (University of Oxford, M.Phil., 1979).

S. Chandra, *The Development of Mountain Warfare in the 19th Century* (University of London, M.Phil., 1968).

R.O. Christiansen, *Conflict and Change Among the Khyber Afridis: A Study of British Policy and Tribal Society on the North-West Frontier 1839–1947* (University of Leicester, Ph.D., 1987).

L. Harris, *British Policy on the North-West Frontier of India, 1889–1901* (University of London, Ph.D., 1960).

M. Jacobson, *The Modernization of the Indian Army, 1925–39* (University of California, Irvine, Ph.D., 1979).

I.D. Leaske, *The Expansion of the Indian Army during the Great War* (London, M.Phil, 1989).

T.R. Moreman, *'Passing it On': The Army in India and the Development of Frontier Warfare 1849–1947* (University of London, Ph.D., 1996).

Namrata Narain, *Co-option and Control: The Role of the Colonial Army in India, 1918–1947* (University of Cambridge, Ph.D., 1993).

D.M. Peers, 'Stocktaking the New Military History of India: Militarism, Orientalism and Explanatory Models for the Company Raj' (Unpublished paper presented to the New Military History of South Asia Conference, Cambridge, 15–17th July 1997).

A.H. Shibly, *The Reorganisation of the Indian Armies, 1858–79* (University of London, Ph.D., 1969).

R.H. Scales, *Artillery in Small Wars* (Duke University, Ph.D., 1976).

D.J.P. Waldie, *Relations between the Army and the Royal Air Force* (University of London, D.Phil., 1980).

Index